DSA®
DRIVING STANDARDS AGENCY
SAFE DRIVING FOR LIFE ™

The OFFICIAL DSA
THEORY TEST
for Car Drivers

and The Official Highway Code

15
Approved by
Plain
English
Campaign

London: TSO

Written and compiled by the Learning Materials Section of the Driving Standards Agency (DSA).

Questions and answers are compiled by the Item Development Team of the DSA.

Published with the permission of the Driving Standards Agency on behalf of the Controller of Her Majesty's Stationery Office.

First published 1996
Thirteenth edition 2009
Second impression 2009

ISBN 978 0 11 553067 8

A CIP catalogue record for this book is available from the British Library.

Other titles in the Driving Skills series

The Official DSA Guide to Driving - the essential skills
The Official DSA Theory Test for Car Drivers
The Official DSA Theory Test for Car Drivers (CD-Rom)
Theory Test Extra - the official DSA guide
Helping Learners to Practise - the official DSA guide
The Official DSA Guide to Learning to Drive
Prepare for your Practical Driving Test DVD
DSA Driving Theory DVD Quiz

The Official DSA Guide to Riding - the essential skills
The Official DSA Theory Test for Motorcyclists
The Official DSA Theory Test for Motorcyclists (CD-Rom)
The Official DSA Guide to Learning to Ride
Better Biking - the Official DSA Training Aid (DVD)

The Official DSA Guide to Driving Buses and Coaches
The Official DSA Guide to Driving Goods Vehicles
The Official DSA Theory Test for Drivers of Large Vehicles
The Official DSA Theory Test for Drivers of Large Vehicles (CD-Rom)
Driver CPC - the Official DSA Guide for Professional Bus and Coach Drivers

The Official DSA Guide to Tractor and Specialist Vehicle Driving Tests

The Official DSA Guide to Hazard Perception (DVD)

Every effort has been made to ensure that the information contained in this publication is accurate at the time of going to press. The Stationery Office cannot be held responsible for any inaccuracies. Information in this book is for guidance only.

All metric and imperial conversions in this book are approximate.

75% recycled
This book is printed
on 75% recycled paper

Directgov

Directgov is the place to find all government motoring information and services. From logbooks to licensing, from driving tests to road tax, go to:

www.direct.gov.uk/motoring

Theory and practical tests

DSA Bookings and enquiries

Online **www.direct.gov.uk/drivingtest**

Practical & Theory Tests
Enquiries & Bookings **0300 200 1122**
Welsh Speakers **0300 200 1133**

Practical Tests
Minicom **0300 200 1144**
Fax **0300 200 1155**

Theory Tests
Minicom **0300 200 1166**
Fax **0300 200 1177**
Customer Enquiry Unit **0300 200 1188**

DVA (Northern Ireland)
Theory test **0845 600 6700**
Practical test **0845 247 2471**

Driving Standards Agency
(Headquarters)

www.dsa.gov.uk

The Axis Building,
112 Upper Parliament Street
Nottingham NG1 6LP

Tel **0115 936 6666**
Fax **0115 936 6570**

Driver & Vehicle Agency (Testing) in Northern Ireland

www.dvani.gov.uk

Balmoral Road, Belfast BT12 6QL

Tel **02890 681 831**
Fax **02890 665 520**

Driver & Vehicle Licensing Agency
(GB licence enquiries)

www.dvla.gov.uk

Longview Road, Swansea SA6 7JL

Tel **0870 240 0009**
Fax **01792 783 071**
Minicom **01792 782 787**

Driver & Vehicle Agency (Licensing) in Northern Ireland

www.dvani.gov.uk

County Hall, Castlerock Road,
Coleraine BT51 3TB

Tel **02870 341 469**
24 hour tel **0345 111 222**
Minicom **02870 341 380**

Office of the Parliamentary Commissioner for Administration
(The Parliamentary Ombudsman)

Millbank Tower, Millbank, London
SW1P 4QP

Tel **020 7217 4163**
Fax **020 7217 4160**

The Driving Standards Agency (DSA) is an executive agency of the Department for Transport. You'll see the DSA logo at theory and practical test centres.

DSA aims to promote road safety through the advancement of driving standards, by

- establishing and developing high standards and best practice in driving and riding on the road; before people start to drive, as they learn, and after they pass their test
- ensuring high standards of instruction for different types of driver and rider
- conducting the statutory theory and practical tests efficiently, fairly and consistently across the country
- providing a centre of excellence for driver training and driving standards
- developing a range of publications and other publicity material designed to promote safe driving for life.

The Driving Standards Agency recognises and values its customers. We will treat all our customers with respect, and deliver our services in an objective, polite and fair way.

www.dsa.gov.uk

The Driver and Vehicle Agency (DVA) is an executive agency within the Department of the Environment for Northern Ireland.

Its primary aim is to promote and improve road safety through the advancement of driving standards and implementation of the Government's policies for improving the mechanical standards of vehicles.

www.dvani.gov.uk

CONTENTS

About the theory test

Annexes

introduction
ABOUT THE THEORY TEST

This section covers

- Getting started
- The Theory Test
- After the Theory Test
- Pass Plus
- Using the questions and answers section

Message from the Chief Driving Examiner

With the ever-increasing volume of traffic on the roads today, it's important to make sure that new drivers have a positive attitude and a broad spread of driving knowledge and ability.

Since July 1996 all new drivers have had to pass a separate theory test before obtaining a full driving licence. In November 2002 the original multiple choice test was extended to include a hazard perception part. The introduction of the separate theory test has been a major step towards improving road safety in Great Britain.

All aspects of the theory test are continually monitored, and the bank of questions is regularly updated to take account of changes to legislation and best driving practices. This book contains the whole theory test question bank, set out in an easy-to-read style, with explanations as to why the answers are correct.

However, to prepare properly for the test, you should study the source material; this consists of

The Highway Code

Know Your Traffic Signs

The Official DSA Guide to Driving - the essential skills

To help you practise for the multiple choice questions, The Official DSA Theory Test for Car Drivers (CD-Rom) contains the full question bank and allows you to practise taking multiple choice tests. You can prepare for the hazard perception part of the test by working through The Official DSA Guide to Hazard Perception (DVD).

Using these training aids will give you an extensive knowledge of driving theory, and will help you towards a better understanding of practical driving skills.

You'll never know all the answers. Throughout your driving career there will always be more to learn.

Remember, as a driver you have a responsibility for the safety of your vehicle, any passengers you carry and other road users. By being reliable, efficient and safe you'll be on your way to becoming a better driver.

Trevor Wedge
Chief Driving Examiner and
Director of Safer Driving

Getting started

Applying for your licence

You must be at least 17 years old to drive a car. As an exception, if you receive Disability Living Allowance at the higher rate, you're allowed to start driving at 16. You must have a valid provisional driving licence before you can drive on the road.

Driving licences are issued by the Driver and Vehicle Licensing Agency (DVLA). Application forms D1 and D750 can be obtained from any Post Office. In Northern Ireland the issuing authority is the Driver and Vehicle Agency (Licensing) and the form is a DL1.

The forms should be sent to the appropriate office, which is shown on the form. You must enclose the required passport-type photos, as all provisional licences now issued are photocard licences.

When you receive your provisional licence, check that all details are correct before you drive on the road. If you need to contact DVLA, their telephone number is 0870 240 0009 (DVA is 02870 341469).

You will need to show your provisional licence when you take your theory test.

Residency requirements

You can't take a test or obtain a full licence unless you are normally resident in this country. Normal residence means the place where you reside because of personal or occupational ties. However, if you moved to the United Kingdom (UK) having recently been permanently resident in another state of the EC/EEA (European Economic Area), you must have been normally resident in the UK for 185 days in the 12 months prior to your application for a driving test or full driving licence.

Choosing an instructor

DSA in Great Britain, and DVA in Northern Ireland, approve instructors who are then able to teach learner drivers in return for payment. These instructors have their standards checked regularly.

Approved Driving Instructors (ADIs) must

- pass a series of difficult examinations
- reach a high standard of instruction
- be registered with DSA or DVA
- display an Approved Driving Instructor's certificate (except in Northern Ireland).

These professional driving instructors will give you guidance on

- your practical skills
- how to study and practise
- when you're ready for your tests
- further training after your practical test under the *Pass Plus* scheme. (Not applicable in Northern Ireland).

DSA and DVA regulate ADIs and both organisations place great emphasis on professional standards and business ethics. A code of practice (not applicable in Northern Ireland) has been created, setting a framework within which all instructors should operate. Details of this can be obtained from DSA (tel 0115 936 6666).

About the theory test

The theory test is a screen-based test, and consists of two parts. It has been devised to test your knowledge of driving theory, in particular the rules of the road and best driving practice.

Your knowledge of this information is tested in the first part, as a series of multiple choice questions. With effect from 28 September 2009 some multiple choice questions may be presented in the form of a case study. More information about this part of the test is given on pages 15 and 400. The questions are given in the main part of the book, beginning on page 22.

The second part is called the hazard perception part, more information about this is given on page 17.

Can I take the practical test first?

No. You have to pass your theory test before you can book a practical test.

Does everyone have to take the theory test?

Most people in the UK who are learning to drive will have to sit a theory test. However, you won't have to if

- you're upgrading in the same category i.e. B (car) to B+E (car with trailer)
- you already have a full B1 entitlement because you have a full motorcycle licence issued before 1 February 2001 (not applicable in Northern Ireland).

Any enquiries about whether you have to take a theory test should be addressed to the Customer Service Unit, DSA, PO Box 280, Newcastle Upon Tyne, NE99 1FP. Tel: 0191 201 8161 email: customer.services@dsa.gsi.gov.uk. (For Northern Ireland, address enquiries to DVA Theory Test Section, Balmoral Road, Belfast BT12 6QL, tel 02890 681 831).

Foreign licence holders: If you hold a foreign driving licence issued outside the EC/EEA, first check with the DVLA (tel 0870 240 0009, for Northern Ireland call 02870 341 469) to see whether you can exchange your driving licence. If you cannot, you will need to apply for a provisional licence and take a theory and practical driving test.

Preparing for your theory test

Although you have to pass your theory test before you can take your practical test, it's recommended that you start studying for your theory test, but don't actually take it until you have some practical driving experience.

To prepare for the multiple choice part of the theory test, we strongly recommend that you study the books from which the questions are taken, as well as the questions themselves. These books are:

The Highway Code - 2007 Edition Essential reading for all road users. This updated edition contains the very latest rules of the road, up-to-date legislation and provides advice on road safety and best practice.

Know Your Traffic Signs - This contains the vast majority of signs and road markings that you are likely to encounter.

Theory Test Extra - This book presents the contents of the theory test in a narrative format. It also includes two question papers.

The Official DSA Guide to Driving - the essential skills - This is the official reference book, giving practical advice and best driving practice for all drivers.

These books will help you to answer the questions correctly and will also help you when studying for your practical test. The information in them will be relevant throughout your driving life so make sure you always have an up-to-date copy that you can refer to.

It's important that you study, not just to pass the test, but to become a safer driver

Other study aids

The Official DSA Theory Test for Car Drivers (CD-Rom) - This is an alternative way of preparing for the multiple choice part of the theory test. It contains all the questions and answers and also allows you to take mock tests.

The Official DSA Guide to Hazard Perception (DVD) - We strongly recommend that you use this, preferably with your instructor, to prepare for the hazard perception part of the test.

The DVD is packed with useful tips, quizzes and expert advice. It also includes interactive hazard perception clips, with feedback on your performance.

The Official DSA Complete Theory Test Kit for Car Drivers - This contains both the above products, giving you all the information you need to prepare for the complete theory test, at a reduced price.

DSA Driving Theory DVD Quiz - A fun way to revise for your theory test - join Vicky Butler-Henderson as you pit your wits against your family and friends to prove who has the best driving knowledge.

Why do the questions keep changing?

To make sure that all candidates are being tested fairly, questions and video clips are under continuous review.

Some questions may be changed as a result of customer feedback. They may also be changed to reflect revised legislation, and DSA publications are updated to reflect such changes.

Can I take a mock test?

You can take a mock test for the multiple choice part of the theory test online at **www.direct.gov.uk/motoring**

All of these training materials are available online at **www.tsoshop.co.uk/dsa** or by mail order from **0870 241 4523**.

They are also available from bookshops and selected computer software retailers.

The Theory Test

Booking your theory test

The easiest ways to book are online or by phone. You can also book by post.

Booking online or by telephone - by using these methods you'll be given the date and time of your test immediately.

Book online at www.direct.gov.uk/drivingtest (for Northern Ireland use www.dvani.gov.uk).

To book by telephone, call 0300 200 1122 (0845 600 6700 for Northern Ireland). If you're deaf and use a minicom machine, call 0300 200 1166 and if you're a Welsh speaker, call 0300 200 1133.

You will need your

- DVLA or DVA driving licence number
- credit or debit card details (the card holder must book the test). We accept Mastercard, Visa, Delta, Switch/Maestro, Visa Electron and Solo.

You'll be given a booking number and should receive an appointment letter within 10 days.

Where can I take the test?

There are over 150 theory test centres throughout England, Scotland and Wales, and six in Northern Ireland. Most people have a test centre within 20 miles of their home, but this will vary depending on the density of population in your area. You can find a list of test centres on page 400.

How do I cancel or postpone my test?

You can cancel or postpone your theory test online or by telephone. You should contact the booking office at least **three clear working days** before your test date, otherwise you'll lose your fee.

Only in exceptional circumstances, such as documented ill-health or family bereavement, can this rule be waived.

What if I don't receive an acknowledgement?

If you don't receive an acknowledgement within the time specified above, please contact the booking office to check that an appointment has been made. We can't take responsibility for postal delays. If you miss your test appointment you'll lose your fee.

When are test centres open?

Test centres are usually open on weekdays, some evenings and some Saturdays.

Booking by post - If you prefer to book by post, you'll need to fill in an application form. These are available from theory or driving test centres, or your instructor may have one.

You should normally receive an appointment letter within 10 days of posting your application form.

If you require a theory test in a language other than English or provision for special needs please turn to page 14.

Taking your theory test

Arriving at the test centre - You must make sure that when you arrive at the test centre you have all the relevant documents with you, or you won't be able to take your test and you'll lose your fee.

You'll need

- your signed photocard licence and paper counterpart; or
- your signed driving licence and valid passport (your passport doesn't have to be British).

No other identification is acceptable.

Other forms of identification may be acceptable in Northern Ireland, please check www.dvani.gov.uk or your appointment letter.

All documents must be original. We can't accept photocopies.

The test centre staff will check your documents and make sure that you take the right category of test.

Remember, if you don't bring your documents, your test will be cancelled and you will lose your fee.

Make sure that you arrive in plenty of time so you aren't rushed. If you arrive after the session has started, you may not be allowed to take the test.

You'll then be ready to start your test. It's a screen-based test and is made up of a multiple choice part and a hazard perception part.

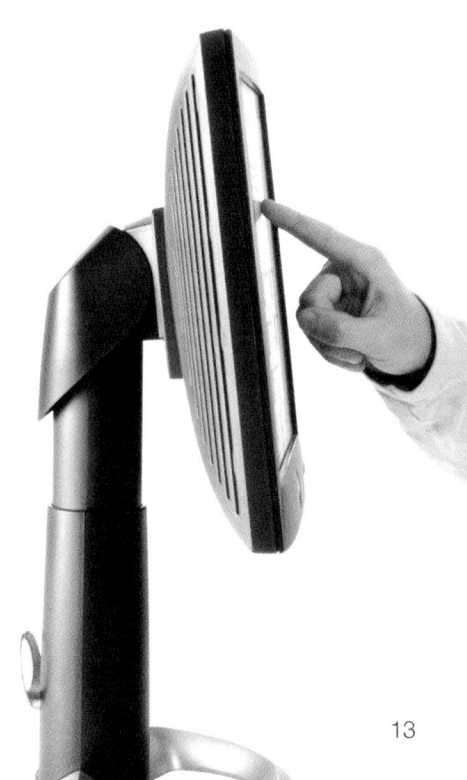

Languages other than English

In Wales, and at theory test centres on the Welsh borders, you can take your theory test with Welsh text on screen. A voiceover can also be provided in Welsh.

You can listen through a headset to the test being read out in one of 20 other languages as well as English. These are: Albanian, Arabic, Bengali, Cantonese, Dari, Farsi, Gujarati, Hindi, Kashmiri, Kurdish, Mirpuri, Polish, Portuguese, Punjabi, Pushto, Spanish, Tamil, Turkish, Urdu and Welsh.

To take your test in any other language, you may bring a translator with you to certain theory test centres. The translator must be approved by DSA (DVA in Northern Ireland) and you must make arrangements when you book your test. You have to arrange and pay for the services of the translator yourself.

Tests with translators can be taken at the following test centres: Aldershot, Birkenhead, Birmingham, Cardiff, Derby, Edinburgh, Glasgow, Ipswich, Leeds, Milton Keynes, Preston, Southgate and all test centres in Northern Ireland.

Provision for special needs

Every effort is made to ensure that the theory test can be taken by all candidates.

It's important that you state your needs when you book your test so that the necessary arrangements can be made.

Reading difficulties - There's an English language voiceover, on a headset, to help you if you have reading difficulties or dyslexia.

You can ask for up to twice the normal time to take the multiple choice part of the test.

You will be asked to provide a letter from a suitable independent person who knows about your reading ability (such as a teacher or employer). Please check with the Special Needs section (on the normal booking number, see page 12), if you're unsure who to ask.

We can't guarantee to return any original documents, so please send copies only.

Hearing difficulties - If you're deaf or have other hearing difficulties, the multiple choice part and the introduction to the hazard perception part of the test can be delivered in British Sign Language (BSL) by an on-screen signer.

A BSL interpreter, signer or lip speaker can be provided if requested at the time of booking. If you have any other requirements please call the Special Needs section on the normal booking number (see page 12).

Physical disabilities - If you have a physical disability which would make it difficult for you to use a mouse button to respond to the clips in the hazard perception part of the test, we may be able to make special arrangements for you to use a different method if you let us know when you book your test.

Multiple choice questions

The first part of the theory test consists of 50 multiple choice questions. Some of these multiple choice questions may be presented to you on test in the form of a case study. You select your answers for this part of the test by simply touching the screen. This 'touch screen' has been carefully designed to make it easy to use.

Before you start this part of your test, you'll be given the chance to work through a practice session for up to 15 minutes to get used to the system. Staff at the test centre will be available to help you if you have any difficulties.

The questions will cover a variety of topics relating to road safety, the environment and documentation. Only one question will appear on the screen at a time.

Most questions will ask you to mark one correct answer from four possible answers given. Some questions may ask for two or more correct answers from a selection, but this is shown clearly on the screen. If you try to move on without marking the correct number of answers you'll be reminded that more answers are needed.

To answer, you need to touch the box alongside the answer or answers you think are correct. If you change your mind and don't want that answer to be selected, touch it again. You can then choose another answer.

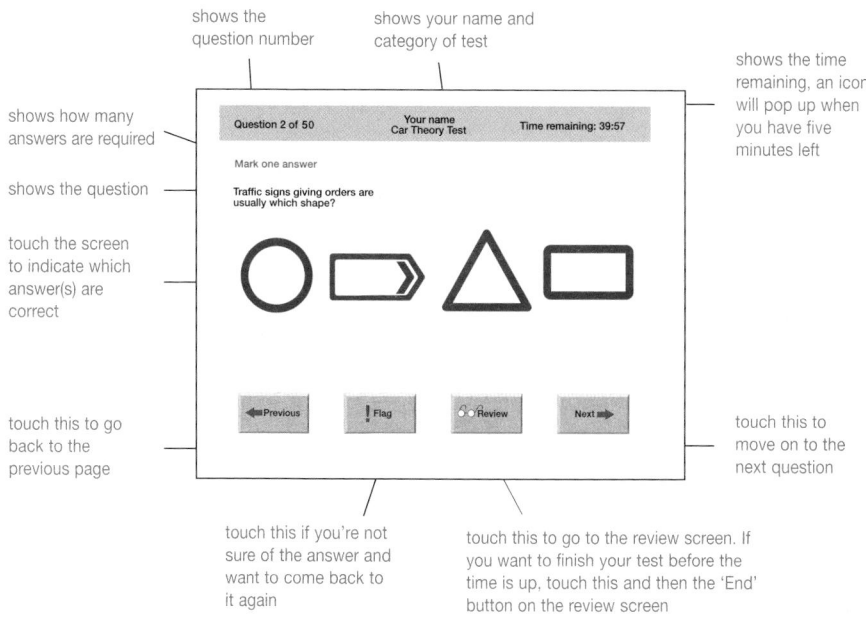

shows the question number

shows your name and category of test

shows the time remaining, an icon will pop up when you have five minutes left

shows how many answers are required

shows the question

touch the screen to indicate which answer(s) are correct

touch this to go back to the previous page

touch this to move on to the next question

touch this if you're not sure of the answer and want to come back to it again

touch this to go to the review screen. If you want to finish your test before the time is up, touch this and then the 'End' button on the review screen

Case studies

From 28 September 2009 DSA are introducing Case Studies into the multiple choice part of the theory test.

Case studies are designed to target

- knowledge (basic recall of facts)
- comprehension (basic understanding)
- application (practical use of knowledge and understanding.

This is done by creating a scenario or a set of circumstances that you may encounter in a real-life situation. You will then be asked a number of questions, relating to the scenario, which will require you to consider how you would react/behave in each case. For an example of a case study, see page 400.

Take your time and read the questions carefully. You're given 57 minutes for this part of the test, so relax and don't rush. Some questions will take longer to answer than others, but there are no trick questions. The time remaining is displayed on screen.

Extra time can be provided if you have special needs and you let us know when you book your test.

You'll be able to move backwards and forwards through the questions and you can also 'flag' questions that you'd like to look at again. It's easy to change your answer if you want to.

Try to answer all the questions. If you're well prepared you shouldn't find them difficult.

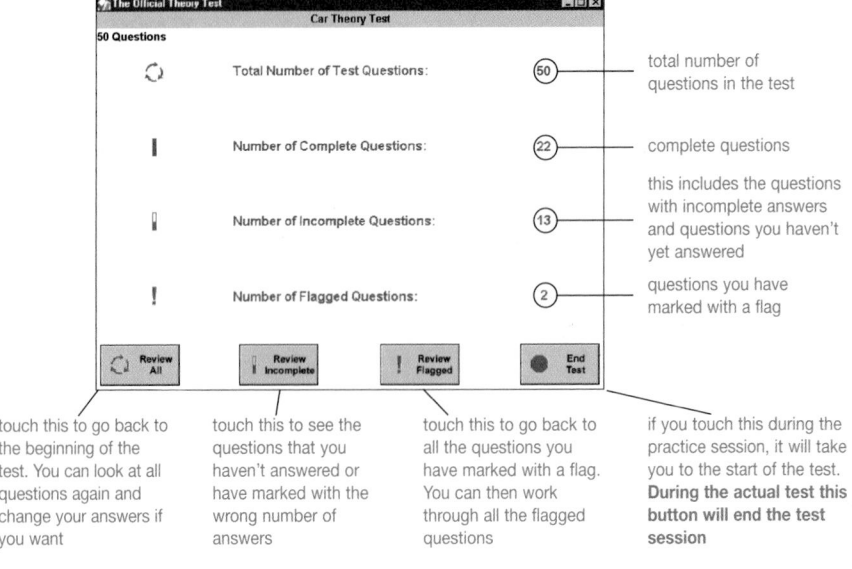

touch this to go back to the beginning of the test. You can look at all questions again and change your answers if you want

touch this to see the questions that you haven't answered or have marked with the wrong number of answers

touch this to go back to all the questions you have marked with a flag. You can then work through all the flagged questions

if you touch this during the practice session, it will take you to the start of the test. **During the actual test this button will end the test session**

Before you finish this part of the test, if you have time, you can use the 'review' feature to check your answers. If you want to finish your test before the full time, touch the 'review' button and then the 'end' button on the review screen. When you touch the review button you will see the following screen.

Hazard perception

After you've finished the multiple choice part, there is a break of up to three minutes before you start the hazard perception part of the test. You cannot leave your seat during this break. This part of the test will consist of a series of film clips, shown from a driver's point of view.

Before you start this part of the test you'll be shown a short tutorial video that explains how the test works and gives you a chance to see a sample film clip. This will help you to understand what you need to do. You can run this video again if you wish.

During the hazard perception part of the test you'll be shown 14 film clips. Each clip contains one or more developing hazards. You should respond by pressing the mouse button **as soon as you see** a hazard developing that may result in you, the driver, having to take some action, such as changing speed or direction.

The earlier you notice a developing hazard and make a response, the higher your score.

There are 15 scoreable hazards in total.

Your response will not cause the scene in the video to change in any way. However, a red flag will appear on the bottom of the screen to show that your response has been noted.

Before each clip starts, there will be a 10-second pause to allow you to see the new road situation.

The hazard perception part of the test lasts about 20 minutes. For this part of the test there is no extra time available, and you can't repeat any of the clips - you don't get a second chance to see a hazard when you're driving on the road.

Trial questions

We're constantly checking the questions and clips to help us decide whether to use them in future tests. After the hazard perception part of the test you may be asked to try a few trial questions and clips. You don't have to do these if you don't want to, and if you answer them they won't count towards your final score.

Customer satisfaction survey

We want to ensure our customers are completely satisfied with the service they receive. At the end of your test you'll be shown some questions designed to give us information about you and how happy you are with the service you received from us.

Your answers will be treated in the strictest confidence. They are not part of the test and they won't be used in determining your final score or for marketing purposes. You'll be asked if you want to complete the survey, there's no obligation to do so.

The result

You should receive your result at the test centre within 10 minutes of completing the test.

You'll be given a score for each part of the test (the multiple choice part and the hazard perception part). You'll need to pass both parts to pass the theory test. If you fail one of the parts you'll have to take the whole test again.

Why do I have to retake both parts of the test if I only fail one?

It's really only one test. The theory test has always included questions relating to hazard awareness – the second part simply tests the same skills in a more effective way. The two parts are only presented separately in the theory test because different scoring methods are used.

What's the pass mark?

To pass the multiple choice part of the theory test you must answer at least 43 questions correctly. For learner car drivers and bike riders the pass mark for the hazard perception part is 44 out of 75.

If I don't pass, when can I take the test again?

If you fail your test, you've shown that you're not fully prepared. You'll have to wait at least three clear working days before you take the theory test again.

Good preparation will save you time and money.

After the theory test

When you pass your theory test you'll be given a certificate. Keep this safe, you'll need it when you go for your practical test.

This certificate has a life of two years from the date of your test. This means that you have to take and pass the practical test within this two-year period. If you don't, you'll have to take and pass the theory test again before you can book your practical test.

Your practical driving test

Your next step is to prepare for and take your practical driving test. To help you prepare for this, DSA has produced a book called *The Official DSA Guide to Learning to Drive* and a DVD called *Prepare for your Practical Driving Test*.

Both products explain the standards required to pass the practical driving test. They include information about each of the 24 key skills examined within the test, with tips from the experts, and they explain what the examiner is looking for during the test.

The DVD also shows a test in action so that you can see what's in store.

Pass Plus
(not applicable in Northern Ireland)

After passing the practical driving test you are at greater risk of being involved in a road accident. That risk is reflected in car insurance premiums.

There may be many driving situations which you have not experienced during your lessons. The *Pass Plus* scheme can help with this by showing you how to deal with these situations so that you can drive with confidence.

Pass Plus is aimed at improving your driving skills and making you a safer driver. It can also lead to insurance discounts.

Pass Plus will take you through driving:

- in town
- on rural roads
- in all weathers
- on dual carriageways and motorways
- in the dark.

The structured syllabus gives you the extra experience you need at a time when you're most likely to be involved in a collision. It builds on your existing skills and there's no test to take at the end.

The amount of money you save on insurance could cover the cost of the course. More than 60% of car insurers recognise the benefits of the scheme and most will give you substantial discounts when you insure your car.

To find out more about the *Pass Plus* scheme, insurance discounts and *Pass Plus* instructors in your area

- ask your driving instructor
- check out the ads in *Drive On* magazine
- visit **www.passplus.org.uk**
- call the *Pass Plus* hotline on **0115 936 6504**
- email **passplus@dsa.gsi.gov.uk**

You can take the *Pass Plus* course at any time in your driving career, but it's mainly aimed at you as a new driver in the first year after passing your test.

Saving money on your car insurance should bring a smile to your face

Using the questions and answers section

The following part of the book contains all the questions that could be used in the multiple choice part of the theory test.

For easy reference, and to help you study, the questions have been divided into topics and put into sections. Although this isn't how you'll find them in your test, it's helpful if you want to refer to particular subjects.

The questions are in the left-hand column with a choice of answers beneath. On the right-hand side of the page you'll find the correct answers and a brief explanation of why they are correct. There will also be some advice on correct driving procedures.

Don't just learn the answers. It's important that you know why the answers are correct. This will help you with your practical skills and prepare you to become a safe and confident driver.

Taking exams or tests is rarely a pleasant experience, but you can make your test less stressful by being confident that you have the knowledge to answer the questions correctly.

Make studying more enjoyable by involving friends and relations. Take part in a question-and-answer game. Test those 'experienced' drivers who've had their licence a while: they might learn something too!

Best wishes with your theory test. Once you're on the road, don't forget everything you've learnt

Some of the questions in this book will not be used in Northern Ireland theory tests. These questions are marked as follows: *NI EXEMPT*

section **one**
ALERTNESS

This section covers

- Observation
- Anticipation
- Concentration
- Awareness
- Distraction
- Boredom

1.1
*Mark **one** answer*

Before you make a U-turn in the road, you should

- ⊙ give an arm signal as well as using your indicators
- ⊙ signal so that other drivers can slow down for you
- ⊙ look over your shoulder for a final check
- ⊙ select a higher gear than normal

⊙ **look over your shoulder for a final check**

If you want to make a U-turn, slow down and ensure that the road is clear in both directions. Make sure that the road is wide enough to carry out the manoeuvre safely.

1.2
*Mark **three** answers*

As you approach this bridge you should

- ⊙ move into the middle of the road to get a better view
- ⊙ slow down
- ⊙ get over the bridge as quickly as possible
- ⊙ consider using your horn
- ⊙ beware of pedestrians

⊙ **slow down**

⊙ **consider using your horn**

⊙ **beware of pedestrians**

This sign gives you a warning. The brow of the hill prevents you seeing oncoming traffic so you must be cautious. The bridge is narrow and there may not be enough room for you to pass an oncoming vehicle at this point. There is no footpath, so pedestrians may be walking in the road. Consider the hidden hazards and be ready to react if necessary.

1.3
*Mark **one** answer*

In which of these situations should you avoid overtaking?

- ⊙ Just after a bend
- ⊙ In a one-way street
- ⊙ On a 30 mph road
- ⊙ Approaching a dip in the road

⊙ **Approaching a dip in the road**

As you begin to think about overtaking, ask yourself if it's really necessary. If you can't see well ahead stay back and wait for a safer place to pull out.

This road marking warns

- ⊙ drivers to use the hard shoulder
- ⊙ overtaking drivers there is a bend to the left
- ⊙ overtaking drivers to move back to the left
- ⊙ drivers that it is safe to overtake

- ⊙ **overtaking drivers to move back to the left**

You should plan your overtaking to take into account any hazards ahead. In this picture the marking indicates that you are approaching a junction. You will not have time to overtake and move back into the left safely.

Your mobile phone rings while you are travelling. You should

- ⊙ stop immediately
- ⊙ answer it immediately
- ⊙ pull up in a suitable place
- ⊙ pull up at the nearest kerb

- ⊙ **pull up in a suitable place**

The safest option is to switch off your mobile phone before you set off, and use a message service. Even hands-free systems are likely to distract your attention. Don't endanger other road users. If you need to make a call, pull up in a safe place when you can, you may need to go some distance before you can find one. It's illegal to use a hand-held mobile or similar device when driving or riding, except in a genuine emergency.

1.6

*Mark **one** answer*

Why are these yellow lines painted across the road?

○ To help you choose the correct lane

○ To help you keep the correct separation distance

○ To make you aware of your speed

○ To tell you the distance to the roundabout

○ **To make you aware of your speed**

These lines are often found on the approach to a roundabout or a dangerous junction. They give you extra warning to adjust your speed. Look well ahead and do this in good time.

1.7

*Mark **one** answer*

You are approaching traffic lights that have been on green for some time. You should

○ accelerate hard

○ maintain your speed

○ be ready to stop

○ brake hard

○ **be ready to stop**

The longer traffic lights have been on green, the greater the chance of them changing. Always allow for this on approach and be prepared to stop.

1.8

*Mark **one** answer*

Which of the following should you do before stopping?

○ Sound the horn

○ Use the mirrors

○ Select a higher gear

○ Flash your headlights

○ **Use the mirrors**

Before pulling up check the mirrors to see what is happening behind you. Also assess what is ahead and make sure you give the correct signal if it helps other road users.

When following a large vehicle you should keep well back because this

- ⊙ allows you to corner more quickly
- ⊙ helps the large vehicle to stop more easily
- ⊙ allows the driver to see you in the mirrors
- ⊙ helps you to keep out of the wind

⊙ **allows the driver to see you in the mirrors**

If you're following a large vehicle but are so close to it that you can't see the exterior mirrors, the driver can't see you. Keeping well back will also allow you to see the road ahead by looking past either side of the large vehicle.

When you see a hazard ahead you should use the mirrors. Why is this?

- ⊙ Because you will need to accelerate out of danger
- ⊙ To assess how your actions will affect following traffic
- ⊙ Because you will need to brake sharply to a stop
- ⊙ To check what is happening on the road ahead

⊙ **To assess how your actions will affect following traffic**

You should be constantly scanning the road for clues about what is going to happen next. Check your mirrors regularly, particularly as soon as you spot a hazard. What is happening behind may affect your response to hazards ahead.

You are waiting to turn right at the end of a road. Your view is obstructed by parked vehicles. What should you do?

- ⊙ Stop and then move forward slowly and carefully for a proper view
- ⊙ Move quickly to where you can see so you only block traffic from one direction
- ⊙ Wait for a pedestrian to let you know when it is safe for you to emerge
- ⊙ Turn your vehicle around immediately and find another junction to use

⊙ **Stop and then move forward slowly and carefully for a proper view**

At junctions your view is often restricted by buildings, trees or parked cars. You need to be able to see in order to judge a safe gap. Edge forward slowly and keep looking all the time. Don't cause other road users to change speed or direction as you emerge.

1.12
*Mark **two** answers*

Objects hanging from your interior mirror may

- restrict your view
- improve your driving
- distract your attention
- help your concentration

- **restrict your view**

- **distract your attention**

Ensure that you can see clearly through the windscreen of your vehicle. Stickers or hanging objects could affect your field of vision or draw your eyes away from the road.

1.13
*Mark **four** answers*

Which of the following may cause loss of concentration on a long journey?

- Loud music
- Arguing with a passenger
- Using a mobile phone
- Putting in a cassette tape
- Stopping regularly to rest
- Pulling up to tune the radio

- **Loud music**

- **Arguing with a passenger**

- **Using a mobile phone**

- **Putting in a cassette tape**

You should not allow yourself to be distracted when driving. You need to concentrate fully in order to be safe on the road. Loud music could mask other sounds, such as the audible warning of an emergency vehicle. Any distraction which causes you to take your hands off the steering wheel or your eyes off the road could be dangerous.

1.14
*Mark **two** answers*

On a long motorway journey boredom can cause you to feel sleepy. You should

- leave the motorway and find a safe place to stop
- keep looking around at the surrounding landscape
- drive faster to complete your journey sooner
- ensure a supply of fresh air into your vehicle
- stop on the hard shoulder for a rest

- **leave the motorway and find a safe place to stop**

- **ensure a supply of fresh air into your vehicle**

Plan your journey to include suitable rest stops. You should take all possible precautions against feeling sleepy while driving. Any lapse of concentration could have serious consequences.

You are driving at dusk. You should switch your lights on

- even when street lights are not lit
- so others can see you
- only when others have done so
- only when street lights are lit

- **even when street lights are not lit**

- **so others can see you**

Your headlights and tail lights help others on the road to see you. It may be necessary to turn on your lights during the day if visibility is reduced, for example due to heavy rain. In these conditions the light might fade before the street lights are timed to switch on. Be seen to be safe.

You are most likely to lose concentration when driving if you

- use a mobile phone
- listen to very loud music
- switch on the heated rear window
- look at the door mirrors

- **use a mobile phone**

- **listen to very loud music**

Distractions which cause you to take your hands off the steering wheel or your eyes off the road are potentially dangerous. You must be in full control of your vehicle at all times.

Which FOUR are most likely to cause you to lose concentration while you are driving?

- Using a mobile phone
- Talking into a microphone
- Tuning your car radio
- Looking at a map
- Checking the mirrors
- Using the demisters

- **Using a mobile phone**

- **Talking into a microphone**

- **Tuning your car radio**

- **Looking at a map**

It's easy to be distracted. Planning your journey before you set off is important. A few sensible precautions are to tune your radio to stations in your area of travel, take planned breaks, and plan your route. Except for emergencies it is illegal to use a hand-held mobile phone while driving. Even using a hands-free kit can distract your attention.

1.18   *Mark **one** answer*

You should ONLY use a mobile phone when

- ⊙ receiving a call
- ⊙ suitably parked
- ⊙ driving at less than 30 mph
- ⊙ driving an automatic vehicle

⊙ **suitably parked**

It is illegal to use a hand-held mobile phone while driving, except in a genuine emergency. Even using hands-free kit can distract your attention. Park in a safe and convenient place before receiving or making a call or using text messaging. Then you will also be free to take notes or refer to papers.

1.19   *Mark **one** answer*

You are driving on a wet road. You have to stop your vehicle in an emergency. You should

- ⊙ apply the handbrake and footbrake together
- ⊙ keep both hands on the wheel
- ⊙ select reverse gear
- ⊙ give an arm signal

⊙ **keep both hands on the wheel**

As you drive, look well ahead and all around so that you're ready for any hazards that might occur. There may be occasions when you have to stop in an emergency. React as soon as you can whilst keeping control of the vehicle.

1.20   *Mark **three** answers*

When you are moving off from behind a parked car you should

- ⊙ look round before you move off
- ⊙ use all the mirrors on the vehicle
- ⊙ look round after moving off
- ⊙ use the exterior mirrors only
- ⊙ give a signal if necessary
- ⊙ give a signal after moving off

⊙ **look round before you move off**

⊙ **use all the mirrors on the vehicle**

⊙ **give a signal if necessary**

Before moving off you should use all the mirrors to check if the road is clear. Look round to check the blind spots and give a signal if it is necessary to warn other road users of your intentions.

You are travelling along this narrow country road. When passing the cyclist you should go

- slowly, sounding the horn as you pass
- quickly, leaving plenty of room
- slowly, leaving plenty of room
- quickly, sounding the horn as you pass

⊙ **slowly, leaving plenty of room**

Look well ahead and only pull out if it is safe. You will need to use all of the road to pass the cyclist, so be extra-cautious. Look out for entrances to fields where tractors or other farm machinery could be waiting to pull out.

Your vehicle is fitted with a hand-held telephone. To use the telephone you should

- reduce your speed
- find a safe place to stop
- steer the vehicle with one hand
- be particularly careful at junctions

⊙ **find a safe place to stop**

Your attention should be on your driving at all times. Except in a genuine emergency never attempt to use a hand-held phone while on the move. It's illegal and very dangerous. Your eyes could wander from the road and at 60 mph your vehicle will travel about 27 metres (89 feet) every second.

To answer a call on your mobile phone while travelling you should

- reduce your speed wherever you are
- stop in a proper and convenient place
- keep the call time to a minimum
- slow down and allow others to overtake

⊙ **stop in a proper and convenient place**

No phone call is important enough to risk endangering lives. It's better to switch your phone off completely when driving. If you must be contactable plan your route to include breaks so you can catch up on messages in safety. Always choose a safe and convenient place to take a break, such as a lay-by or service area.

1.24   *Mark **one** answer*

You lose your way on a busy road. What is the best action to take?

- ◉ Stop at traffic lights and ask pedestrians
- ◉ Shout to other drivers to ask them the way
- ◉ Turn into a side road, stop and check a map
- ◉ Check a map, and keep going with the traffic flow

◉ **Turn into a side road, stop and check a map**

It's easy to lose your way in an unfamiliar area. If you need to check a map or ask for directions, first find a safe place to stop.

1.25   *Mark **one** answer*

Windscreen pillars can obstruct your view. You should take particular care when

- ◉ driving on a motorway
- ◉ driving on a dual carriageway
- ◉ approaching a one-way street
- ◉ approaching bends and junctions

◉ **approaching bends and junctions**

Windscreen pillars can obstruct your view, particularly at bends and junctions. Look out for other road users, particularly cyclists and pedestrians, as they can be hard to see.

1.26   *Mark **one** answer*

You cannot see clearly behind when reversing. What should you do?

- ◉ Open your window to look behind
- ◉ Open the door and look behind
- ◉ Look in the nearside mirror
- ◉ Ask someone to guide you

◉ **Ask someone to guide you**

If you want to turn your car around try to find a place where you have good all-round vision. If this isn't possible and you're unable to see clearly, then get someone to guide you.

*Mark **one** answer*

What does the term 'blind spot' mean for a driver?

⊙ An area covered by your right-hand mirror

⊙ An area not covered by your headlights

⊙ An area covered by your left-hand mirror

⊙ An area not covered by your mirrors

⊙ **An area not covered by your mirrors**

Modern vehicles provide the driver with well-positioned mirrors which are essential to safe driving. However, they cannot see every angle of the scene behind and to the sides of the vehicle. This is why it is essential that you check over your shoulder, so that you are aware of any hazards not reflected in your mirrors.

---

*Mark **one** answer*

Your vehicle is fitted with a hands-free phone system. Using this equipment whilst driving

⊙ is quite safe as long as you slow down

⊙ could distract your attention from the road

⊙ is recommended by The Highway Code

⊙ could be very good for road safety

⊙ **could distract your attention from the road**

Using a hands-free system doesn't mean that you can safely drive and use a mobile phone. This type of mobile phone can still distract your attention from the road. As a driver, it is your responsibility to keep yourself and other road users safe at all times.

---

*Mark **one** answer*

Using a hands-free phone is likely to

⊙ improve your safety

⊙ increase your concentration

⊙ reduce your view

⊙ divert your attention

⊙ **divert your attention**

Unlike someone in the car with you, the person on the other end of the line is unable to see the traffic situations you are dealing with. They will not stop speaking to you even if you are approaching a hazardous situation. You need to be concentrating on your driving all of the time, but especially so when dealing with a hazard.

1.30

*Mark **one** answer*

What is the safest way to use a mobile phone in your vehicle?

- ⊙ Use hands-free equipment
- ⊙ Find a suitable place to stop
- ⊙ Drive slowly on a quiet road
- ⊙ Direct your call through the operator

⊙ **Find a suitable place to stop**

It's illegal to use a hand-held mobile phone while driving, except in genuine emergencies. Even using hands-free kit is very likely to take your mind off your driving. If the use of a mobile causes you to drive in a careless or dangerous manner, you could be prosecuted for those offences. The penalties include an unlimited fine, disqualification and up to two years' imprisonment.

1.31

*Mark **one** answer*

Your mobile phone rings while you are on the motorway. Before answering you should

- ⊙ reduce your speed to 30 mph
- ⊙ pull up on the hard shoulder
- ⊙ move into the left-hand lane
- ⊙ stop in a safe place

⊙ **stop in a safe place**

When driving on motorways, you can't just pull up to answer your mobile phone. Do not stop on the hard shoulder or slip road. To avoid being distracted it's safer to switch it off when driving. If you need to be contacted plan your journey to include breaks at service areas so you can pick up any messages when you stop.

1.32

*Mark **one** answer*

You are turning right onto a dual carriageway. What should you do before emerging?

- ⊙ Stop, apply the handbrake and then select a low gear
- ⊙ Position your vehicle well to the left of the side road
- ⊙ Check that the central reservation is wide enough for your vehicle
- ⊙ Make sure that you leave enough room for a vehicle behind

⊙ **Check that the central reservation is wide enough for your vehicle**

Before emerging right onto a dual carriageway make sure that the central reserve is deep enough to protect your vehicle. If it's not, you should treat it as one road and check that it's clear in both directions before pulling out. Neglecting to do this could place part or all of your vehicle in the path of approaching traffic and cause a collision.

You are waiting to emerge from a junction. The windscreen pillar is restricting your view. What should you be particularly aware of?

- ⊙ Lorries
- ⊙ Buses
- ⊙ Motorcyclists
- ⊙ Coaches

⊙ **Motorcyclists**

Windscreen pillars can completely block your view of pedestrians, motorcyclists and pedal cyclists. You should particularly watch out for these road users; don't just rely on a quick glance. Where possible make eye contact with them so you can be sure they have seen you too.

When emerging from junctions, which is most likely to obstruct your view?

- ⊙ Windscreen pillars
- ⊙ Steering wheel
- ⊙ Interior mirror
- ⊙ Windscreen wipers

⊙ **Windscreen pillars**

Windscreen pillars can block your view, particularly at junctions. Those road users most at risk of not being seen are cyclists, motorcyclists and pedestrians. Never rely on just a quick glance.

Your vehicle is fitted with a navigation system. How should you avoid letting this distract you while driving?

- ⊙ Keep going and input your destination into the system
- ⊙ Keep going as the system will adjust to your route
- ⊙ Stop immediately to view and use the system
- ⊙ Stop in a safe place before using the system

⊙ **Stop in a safe place before using the system**

Vehicle navigation systems can be useful when driving on unfamiliar routes. However they can also distract you and cause you to lose control if you look at or adjust them while driving. Pull up in a convenient and safe place before adjusting them.

1.36

*Mark **one** answer*

You are driving on a motorway and want to use your mobile phone. What should you do?

- ⊙ Try to find a safe place on the hard shoulder
- ⊙ Leave the motorway and stop in a safe place
- ⊙ Use the next exit and pull up on the slip road
- ⊙ Move to the left lane and reduce your speed

⊙ **Leave the motorway and stop in a safe place**

Except in a genuine emergency you MUST NOT use your mobile phone when driving. If you need to use it leave the motorway and find a safe place to stop. Even a hands-free phone can distract your attention. Use your voicemail to receive calls. Driving requires all of your attention, all of the time.

1.37

*Mark **one** answer*

You must not use a hand-held phone while driving. Using a hands-free system

- ⊙ is acceptable in a vehicle with power steering
- ⊙ will significantly reduce your field of vision
- ⊙ will affect your vehicle's electronic systems
- ⊙ is still likely to distract your attention from the road

⊙ **is still likely to distract your attention from the road**

While driving your concentration is required all the time. Even using a hands-free kit can still distract your attention from the road. Any distraction, however brief, is potentially dangerous and could cause you to lose control. Except in a genuine emergency, it is an offence to use a hand-held phone while driving.

35

section **two**
ATTITUDE

This section covers

- Consideration
- Close following
- Courtesy
- Priority

2.1

*Mark **one** answer*

At a pelican crossing the flashing amber light means you MUST

○ stop and wait for the green light

○ stop and wait for the red light

○ give way to pedestrians waiting to cross

○ give way to pedestrians already on the crossing

○ **give way to pedestrians already on the crossing**

Pelican crossings are signal-controlled crossings operated by pedestrians. Push-button controls change the signals. Pelican crossings have no red-and-amber stage before green. Instead, they have a flashing amber light, which means you MUST give way to pedestrians already on the crossing, but if it is clear, you may continue.

2.2

*Mark **one** answer*

You should never wave people across at pedestrian crossings because

○ there may be another vehicle coming

○ they may not be looking

○ it is safer for you to carry on

○ they may not be ready to cross

○ **there may be another vehicle coming**

If people are waiting to use a pedestrian crossing, slow down and be prepared to stop. Don't wave them across the road since another driver may not have seen them, not have seen your signal and may not be able to stop safely.

2.3

*Mark **one** answer*

'Tailgating' means

○ using the rear door of a hatchback car

○ reversing into a parking space

○ following another vehicle too closely

○ driving with rear fog lights on

○ **following another vehicle too closely**

'Tailgating' is used to describe this dangerous practice, often seen in fast-moving traffic and on motorways. Following the vehicle in front too closely is dangerous because it

• restricts your view of the road ahead

• leaves you no safety margin if the vehicle in front slows down or stops suddenly.

Following this vehicle too closely is unwise because

⊙ your brakes will overheat

⊙ your view ahead is increased

⊙ your engine will overheat

⊙ your view ahead is reduced

⊙ **your view ahead is reduced**

Staying back will increase your view of the road ahead. This will help you to see any hazards that might occur and allow you more time to react.

You are following a vehicle on a wet road. You should leave a time gap of at least

⊙ one second

⊙ two seconds

⊙ three seconds

⊙ four seconds

⊙ **four seconds**

Wet roads will reduce your tyres' grip on the road. The safe separation gap of at least two seconds in dry conditions should be doubled in wet weather.

A long, heavily-laden lorry is taking a long time to overtake you. What should you do?

⊙ Speed up

⊙ Slow down

⊙ Hold your speed

⊙ Change direction

⊙ **Slow down**

A long lorry with a heavy load will need more time to pass you than a car, especially on an uphill stretch of road. Slow down and allow the lorry to pass.

2.7 — Mark **three** answers

Which of the following vehicles will use blue flashing beacons?

- Motorway maintenance
- Bomb disposal
- Blood transfusion
- Police patrol
- Breakdown recovery

- **Bomb disposal**
- **Blood transfusion**
- **Police patrol**

When you see emergency vehicles with blue flashing beacons, move out of the way as soon as it is safe to do so.

2.8 — Mark **three** answers

Which THREE of these emergency services might have blue flashing beacons?

- Coastguard
- Bomb disposal
- Gritting lorries
- Animal ambulances
- Mountain rescue
- Doctors' cars

- **Coastguard**
- **Bomb disposal**
- **Mountain rescue**

When attending an emergency these vehicles will be travelling at speed. You should help their progress by pulling over and allowing them to pass. Do so safely. Don't stop suddenly or in a dangerous position.

2.9 — Mark **one** answer

When being followed by an ambulance showing a flashing blue beacon you should

- pull over as soon as safely possible to let it pass
- accelerate hard to get away from it
- maintain your speed and course
- brake harshly and immediately stop in the road

- **pull over as soon as safely possible to let it pass**

Pull over in a place where the ambulance can pass safely. Check that there are no bollards or obstructions in the road that will prevent it from doing so.

What type of emergency vehicle is fitted with a green flashing beacon?

- ◉ Fire engine
- ◉ Road gritter
- ◉ Ambulance
- ◉ Doctor's car

◉ **Doctor's car**

A green flashing beacon on a vehicle means the driver or passenger is a doctor on an emergency call. Give way to them if it's safe to do so. Be aware that the vehicle may be travelling quickly or may stop in a hurry.

A flashing green beacon on a vehicle means

- ◉ police on non-urgent duties
- ◉ doctor on an emergency call
- ◉ road safety patrol operating
- ◉ gritting in progress

◉ **doctor on an emergency call**

If you see a vehicle with a flashing green beacon approaching, allow it to pass when you can do so safely. Be aware that someone's life could depend on the driver making good progress through traffic.

Diamond-shaped signs give instructions to

- ◉ tram drivers
- ◉ bus drivers
- ◉ lorry drivers
- ◉ taxi drivers

◉ **tram drivers**

These signs only apply to trams. They are directed at tram drivers but you should know their meaning so that you're aware of the priorities and are able to anticipate the actions of the driver.

2.13 — *Mark **one** answer*

On a road where trams operate, which of these vehicles will be most at risk from the tram rails?

- ⊙ Cars
- ⊙ Cycles
- ⊙ Buses
- ⊙ Lorries

⊙ **Cycles**

The narrow wheels of a bicycle can become stuck in the tram rails, causing the cyclist to stop suddenly, wobble or even lose balance altogether. The tram lines are also slippery which could cause a cyclist to slide or fall off.

2.14 — *Mark **one** answer*

What should you use your horn for?

- ⊙ To alert others to your presence
- ⊙ To allow you right of way
- ⊙ To greet other road users
- ⊙ To signal your annoyance

⊙ **To alert others to your presence**

Your horn must not be used between 11.30 pm and 7 am in a built-up area or when you are stationary, unless a moving vehicle poses a danger. Its function is to alert other road users to your presence.

2.15 — *Mark **one** answer*

You are in a one-way street and want to turn right. You should position yourself

- ⊙ in the right-hand lane
- ⊙ in the left-hand lane
- ⊙ in either lane, depending on the traffic
- ⊙ just left of the centre line

⊙ **in the right-hand lane**

If you're travelling in a one-way street and wish to turn right you should take up a position in the right-hand lane. This will enable other road users not wishing to turn to proceed on the left. Indicate your intention and take up your position in good time.

2.16
Mark **one** answer

You wish to turn right ahead. Why should you take up the correct position in good time?

- To allow other drivers to pull out in front of you
- To give a better view into the road that you're joining
- To help other road users know what you intend to do
- To allow drivers to pass you on the right

⊙ **To help other road users know what you intend to do**

If you wish to turn right into a side road take up your position in good time. Move to the centre of the road when it's safe to do so. This will allow vehicles to pass you on the left. Early planning will show other traffic what you intend to do.

2.17
Mark **one** answer

At which type of crossing are cyclists allowed to ride across with pedestrians?

- Toucan
- Puffin
- Pelican
- Zebra

⊙ **Toucan**

A toucan crossing is designed to allow pedestrians and cyclists to cross at the same time. Look out for cyclists approaching the crossing at speed.

2.18
Mark **one** answer

You are travelling at the legal speed limit. A vehicle comes up quickly behind, flashing its headlights. You should

- accelerate to make a gap behind you
- touch the brakes sharply to show your brake lights
- maintain your speed to prevent the vehicle from overtaking
- allow the vehicle to overtake

⊙ **allow the vehicle to overtake**

Don't enforce the speed limit by blocking another vehicle's progress. This will only lead to the other driver becoming more frustrated. Allow the other vehicle to pass when you can do so safely.

2.19
*Mark **one** answer*

You should ONLY flash your headlights to other road users

- to show that you are giving way
- to show that you are about to turn
- to tell them that you have right of way
- to let them know that you are there

⊙ **to let them know that you are there**

You should only flash your headlights to warn others of your presence. Don't use them to greet others, show impatience or give priority to other road users. They could misunderstand your signal.

2.20
*Mark **one** answer*

You are approaching unmarked crossroads. How should you deal with this type of junction?

- Accelerate and keep to the middle
- Slow down and keep to the right
- Accelerate looking to the left
- Slow down and look both ways

⊙ **Slow down and look both ways**

Be extra-cautious, especially when your view is restricted by hedges, bushes, walls and large vehicles etc. In the summer months these junctions can become more difficult to deal with when growing foliage may obscure your view.

2.21
*Mark **one** answer*

You are approaching a pelican crossing. The amber light is flashing. You must

- give way to pedestrians who are crossing
- encourage pedestrians to cross
- not move until the green light appears
- stop even if the crossing is clear

⊙ **give way to pedestrians who are crossing**

While the pedestrians are crossing don't encourage them to cross by waving or flashing your headlights: other road users may misunderstand your signal. Don't harass them by creeping forward or revving your engine.

The conditions are good and dry. You could use the 'two-second rule'

- ⊙ before restarting the engine after it has stalled
- ⊙ to keep a safe gap from the vehicle in front
- ⊙ before using the 'Mirror-Signal-Manoeuvre' routine
- ⊙ when emerging on wet roads

⊙ **to keep a safe gap from the vehicle in front**

To measure this, choose a fixed reference point such as a bridge, sign or tree. When the vehicle ahead passes the object, say to yourself 'Only a fool breaks the two-second rule.' If you reach the object before you finish saying this, you're TOO CLOSE.

At a puffin crossing, which colour follows the green signal?

- ⊙ Steady red
- ⊙ Flashing amber
- ⊙ Steady amber
- ⊙ Flashing green

⊙ **Steady amber**

Puffin crossings have infra-red sensors which detect when pedestrians are crossing and hold the red traffic signal until the crossing is clear. The use of a sensor means there is no flashing amber phase as there is with a pelican crossing.

You are in a line of traffic. The driver behind you is following very closely. What action should you take?

- ⊙ Ignore the following driver and continue to travel within the speed limit
- ⊙ Slow down, gradually increasing the gap between you and the vehicle in front
- ⊙ Signal left and wave the following driver past
- ⊙ Move over to a position just left of the centre line of the road

⊙ **Slow down, gradually increasing the gap between you and the vehicle in front**

It can be worrying to see that the car behind is following you too closely. Give yourself a greater safety margin by easing back from the vehicle in front.

2.25
Mark **one** answer

A vehicle has a flashing green beacon. What does this mean?

- ⊙ A doctor is answering an emergency call
- ⊙ The vehicle is slow-moving
- ⊙ It is a motorway police patrol vehicle
- ⊙ The vehicle is carrying hazardous chemicals

⊙ **A doctor is answering an emergency call**

A doctor attending an emergency may show a green flashing beacon on their vehicle. Give way to them when you can do so safely as they will need to reach their destination quickly. Be aware that they might pull over suddenly.

2.26
Mark **one** answer

A bus has stopped at a bus stop ahead of you. Its right-hand indicator is flashing. You should

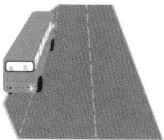

- ⊙ flash your headlights and slow down
- ⊙ slow down and give way if it is safe to do so
- ⊙ sound your horn and keep going
- ⊙ slow down and then sound your horn

⊙ **slow down and give way if it is safe to do so**

Give way to buses whenever you can do so safely, especially when they signal to pull away from bus stops. Look out for people leaving the bus and crossing the road.

2.27
Mark **one** answer

You are driving on a clear night. There is a steady stream of oncoming traffic. The national speed limit applies. Which lights should you use?

- ⊙ Full beam headlights
- ⊙ Sidelights
- ⊙ Dipped headlights
- ⊙ Fog lights

⊙ **Dipped headlights**

Use the full beam headlights only when you can be sure that you won't dazzle other road users.

You are driving behind a large goods vehicle. It signals left but steers to the right. You should

- ⊙ slow down and let the vehicle turn
- ⊙ drive on, keeping to the left
- ⊙ overtake on the right of it
- ⊙ hold your speed and sound your horn

⊙ **slow down and let the vehicle turn**

Large, long vehicles need extra room when making turns at junctions. They may move out to the right in order to make a left turn. Keep well back and don't attempt to pass on the left.

You are driving along this road. The red van cuts in close in front of you. What should you do?

- ⊙ Accelerate to get closer to the red van
- ⊙ Give a long blast on the horn
- ⊙ Drop back to leave the correct separation distance
- ⊙ Flash your headlights several times

⊙ **Drop back to leave the correct separation distance**

There are times when other drivers make incorrect or ill-judged decisions. Be tolerant and try not to retaliate or react aggressively. Always consider the safety of other road users, your passengers and yourself.

You are waiting in a traffic queue at night. To avoid dazzling following drivers you should

- ⊙ apply the handbrake only
- ⊙ apply the footbrake only
- ⊙ switch off your headlights
- ⊙ use both the handbrake and footbrake

⊙ **apply the handbrake only**

You should consider drivers behind as brake lights can dazzle. However, if you are driving in fog it's safer to keep your foot on the footbrake. In this case it will give the vehicle behind extra warning of your presence.

2.31 Mark **one** answer

You are driving in traffic at the speed limit for the road. The driver behind is trying to overtake. You should

- ⊙ move closer to the car ahead, so the driver behind has no room to overtake
- ⊙ wave the driver behind to overtake when it is safe
- ⊙ keep a steady course and allow the driver behind to overtake
- ⊙ accelerate to get away from the driver behind

⊙ **keep a steady course and allow the driver behind to overtake**

Keep a steady course to give the driver behind an opportunity to overtake safely. If necessary, slow down. Reacting incorrectly to another driver's impatience can lead to danger.

2.32 Mark **one** answer

A bus lane on your left shows no times of operation. This means it is

- ⊙ not in operation at all
- ⊙ only in operation at peak times
- ⊙ in operation 24 hours a day
- ⊙ only in operation in daylight hours

⊙ **in operation 24 hours a day**

Don't drive or park in a bus lane when it's in operation. This can cause disruption to traffic and delays to public transport.

2.33 Mark **two** answers

You are driving along a country road. A horse and rider are approaching. What should you do?

- ⊙ Increase your speed
- ⊙ Sound your horn
- ⊙ Flash your headlights
- ⊙ Drive slowly past
- ⊙ Give plenty of room
- ⊙ Rev your engine

⊙ **Drive slowly past**

⊙ **Give plenty of room**

It's important that you reduce your speed. Passing too closely at speed could startle the horse and unseat the rider.

2.34

A person herding sheep asks you to stop. You should

- ignore them as they have no authority
- stop and switch off your engine
- continue on but drive slowly
- try and get past quickly

⊙ **stop and switch off your engine**

Allow the sheep to clear the road before you proceed. Animals are unpredictable and startle easily; they could turn and run into your path or into the path of another moving vehicle.

2.35

When overtaking a horse and rider you should

- sound your horn as a warning
- go past as quickly as possible
- flash your headlights as a warning
- go past slowly and carefully

⊙ **go past slowly and carefully**

Horses can become startled by the sound of a car engine or the rush of air caused by passing too closely. Keep well back and only pass when it is safe; leave them plenty of room. You may have to use the other side of the road to go past: if you do, first make sure there is no oncoming traffic.

2.36

You are approaching a zebra crossing. Pedestrians are waiting to cross. You should

- give way to the elderly and infirm only
- slow down and prepare to stop
- use your headlights to indicate they can cross
- wave at them to cross the road

⊙ **slow down and prepare to stop**

Look out on the approach especially for children and older pedestrians. They may walk across without looking. Zebra crossings have flashing amber beacons on both sides of the road, black and white stripes on the crossing and white zigzag markings on both sides of the crossing. Where you can see pedestrians waiting to cross, slow down and prepare to stop.

2.37
*Mark **one** answer*

A vehicle pulls out in front of you at a junction. What should you do?

- Swerve past it and sound your horn
- Flash your headlights and drive up close behind
- Slow down and be ready to stop
- Accelerate past it immediately

◉ **Slow down and be ready to stop**

Try to be ready for the unexpected. Plan ahead and learn to anticipate hazards. You'll then give yourself more time to react to any problems that might occur.

Be tolerant of the behaviour of other road users who don't behave correctly.

2.38
*Mark **one** answer*

You stop for pedestrians waiting to cross at a zebra crossing. They do not start to cross. What should you do?

- Be patient and wait
- Sound your horn
- Carry on
- Wave them to cross

◉ **Be patient and wait**

If you stop for pedestrians and they don't start to cross don't wave them across or sound your horn. This could be dangerous if another vehicle is approaching which hasn't seen or heard your signal.

2.39
*Mark **one** answer*

You are following this lorry. You should keep well back from it to

- give you a good view of the road ahead
- stop following traffic from rushing through the junction
- prevent traffic behind you from overtaking
- allow you to hurry through the traffic lights if they change

◉ **give you a good view of the road ahead**

By keeping well back you will increase your width of vision around the rear of the lorry. This will allow you to see further down the road and be prepared for any hazards.

2.40 *Mark **one** answer*

You are approaching a red light at a puffin crossing. Pedestrians are on the crossing. The red light will stay on until

- ⊙ you start to edge forward on to the crossing
- ⊙ the pedestrians have reached a safe position
- ⊙ the pedestrians are clear of the front of your vehicle
- ⊙ a driver from the opposite direction reaches the crossing

⊙ **the pedestrians have reached a safe position**

The electronic device will automatically detect that the pedestrians have reached a safe position. Don't proceed until the green light shows it is safe for vehicles to do so.

2.41 *Mark **one** answer*

Which instrument panel warning light would show that headlights are on full beam?

You should be aware of where all the warning lights and visual aids are on the vehicle you are driving. If you are driving a vehicle for the first time you should take time to check all the controls.

2.42 *Mark **one** answer*

At puffin crossings, which light will not show to a driver?

- ⊙ Flashing amber
- ⊙ Red
- ⊙ steady amber
- ⊙ green

⊙ **Flashing amber**

A flashing amber light is shown at pelican crossings, but puffin crossings are different. They are controlled electronically and automatically detect when pedestrians are on the crossing. The phase is shortened or lengthened according to the position of the pedestrians.

2.43

You should leave at least a two-second gap between your vehicle and the one in front when conditions are

- wet
- good
- damp
- foggy

⊙ **good**

In good, dry conditions an alert driver who's driving a vehicle with tyres and brakes in good condition, needs to keep a distance of at least two seconds from the car in front.

2.44

You are driving at night on an unlit road behind another vehicle. You should

- flash your headlights
- use dipped beam headlights
- switch off your headlights
- use full beam headlights

⊙ **use dipped beam headlights**

If you follow another vehicle with your headlights on full beam they could dazzle the driver. Leave a safe distance and ensure that the light from your dipped beam falls short of the vehicle in front.

2.45

You are driving a slow-moving vehicle on a narrow winding road. You should

- keep well out to stop vehicles overtaking dangerously
- wave following vehicles past you if you think they can overtake quickly
- pull in safely when you can, to let following vehicles overtake
- give a left signal when it is safe for vehicles to overtake you

⊙ **pull in safely when you can, to let following vehicles overtake**

Try not to hold up a queue of traffic. Other road users may become impatient and this could lead to reckless actions. If you're driving a slow-moving vehicle and the road is narrow, look for a safe place to pull in. DON'T wave other traffic past since this could be dangerous if you or they haven't seen an oncoming vehicle.

You have a loose filler cap on your diesel fuel tank. This will

- ◉ waste fuel and money
- ◉ make roads slippery for other road users
- ◉ improve your vehicle's fuel consumption
- ◉ increase the level of exhaust emissions

◉ **waste fuel and money**

◉ **make roads slippery for other road users**

Diesel fuel is especially slippery if spilled on a wet road. At the end of a dry spell of weather you should be aware that the road surfaces may have a high level of diesel spillage that hasn't been washed away by rain.

To avoid spillage after refuelling, you should make sure that

- ◉ your tank is only three quarters full
- ◉ you have used a locking filler cap
- ◉ you check your fuel gauge is working
- ◉ your filler cap is securely fastened

◉ **your filler cap is securely fastened**

When learning to drive it is a good idea to practise filling your car with fuel. Ask your instructor if you can use a petrol station and fill the fuel tank yourself. You need to know where the filler cap is located on the car you are driving in order to park on the correct side of the pump. Take care not to overfill the tank or spill fuel. Make sure you secure the filler cap as soon as you have replaced the fuel nozzle.

If your vehicle uses diesel fuel, take extra care when refuelling. Diesel fuel when spilt is

- ◉ sticky
- ◉ odourless
- ◉ clear
- ◉ slippery

◉ **slippery**

If you are using diesel, or are at a pump which has a diesel facility, be aware that there may be spilt fuel on the ground. Fuel contamination on the soles of your shoes may cause them to slip when using the foot pedals.

2.49
*Mark **one** answer*

What style of driving causes increased risk to everyone?

- Considerate
- Defensive
- Competitive
- Responsible

○ **Competitive**

Competitive driving increases the risks to everyone and is the opposite of responsible, considerate and defensive driving. Defensive driving is about questioning the actions of other road users and being prepared for the unexpected. Don't be taken by surprise.

2.50
*Mark **one** answer*

Young, inexperienced and newly qualified drivers can often be involved in crashes. This is due to

- being too cautious at junctions
- driving in the middle of their lane
- showing off and being competitive
- staying within the speed limit

○ **showing off and being competitive**

Newly qualified, and particularly young drivers, are more vulnerable in the first year after passing the test. Inexperience plays a part in this but it's essential to have the correct attitude. Be responsible and always show courtesy and consideration to other road users.

section **three**
SAFETY AND YOUR VEHICLE

This section covers

- Fault detection
- Defects
- Safety equipment
- Emissions
- Noise

3.1

*Mark **two** answers*

Which TWO are badly affected if the tyres are under-inflated?

⊙ Braking

⊙ Steering

⊙ Changing gear

⊙ Parking

⊙ **Braking**

⊙ **Steering**

Your tyres are your only contact with the road so it is very important to ensure that they are free from defects, have sufficient tread depth and are correctly inflated. Correct tyre pressures help reduce the risk of skidding and provide a safer and more comfortable drive or ride.

3.2

*Mark **one** answer*

You must NOT sound your horn

⊙ between 10 pm and 6 am in a built-up area

⊙ at any time in a built-up area

⊙ between 11.30 pm and 7 am in a built-up area

⊙ between 11.30 pm and 6 am on any road

⊙ **between 11.30 pm and 7 am in a built-up area**

Vehicles can be noisy. Every effort must be made to prevent excessive noise, especially in built-up areas at night. Don't

• rev the engine

• sound the horn

unnecessarily.

It is illegal to sound your horn in a built-up area between 11.30 pm and 7 am, except when another vehicle poses a danger.

The pictured vehicle is 'environmentally friendly' because it

- ⊙ reduces noise pollution
- ⊙ uses diesel fuel
- ⊙ uses electricity
- ⊙ uses unleaded fuel
- ⊙ reduces parking spaces
- ⊙ reduces town traffic

⊙ **reduces noise pollution**

⊙ **uses electricity**

⊙ **reduces town traffic**

Trams are powered by electricity and therefore do not emit exhaust fumes. They are also much quieter than petrol or diesel engined vehicles and can carry a large number of passengers.

Supertrams or Light Rapid Transit (LRT) systems are environmentally friendly because

- ⊙ they use diesel power
- ⊙ they use quieter roads
- ⊙ they use electric power
- ⊙ they do not operate during rush hour

⊙ **they use electric power**

This means that they do not emit toxic fumes, which add to city pollution problems. They are also a lot quieter and smoother to ride on.

'Red routes' in major cities have been introduced to

- ⊙ raise the speed limits
- ⊙ help the traffic flow
- ⊙ provide better parking
- ⊙ allow lorries to load more freely

⊙ **help the traffic flow**

Traffic jams today are often caused by the volume of traffic. However, inconsiderate parking can lead to the closure of an inside lane or traffic having to wait for oncoming vehicles. Driving slowly in traffic increases fuel consumption and causes a build-up of exhaust fumes.

3.6
*Mark **one** answer*

Road humps, chicanes, and narrowings are

- ⊙ always at major road works
- ⊙ used to increase traffic speed
- ⊙ at toll-bridge approaches only
- ⊙ traffic calming measures

⊙ **traffic calming measures**

Traffic calming measures help keep vehicle speeds low in congested areas where there are pedestrians and children. A pedestrian is much more likely to survive a collision with a vehicle travelling at 20 mph than at 40 mph.

3.7
*Mark **one** answer*

The purpose of a catalytic converter is to reduce

- ⊙ fuel consumption
- ⊙ the risk of fire
- ⊙ toxic exhaust gases
- ⊙ engine wear

⊙ **toxic exhaust gases**

Catalytic converters are designed to reduce a large percentage of toxic emissions. They work more efficiently when the engine has reached its normal working temperature.

3.8
*Mark **one** answer*

Catalytic converters are fitted to make the

- ⊙ engine produce more power
- ⊙ exhaust system easier to replace
- ⊙ engine run quietly
- ⊙ exhaust fumes cleaner

⊙ **exhaust fumes cleaner**

Harmful gases in the exhaust system pollute the atmosphere. These gases are reduced by up to 90% if a catalytic converter is fitted. Cleaner air benefits everyone, especially people who live or work near congested roads.

It is essential that tyre pressures are checked regularly. When should this be done?

- After any lengthy journey
- After travelling at high speed
- When tyres are hot
- When tyres are cold

⊙ **When tyres are cold**

When you check the tyre pressures do so when the tyres are cold. This will give you a more accurate reading. The heat generated from a long journey will raise the pressure inside the tyre.

When should you NOT use your horn in a built-up area?

- Between 8 pm and 8 am
- Between 9 pm and dawn
- Between dusk and 8 am
- Between 11.30 pm and 7 am

⊙ **Between 11.30 pm and 7 am**

By law you must not sound your horn in a built-up area between 11.30 pm and 7.00 am. The exception to this is when another road user poses a danger.

You will use more fuel if your tyres are

- under-inflated
- of different makes
- over-inflated
- new and hardly used

⊙ **under-inflated**

Check your tyre pressures frequently – normally once a week. If pressures are lower than those recommended by the manufacturer, there will be more 'rolling resistance'. The engine will have to work harder to overcome this, leading to increased fuel consumption.

3.12
*Mark **two** answers*

How should you dispose of a used battery?

- ⊙ Take it to a local authority site
- ⊙ Put it in the dustbin
- ⊙ Break it up into pieces
- ⊙ Leave it on waste land
- ⊙ Take it to a garage
- ⊙ Burn it on a fire

⊙ **Take it to a local authority site**

⊙ **Take it to a garage**

Batteries contain acid which is hazardous and must be disposed of safely.

3.13
*Mark **one** answer*

What is most likely to cause high fuel consumption?

- ⊙ Poor steering control
- ⊙ Accelerating around bends
- ⊙ Staying in high gears
- ⊙ Harsh braking and accelerating

⊙ **Harsh braking and accelerating**

Accelerating and braking gently and smoothly will help to save fuel, reduce wear on your vehicle and is better for the environment.

3.14
*Mark **one** answer*

The fluid level in your battery is low. What should you top it up with?

- ⊙ Battery acid
- ⊙ Distilled water
- ⊙ Engine oil
- ⊙ Engine coolant

⊙ **Distilled water**

Some modern batteries are maintenance-free. Check your vehicle handbook and, if necessary, make sure that the plates in each battery cell are covered.

You are parked on the road at night. Where must you use parking lights?

- ⊙ Where there are continuous white lines in the middle of the road
- ⊙ Where the speed limit exceeds 30 mph
- ⊙ Where you are facing oncoming traffic
- ⊙ Where you are near a bus stop

⊙ **Where the speed limit exceeds 30 mph**

When parking at night, park in the direction of the traffic. This will enable other road users to see the reflectors on the rear of your vehicle. Use your parking lights if the speed limit is over 30 mph.

Motor vehicles can harm the environment. This has resulted in

- ⊙ air pollution
- ⊙ damage to buildings
- ⊙ less risk to health
- ⊙ improved public transport
- ⊙ less use of electrical vehicles
- ⊙ using up of natural resources

⊙ **air pollution**

⊙ **damage to buildings**

⊙ **using up of natural resources**

Exhaust emissions are harmful to health. Together with vibration from heavy traffic this can result in damage to buildings. Most petrol and diesel fuels come from a finite and non-renewable source. Anything you can do to reduce your use of these fuels will help the environment.

Excessive or uneven tyre wear can be caused by faults in which THREE of the following?

- ⊙ The gearbox
- ⊙ The braking system
- ⊙ The accelerator
- ⊙ The exhaust system
- ⊙ Wheel alignment
- ⊙ The suspension

⊙ **The braking system**

⊙ **Wheel alignment**

⊙ **The suspension**

Regular servicing will help to detect faults at an early stage and this will avoid the risk of minor faults becoming serious or even dangerous.

3.18

You need to top up your battery. What level should you fill to?

- ⊙ The top of the battery
- ⊙ Half-way up the battery
- ⊙ Just below the cell plates
- ⊙ Just above the cell plates

⊙ **Just above the cell plates**

Top up the battery with distilled water and make sure each cell plate is covered.

3.19

You are parking on a two-way road at night. The speed limit is 40 mph. You should park on the

- ⊙ left with parking lights on
- ⊙ left with no lights on
- ⊙ right with parking lights on
- ⊙ right with dipped headlights on

⊙ **left with parking lights on**

At night all vehicles must display parking lights when parked on a road with a speed limit greater than 30 mph. They should be close to the kerb, facing in the direction of the traffic flow and not within a distance as specified in The Highway Code.

3.20

Before starting a journey it is wise to plan your route. How can you do this?

- ⊙ Look at a map
- ⊙ Contact your local garage
- ⊙ Look in your vehicle handbook
- ⊙ Check your vehicle registration document

⊙ **Look at a map**

Planning your journey before you set out can help to make it much easier, more pleasant and may help to ease traffic congestion. Look at a map to help you to do this. You may need different scale maps depending on where and how far you're going. Printing or writing out the route can also help.

It can help to plan your route before starting a journey. You can do this by contacting

⊙ your local filling station

⊙ a motoring organisation

⊙ the Driver Vehicle Licensing Agency

⊙ your vehicle manufacturer

⊙ **a motoring organisation**

Most motoring organisations will give you a detailed plan of your trip showing directions and distance. Some will also include advice on rest and fuel stops. The Highways Agency website will also give you information on roadworks and incidents and gives expected delay times.

How can you plan your route before starting a long journey?

⊙ Check your vehicle's workshop manual

⊙ Ask your local garage

⊙ Use a route planner on the internet

⊙ Consult your travel agents

⊙ **Use a route planner on the internet**

Various route planners are available on the internet. Most of them give you various options allowing you to choose the most direct, quickest or scenic route. They can also include rest and fuel stops and distances. Print them off and take them with you.

Planning your route before setting out can be helpful. How can you do this?

⊙ Look in a motoring magazine

⊙ Only visit places you know

⊙ Try to travel at busy times

⊙ Print or write down the route

⊙ **Print or write down the route**

Print or write down your route before setting out. Some places are not well signed so using place names and road numbers may help you avoid problems en route. Try to get an idea of how far you're going before you leave. You can also use it to re-check the next stage at each rest stop.

3.24 *Mark **one** answer*

Why is it a good idea to plan your journey to avoid busy times?

- You will have an easier journey
- You will have a more stressful journey
- Your journey time will be longer
- It will cause more traffic congestion

⊙ **You will have an easier journey**

No one likes to spend time in traffic queues. Try to avoid busy times related to school or work travel. As well as moving vehicles you should also consider congestion caused by parked cars, buses and coaches around schools.

3.25 *Mark **one** answer*

Planning your journey to avoid busy times has a number of advantages. One of these is

- your journey will take longer
- you will have a more pleasant journey
- you will cause more pollution
- your stress level will be greater

⊙ **you will have a more pleasant journey**

Having a pleasant journey can have safety benefits. You will be less tired and stressed and this will allow you to concentrate more on your driving or riding.

3.26 *Mark **one** answer*

It is a good idea to plan your journey to avoid busy times. This is because

- your vehicle will use more fuel
- you will see less road works
- it will help to ease congestion
- you will travel a much shorter distance

⊙ **it will help to ease congestion**

Avoiding busy times means that you are not adding needlessly to traffic congestion. Other advantages are that you will use less fuel and feel less stressed.

By avoiding busy times when travelling

- you are more likely to be held up
- your journey time will be longer
- you will travel a much shorter distance
- you are less likely to be delayed

⊙ **you are less likely to be delayed**

If possible, avoid the early morning and, late afternoon/early evening 'rush hour'. Doing this should allow you to travel in a more relaxed frame of mind, concentrate solely on what you're doing and arrive at your destination feeling less stressed.

It can help to plan your route before starting a journey. Why should you also plan an alternative route?

- Your original route may be blocked
- Your maps may have different scales
- You may find you have to pay a congestion charge
- Because you may get held up by a tractor

⊙ **Your original route may be blocked**

It can be frustrating and worrying to find your planned route is blocked by roadworks or diversions. If you have planned an alternative you will feel less stressed and more able to concentrate fully on your driving or riding. If your original route is mostly on motorways it's a good idea to plan an alternative using non-motorway roads. Always carry a map with you just in case you need to refer to it.

As well as planning your route before starting a journey, you should also plan an alternative route. Why is this?

- To let another driver overtake
- Your first route may be blocked
- To avoid a railway level crossing
- In case you have to avoid emergency vehicles

⊙ **Your first route may be blocked**

It's a good idea to plan an alternative route in case your original route is blocked for any reason. You're less likely to feel worried and stressed if you've got an alternative in mind. This will enable you to concentrate fully on your driving or riding. Always carry a map that covers the area you will travel in.

3.30
*Mark **one** answer*

You are making an appointment and will have to travel a long distance. You should

- allow plenty of time for your journey
- plan to go at busy times
- avoid all national speed limit roads
- prevent other drivers from overtaking

- **allow plenty of time for your journey**

Always allow plenty of time for your journey in case of unforeseen problems. Anything can happen, punctures, breakdowns, road closures, diversions etc. You will feel less stressed and less inclined to take risks if you are not 'pushed for time'.

3.31
*Mark **one** answer*

Rapid acceleration and heavy braking can lead to

- reduced pollution
- increased fuel consumption
- reduced exhaust emissions
- increased road safety

- **increased fuel consumption**

Using the controls smoothly can reduce fuel consumption by about 15% as well as reducing wear and tear on your vehicle. Plan ahead and anticipate changes of speed well in advance. This will reduce the need to accelerate rapidly or brake sharply.

3.32
*Mark **one** answer*

What percentage of all emissions does road transport account for?

- 10%
- 20%
- 30%
- 40%

- **20%**

Transport is an essential part of modern life but it does have environmental effects. In heavily populated areas traffic is the biggest source of air pollution. Eco-safe driving and riding will reduce emissions and can make a surprising difference to local air quality.

Which of these, if allowed to get low, could cause you to crash?

- Anti-freeze level
- Brake fluid level
- Battery water level
- Radiator coolant level

○ **Brake fluid level**

You should carry out frequent checks on all fluid levels but particularly brake fluid. As the brake pads or shoes wear down the brake fluid level will drop. If it drops below the minimum mark on the fluid reservoir, air could enter the hydraulic system and lead to a loss of braking efficiency or complete brake failure.

New petrol-engined cars must be fitted with catalytic converters. The reason for this is to

- control exhaust noise levels
- prolong the life of the exhaust system
- allow the exhaust system to be recycled
- reduce harmful exhaust emissions

○ **reduce harmful exhaust emissions**

We should all be concerned about the effect traffic has on our environment. Fumes from vehicles are polluting the air around us. Catalytic converters act like a filter, removing some of the toxic waste from exhaust gases.

What can cause heavy steering?

- Driving on ice
- Badly worn brakes
- Over-inflated tyres
- Under-inflated tyres

○ **Under-inflated tyres**

If your tyre pressures are low this will increase the drag on the road surface and make the steering feel heavy. Your vehicle will also use more fuel. Incorrectly inflated tyres can affect the braking, cornering and handling of your vehicle to a dangerous level.

3.36
*Mark **two** answers*

Driving with under-inflated tyres can affect

- ⊙ engine temperature
- ⊙ fuel consumption
- ⊙ braking
- ⊙ oil pressure

⊙ **fuel consumption**

⊙ **braking**

Keeping your vehicle's tyres correctly inflated is a legal requirement.

Driving with correctly inflated tyres will use less fuel and your vehicle will brake more safely.

3.37
*Mark **two** answers*

Excessive or uneven tyre wear can be caused by faults in the

- ⊙ gearbox
- ⊙ braking system
- ⊙ suspension
- ⊙ exhaust system

⊙ **braking system**

⊙ **suspension**

Uneven wear on your tyres can be caused by the condition of your vehicle. Having it serviced regularly will ensure that the brakes, steering and wheel alignment are maintained in good order.

3.38
*Mark **one** answer*

The main cause of brake fade is

- ⊙ the brakes overheating
- ⊙ air in the brake fluid
- ⊙ oil on the brakes
- ⊙ the brakes out of adjustment

⊙ **the brakes overheating**

If your vehicle is fitted with drum brakes they can get hot and lose efficiency. This happens when they're used continually, such as on a long, steep, downhill stretch of road. Using a lower gear will assist the braking and help prevent the vehicle gaining momentum.

Your anti-lock brakes warning light stays on. You should

- check the brake fluid level
- check the footbrake free play
- check that the handbrake is released
- have the brakes checked immediately

⊙ **have the brakes checked immediately**

Consult the vehicle handbook or garage before driving the vehicle. Only drive to a garage if it is safe to do so. If you're not sure get expert help.

While driving, this warning light on your dashboard comes on. It means

- a fault in the braking system
- the engine oil is low
- a rear light has failed
- your seat belt is not fastened

⊙ **a fault in the braking system**

Don't ignore this warning light. A fault in your braking system could have dangerous consequences.

It is important to wear suitable shoes when you are driving. Why is this?

- To prevent wear on the pedals
- To maintain control of the pedals
- To enable you to adjust your seat
- To enable you to walk for assistance if you break down

⊙ **To maintain control of the pedals**

When you're going to drive, ensure that you're wearing suitable clothing.

Comfortable shoes will ensure that you have proper control of the foot pedals.

3.42
*Mark **one** answer*

What will reduce the risk of neck injury resulting from a collision?

- ⊙ An air-sprung seat
- ⊙ Anti-lock brakes
- ⊙ A collapsible steering wheel
- ⊙ A properly adjusted head restraint

⊙ **A properly adjusted head restraint**

If you're involved in a collision, head restraints will reduce the risk of neck injury. They must be properly adjusted. Make sure they aren't positioned too low, in a crash this could cause damage to the neck or spine.

3.43
*Mark **one** answer*

You are testing your suspension. You notice that your vehicle keeps bouncing when you press down on the front wing. What does this mean?

- ⊙ Worn tyres
- ⊙ Tyres under-inflated
- ⊙ Steering wheel not located centrally
- ⊙ Worn shock absorbers

⊙ **Worn shock absorbers**

If you find that your vehicle bounces as you drive around a corner or bend in the road, the shock absorbers might be worn. Press down on the front wing and, if the vehicle continues to bounce, take it to be checked by a qualified mechanic.

3.44
*Mark **one** answer*

A roof rack fitted to your car will

- ⊙ reduce fuel consumption
- ⊙ improve the road handling
- ⊙ make your car go faster
- ⊙ increase fuel consumption

⊙ **increase fuel consumption**

If you are carrying anything on a roof rack, make sure that any cover is securely fitted and does not flap about while driving. Aerodynamically designed roof boxes are available which reduce wind resistance and, in turn, fuel consumption.

It is illegal to drive with tyres that

- ⊙ have been bought second-hand
- ⊙ have a large deep cut in the side wall
- ⊙ are of different makes
- ⊙ are of different tread patterns

⊙ **have a large deep cut in the side wall**

When checking your tyres for cuts and bulges in the side walls, don't forget the inner walls (ie. those facing each other under the vehicle).

The legal minimum depth of tread for car tyres over three quarters of the breadth is

- ⊙ 1 mm
- ⊙ 1.6 mm
- ⊙ 2.5 mm
- ⊙ 4 mm

⊙ **1.6 mm**

Tyres must have sufficient depth of tread to give them a good grip on the road surface. The legal minimum for cars is 1.6 mm.

This depth should be across the central three quarters of the breadth of the tyre and around the entire circumference.

You are carrying two 13 year old children and their parents in your car. Who is responsible for seeing that the children wear seat belts?

- ⊙ The children's parents
- ⊙ You, the driver
- ⊙ The front-seat passenger
- ⊙ The children

⊙ **You, the driver**

Seat belts save lives and reduce the risk of injury. If you are carrying passengers under 14 years of age it's your responsibility as the driver to ensure that their seat belts are fastened or they are seated in an approved child restraint.

When a roof rack is not in use it should be removed. Why is this?

- ⊙ It will affect the suspension
- ⊙ It is illegal
- ⊙ It will affect your braking
- ⊙ It will waste fuel

⊙ **It will waste fuel**

We are all responsible for the environment we live in. If each driver takes responsibility for conserving fuel, together it will make a difference.

3.49　*Mark **three** answers*

How can you, as a driver, help the environment?

- ⊙ By reducing your speed
- ⊙ By gentle acceleration
- ⊙ By using leaded fuel
- ⊙ By driving faster
- ⊙ By harsh acceleration
- ⊙ By servicing your vehicle properly

- ⊙ **By reducing your speed**
- ⊙ **By gentle acceleration**
- ⊙ **By servicing your vehicle properly**

Rapid acceleration and heavy braking lead to greater fuel consumption. They also increase wear and tear on your vehicle.

Having your vehicle regularly serviced means your engine will maintain its efficiency, produce cleaner emissions and lengthen its life.

3.50　*Mark **three** answers*

To help the environment, you can avoid wasting fuel by

- ⊙ having your vehicle properly serviced
- ⊙ making sure your tyres are correctly inflated
- ⊙ not over-revving in the lower gears
- ⊙ driving at higher speeds where possible
- ⊙ keeping an empty roof rack properly fitted
- ⊙ servicing your vehicle less regularly

- ⊙ **having your vehicle properly serviced**
- ⊙ **making sure your tyres are correctly inflated**
- ⊙ **not over-revving in the lower gears**

If you don't have your vehicle serviced regularly, the engine will not burn all the fuel efficiently. This will cause excess gases to be discharged into the atmosphere.

3.51　*Mark **three** answers*

To reduce the volume of traffic on the roads you could

- ⊙ use public transport more often
- ⊙ share a car when possible
- ⊙ walk or cycle on short journeys
- ⊙ travel by car at all times
- ⊙ use a car with a smaller engine
- ⊙ drive in a bus lane

- ⊙ **use public transport more often**
- ⊙ **share a car when possible**
- ⊙ **walk or cycle on short journeys**

Walking or cycling are good ways to get exercise. Using public transport also gives the opportunity for exercise if you walk to the railway station or bus stop. Leave the car at home whenever you can.

*Mark **three** answers*

Which THREE of the following are most likely to waste fuel?

- ⊙ Reducing your speed
- ⊙ Carrying unnecessary weight
- ⊙ Using the wrong grade of fuel
- ⊙ Under-inflated tyres
- ⊙ Using different brands of fuel
- ⊙ A fitted, empty roof rack

- ⊙ **Carrying unnecessary weight**
- ⊙ **Under-inflated tyres**
- ⊙ **A fitted, empty roof rack**

Wasting fuel costs you money and also causes unnecessary pollution. Ensuring your tyres are correctly inflated, avoiding carrying unnecessary weight, and removing a roof rack that is not in use, will all help to reduce your fuel consumption.

---

*Mark **three** answers*

Which THREE things can you, as a road user, do to help the environment?

- ⊙ Cycle when possible
- ⊙ Drive on under-inflated tyres
- ⊙ Use the choke for as long as possible on a cold engine
- ⊙ Have your vehicle properly tuned and serviced
- ⊙ Watch the traffic and plan ahead
- ⊙ Brake as late as possible without skidding

- ⊙ **Cycle when possible**
- ⊙ **Have your vehicle properly tuned and serviced**
- ⊙ **Watch the traffic and plan ahead**

Although the car is a convenient form of transport it can also cause damage to health and the environment, especially when used on short journeys. Before you travel consider other types of transport. Walking and cycling are better for your health and public transport can be quicker, more convenient and less stressful than driving.

---

*Mark **one** answer*

To help protect the environment you should NOT

- ⊙ remove your roof rack when unloaded
- ⊙ use your car for very short journeys
- ⊙ walk, cycle, or use public transport
- ⊙ empty the boot of unnecessary weight

- ⊙ **use your car for very short journeys**

Try not to use your car as a matter of routine. For shorter journeys, consider walking or cycling instead – this is much better for both you and the environment.

3.55
*Mark **three** answers*

Which THREE does the law require you to keep in good condition?

⊙ Gears

⊙ Transmission

⊙ Headlights

⊙ Windscreen

⊙ Seat belts

⊙ **Headlights**

⊙ **Windscreen**

⊙ **Seat belts**

Other things to check include lights, get someone to help you check the brake lights and indicators. Battery, a lot of these are now maintenance-free. Steering, check for play in the steering. Oil, water and suspension also need checking. Always check that the speedometer is working once you've moved off.

3.56
*Mark **one** answer*

Driving at 70 mph uses more fuel than driving at 50 mph by up to

⊙ 10%

⊙ 30%

⊙ 75%

⊙ 100%

⊙ **30%**

Your vehicle will use less fuel if you avoid heavy acceleration. The higher the engine revs, the more fuel you will use. Using the same gear, a vehicle travelling at 70mph will use up to 30% more fuel to cover the same distance, than at 50mph. However, don't travel so slowly that you inconvenience or endanger other road users.

3.57
*Mark **one** answer*

Your vehicle pulls to one side when braking. You should

⊙ change the tyres around

⊙ consult your garage as soon as possible

⊙ pump the pedal when braking

⊙ use your handbrake at the same time

⊙ **consult your garage as soon as possible**

The brakes on your vehicle must be effective and properly adjusted. If your vehicle pulls to one side when braking, take it to be checked by a qualified mechanic. Don't take risks.

3.58 Mark **one** answer

Unbalanced wheels on a car may cause

- the steering to pull to one side
- the steering to vibrate
- the brakes to fail
- the tyres to deflate

⊙ **the steering to vibrate**

If your wheels are out of balance it will cause the steering to vibrate at certain speeds. It is not a fault that will rectify itself. You will have to take your vehicle to a garage or tyre fitting firm as this is specialist work.

3.59 Mark **two** answers

Turning the steering wheel while your car is stationary can cause damage to the

- gearbox
- engine
- brakes
- steering
- tyres

⊙ **steering**

⊙ **tyres**

Turning the steering wheel when the car is not moving can cause unnecessary wear to the tyres and steering mechanism. This is known as 'dry' steering.

3.60 Mark **one** answer

You have to leave valuables in your car. It would be safer to

- put them in a carrier bag
- park near a school entrance
- lock them out of sight
- park near a bus stop

⊙ **lock them out of sight**

If you have to leave valuables in your car, always lock them out of sight. If you can see them, so can a thief.

3.61 Mark **one** answer

How could you deter theft from your car when leaving it unattended?

- Leave valuables in a carrier bag
- Lock valuables out of sight
- Put valuables on the seats
- Leave valuables on the floor

⊙ **Lock valuables out of sight**

If you can see valuables in your car so can a thief. If you can't take them with you lock them out of sight or you risk losing them, as well as having your car damaged.

3.62
*Mark **one** answer*

Which of the following may help to deter a thief from stealing your car?

- Always keeping the headlights on
- Fitting reflective glass windows
- Always keeping the interior light on
- Etching the car number on the windows

⊙ **Etching the car number on the windows**

Having your car registration number etched on all your windows is a cheap and effective way to deter professional car thieves.

3.63
*Mark **one** answer*

Which of the following should not be kept in your vehicle?

- A first aid kit
- A road atlas
- The tax disc
- The vehicle documents

⊙ **The vehicle documents**

Never leave the vehicle's documents inside it. They would help a thief dispose of the vehicle more easily.

3.64
*Mark **one** answer*

What should you do when leaving your vehicle?

- Put valuable documents under the seats
- Remove all valuables
- Cover valuables with a blanket
- Leave the interior light on

⊙ **Remove all valuables**

When leaving your vehicle unattended it is best to take valuables with you. If you can't, then lock them out of sight in the boot. If you can see valuables in your car, so can a thief.

3.65
*Mark **one** answer*

Which of these is most likely to deter the theft of your vehicle?

- An immobiliser
- Tinted windows
- Locking wheel nuts
- A sun screen

⊙ **An immobiliser**

An immobiliser makes it more difficult for your vehicle to be driven off by a thief. It is a particular deterrent to opportunist thieves.

3.66
*Mark **one** answer*

When parking and leaving your car you should

- park under a shady tree
- remove the tax disc
- park in a quiet road
- engage the steering lock

⊙ **engage the steering lock**

When you leave your car always engage the steering lock. This increases the security of your vehicle, as the ignition key is needed to release the steering lock.

3.67
*Mark **one** answer*

When leaving your vehicle parked and unattended you should

- park near a busy junction
- park in a housing estate
- remove the key and lock it
- leave the left indicator on

⊙ **remove the key and lock it**

An unlocked car is an open invitation to thieves. Leaving the keys in the ignition not only makes your car easy to steal, it could also invalidate your insurance.

3.68
*Mark **two** answers*

Which TWO of the following will improve fuel consumption?

- Reducing your road speed
- Planning well ahead
- Late and harsh braking
- Driving in lower gears
- Short journeys with a cold engine
- Rapid acceleration

⊙ **Reducing your road speed**

⊙ **Planning well ahead**

Harsh braking, constant gear changes and harsh acceleration increase fuel consumption. An engine uses less fuel when travelling at a constant low speed.

You need to look well ahead so you are able to anticipate hazards early. Easing off the accelerator and timing your approach, at junctions, for example, could actually improve the fuel consumption of your vehicle.

3.69 *Mark **one** answer*

You service your own vehicle. How should you get rid of the old engine oil?

- ⊙ Take it to a local authority site
- ⊙ Pour it down a drain
- ⊙ Tip it into a hole in the ground
- ⊙ Put it into your dustbin

⊙ **Take it to a local authority site**

It is illegal to pour engine oil down any drain. Oil is a pollutant and harmful to wildlife. Dispose of it safely at an authorised site.

3.70 *Mark **one** answer*

Why do MOT tests include a strict exhaust emission test?

- ⊙ To recover the cost of expensive garage equipment
- ⊙ To help protect the environment against pollution
- ⊙ To discover which fuel supplier is used the most
- ⊙ To make sure diesel and petrol engines emit the same fumes

⊙ **To help protect the environment against pollution**

Emission tests are carried out to ensure your vehicle's engine is operating efficiently. This ensures the pollution produced by the engine is kept to a minimum. If your vehicle is not serviced regularly, it may fail the annual MOT test.

3.71 *Mark **three** answers*

To reduce the damage your vehicle causes to the environment you should

- ⊙ use narrow side streets
- ⊙ avoid harsh acceleration
- ⊙ brake in good time
- ⊙ anticipate well ahead
- ⊙ use busy routes

⊙ **avoid harsh acceleration**

⊙ **brake in good time**

⊙ **anticipate well ahead**

By looking well ahead and recognising hazards early you can avoid last-minute harsh braking. Watch the traffic flow and look well ahead for potential hazards so you can control your speed accordingly. Avoid over-revving the engine and accelerating harshly as this increases wear to the engine and uses more fuel.

Your vehicle has a catalytic converter. Its purpose is to reduce

- ⊙ exhaust noise
- ⊙ fuel consumption
- ⊙ exhaust emissions
- ⊙ engine noise

⊙ **exhaust emissions**

Catalytic converters reduce the harmful gases given out by the engine. The gases are changed by a chemical process as they pass through a special filter.

A properly serviced vehicle will give

- ⊙ lower insurance premiums
- ⊙ you a refund on your road tax
- ⊙ better fuel economy
- ⊙ cleaner exhaust emissions

⊙ **better fuel economy**

⊙ **cleaner exhaust emissions**

When you purchase your vehicle, check at what intervals you should have it serviced. This can vary depending on model and manufacturer. Use the service manual and keep it up to date. The cost of a service may well be less than the cost of running a poorly maintained vehicle.

You enter a road where there are road humps. What should you do?

- ⊙ Maintain a reduced speed throughout
- ⊙ Accelerate quickly between each one
- ⊙ Always keep to the maximum legal speed
- ⊙ Drive slowly at school times only

⊙ **Maintain a reduced speed throughout**

The humps are there for a reason – to reduce the speed of the traffic. Don't accelerate harshly between them as this means you will only have to brake harshly to negotiate the next hump. Harsh braking and accelerating uses more fuel.

3.75

*Mark **one** answer*

When should you especially check the engine oil level?

- Before a long journey
- When the engine is hot
- Early in the morning
- Every 6000 miles

⊙ **Before a long journey**

During long journeys an engine can use more oil than on shorter trips. Insufficient oil is potentially dangerous: it can lead to excessive wear and expensive repairs.

Most cars have a dipstick to allow the oil level to be checked. If not, you should refer to the vehicle's handbook. Also make checks on

- fuel
- water
- tyres.

3.76

*Mark **one** answer*

You are having difficulty finding a parking space in a busy town. You can see there is space on the zigzag lines of a zebra crossing. Can you park there?

- No, unless you stay with your car
- Yes, in order to drop off a passenger
- Yes, if you do not block people from crossing
- No, not in any circumstances

⊙ **No, not in any circumstances**

It's an offence to park there. You will be causing an obstruction by obscuring the view of both pedestrians and drivers.

3.77

*Mark **one** answer*

When leaving your car unattended for a few minutes you should

- leave the engine running
- switch the engine off but leave the key in
- lock it and remove the key
- park near a traffic warden

⊙ **lock it and remove the key**

Always switch off the engine, remove the key and lock your car, even if you are only leaving it for a few minutes.

*Mark **one** answer*

When parking and leaving your car for a few minutes you should

- ⊙ leave it unlocked
- ⊙ lock it and remove the key
- ⊙ leave the hazard warning lights on
- ⊙ leave the interior light on

⊙ **lock it and remove the key**

Always remove the key and lock your car even if you only leave it for a few minutes.

3.79 *Mark **one** answer*

When leaving your vehicle where should you park if possible?

- ⊙ Opposite a traffic island
- ⊙ In a secure car park
- ⊙ On a bend
- ⊙ At or near a taxi rank

⊙ **In a secure car park**

Whenever possible leave your car in a secure car park. This will help stop thieves.

3.80 *Mark **three** answers*

In which THREE places would parking your vehicle cause danger or obstruction to other road users?

- ⊙ In front of a property entrance
- ⊙ At or near a bus stop
- ⊙ On your driveway
- ⊙ In a marked parking space
- ⊙ On the approach to a level crossing

⊙ **In front of a property entrance**

⊙ **At or near a bus stop**

⊙ **On the approach to a level crossing**

Don't park your vehicle where parking restrictions apply. Think carefully before you slow down and stop. Look at road markings and signs to ensure that you aren't parking illegally.

3.81
*Mark **three** answers*

In which THREE places would parking cause an obstruction to others?

- Near the brow of a hill
- In a lay-by
- Where the kerb is raised
- Where the kerb has been lowered for wheelchairs
- At or near a bus stop

- **Near the brow of a hill**

- **Where the kerb has been lowered for wheelchairs**

- **At or near a bus stop**

Think about the effect your parking will have on other road users. Don't forget that not all vehicles are the size of a car. Large vehicles will need more room to pass and might need more time too.

Parking out of the view of traffic, such as before the brow of a hill, causes unnecessary risks. Think before you park.

3.82
*Mark **one** answer*

You are away from home and have to park your vehicle overnight. Where should you leave it?

- Opposite another parked vehicle
- In a quiet road
- Opposite a traffic island
- In a secure car park

- **In a secure car park**

When leaving your vehicle unattended, use a secure car park whenever possible.

3.83
*Mark **one** answer*

The most important reason for having a properly adjusted head restraint is to

- make you more comfortable
- help you to avoid neck injury
- help you to relax
- help you to maintain your driving position

- **help you to avoid neck injury**

The restraint should be adjusted so that it gives maximum protection to the head and neck. This will help in the event of a rear-end collision.

As a driver you can cause more damage to the environment by

- ⊙ choosing a fuel-efficient vehicle
- ⊙ making a lot of short journeys
- ⊙ driving in as high a gear as possible
- ⊙ accelerating as quickly as possible
- ⊙ having your vehicle regularly serviced

⊙ **making a lot of short journeys**

⊙ **accelerating as quickly as possible**

For short journeys it may be quicker to walk, or cycle, which is far better for your health. Time spent stationary in traffic with the engine running is damaging to health, the environment and expensive in fuel costs.

As a driver, you can help reduce pollution levels in town centres by

- ⊙ driving more quickly
- ⊙ over-revving in a low gear
- ⊙ walking or cycling
- ⊙ driving short journeys

⊙ **walking or cycling**

Using a vehicle for short journeys means the engine does not have time to reach its normal running temperature. When an engine is running below its normal running temperature it produces increased amounts of pollution. Walking and cycling do not create pollution and have health benefits as well.

How can you reduce the chances of your car being broken into when leaving it unattended?

- ⊙ Take all valuables with you
- ⊙ Park near a taxi rank
- ⊙ Place any valuables on the floor
- ⊙ Park near a fire station

⊙ **Take all valuables with you**

When leaving your car take all valuables with you if you can, otherwise lock them out of sight.

3.87 *Mark **one** answer*

How can you help to prevent your car radio being stolen?

⊙ Park in an unlit area

⊙ Hide the radio with a blanket

⊙ Park near a busy junction

⊙ Install a security-coded radio

⊙ **Install a security-coded radio**

A security-coded radio can deter thieves as it is likely to be of little use when removed from the vehicle.

3.88 *Mark **one** answer*

You are parking your car. You have some valuables which you are unable to take with you. What should you do?

⊙ Park near a police station

⊙ Put them under the driver's seat

⊙ Lock them out of sight

⊙ Park in an unlit side road

⊙ **Lock them out of sight**

Your vehicle is like a shop window for thieves. Either remove all valuables or lock them out of sight.

3.89 *Mark **one** answer*

Wherever possible, which one of the following should you do when parking at night?

⊙ Park in a quiet car park

⊙ Park in a well-lit area

⊙ Park facing against the flow of traffic

⊙ Park next to a busy junction

⊙ **Park in a well-lit area**

If you are away from home, try to avoid leaving your vehicle unattended in poorly-lit areas. If possible park in a secure, well-lit car park.

*Mark **one** answer*

How can you lessen the risk of your vehicle being broken into at night?

- ⊙ Leave it in a well-lit area
- ⊙ Park in a quiet side road
- ⊙ Don't engage the steering lock
- ⊙ Park in a poorly-lit area

⊙ **Leave it in a well-lit area**

Having your vehicle broken into or stolen can be very distressing and inconvenient. Avoid leaving your vehicle unattended in poorly-lit areas.

*Mark **one** answer*

To help keep your car secure you could join a

- ⊙ vehicle breakdown organisation
- ⊙ vehicle watch scheme
- ⊙ advanced driver's scheme
- ⊙ car maintenance class

⊙ **vehicle watch scheme**

The vehicle watch scheme helps reduce the risk of having your car stolen. By displaying high visibility vehicle watch stickers in your car you are inviting the police to stop your vehicle if seen in use between midnight and 5 am.

*Mark **one** answer*

On a vehicle, where would you find a catalytic converter?

- ⊙ In the fuel tank
- ⊙ In the air filter
- ⊙ On the cooling system
- ⊙ On the exhaust system

⊙ **On the exhaust system**

Although carbon dioxide is still produced, a catalytic converter reduces the toxic and polluting gases by up to 90%. Unleaded fuel must be used in vehicles fitted with a catalytic converter.

*Mark **one** answer*

When leaving your car to help keep it secure you should

- ⊙ leave the hazard warning lights on
- ⊙ lock it and remove the key
- ⊙ park on a one-way street
- ⊙ park in a residential area

⊙ **lock it and remove the key**

To help keep your car secure when you leave it, you should always remove the key from the ignition, lock it and take the key with you. Don't make it easy for thieves.

3.94   *Mark **one** answer*

You will find that driving smoothly can

- ⊙ reduce journey times by about 15%
- ⊙ increase fuel consumption by about 15%
- ⊙ reduce fuel consumption by about 15%
- ⊙ increase journey times by about 15%

⊙ **reduce fuel consumption by about 15%**

Not only will you save about 15% of your fuel by driving smoothly, but you will also reduce the amount of wear and tear on your vehicle as well as reducing pollution. You will also feel more relaxed and have a more pleasant journey.

3.95   *Mark **one** answer*

You can save fuel when conditions allow by

- ⊙ using lower gears as often as possible
- ⊙ accelerating sharply in each gear
- ⊙ using each gear in turn
- ⊙ missing out some gears

⊙ **missing out some gears**

Missing out intermediate gears when appropriate, helps to reduce the amount of time spent accelerating and decelerating - the time when your vehicle uses most fuel.

3.96   *Mark **one** answer*

How can driving in an Eco-safe manner help protect the environment?

- ⊙ Through the legal enforcement of speed regulations
- ⊙ By increasing the number of cars on the road
- ⊙ Through increased fuel bills
- ⊙ By reducing exhaust emissions

⊙ **By reducing exhaust emissions**

Eco-safe driving is all about becoming a more environmentally-friendly driver. This will make your journeys more comfortable as well as considerably reducing your fuel bills and reducing emissions that can damage the environment.

What does Eco-safe driving achieve?

⊙ Increased fuel consumption

⊙ Improved road safety

⊙ Damage to the environment

⊙ Increased exhaust emissions

⊙ **Improved road safety**

The emphasis is on hazard awareness and planning ahead. By looking well ahead you will have plenty of time to deal with hazards safely and won't need to brake sharply. This will also reduce damage to the environment.

How can missing out some gear changes save fuel?

⊙ By reducing the amount of time you are accelerating

⊙ Because there is less need to use the footbrake

⊙ By controlling the amount of steering

⊙ Because coasting is kept to a minimum

⊙ **By reducing the amount of time you are accelerating**

Missing out some gears helps to reduce the amount of time you are accelerating and this saves fuel. You don't always need to change up or down through each gear. As you accelerate between each gear more fuel is injected into the engine than if you had maintained constant acceleration. Fewer gear changes means less fuel used.

Missing out some gears saves fuel by reducing the amount of time you spend

⊙ braking

⊙ coasting

⊙ steering

⊙ accelerating

⊙ **accelerating**

It is not always necessary to change up or down through each gear. Missing out intermediate gears helps to reduce the amount of time you are accelerating. Because fuel consumption is at its highest when accelerating this can save fuel.

3.100 *Mark **one** answer*

You are checking your trailer tyres. What is the legal minimum tread depth over the central three quarters of its breadth?

- ⊙ 1 mm
- ⊙ 1.6 mm
- ⊙ 2 mm
- ⊙ 2.6 mm

⊙ **1.6 mm**

Trailers and caravans may be left in storage over the winter months and tyres can deteriorate. It's important to check their tread depth and also the pressures and general condition. The legal tread depth applies to the central three quarters of its breadth over its entire circumference.

3.101 *Mark **one** answer*

Fuel consumption is at its highest when you are

- ⊙ braking
- ⊙ coasting
- ⊙ accelerating
- ⊙ steering

⊙ **accelerating**

Always try to use the accelerator smoothly. Taking your foot off the accelerator allows the momentum of the car to take you forward, especially when going downhill. This can save a considerable amount of fuel without any loss of control over the vehicle.

3.102 *Mark **one** answer*

Car passengers MUST wear a seat belt/restraint if one is available, unless they are

- ⊙ under 14 years old
- ⊙ under 1.5 metres (5 feet) in height
- ⊙ sitting in the rear seat
- ⊙ exempt for medical reasons

⊙ **exempt for medical reasons**

If you have adult passengers it is their responsibility to wear a seat belt, but you should still remind them to use them as they get in the car. It is your responsibility to ensure that all children in your car are secured with an appropriate restraint.

Car passengers MUST wear a seat belt if one is available, unless they are

- ⊙ in a vehicle fitted with air bags
- ⊙ travelling within a congestion charging zone
- ⊙ sitting in the rear seat
- ⊙ exempt for medical reasons

⊙ **exempt for medical reasons**

When adult passengers are travelling in a vehicle, it is their own responsibility to wear a seat belt. However, you should still remind them to use a seat belt.

You are driving the children of a friend home from school. They are both under 14 years old. Who is responsible for making sure they wear a seat belt or approved child restraint where required?

- ⊙ An adult passenger
- ⊙ The children
- ⊙ You, the driver
- ⊙ Your friend

⊙ **You, the driver**

Passengers should always be secured and safe. Children should be encouraged to fasten their seat belts or approved restraints themselves from an early age so that it becomes a matter of routine. As the driver you must check that they are fastened securely. It's your responsibility.

You have too much oil in your engine. What could this cause?

- ⊙ Low oil pressure
- ⊙ Engine overheating
- ⊙ Chain wear
- ⊙ Oil leaks

⊙ **Oil leaks**

Too much oil in the engine will create excess pressure and could damage engine seals and cause oil leaks. Any excess oil should be drained off.

3.106
*Mark **one** answer*

You are carrying a 5 year-old child in the back seat of your car. They are under 1.35 metres (4 feet 5 inches). A correct child restraint is NOT available. They MUST

- ⊙ sit behind the passenger seat
- ⊙ use an adult seat belt
- ⊙ share a belt with an adult
- ⊙ sit between two other children

⊙ **use an adult seat belt**

Usually a correct child restraint MUST be used. In a few exceptional cases if one is not available an adult seat belt MUST be used. In a collision unrestrained objects and people can cause serious injury or even death.

3.107
*Mark **one** answer*

You are carrying a child using a rear-facing baby seat. You want to put it on the front passenger seat. What MUST you do before setting off?

- ⊙ Deactivate all front and rear airbags
- ⊙ Make sure any front passenger airbag is deactivated
- ⊙ Make sure all the child safety locks are off
- ⊙ Recline the front passenger seat

⊙ **Make sure any front passenger airbag is deactivated**

You MUST deactivate any frontal passenger airbag when using a rear-facing baby seat in a front passenger seat. It is ILLEGAL if you don't. If activated in a crash it could cause serious injury or death. Ensure you follow the manufacturer's instructions. In some cars this is now done automatically.

3.108
*Mark **one** answer*

You are carrying an 11 year old child in the back seat of your car. They are under 1.35 metres (4 feet 5 inches) in height. You MUST make sure that

- ⊙ they sit between two belted people
- ⊙ they can fasten their own seat belt
- ⊙ a suitable child restraint is available
- ⊙ they can see clearly out of the front window

⊙ **a suitable child restraint is available**

It is your responsibility as a driver to ensure that children are secure and safe in your vehicle. Make sure you are familiar with the rules. In a few very exceptional cases when a child restraint is not available, an adult seat belt MUST be used. Child restraints and seat belts save lives!

3.109

Mark **one** answer

You are parked at the side of the road. You will be waiting for some time for a passenger. What should you do?

- ⊙ Switch off the engine
- ⊙ Apply the steering lock
- ⊙ Switch off the radio
- ⊙ Use your headlights

⊙ **Switch off the engine**

If your vehicle is stationary and is likely to remain so for some time, switch off the engine. We should all try to reduce global warming and pollution.

3.110

Mark **one** answer

You are using a rear-facing baby seat. You want to put it on the front passenger seat which is protected by a frontal airbag. What MUST you do before setting off?

- ⊙ Deactivate the airbag
- ⊙ Turn the seat to face sideways
- ⊙ Ask a passenger to hold the baby
- ⊙ Put the child in an adult seat belt

⊙ **Deactivate the airbag**

If the airbag activates near a baby seat, it could cause serious injury or even death to the child. It is illegal to fit a rear-facing baby seat into a passenger seat protected by an active frontal airbag. You MUST secure it in a different seat or deactivate the relevant airbag. Follow the manufacturer's advice when fitting a baby seat.

3.111

Mark **one** answer

You are carrying a five year-old child in the back seat of your car. They are under 1.35 metres (4 feet 5 inches) in height. They MUST use an adult seat belt ONLY if

- ⊙ a correct child restraint is not available
- ⊙ it is a lap type belt
- ⊙ they sit between two adults
- ⊙ it can be shared with another adult

⊙ **a correct child restraint is not available**

You should make all efforts to ensure a correct child restraint is used, with very few exceptions. If in specific circumstances one is not available, then an adult seat belt MUST be used. Unrestrained objects, including people, can be thrown violently around in a collision, and may cause serious injury or even death!

3.112 *Mark **one** answer*

You are leaving your vehicle parked on a road unattended. When may you leave the engine running?

- ⊙ If you will be parking for less than five minutes
- ⊙ If the battery keeps going flat
- ⊙ When parked in a 20 mph zone
- ⊙ Never if you are away from the vehicle

⊙ **Never if you are away from the vehicle**

When you leave your vehicle parked on a road, switch off the engine and secure the vehicle. Make sure there aren't any valuables visible, shut all the windows, lock the vehicle, set the alarm if it has one and use an anti-theft device such as a steering wheel lock.

section **four**
SAFETY MARGINS

This section covers

- Stopping distances
- Road surfaces
- Skidding
- Weather conditions

4.1

*Mark **one** answer*

Braking distances on ice can be

- ⊙ twice the normal distance
- ⊙ five times the normal distance
- ⊙ seven times the normal distance
- ⊙ ten times the normal distance

⊙ **ten times the normal distance**

In icy and snowy weather, your stopping distance will increase by up to ten times compared to good, dry conditions.

Take extra care when braking, accelerating and steering, to cut down the risk of skidding.

4.2

*Mark **one** answer*

Freezing conditions will affect the distance it takes you to come to a stop. You should expect stopping distances to increase by up to

- ⊙ two times
- ⊙ three times
- ⊙ five times
- ⊙ ten times

⊙ **ten times**

Your tyre grip is greatly reduced on icy roads and you need to allow up to ten times the normal stopping distance.

4.3

*Mark **one** answer*

In windy conditions you need to take extra care when

- ⊙ using the brakes
- ⊙ making a hill start
- ⊙ turning into a narrow road
- ⊙ passing pedal cyclists

⊙ **passing pedal cyclists**

You should always give cyclists plenty of room when overtaking. When it's windy, a sudden gust could blow them off course.

When approaching a right-hand bend you should keep well to the left. Why is this?

⊙ To improve your view of the road

⊙ To overcome the effect of the road's slope

⊙ To let faster traffic from behind overtake

⊙ To be positioned safely if you skid

⊙ **To improve your view of the road**

Doing this will give you an earlier view around the bend and enable you to see any hazards sooner.

It also reduces the risk of collision with an oncoming vehicle that may have drifted over the centre line while taking the bend.

You have just gone through deep water. To dry off the brakes you should

⊙ accelerate and keep to a high speed for a short time

⊙ go slowly while gently applying the brakes

⊙ avoid using the brakes at all for a few miles

⊙ stop for at least an hour to allow them time to dry

⊙ **go slowly while gently applying the brakes**

Water on the brakes will act as a lubricant, causing them to work less efficiently. Using the brakes lightly as you go along will dry them out.

In very hot weather the road surface can become soft. Which TWO of the following will be most affected?

⊙ The suspension

⊙ The grip of the tyres

⊙ The braking

⊙ The exhaust

⊙ **The grip of the tyres**

⊙ **The braking**

Only a small part of your tyres is in contact with the road. This is why you must consider the surface on which you're travelling, and alter your speed to suit the road conditions.

4.7
*Mark **one** answer*

Where are you most likely to be affected by a side wind?

- ⊙ On a narrow country lane
- ⊙ On an open stretch of road
- ⊙ On a busy stretch of road
- ⊙ On a long, straight road

⊙ **On an open stretch of road**

In windy conditions, care must be taken on exposed roads. A strong gust of wind can blow you off course. Watch out for other road users who are particularly likely to be affected, such as cyclists, motorcyclists, high-sided lorries and vehicles towing trailers.

4.8
*Mark **one** answer*

In good conditions, what is the typical stopping distance at 70 mph?

- ⊙ 53 metres (175 feet)
- ⊙ 60 metres (197 feet)
- ⊙ 73 metres (240 feet)
- ⊙ 96 metres (315 feet)

⊙ **96 metres (315 feet)**

Note that this is the typical stopping distance. It will take at least this distance to think, brake and stop in good conditions. In poor conditions it will take much longer.

4.9
*Mark **one** answer*

What is the shortest overall stopping distance on a dry road at 60 mph?

- ⊙ 53 metres (175 feet)
- ⊙ 58 metres (190 feet)
- ⊙ 73 metres (240 feet)
- ⊙ 96 metres (315 feet)

⊙ **73 metres (240 feet)**

This distance is the equivalent of 18 car lengths. Try pacing out 73 metres and then look back. It's probably further than you think.

*Mark **one** answer*

You are following a vehicle at a safe distance on a wet road. Another driver overtakes you and pulls into the gap you have left. What should you do?

◉ Flash your headlights as a warning

◉ Try to overtake safely as soon as you can

◉ Drop back to regain a safe distance

◉ Stay close to the other vehicle until it moves on

◉ **Drop back to regain a safe distance**

Wet weather will affect the time it takes for you to stop and can affect your control. Your speed should allow you to stop safely and in good time. If another vehicle pulls into the gap you've left, ease back until you've regained your stopping distance.

*Mark **one** answer*

You are travelling at 50 mph on a good, dry road. What is your typical overall stopping distance?

◉ 36 metres (118 feet)

◉ 53 metres (175 feet)

◉ 75 metres (245 feet)

◉ 96 metres (315 feet)

◉ **53 metres (175 feet)**

Even in good conditions it will usually take you further than you think to stop. Don't just learn the figures, make sure you understand how far the distance is.

*Mark **one** answer*

You are on a good, dry, road surface. Your brakes and tyres are good. What is the typical overall stopping distance at 40 mph?

◉ 23 metres (75 feet)

◉ 36 metres (118 feet)

◉ 53 metres (175 feet)

◉ 96 metres (315 feet)

◉ **36 metres (118 feet)**

Stopping distances are affected by a number of variable factors. These include the type, model and condition of your vehicle, road and weather conditions, and your reaction time. Look well ahead for hazards and leave enough space between you and the vehicle in front. This should allow you to pull up safely if you have to, without braking sharply.

4.13

*Mark **one** answer*

What should you do when overtaking a motorcyclist in strong winds?

- ⊙ Pass close
- ⊙ Pass quickly
- ⊙ Pass wide
- ⊙ Pass immediately

⊙ **Pass wide**

In strong winds riders of two-wheeled vehicles are particularly vulnerable. When you overtake them allow plenty of room. Always check to the left as you pass.

4.14

*Mark **one** answer*

You are overtaking a motorcyclist in strong winds? What should you do?

- ⊙ Allow extra room
- ⊙ Give a thank you wave
- ⊙ Move back early
- ⊙ Sound your horn

⊙ **Allow extra room**

It is easy for motorcyclists to be blown off course. Always give them plenty of room if you decide to overtake, especially in strong winds. Decide whether you need to overtake at all. Always check to the left as you pass.

4.15

*Mark **one** answer*

Overall stopping distance is made up of thinking and braking distance. You are on a good, dry road surface with good brakes and tyres. What is the typical BRAKING distance from 50 mph?

- ⊙ 14 metres (46 feet)
- ⊙ 24 metres (80 feet)
- ⊙ 38 metres (125 feet)
- ⊙ 55 metres (180 feet)

⊙ **38 metres (125 feet)**

Be aware this is just the braking distance. You need to add the thinking distance to this to give the OVERALL STOPPING DISTANCE. At 50 mph the typical thinking distance will be 15 metres (50 feet), plus a braking distance of 38 metres (125 feet), giving an overall stopping distance of 53 metres (175 feet). The distance could be greater than this depending on your attention and response to any hazards. These figures are a general guide.

*Mark **one** answer*

In heavy motorway traffic the vehicle behind you is following too closely. How can you lower the risk of a collision?

⊙ Increase your distance from the vehicle in front

⊙ Operate the brakes sharply

⊙ Switch on your hazard lights

⊙ Move onto the hard shoulder and stop

⊙ **Increase your distance from the vehicle in front**

On busy roads traffic may still travel at high speeds despite being close together. Don't follow too closely to the vehicle in front. If a driver behind seems to be 'pushing' you, gradually increase your distance from the vehicle in front by slowing down gently. This will give you more space in front if you have to brake, and lessen the risk of a collision involving several vehicles.

*Mark **one** answer*

You are following other vehicles in fog. You have your lights on. What else can you do to reduce the chances of being in a collision?

⊙ Keep close to the vehicle in front

⊙ Use your main beam instead of dipped headlights

⊙ Keep up with the faster vehicles

⊙ Reduce your speed and increase the gap in front

⊙ **Reduce your speed and increase the gap in front**

When it's foggy use dipped headlights. This will help you see and be seen by other road users. If visibility is seriously reduced consider using front and rear fog lights. Keep a sensible speed and don't follow the vehicle in front too closely. If the road is wet and slippery you'll need to allow twice the normal stopping distance.

4.18

*Mark **three** answers*

To avoid a collision when entering a contraflow system, you should

- ⊙ reduce speed in good time
- ⊙ switch lanes at any time to make progress
- ⊙ choose an appropriate lane in good time
- ⊙ keep the correct separation distance
- ⊙ increase speed to pass through quickly
- ⊙ follow other motorists closely to avoid long queues

- ⊙ **reduce speed in good time**

- ⊙ **choose an appropriate lane in good time**

- ⊙ **keep the correct separation distance**

In a contraflow system you will be travelling close to oncoming traffic and sometimes in narrow lanes. You should obey the temporary speed limit signs, get into the correct lane at the proper time and keep a safe separation distance from the vehicle ahead. When traffic is at a very low speed, merging in turn is recommended if it's safe and appropriate.

4.19

*Mark **one** answer*

What is the most common cause of skidding?

- ⊙ Worn tyres
- ⊙ Driver error
- ⊙ Other vehicles
- ⊙ Pedestrians

- ⊙ **Driver error**

A skid happens when the driver changes the speed or direction of their vehicle so suddenly that the tyres can't keep their grip on the road.

Remember that the risk of skidding on wet or icy roads is much greater than in dry conditions.

4.20

*Mark **one** answer*

You are driving on an icy road. How can you avoid wheelspin?

- ⊙ Drive at a slow speed in as high a gear as possible
- ⊙ Use the handbrake if the wheels start to slip
- ⊙ Brake gently and repeatedly
- ⊙ Drive in a low gear at all times

- ⊙ **Drive at a slow speed in as high a gear as possible**

If you're travelling on an icy road extra caution will be required to avoid loss of control. Keeping your speed down and using the highest gear possible will reduce the risk of the tyres losing their grip on this slippery surface.

4.21

*Mark **one** answer*

Skidding is mainly caused by

- ⊙ the weather
- ⊙ the driver
- ⊙ the vehicle
- ⊙ the road

⊙ **the driver**

You should always consider the conditions and drive accordingly.

4.22

*Mark **two** answers*

You are driving in freezing conditions. What should you do when approaching a sharp bend?

- ⊙ Slow down before you reach the bend
- ⊙ Gently apply your handbrake
- ⊙ Firmly use your footbrake
- ⊙ Coast into the bend
- ⊙ Avoid sudden steering movements

⊙ **Slow down before you reach the bend**

⊙ **Avoid sudden steering movements**

Harsh use of the accelerator, brakes or steering are likely to lead to skidding, especially on slippery surfaces. Avoid steering and braking at the same time.

In icy conditions it's very important that you constantly assess what's ahead, so that you can take appropriate action in plenty of time.

4.23

*Mark **one** answer*

You are turning left on a slippery road. The back of your vehicle slides to the right. You should

- ⊙ brake firmly and not turn the steering wheel
- ⊙ steer carefully to the left
- ⊙ steer carefully to the right
- ⊙ brake firmly and steer to the left

⊙ **steer carefully to the right**

Steer into the skid but be careful not to overcorrect with too much steering. Too much movement may lead to a skid in the opposite direction. Skids don't just happen, they are caused. The three important factors in order are the driver, the vehicle and the road conditions.

4.24
*Mark **four** answers*

Before starting a journey in freezing weather you should clear ice and snow from your vehicle's

- ⊙ aerial
- ⊙ windows
- ⊙ bumper
- ⊙ lights
- ⊙ mirrors
- ⊙ number plates

- ⊙ **windows**
- ⊙ **lights**
- ⊙ **mirrors**
- ⊙ **number plates**

Don't travel unless you have no choice. Making unnecessary journeys in bad weather can increase the risk of having a collision. It's important that you can see and be seen. Make sure any snow or ice is cleared from lights, mirrors, number plates and windows.

4.25
*Mark **one** answer*

You are trying to move off on snow. You should use

- ⊙ the lowest gear you can
- ⊙ the highest gear you can
- ⊙ a high engine speed
- ⊙ the handbrake and footbrake together

- ⊙ **the highest gear you can**

If you attempt to move off in a low gear, such as first, the engine will rev at a higher speed. This could cause the wheels to spin and dig further into the snow.

4.26
*Mark **one** answer*

When driving in falling snow you should

- ⊙ brake firmly and quickly
- ⊙ be ready to steer sharply
- ⊙ use sidelights only
- ⊙ brake gently in plenty of time

- ⊙ **brake gently in plenty of time**

Braking on snow can be extremely dangerous. Be gentle with both the accelerator and brake to prevent wheel-spin.

The MAIN benefit of having four-wheel drive is to improve

- ⊙ road holding
- ⊙ fuel consumption
- ⊙ stopping distances
- ⊙ passenger comfort

⊙ **road holding**

By driving all four wheels there is improved grip, but this does not replace the skills you need to drive safely. The extra grip helps road holding when travelling on slippery or uneven roads.

You are about to go down a steep hill. To control the speed of your vehicle you should

- ⊙ select a high gear and use the brakes carefully
- ⊙ select a high gear and use the brakes firmly
- ⊙ select a low gear and use the brakes carefully
- ⊙ select a low gear and avoid using the brakes

⊙ **select a low gear and use the brakes carefully**

When going down a steep hill your vehicle will speed up. This will make it more difficult for you to stop. Select a lower gear to give you more engine braking and control. Use this in combination with careful use of the brakes.

You wish to park facing DOWNHILL. Which TWO of the following should you do?

- ⊙ Turn the steering wheel towards the kerb
- ⊙ Park close to the bumper of another car
- ⊙ Park with two wheels on the kerb
- ⊙ Put the handbrake on firmly
- ⊙ Turn the steering wheel away from the kerb

⊙ **Turn the steering wheel towards the kerb**

⊙ **Put the handbrake on firmly**

Turning the wheels towards the kerb will allow it to act as a chock, preventing any forward movement of the vehicle. It will also help to leave it in gear, or select Park if you have an automatic.

4.30
*Mark **one** answer*

You are driving in a built-up area. You approach a speed hump. You should

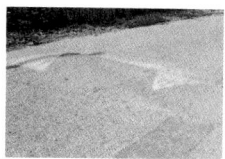

- ⊙ move across to the left-hand side of the road
- ⊙ wait for any pedestrians to cross
- ⊙ slow your vehicle right down
- ⊙ stop and check both pavements

⊙ **slow your vehicle right down**

Many towns have speed humps to slow down traffic. Slow down when driving over them. If you go too fast they may affect your steering and suspension, causing you to lose control or even damaging it. Be aware of pedestrians in these areas.

4.31
*Mark **one** answer*

You are on a long, downhill slope. What should you do to help control the speed of your vehicle?

- ⊙ Select neutral
- ⊙ Select a lower gear
- ⊙ Grip the handbrake firmly
- ⊙ Apply the parking brake gently

⊙ **Select a lower gear**

Selecting a low gear when travelling downhill will help you to control your speed. The engine will assist the brakes and help prevent your vehicle gathering speed.

4.32
*Mark **one** answer*

Anti-lock brakes prevent wheels from locking. This means the tyres are less likely to

- ⊙ aquaplane
- ⊙ skid
- ⊙ puncture
- ⊙ wear

⊙ **skid**

If an anti-lock braking system is fitted it activates automatically when maximum braking pressure is applied or when it senses that the wheels are about to lock. It prevents the wheels from locking so you can continue to steer the vehicle during braking. It does not remove the need for good driving practices such as anticipation and correct speed for the conditions.

*Mark **one** answer*

Anti-lock brakes reduce the chances of a skid occurring particularly when

- ⊙ driving down steep hills
- ⊙ braking during normal driving
- ⊙ braking in an emergency
- ⊙ driving on good road surfaces

⊙ **braking in an emergency**

The anti-lock braking system will operate when the brakes have been applied harshly.

It will reduce the chances of your car skidding, but it is not a miracle cure for careless driving.

---

*Mark **one** answer*

Vehicles fitted with anti-lock brakes

- ⊙ are impossible to skid
- ⊙ can be steered while you are braking
- ⊙ accelerate much faster
- ⊙ are not fitted with a handbrake

⊙ **can be steered while you are braking**

Preventing the wheels from locking means that the vehicle's steering and stability can be maintained, leading to safer stopping. However, you must ensure that the engine does not stall, as this could disable the power steering. Look in your vehicle handbook for the correct method when stopping in an emergency.

---

*Mark **two** answers*

Anti-lock brakes may not work as effectively if the road surface is

- ⊙ dry
- ⊙ loose
- ⊙ wet
- ⊙ good
- ⊙ firm

⊙ **loose**

⊙ **wet**

Poor contact with the road surface could cause one or more of the tyres to lose grip on the road. This is more likely to happen when braking in poor weather conditions, when the road surface is uneven or has loose chippings.

4.36
*Mark **one** answer*

Anti-lock brakes are of most use when you are

- ⊙ braking gently
- ⊙ driving on worn tyres
- ⊙ braking excessively
- ⊙ driving normally

⊙ **braking excessively**

Anti-lock brakes will not be required when braking normally. Looking well down the road and anticipating possible hazards could prevent you having to brake late and harshly. Knowing that you have anti-lock brakes is not an excuse to drive in a careless or reckless way.

4.37
*Mark **one** answer*

Driving a vehicle fitted with anti-lock brakes allows you to

- ⊙ brake harder because it is impossible to skid
- ⊙ drive at higher speeds
- ⊙ steer and brake at the same time
- ⊙ pay less attention to the road ahead

⊙ **steer and brake at the same time**

When stopping in an emergency anti-lock brakes will help you continue to steer when braking. In poor weather conditions this may be less effective. You need to depress the clutch pedal to prevent the car stalling as most power steering systems use an engine-driven pump and will only operate when the engine is running. Look in your vehicle handbook for the correct method when stopping in an emergency.

4.38
*Mark **one** answer*

Anti-lock brakes can greatly assist with

- ⊙ a higher cruising speed
- ⊙ steering control when braking
- ⊙ control when accelerating
- ⊙ motorway driving

⊙ **steering control when braking**

If the wheels of your vehicle lock they will not grip the road and you will lose steering control. In good conditions the anti-lock system will prevent the wheels locking and allow you to retain steering control.

You are driving a vehicle fitted with anti-lock brakes. You need to stop in an emergency. You should apply the footbrake

- ⊙ slowly and gently
- ⊙ slowly but firmly
- ⊙ rapidly and gently
- ⊙ rapidly and firmly

⊙ **rapidly and firmly**

Look well ahead down the road as you drive and give yourself time and space to react safely to any hazards. You may have to stop in an emergency due to a misjudgement by another driver or a hazard arising suddenly such as a child running out into the road. In this case, if your vehicle has anti-lock brakes, you should apply the brakes immediately and keep them firmly applied until you stop.

Your vehicle has anti-lock brakes, but they may not always prevent skidding. This is most likely to happen when driving

- ⊙ in foggy conditions
- ⊙ on surface water
- ⊙ on loose road surfaces
- ⊙ on dry tarmac
- ⊙ at night on unlit roads

⊙ **on surface water**

⊙ **on loose road surfaces**

In very wet weather water can build up between the tyre and the road surface. As a result your vehicle actually rides on a thin film of water and your tyres will not grip the road. Gravel or shingle surfaces also offer less grip and can present problems when braking. An anti-lock braking system may be ineffective in these conditions.

You are driving along a country road. You see this sign. AFTER dealing safely with the hazard you should always

- ⊙ check your tyre pressures
- ⊙ switch on your hazard warning lights
- ⊙ accelerate briskly
- ⊙ test your brakes

⊙ **test your brakes**

Deep water can affect your brakes, so you should check that they're working properly before you build up speed again. Before you do this, remember to check your mirrors and consider what's behind you.

4.42
*Mark **one** answer*

You are driving in heavy rain. Your steering suddenly becomes very light. You should

- steer towards the side of the road
- apply gentle acceleration
- brake firmly to reduce speed
- ease off the accelerator

⊙ **ease off the accelerator**

If the steering becomes light in these conditions it is probably due to a film of water that has built up between your tyres and the road surface. Easing off the accelerator should allow your tyres to displace the film of water and they should then regain their grip on the road.

4.43
*Mark **one** answer*

The roads are icy. You should drive slowly

- in the highest gear possible
- in the lowest gear possible
- with the handbrake partly on
- with your left foot on the brake

⊙ **in the highest gear possible**

Driving at a slow speed in a high gear will reduce the likelihood of wheel-spin and help your vehicle maintain the best possible grip.

4.44
*Mark **one** answer*

You are driving along a wet road. How can you tell if your vehicle is aquaplaning?

- The engine will stall
- The engine noise will increase
- The steering will feel very heavy
- The steering will feel very light

⊙ **The steering will feel very light**

If you drive at speed in very wet conditions your steering may suddenly feel 'light'. This means that the tyres have lifted off the surface of the road and are skating on the surface of the water. This is known as aquaplaning. Reduce speed by easing off the accelerator, but don't brake until your steering returns to normal.

How can you tell if you are driving on ice?

- ⊙ The tyres make a rumbling noise
- ⊙ The tyres make hardly any noise
- ⊙ The steering becomes heavier
- ⊙ The steering becomes lighter

⊙ **The tyres make hardly any noise**

⊙ **The steering becomes lighter**

Drive extremely carefully when the roads are icy. When travelling on ice, tyres make virtually no noise and the steering feels unresponsive.

In icy conditions, avoid harsh braking, acceleration and steering.

You are driving along a wet road. How can you tell if your vehicle's tyres are losing their grip on the surface?

- ⊙ The engine will stall
- ⊙ The steering will feel very heavy
- ⊙ The engine noise will increase
- ⊙ The steering will feel very light

⊙ **The steering will feel very light**

If you drive at speed in very wet conditions your steering may suddenly feel lighter than usual. This means that the tyres have lifted off the surface of the road and are skating on the surface of the water. This is known as aquaplaning. Reduce speed but don't brake until your steering returns to a normal feel.

Your overall stopping distance will be much longer when driving

- ⊙ in the rain
- ⊙ in fog
- ⊙ at night
- ⊙ in strong winds

⊙ **in the rain**

Extra care should be taken in wet weather as, on wet roads, your stopping distance could be double that necessary for dry conditions.

4.48
*Mark **one** answer*

You have driven through a flood. What is the first thing you should do?

○ Stop and check the tyres

○ Stop and dry the brakes

○ Check your exhaust

○ Test your brakes

⊙ **Test your brakes**

Before you test your brakes you must check for following traffic. If it is safe, gently apply the brakes to clear any water that may be covering the braking surfaces.

4.49
*Mark **one** answer*

You are on a fast, open road in good conditions. For safety, the distance between you and the vehicle in front should be

○ a two-second time gap

○ one car length

○ 2 metres (6 feet 6 inches)

○ two car lengths

⊙ **a two-second time gap**

One useful method of checking that you've allowed enough room between you and the vehicle in front is the two-second rule.

To check for a two-second time gap, choose a stationary object ahead, such as a bridge or road sign. When the car in front passes the object say 'Only a fool breaks the two-second rule'. If you reach the object before you finish saying it you're too close.

4.50
*Mark **one** answer*

How can you use your vehicle's engine as a brake?

○ By changing to a lower gear

○ By selecting reverse gear

○ By changing to a higher gear

○ By selecting neutral gear

⊙ **By changing to a lower gear**

When driving on downhill stretches of road selecting a lower gear gives increased engine braking. This will prevent excess use of the brakes, which become less effective if they overheat.

Anti-lock brakes are most effective when you

- keep pumping the foot brake to prevent skidding
- brake normally, but grip the steering wheel tightly
- brake promptly and firmly until you have slowed down
- apply the handbrake to reduce the stopping distance

⊙ **brake promptly and firmly until you have slowed down**

Releasing the brake before you have slowed right down will disable the system. If you have to brake in an emergency ensure that you keep your foot firmly on the brake pedal until the vehicle has stopped.

Your car is fitted with anti-lock brakes. You need to stop in an emergency. You should

- brake normally and avoid turning the steering wheel
- press the brake pedal promptly and firmly until you have stopped
- keep pushing and releasing the foot brake quickly to prevent skidding
- apply the handbrake to reduce the stopping distance

⊙ **press the brake pedal promptly and firmly until you have stopped**

Keep pressure on the brake pedal until you have come to a stop. The anti-lock mechanism will activate automatically if it senses the wheels are about to lock.

When would an anti-lock braking system start to work?

- After the parking brake has been applied
- Whenever pressure on the brake pedal is applied
- Just as the wheels are about to lock
- When the normal braking system fails to operate

⊙ **Just as the wheels are about to lock**

The anti-lock braking system has sensors that detect when the wheels are about to lock. It releases the brakes momentarily to allow the wheels to revolve and grip, then automatically reapplies them. This cycle is repeated several times a second to maximise braking performance.

4.54
*Mark **one** answer*

Anti-lock brakes will take effect when

- ⊙ you do not brake quickly enough
- ⊙ maximum brake pressure has been applied
- ⊙ you have not seen a hazard ahead
- ⊙ speeding on slippery road surfaces

⊙ **maximum brake pressure has been applied**

If your car is fitted with anti-lock brakes they will take effect when you use them very firmly in an emergency. The system will only activate when it senses the wheels are about to lock.

4.55
*Mark **one** answer*

You are on a wet motorway with surface spray. You should use

- ⊙ hazard flashers
- ⊙ dipped headlights
- ⊙ rear fog lights
- ⊙ sidelights

⊙ **dipped headlights**

When surface spray reduces visibility switch on your dipped headlights. This will help other road users to see you.

4.56
*Mark **one** answer*

Your vehicle is fitted with anti-lock brakes. To stop quickly in an emergency you should

- ⊙ brake firmly and pump the brake pedal on and off
- ⊙ brake rapidly and firmly without releasing the brake pedal
- ⊙ brake gently and pump the brake pedal on and off
- ⊙ brake rapidly once, and immediately release the brake pedal

⊙ **brake rapidly and firmly without releasing the brake pedal**

Once you have applied the brake keep your foot firmly on the pedal. Releasing the brake and reapplying it will disable the anti-lock brake system.

4.57

Travelling for long distances in neutral (known as coasting)

- ⊙ improves the driver's control
- ⊙ makes steering easier
- ⊙ reduces the driver's control
- ⊙ uses more fuel

⊙ **reduces the driver's control**

Coasting, is the term used when the clutch is held down, or the gear lever is in neutral, and the vehicle is allowed to freewheel. This reduces the driver's control of the vehicle. When you coast, the engine can't drive the wheels to pull you through a corner. Coasting also removes the assistance of engine braking that helps to slow the car.

4.58

How can you tell when you are driving over black ice?

- ⊙ It is easier to brake
- ⊙ The noise from your tyres sounds louder
- ⊙ You will see tyre tracks on the road
- ⊙ Your steering feels light

⊙ **Your steering feels light**

Sometimes you may not be able to see that the road is icy. Black ice makes a road look damp. The signs that you're travelling on black ice can be that

- the steering feels light
- the noise from your tyres suddenly goes quiet.

4.59

When driving in fog, which THREE of these are correct?

- ⊙ Use dipped headlights
- ⊙ Position close to the centre line
- ⊙ Allow more time for your journey
- ⊙ Keep close to the car in front
- ⊙ Slow down
- ⊙ Use side lights only

⊙ **Use dipped headlights**

⊙ **Allow more time for your journey**

⊙ **Slow down**

Don't venture out if your journey is not necessary. If you have to travel and someone is expecting you at the other end, let them know that you will be taking longer than usual for your journey. This will stop them worrying if you don't turn up on time and will also take the pressure off you, so you don't feel you have to rush.

section **five**
HAZARD AWARENESS

This section covers

- Anticipation
- Attention
- Speed and distance
- Reaction time
- Alcohol and drugs
- Tiredness

5.1

*Mark **two** answers*

Where would you expect to see these markers?

- On a motorway sign
- At the entrance to a narrow bridge
- On a large goods vehicle
- On a builder's skip placed on the road

⊙ **On a large goods vehicle**

⊙ **On a builder's skip placed on the road**

These markers must be fitted to vehicles over 13 metres long, large goods vehicles, and rubbish skips placed in the road. They are reflective to make them easier to see in the dark.

5.2

*Mark **one** answer*

What is the main hazard shown in this picture?

- Vehicles turning right
- Vehicles doing U-turns
- The cyclist crossing the road
- Parked cars around the corner

⊙ **The cyclist crossing the road**

Look at the picture carefully and try to imagine you're there. The cyclist in this picture appears to be trying to cross the road. You must be able to deal with the unexpected, especially when you're approaching a hazardous junction. Look well ahead to give yourself time to deal with any hazards.

Which road user has caused a hazard?

- The parked car (arrowed A)
- The pedestrian waiting to cross (arrowed B)
- The moving car (arrowed C)
- The car turning (arrowed D)

⊙ **The parked car (arrowed A)**

The car arrowed A is parked within the area marked by zigzag lines at the pedestrian crossing. Parking here is illegal. It also

- blocks the view for pedestrians wishing to cross the road
- restricts the view of the crossing for approaching traffic.

What should the driver of the car approaching the crossing do?

- Continue at the same speed
- Sound the horn
- Drive through quickly
- Slow down and get ready to stop

⊙ **Slow down and get ready to stop**

Look well ahead to see if any hazards are developing. This will give you more time to deal with them in the correct way. The man in the picture is clearly intending to cross the road. You should be travelling at a speed that allows you to check your mirror, slow down and stop in good time. You shouldn't have to brake harshly.

5.5
*Mark **three** answers*

What THREE things should the driver of the grey car (arrowed) be especially aware of?

- ⊙ Pedestrians stepping out between cars
- ⊙ Other cars behind the grey car
- ⊙ Doors opening on parked cars
- ⊙ The bumpy road surface
- ⊙ Cars leaving parking spaces
- ⊙ Empty parking spaces

- ⊙ **Pedestrians stepping out between cars**

- ⊙ **Doors opening on parked cars**

- ⊙ **Cars leaving parking spaces**

You need to be aware that other road users may not have seen you. Always be on the lookout for hazards that may develop suddenly and need you to take avoiding action.

5.6
*Mark **one** answer*

You see this sign ahead. You should expect the road to

- ⊙ go steeply uphill
- ⊙ go steeply downhill
- ⊙ bend sharply to the left
- ⊙ bend sharply to the right

- ⊙ **bend sharply to the left**

Adjust your speed in good time and select the correct gear for your speed. Going too fast into the bend could cause you to lose control.

Braking late and harshly while changing direction reduces your vehicle's grip on the road, and is likely to cause a skid.

117

You are approaching this cyclist. You should

- ⊙ overtake before the cyclist gets to the junction
- ⊙ flash your headlights at the cyclist
- ⊙ slow down and allow the cyclist to turn
- ⊙ overtake the cyclist on the left-hand side

⊙ **slow down and allow the cyclist to turn**

Keep well back and allow the cyclist room to take up the correct position for the turn. Don't get too close behind or try to squeeze past.

Why must you take extra care when turning right at this junction?

- ⊙ Road surface is poor
- ⊙ Footpaths are narrow
- ⊙ Road markings are faint
- ⊙ There is reduced visibility

⊙ **There is reduced visibility**

You may have to pull forward slowly until you can see up and down the road. Be aware that the traffic approaching the junction can't see you either. If you don't know that it's clear, don't go.

5.9

*Mark **one** answer*

When approaching this bridge you should give way to

○ bicycles

○ buses

○ motorcycles

○ cars

○ **buses**

A double-deck bus or high-sided lorry will have to take up a position in the centre of the road so that it can clear the bridge. There is normally a sign to indicate this.

Look well down the road, through the bridge and be aware you may have to stop and give way to an oncoming large vehicle.

5.10

*Mark **one** answer*

What type of vehicle could you expect to meet in the middle of the road?

○ Lorry

○ Bicycle

○ Car

○ Motorcycle

○ **Lorry**

The highest point of the bridge is in the centre so a large vehicle might have to move to the centre of the road to allow it enough room to pass under the bridge.

At this blind junction you must stop

- behind the line, then edge forward to see clearly
- beyond the line at a point where you can see clearly
- only if there is traffic on the main road
- only if you are turning to the right

- **behind the line, then edge forward to see clearly**

The 'stop' sign has been put here because there is a poor view into the main road. You must stop because it will not be possible to assess the situation on the move, however slowly you are travelling.

A driver pulls out of a side road in front of you. You have to brake hard. You should

- ignore the error and stay calm
- flash your lights to show your annoyance
- sound your horn to show your annoyance
- overtake as soon as possible

- **ignore the error and stay calm**

Where there are a number of side roads, be alert. Be especially careful if there are a lot of parked vehicles because they can make it more difficult for drivers emerging to see you. Try to be tolerant if a vehicle does emerge and you have to brake quickly. Don't react aggressively.

An elderly person's driving ability could be affected because they may be unable to

- obtain car insurance
- understand road signs
- react very quickly
- give signals correctly

- **react very quickly**

Be tolerant of older drivers. Poor eyesight and hearing could affect the speed with which they react to a hazard and may cause them to be hesitant.

5.14 Mark **one** answer

You have just passed these warning lights. What hazard would you expect to see next?

⊙ A level crossing with no barrier

⊙ An ambulance station

⊙ A school crossing patrol

⊙ An opening bridge

⊙ **A school crossing patrol**

These lights warn that children may be crossing the road to a nearby school. Slow down so that you're ready to stop if necessary.

5.15 Mark **one** answer

You are planning a long journey. Do you need to plan rest stops?

⊙ Yes, you should plan to stop every half an hour

⊙ Yes, regular stops help concentration

⊙ No, you will be less tired if you get there as soon as possible

⊙ No, only fuel stops will be needed

⊙ **Yes, regular stops help concentration**

Try to plan your journey so that you can take rest stops. It's recommended that you take a break of at least 15 minutes after every two hours of driving. This should help to maintain your concentration.

5.16 Mark **one** answer

A driver does something that upsets you. You should

⊙ try not to react

⊙ let them know how you feel

⊙ flash your headlights several times

⊙ sound your horn

⊙ **try not to react**

There are times when other road users make a misjudgement or mistake. When this happens try not to get annoyed and don't react by showing anger. Sounding your horn, flashing your headlights or shouting won't help the situation. Good anticipation will help to prevent these incidents becoming collisions.

The red lights are flashing. What should you do when approaching this level crossing?

- ⊙ Go through quickly
- ⊙ Go through carefully
- ⊙ Stop before the barrier
- ⊙ Switch on hazard warning lights

⊙ **Stop before the barrier**

At level crossings the red lights flash before and when the barrier is down. At most crossings an amber light will precede the red lights. You must stop behind the white line unless you have already crossed it when the amber light comes on. NEVER zigzag around half-barriers.

You are approaching crossroads. The traffic lights have failed. What should you do?

- ⊙ Brake and stop only for large vehicles
- ⊙ Brake sharply to a stop before looking
- ⊙ Be prepared to brake sharply to a stop
- ⊙ Be prepared to stop for any traffic.

⊙ **Be prepared to stop for any traffic.**

When approaching a junction where the traffic lights have failed, you should proceed with caution. Treat the situation as an unmarked junction and be prepared to stop.

5.19
*Mark **one** answer*

What should the driver of the red car
(arrowed) do?

⊙ Wave the pedestrians who are waiting
to cross

⊙ Wait for the pedestrian in the road to
cross

⊙ Quickly drive behind the pedestrian in
the road

⊙ Tell the pedestrian in the road she
should not have crossed

⊙ **Wait for the pedestrian in the
road to cross**

Some people might take longer to cross
the road. They may be older or have a
disability. Be patient and don't hurry them
by showing your impatience. They might
have poor eyesight or not be able to hear
traffic approaching. If pedestrians are
standing at the side of the road, don't
signal or wave them to cross. Other road
users may not have seen your signal and
this could lead the pedestrians into a
hazardous situation.

5.20
*Mark **one** answer*

You are following a slower-moving vehicle
on a narrow country road. There is a
junction just ahead on the right. What
should you do?

⊙ Overtake after checking your mirrors
and signalling

⊙ Stay behind until you are past the
junction

⊙ Accelerate quickly to pass before the
junction

⊙ Slow down and prepare to overtake on
the left

⊙ **Stay behind until you are past
the junction**

You should never overtake as you
approach a junction. If a vehicle emerged
from the junction while you were
overtaking, a dangerous situation could
develop very quickly.

What should you do as you approach this overhead bridge?

- Move out to the centre of the road before going through

- Find another route, this is only for high vehicles

- Be prepared to give way to large vehicles in the middle of the road

- Move across to the right hand side before going through

⊙ **Be prepared to give way to large vehicles in the middle of the road**

Oncoming large vehicles may need to move to the middle of the road so that they can pass safely under the bridge. There will not be enough room for you to continue and you should be ready to stop and wait.

Why are mirrors often slightly curved (convex)?

- They give a wider field of vision

- They totally cover blind spots

- They make it easier to judge the speed of following traffic

- They make following traffic look bigger

⊙ **They give a wider field of vision**

Although a convex mirror gives a wide view of the scene behind, you should be aware that it will not show you everything behind or to the side of the vehicle. Before you move off you will need to check over your shoulder to look for anything not visible in the mirrors.

5.23   *Mark **one** answer*

You see this sign on the rear of a slow-moving lorry that you want to pass. It is travelling in the middle lane of a three-lane motorway. You should

⊙ cautiously approach the lorry then pass on either side

⊙ follow the lorry until you can leave the motorway

⊙ wait on the hard shoulder until the lorry has stopped

⊙ approach with care and keep to the left of the lorry

⊙ **approach with care and keep to the left of the lorry**

This sign is found on slow-moving or stationary works vehicles. If you wish to overtake, do so on the left, as indicated. Be aware that there might be workmen in the area.

5.24   *Mark **one** answer*

You think the driver of the vehicle in front has forgotten to cancel their right indicator. You should

⊙ flash your lights to alert the driver

⊙ sound your horn before overtaking

⊙ overtake on the left if there is room

⊙ stay behind and not overtake

⊙ **stay behind and not overtake**

The driver may be unsure of the location of a junction and turn suddenly. Be cautious and don't attempt to overtake.

What is the main hazard the driver of the red car (arrowed) should be aware of?

- ⊙ Glare from the sun may affect the driver's vision
- ⊙ The black car may stop suddenly
- ⊙ The bus may move out into the road
- ⊙ Oncoming vehicles will assume the driver is turning right

⊙ **The bus may move out into the road**

If you can do so safely give way to buses signalling to move off at bus stops. Try to anticipate the actions of other road users around you. The driver of the red car should be prepared for the bus pulling out. As you approach a bus stop look to see how many passengers are waiting to board. If the last one has just got on, the bus is likely to move off.

This yellow sign on a vehicle indicates this is

- ⊙ a broken-down vehicle
- ⊙ a school bus
- ⊙ an ice cream van
- ⊙ a private ambulance

⊙ **a school bus**

Buses which carry children to and from school may stop at places other than scheduled bus stops. Be aware that they might pull over at any time to allow children to get on or off. This will normally be when traffic is heavy during rush hour.

5.27 *Mark **two** answers*

What TWO main hazards should you be aware of when going along this street?

- ⊙ Glare from the sun
- ⊙ Car doors opening suddenly
- ⊙ Lack of road markings
- ⊙ The headlights on parked cars being switched on
- ⊙ Large goods vehicles
- ⊙ Children running out from between vehicles

⊙ **Car doors opening suddenly**

⊙ **Children running out from between vehicles**

On roads where there are many parked vehicles you should take extra care. You might not be able to see children between parked cars and they may run out into the road without looking.

People may open car doors without realising the hazard this can create. You will also need to look well down the road for oncoming traffic.

5.28 *Mark **one** answer*

What is the main hazard you should be aware of when following this cyclist?

- ⊙ The cyclist may move to the left and dismount
- ⊙ The cyclist may swerve out into the road
- ⊙ The contents of the cyclist's carrier may fall onto the road
- ⊙ The cyclist may wish to turn right at the end of the road

⊙ **The cyclist may swerve out into the road**

When following a cyclist be aware that they have to deal with the hazards around them. They may wobble or swerve to avoid a pothole in the road or see a potential hazard and change direction suddenly. Don't follow them too closely or rev your engine impatiently.

A driver's behaviour has upset you. It may help if you

- ⊙ stop and take a break
- ⊙ shout abusive language
- ⊙ gesture to them with your hand
- ⊙ follow their car, flashing your headlights

⊙ **stop and take a break**

Tiredness may make you more irritable than you would be normally. You might react differently to situations because of it. If you feel yourself becoming tense, take a break.

In areas where there are 'traffic calming' measures you should

- ⊙ travel at a reduced speed
- ⊙ always travel at the speed limit
- ⊙ position in the centre of the road
- ⊙ only slow down if pedestrians are near

⊙ **travel at a reduced speed**

Traffic calming measures such as road humps, chicanes and narrowings are intended to slow you down. Maintain a reduced speed until you reach the end of these features. They are there to protect pedestrians. Kill your speed!

When approaching this hazard why should you slow down?

- ⊙ Because of the bend
- ⊙ Because it's hard to see to the right
- ⊙ Because of approaching traffic
- ⊙ Because of animals crossing
- ⊙ Because of the level crossing

⊙ **Because of the bend**

⊙ **Because of the level crossing**

There are two hazards clearly signed in this picture. You should be preparing for the bend by slowing down and selecting the correct gear. You might also have to stop at the level crossing, so be alert and be prepared to stop if necessary.

5.32
*Mark **one** answer*

Why are place names painted on the road surface?

- To restrict the flow of traffic
- To warn you of oncoming traffic
- To enable you to change lanes early
- To prevent you changing lanes

⊙ **To enable you to change lanes early**

The names of towns and cities may be painted on the road at busy junctions and complex road systems. Their purpose is to let you move into the correct lane in good time, allowing traffic to flow more freely.

5.33
*Mark **one** answer*

Some two-way roads are divided into three lanes. Why are these particularly dangerous?

- Traffic in both directions can use the middle lane to overtake
- Traffic can travel faster in poor weather conditions
- Traffic can overtake on the left
- Traffic uses the middle lane for emergencies only

⊙ **Traffic in both directions can use the middle lane to overtake**

If you intend to overtake you must consider that approaching traffic could be planning the same manoeuvre. When you have considered the situation and have decided it is safe, indicate your intentions early. This will show the approaching traffic that you intend to pull out.

5.34
*Mark **one** answer*

You are on a dual carriageway. Ahead you see a vehicle with an amber flashing light. What could this be?

- An ambulance
- A fire engine
- A doctor on call
- A disabled person's vehicle

⊙ **A disabled person's vehicle**

An amber flashing light on a vehicle indicates that it is slow-moving. Battery powered vehicles used by disabled people are limited to 8 mph. It's not advisable for them to be used on dual carriageways where the speed limit exceeds 50 mph. If they are then an amber flashing light must be used.

What does this signal from a police officer mean to oncoming traffic?

- ⊙ Go ahead
- ⊙ Stop
- ⊙ Turn left
- ⊙ Turn right

⊙ **Stop**

Police officers may need to direct traffic, for example, at a junction where the traffic lights have broken down. Check your copy of The Highway Code for the signals that they use.

Why should you be especially cautious when going past this stationary bus?

- ⊙ There is traffic approaching in the distance
- ⊙ The driver may open the door
- ⊙ It may suddenly move off
- ⊙ People may cross the road in front of it
- ⊙ There are bicycles parked on the pavement

⊙ **It may suddenly move off**

⊙ **People may cross the road in front of it**

A stationary bus at a bus stop can hide pedestrians just in front of it who might be about to cross the road. Only go past at a speed that will enable you to stop safely if you need to.

5.37
*Mark **three** answers*

Overtaking is a major cause of collisions. In which THREE of these situations should you NOT overtake?

- ⊙ If you are turning left shortly afterwards
- ⊙ When you are in a one-way street
- ⊙ When you are approaching a junction
- ⊙ If you are travelling up a long hill
- ⊙ When your view ahead is blocked

- ⊙ **If you are turning left shortly afterwards**

- ⊙ **When you are approaching a junction**

- ⊙ **When your view ahead is blocked**

You should not overtake unless it is really necessary. Arriving safely is more important than taking risks. Also look out for road signs and markings that show it is illegal or would be unsafe to overtake. In many cases overtaking is unlikely to significantly improve journey times.

5.38
*Mark **three** answers*

Which THREE result from drinking alcohol?

- ⊙ Less control
- ⊙ A false sense of confidence
- ⊙ Faster reactions
- ⊙ Poor judgement of speed
- ⊙ Greater awareness of danger

- ⊙ **Less control**

- ⊙ **A false sense of confidence**

- ⊙ **Poor judgement of speed**

You must understand the serious dangers of mixing alcohol with driving or riding. Alcohol will severely reduce your ability to drive or ride safely. Just one drink could put you over the limit. Don't risk people's lives – DON'T DRINK AND DRIVE OR RIDE!

What does the solid white line at the side of the road indicate?

- ⊙ Traffic lights ahead
- ⊙ Edge of the carriageway
- ⊙ Footpath on the left
- ⊙ Cycle path

⊙ **Edge of the carriageway**

The continuous white line shows the edge of the carriageway. It can be especially useful when visibility is restricted, for example at night or in bad weather. It is discontinued where it crosses junctions, lay-bys etc.

You are driving towards this level crossing. What would be the first warning of an approaching train?

- ⊙ Both half barriers down
- ⊙ A steady amber light
- ⊙ One half barrier down
- ⊙ Twin flashing red lights

⊙ **A steady amber light**

The steady amber light will be followed by twin flashing red lights that mean you must stop. An alarm will also sound to alert you to the fact that a train is approaching.

5.41 *Mark **one** answer*

You are behind this cyclist. When the traffic lights change, what should you do?

- ⊙ Try to move off before the cyclist
- ⊙ Allow the cyclist time and room
- ⊙ Turn right but give the cyclist room
- ⊙ Tap your horn and drive through first

⊙ **Allow the cyclist time and room**

Hold back and allow the cyclist to move off. In some towns, junctions have special areas marked across the front of the traffic lane. These allow cyclists to wait for the lights to change and move off ahead of other traffic.

5.42 *Mark **one** answer*

While driving, you see this sign ahead. You should

- ⊙ stop at the sign
- ⊙ slow, but continue around the bend
- ⊙ slow to a crawl and continue
- ⊙ stop and look for open farm gates

⊙ **slow, but continue around the bend**

Drive around the bend at a steady speed in the correct gear. Be aware that you might have to stop for approaching trains.

When the traffic lights change to green the white car should

- ⊙ wait for the cyclist to pull away
- ⊙ move off quickly and turn in front of the cyclist
- ⊙ move close up to the cyclist to beat the lights
- ⊙ sound the horn to warn the cyclist

⊙ **wait for the cyclist to pull away**

If you are waiting at traffic lights, check all around you before you move away, as cyclists often filter through waiting traffic. Allow the cyclist to move off safely.

You intend to turn left at the traffic lights. Just before turning you should

- ⊙ check your right mirror
- ⊙ move close up to the white car
- ⊙ straddle the lanes
- ⊙ check for bicycles on your left

⊙ **check for bicycles on your left**

Check your nearside for cyclists before moving away. This is especially important if you have been in a stationary queue of traffic and are about to move off, as cyclists often try to filter past on the nearside of stationary vehicles.

5.45
Mark **one** answer

You should reduce your speed when driving along this road because

- ⊙ there is a staggered junction ahead
- ⊙ there is a low bridge ahead
- ⊙ there is a change in the road surface
- ⊙ the road ahead narrows

⊙ **there is a staggered junction ahead**

Traffic could be turning off ahead of you, to the left or right.

Vehicles turning left will be slowing down before the junction and any vehicles turning right may have to stop to allow oncoming traffic to clear. Be prepared for this as you might have to slow down or stop behind them.

5.46
Mark **one** answer

You are driving at 60 mph. As you approach this hazard you should

- ⊙ maintain your speed
- ⊙ reduce your speed
- ⊙ take the next right turn
- ⊙ take the next left turn

⊙ **reduce your speed**

There could be stationary traffic ahead, waiting to turn right. Other traffic could be emerging and it may take time for them to gather speed.

What might you expect to happen in this situation?

- ⊙ Traffic will move into the right-hand lane
- ⊙ Traffic speed will increase
- ⊙ Traffic will move into the left-hand lane
- ⊙ Traffic will not need to change position

⊙ **Traffic will move into the left-hand lane**

Be courteous and allow the traffic to merge into the left-hand lane.

You are driving on a road with several lanes. You see these signs above the lanes. What do they mean?

- ⊙ The two right lanes are open
- ⊙ The two left lanes are open
- ⊙ Traffic in the left lanes should stop
- ⊙ Traffic in the right lanes should stop

⊙ **The two left lanes are open**

If you see a red cross above your lane it means that there is an obstruction ahead. You will have to move into one of the lanes which is showing the green light. If all the lanes are showing a red cross, then you must stop.

5.49
*Mark **one** answer*

You are invited to a pub lunch. You know that you will have to drive in the evening. What is your best course of action?

- ⊙ Avoid mixing your alcoholic drinks
- ⊙ Not drink any alcohol at all
- ⊙ Have some milk before drinking alcohol
- ⊙ Eat a hot meal with your alcoholic drinks

⊙ **Not drink any alcohol at all**

Alcohol will stay in the body for several hours and may make you unfit to drive later in the day. Drinking during the day will also affect your performance at work or study.

5.50
*Mark **one** answer*

You have been convicted of driving whilst unfit through drink or drugs. You will find this is likely to cause the cost of one of the following to rise considerably. Which one?

- ⊙ Road fund licence
- ⊙ Insurance premiums
- ⊙ Vehicle test certificate
- ⊙ Driving licence

⊙ **Insurance premiums**

You have shown that you are a risk to yourself and others on the road. For this reason insurance companies may charge you a higher premium.

5.51
*Mark **one** answer*

What advice should you give to a driver who has had a few alcoholic drinks at a party?

- ⊙ Have a strong cup of coffee and then drive home
- ⊙ Drive home carefully and slowly
- ⊙ Go home by public transport
- ⊙ Wait a short while and then drive home

⊙ **Go home by public transport**

Drinking black coffee or waiting a few hours won't make any difference. Alcohol takes time to leave the body.

A driver who has been drinking should go home by public transport or taxi. They might even be unfit to drive the following morning.

You have been taking medicine for a few days which made you feel drowsy. Today you feel better but still need to take the medicine. You should only drive

- ⊙ if your journey is necessary
- ⊙ at night on quiet roads
- ⊙ if someone goes with you
- ⊙ after checking with your doctor

⊙ **after checking with your doctor**

Take care – it's not worth taking risks. Always check with your doctor to be really sure. You may not feel drowsy now, but the medicine could have an effect on you later in the day.

You are about to return home from holiday when you become ill. A doctor prescribes drugs which are likely to affect your driving. You should

- ⊙ drive only if someone is with you
- ⊙ avoid driving on motorways
- ⊙ not drive yourself
- ⊙ never drive at more than 30 mph

⊙ **not drive yourself**

Find another way to get home even if this proves to be very inconvenient. You must not put other road users, your passengers or yourself at risk.

During periods of illness your ability to drive may be impaired. You MUST

- ⊙ see your doctor each time before you drive
- ⊙ only take smaller doses of any medicines
- ⊙ be medically fit to drive
- ⊙ not drive after taking certain medicines
- ⊙ take all your medicines with you when you drive

⊙ **be medically fit to drive**

⊙ **not drive after taking certain medicines**

Be responsible and only drive if you are fit to do so. Some medication can affect your concentration and judgement when dealing with hazards. It may also cause you to become drowsy or even fall asleep. Driving while taking such medication is highly dangerous.

5.55   Mark **two** answers

You feel drowsy when driving. You should

- stop and rest as soon as possible
- turn the heater up to keep you warm and comfortable
- make sure you have a good supply of fresh air
- continue with your journey but drive more slowly
- close the car windows to help you concentrate

⊙ **stop and rest as soon as possible**

⊙ **make sure you have a good supply of fresh air**

You will be putting other road users at risk if you continue to drive when drowsy. Pull over and stop in a safe place. If you are driving a long distance, think about finding some accommodation so you can get some sleep before continuing your journey.

5.56   Mark **two** answers

You are driving along a motorway and become tired. You should

- stop at the next service area and rest
- leave the motorway at the next exit and rest
- increase your speed and turn up the radio volume
- close all your windows and set heating to warm
- pull up on the hard shoulder and change drivers

⊙ **stop at the next service area and rest**

⊙ **leave the motorway at the next exit and rest**

If you have planned your journey properly, to include rest stops, you should arrive at your destination in good time.

5.57   Mark **one** answer

You are taking drugs that are likely to affect your driving. What should you do?

- Seek medical advice before driving
- Limit your driving to essential journeys
- Only drive if accompanied by a full licence-holder
- Drive only for short distances

⊙ **Seek medical advice before driving**

Check with your doctor or pharmacist if you think that the drugs you're taking are likely to make you feel drowsy or impair your judgement.

139

5.58

Mark *one* answer

You are about to drive home. You feel very tired and have a severe headache. You should

- wait until you are fit and well before driving
- drive home, but take a tablet for headaches
- drive home if you can stay awake for the journey
- wait for a short time, then drive home slowly

⊙ **wait until you are fit and well before driving**

All your concentration should be on your driving. Any pain you feel will distract you and you should avoid driving when drowsy. The safest course of action is to wait until you have rested and feel better.

5.59

Mark *one* answer

If you are feeling tired it is best to stop as soon as you can. Until then you should

- increase your speed to find a stopping place quickly
- ensure a supply of fresh air
- gently tap the steering wheel
- keep changing speed to improve concentration

⊙ **ensure a supply of fresh air**

If you're going on a long journey plan your route before you leave. This will help you to be decisive at intersections and junctions, plan rest stops and have an idea of how long the journey will take.

Make sure your vehicle is well-ventilated to stop you becoming drowsy. You need to maintain concentration so that your judgement is not impaired.

5.60

Mark *three* answers

Driving long distances can be tiring. You can prevent this by

- stopping every so often for a walk
- opening a window for some fresh air
- ensuring plenty of refreshment breaks
- completing the journey without stopping
- eating a large meal before driving

⊙ **stopping every so often for a walk**

⊙ **opening a window for some fresh air**

⊙ **ensuring plenty of refreshment breaks**

Long-distance driving can be boring. This, coupled with a stuffy, warm vehicle, can make you feel tired. Make sure you take rest breaks to keep yourself awake and alert. Stop in a safe place before you get to the stage of fighting sleep.

5.61

*Mark **one** answer*

You go to a social event and need to drive a short time after. What precaution should you take?

- ⊙ Avoid drinking alcohol on an empty stomach
- ⊙ Drink plenty of coffee after drinking alcohol
- ⊙ Avoid drinking alcohol completely
- ⊙ Drink plenty of milk before drinking alcohol

⊙ **Avoid drinking alcohol completely**

This is always going to be the safest option. Just one drink could put you over the limit and dangerously impair your judgement and reactions.

5.62

*Mark **one** answer*

You take some cough medicine given to you by a friend. What should you do before driving?

- ⊙ Ask your friend if taking the medicine affected their driving
- ⊙ Drink some strong coffee one hour before driving
- ⊙ Check the label to see if the medicine will affect your driving
- ⊙ Drive a short distance to see if the medicine is affecting your driving

⊙ **Check the label to see if the medicine will affect your driving**

Never drive if you have taken drugs, without first checking what the side effects might be. They might affect your judgement and perception, and therefore endanger lives.

You take the wrong route and find you are on a one-way street. You should

- ⊙ reverse out of the road
- ⊙ turn round in a side road
- ⊙ continue to the end of the road
- ⊙ reverse into a driveway

⊙ **continue to the end of the road**

Never reverse or turn your vehicle around in a one-way street. This is highly dangerous. Carry on and find another route, checking the direction signs as you drive. If you need to check a map, first stop in a safe place.

Which THREE are likely to make you lose concentration while driving?

- ⊙ Looking at road maps
- ⊙ Listening to loud music
- ⊙ Using your windscreen washers
- ⊙ Looking in your wing mirror
- ⊙ Using a mobile phone

⊙ **Looking at road maps**

⊙ **Listening to loud music**

⊙ **Using a mobile phone**

Looking at road maps while driving is very dangerous. If you aren't sure of your route stop in a safe place and check the map. You must not allow anything to take your attention away from the road.

If you need to use a mobile phone, stop in a safe place before doing so.

5.65

You are driving along this road. The driver on the left is reversing from a driveway. You should

⊙ move to the opposite side of the road

⊙ drive through as you have priority

⊙ sound your horn and be prepared to stop

⊙ speed up and drive through quickly

⊙ **sound your horn and be prepared to stop**

White lights at the rear of a car show that it is about to reverse. Sound your horn to warn of your presence and reduce your speed as a precaution.

5.66

You have been involved in an argument before starting your journey. This has made you feel angry. You should

⊙ start to drive, but open a window

⊙ drive slower than normal and turn your radio on

⊙ have an alcoholic drink to help you relax before driving

⊙ calm down before you start to drive

⊙ **calm down before you start to drive**

If you are feeling upset or angry you should wait until you have calmed down before setting out on a journey.

5.67

You start to feel tired while driving. What should you do?

⊙ Increase your speed slightly

⊙ Decrease your speed slightly

⊙ Find a less busy route

⊙ Pull over at a safe place to rest

⊙ **Pull over at a safe place to rest**

If you start to feel tired, stop at a safe place for a rest break.

Every year many fatal incidents are caused by drivers falling asleep at the wheel.

You are driving on this dual carriageway. Why may you need to slow down?

- ⊙ There is a broken white line in the centre
- ⊙ There are solid white lines either side
- ⊙ There are roadworks ahead of you
- ⊙ There are no footpaths

⊙ **There are roadworks ahead of you**

Look well ahead and read any road signs as you drive. They are there to inform you of what is ahead. In this case you may need to slow right down and change direction.

Make sure you can take whatever action is necessary in plenty of time. Check your mirrors so you know what is happening around you before you change speed or direction.

You have just been overtaken by this motorcyclist who is cutting in sharply. You should

- ⊙ sound the horn
- ⊙ brake firmly
- ⊙ keep a safe gap
- ⊙ flash your lights

⊙ **keep a safe gap**

If another vehicle cuts in too sharply, ease off the accelerator and drop back to allow a safe separation distance. Try not to overreact by braking sharply or swerving, as you could lose control. If vehicles behind you are too close or unprepared, it could lead to a crash.

5.70
*Mark **one** answer*

You are about to drive home. You cannot find the glasses you need to wear. You should

- drive home slowly, keeping to quiet roads
- borrow a friend's glasses and use those
- drive home at night, so that the lights will help you
- find a way of getting home without driving

- **find a way of getting home without driving**

Don't be tempted to drive if you've lost or forgotten your glasses. You must be able to see clearly when driving.

5.71
*Mark **three** answers*

Which THREE of these are likely effects of drinking alcohol?

- Reduced co-ordination
- Increased confidence
- Poor judgement
- Increased concentration
- Faster reactions
- Colour blindness

- **Reduced co-ordination**

- **Increased confidence**

- **Poor judgement**

Alcohol can increase confidence to a point where a driver's behaviour might become 'out of character'. Someone who normally behaves sensibly suddenly takes risks and enjoys it. Never let yourself or your friends get into this situation.

5.72
*Mark **one** answer*

How does alcohol affect you?

- It speeds up your reactions
- It increases your awareness
- It improves your co-ordination
- It reduces your concentration

- **It reduces your concentration**

Concentration and good judgement are needed at all times to be a good, safe driver. Don't put yourself or others at risk by drinking and driving.

Your doctor has given you a course of medicine. Why should you ask how it will affect you?

- Drugs make you a better driver by quickening your reactions
- You will have to let your insurance company know about the medicine
- Some types of medicine can cause your reactions to slow down
- The medicine you take may affect your hearing

- **Some types of medicine can cause your reactions to slow down**

Always check the label of any medication container. The contents might affect your driving. If you aren't sure, ask your doctor or pharmacist.

You are on a motorway. You feel tired. You should

- carry on but go slowly
- leave the motorway at the next exit
- complete your journey as quickly as possible
- stop on the hard shoulder

- **leave the motorway at the next exit**

If you do feel tired and there's no service station for many miles, leave the motorway at the next exit. Find a road off the motorway where you can pull up and stop safely.

You find that you need glasses to read vehicle number plates at the required distance. When MUST you wear them?

- Only in bad weather conditions
- At all times when driving
- Only when you think it necessary
- Only in bad light or at night time

- **At all times when driving**

Have your eyesight tested before you start your practical training. Then, throughout your driving life, have checks periodically to ensure that your eyes haven't deteriorated.

5.76
*Mark **two** answers*

Which TWO things would help to keep you alert during a long journey?

- Finishing your journey as fast as you can
- Keeping off the motorways and using country roads
- Making sure that you get plenty of fresh air
- Making regular stops for refreshments

- **Making sure that you get plenty of fresh air**

- **Making regular stops for refreshments**

Make sure that the vehicle you're driving is well ventilated. A warm, stuffy atmosphere will make you feel drowsy. Open a window and turn down the heating.

5.77
*Mark **one** answer*

Which of the following types of glasses should NOT be worn when driving at night?

- Half-moon
- Round
- Bi-focal
- Tinted

- **Tinted**

If you are driving at night or in poor visibility, tinted lenses will reduce the efficiency of your vision, by reducing the amount of available light reaching your eyes.

5.78
*Mark **three** answers*

Drinking any amount of alcohol is likely to

- slow down your reactions to hazards
- increase the speed of your reactions
- worsen your judgement of speed
- improve your awareness of danger
- give a false sense of confidence

- **slow down your reactions to hazards**

- **worsen your judgement of speed**

- **give a false sense of confidence**

If you are going to drive it's always the safest option not to drink at all. Don't be tempted – it's not worth it.

*Mark **three** answers*

What else can seriously affect your concentration, other than alcoholic drinks?

- Drugs
- Tiredness
- Tinted windows
- Contact lenses
- Loud music

⊙ **Drugs**

⊙ **Tiredness**

⊙ **Loud music**

Even a slight distraction can allow your concentration to drift. Maintain full concentration at all times so you stay in full control of your vehicle.

---

*Mark **one** answer*

As a driver you find that your eyesight has become very poor. Your optician says they cannot help you. The law says that you should tell

- the licensing authority
- your own doctor
- the local police station
- another optician

⊙ **the licensing authority**

This will have a serious effect on your judgement and concentration. If you cannot meet the eyesight requirements you must tell DVLA (or DVA in Northern Ireland).

---

*Mark **one** answer*

When should you use hazard warning lights?

- When you are double-parked on a two way road
- When your direction indicators are not working
- When warning oncoming traffic that you intend to stop
- When your vehicle has broken down and is causing an obstruction

⊙ **When your vehicle has broken down and is causing an obstruction**

Hazard warning lights are an important safety feature and should be used if you have broken down and are causing an obstruction. Don't use them as an excuse to park illegally such as when using a cash machine or post box. You may also use them on motorways to warn traffic behind you of danger ahead.

5.82
*Mark **one** answer*

You want to turn left at this junction. The view of the main road is restricted. What should you do?

- Stay well back and wait to see if something comes
- Build up your speed so that you can emerge quickly
- Stop and apply the handbrake even if the road is clear
- Approach slowly and edge out until you can see more clearly

⊙ **Approach slowly and edge out until you can see more clearly**

You should slow right down, and stop if necessary, at any junction where the view is restricted. Edge forward until you can see properly. Only then can you decide if it is safe to go.

5.83
*Mark **one** answer*

When may you use hazard warning lights?

- To park alongside another car
- To park on double yellow lines
- When you are being towed
- When you have broken down

⊙ **When you have broken down**

Hazard warning lights may be used to warn other road users when you have broken down and are causing an obstruction, or are on a motorway and want to warn following traffic of a hazard ahead. Don't use them when being towed or when parking illegally.

5.84
*Mark **one** answer*

Hazard warning lights should be used when vehicles are

- broken down and causing an obstruction
- faulty and moving slowly
- being towed along a road
- reversing into a side road

⊙ **broken down and causing an obstruction**

Don't use hazard lights as an excuse for illegal parking. If you do use them, don't forget to switch them off when you move away. There must be a warning light on the control panel to show when the hazard lights are in operation.

When driving a car fitted with automatic transmission what would you use 'kick down' for?

⊙ Cruise control

⊙ Quick acceleration

⊙ Slow braking

⊙ Fuel economy

⊙ **Quick acceleration**

'Kick down' selects a lower gear, enabling the vehicle to accelerate faster.

You are driving along this motorway. It is raining. When following this lorry you should

⊙ allow at least a two-second gap

⊙ move left and drive on the hard shoulder

⊙ allow at least a four-second gap

⊙ be aware of spray reducing your vision

⊙ move right and stay in the right-hand lane

⊙ **allow at least a four-second gap**

⊙ **be aware of spray reducing your vision**

The usual two second time gap will increase to four seconds when the roads are wet. If you stay well back you will

• be able to see past the vehicle

• be out of the spray thrown up by the lorry's tyres

• give yourself more time to stop if the need arises

• increase your chances of being seen by the lorry driver.

5.87
*Mark **one** answer*

You are driving towards this left-hand bend. What dangers should you be aware of?

⊙ A vehicle overtaking you

⊙ No white lines in the centre of the road

⊙ No sign to warn you of the bend

⊙ Pedestrians walking towards you

⊙ **Pedestrians walking towards you**

Pedestrians walking on a road with no pavement should walk against the direction of the traffic. You can't see around this bend: there may be hidden dangers. Always keep this in mind so you give yourself time to react if a hazard does arise.

5.88
*Mark **two** answers*

The traffic ahead of you in the left-hand lane is slowing. You should

⊙ be wary of cars on your right cutting in

⊙ accelerate past the vehicles in the left-hand lane

⊙ pull up on the left-hand verge

⊙ move across and continue in the right-hand lane

⊙ slow down, keeping a safe separation distance

⊙ **be wary of cars on your right cutting in**

⊙ **slow down, keeping a safe separation distance**

Allow the traffic to merge into the nearside lane. Leave enough room so that your separation distance is not reduced drastically if a vehicle pulls in ahead of you.

Mark **two** answers

As a provisional licence holder, you must not drive a motor car

- at more than 40 mph
- on your own
- on the motorway
- under the age of 18 years at night
- with passengers in the rear seats

- **on your own**

- **on the motorway**

When you have passed your practical test you will be able to drive on a motorway. It is recommended that you have instruction on motorway driving before you venture out on your own. Ask your instructor about this.

Mark **two** answers

You are not sure if your cough medicine will affect you. What TWO things should you do?

- Ask your doctor
- Check the medicine label
- Drive if you feel alright
- Ask a friend or relative for advice

- **Ask your doctor**

- **Check the medicine label**

If you're taking medicine or drugs prescribed by your doctor, check to ensure that they won't make you drowsy. If you forget to ask at the time of your visit to the surgery, check with your pharmacist.

Some over-the-counter medication can also cause drowsiness. Read the label and don't drive if you are affected.

Mark **one** answer

For which of these may you use hazard warning lights?

- When driving on a motorway to warn traffic behind of a hazard ahead
- When you are double-parked on a two-way road
- When your direction indicators are not working
- When warning oncoming traffic that you intend to stop

- **When driving on a motorway to warn traffic behind of a hazard ahead**

Hazard warning lights are an important safety feature. Use them when driving on a motorway to warn traffic behind you of danger ahead.

You should also use them if your vehicle has broken down and is causing an obstruction.

5.92
*Mark **one** answer*

You are waiting to emerge at a junction.
Your view is restricted by parked vehicles.
What can help you to see traffic on the road
you are joining?

- Looking for traffic behind you
- Reflections of traffic in shop windows
- Making eye contact with other road users
- Checking for traffic in your interior mirror

⊙ **Reflections of traffic in shop windows**

When your view is restricted into the new road you must still be completely sure it is safe to emerge. Try to look for traffic through the windows of the parked cars or the reflections in shop windows. Keep looking in all directions as you slowly edge forwards until you can see it is safe.

5.93
*Mark **one** answer*

After passing your driving test, you suffer
from ill health. This affects your driving. You
MUST

- inform your local police station
- avoid using motorways
- always drive accompanied
- inform the licensing authority

⊙ **inform the licensing authority**

The licensing authority won't automatically take away your licence without investigation. For advice, contact the Driver and Vehicle Licensing Agency (or DVA in Northern Ireland).

5.94
*Mark **one** answer*

Why should the junction on the left be kept
clear?

- To allow vehicles to enter and emerge
- To allow the bus to reverse
- To allow vehicles to make a U-turn
- To allow vehicles to park

⊙ **To allow vehicles to enter and emerge**

You should always try to keep junctions clear. If you are in queuing traffic make sure that when you stop you leave enough space for traffic to flow in and out of the junction.

Your motorway journey seems boring and you feel drowsy. What should you do?

- ⊙ Stop on the hard shoulder for a sleep
- ⊙ Open a window and stop as soon as it's safe and legal
- ⊙ Speed up to arrive at your destination sooner
- ⊙ Slow down and let other drivers overtake

⊙ **Open a window and stop as soon as it's safe and legal**

Never stop on the hard shoulder to rest. If there is no service station for several miles, leave the motorway at the next exit and find somewhere safe and legal to pull over.

You are driving on a motorway. The traffic ahead is braking sharply because of an incident. How could you warn traffic behind you?

- ⊙ Briefly use the hazard warning lights
- ⊙ Switch on the hazard warning lights continuously
- ⊙ Briefly use the rear fog lights
- ⊙ Switch on the headlights continuously

⊙ **Briefly use the hazard warning lights**

The only time you are permitted to use your hazard warning lights while moving is if you are on a motorway or dual carriageway and you need to warn other road users, particularly those behind, of a hazard or obstruction ahead. Only use them long enough to ensure your warning has been seen.

section **six**
VULNERABLE ROAD USERS

This section covers

- Pedestrians
- Children
- Older drivers
- Disabled people
- Cyclists
- Motorcyclists
- Animals
- New drivers

6.1 *Mark **one** answer*

Which sign means that there may be people walking along the road?

Always check the road signs. Triangular signs are warning signs and they'll keep you informed of hazards ahead and help you to anticipate any problems. There are a number of different signs showing pedestrians. Learn the meaning of each one.

6.2 *Mark **one** answer*

You are turning left at a junction. Pedestrians have started to cross the road. You should

- go on, giving them plenty of room
- stop and wave at them to cross
- blow your horn and proceed
- give way to them

⊙ **give way to them**

If you're turning into a side road, pedestrians already crossing the road have priority and you should give way to them. Don't wave them across the road, sound your horn, flash your lights or give any other misleading signal. Other road users may misinterpret your signal and this may lead the pedestrians into a dangerous situation. If a pedestrian is slow or indecisive be patient and wait. Don't hurry them across by revving your engine.

You are turning left from a main road into a side road. People are already crossing the road into which you are turning. You should

- continue, as it is your right of way
- signal to them to continue crossing
- wait and allow them to cross
- sound your horn to warn them of your presence

⊙ **wait and allow them to cross**

Always check the road into which you are turning. Approaching at the correct speed will allow you enough time to observe and react.

Give way to any pedestrians already crossing the road.

You are at a road junction, turning into a minor road. There are pedestrians crossing the minor road. You should

- stop and wave the pedestrians across
- sound your horn to let the pedestrians know that you are there
- give way to the pedestrians who are already crossing
- carry on; the pedestrians should give way to you

⊙ **give way to the pedestrians who are already crossing**

Always look into the road into which you are turning. If there are pedestrians crossing, give way to them, but don't wave or signal to them to cross. Signal your intention to turn as you approach.

6.5
Mark **one** answer

You are turning left into a side road. What hazards should you be especially aware of?

- ⊙ One way street
- ⊙ Pedestrians
- ⊙ Traffic congestion
- ⊙ Parked vehicles

⊙ **Pedestrians**

Make sure that you have reduced your speed and are in the correct gear for the turn. Look into the road before you turn and always give way to any pedestrians who are crossing.

6.6
Mark **one** answer

You intend to turn right into a side road. Just before turning you should check for motorcyclists who might be

- ⊙ overtaking on your left
- ⊙ following you closely
- ⊙ emerging from the side road
- ⊙ overtaking on your right

⊙ **overtaking on your right**

Never attempt to change direction to the right without first checking your right-hand mirror. A motorcyclist might not have seen your signal and could be hidden by the car behind you. This action should become a matter of routine.

6.7
Mark **one** answer

A toucan crossing is different from other crossings because

- ⊙ moped riders can use it
- ⊙ it is controlled by a traffic warden
- ⊙ it is controlled by two flashing lights
- ⊙ cyclists can use it

⊙ **cyclists can use it**

Toucan crossings are shared by pedestrians and cyclists and they are shown the green light together. Cyclists are permitted to cycle across.

The signals are push-button operated and there is no flashing amber phase.

How will a school crossing patrol signal you to stop?

- ⊙ By pointing to children on the opposite pavement
- ⊙ By displaying a red light
- ⊙ By displaying a stop sign
- ⊙ By giving you an arm signal

⊙ **By displaying a stop sign**

If a school crossing patrol steps out into the road with a stop sign you must stop. Don't wave anyone across the road and don't get impatient or rev your engine.

Where would you see this sign?

- ⊙ In the window of a car taking children to school
- ⊙ At the side of the road
- ⊙ At playground areas
- ⊙ On the rear of a school bus or coach

⊙ **On the rear of a school bus or coach**

Vehicles that are used to carry children to and from school will be travelling at busy times of the day. If you're following a vehicle with this sign be prepared for it to make frequent stops. It might pick up or set down passengers in places other than normal bus stops.

6.10   *Mark **one** answer*

Which sign tells you that pedestrians may be walking in the road as there is no pavement?

Give pedestrians who are walking at the side of the road plenty of room when you pass them. They may turn around when they hear your engine and unintentionally step into the path of your vehicle.

6.11   *Mark **one** answer*

What does this sign mean?

○ No route for pedestrians and cyclists

○ A route for pedestrians only

○ A route for cyclists only

○ A route for pedestrians and cyclists

○ **A route for pedestrians and cyclists**

This sign shows a shared route for pedestrians and cyclists: when it ends, the cyclists will be rejoining the main road.

6.12   *Mark **one** answer*

You see a pedestrian with a white stick and red band. This means that the person is

○ physically disabled

○ deaf only

○ blind only

○ deaf and blind

○ **deaf and blind**

If someone is deaf as well as blind, they may be carrying a white stick with a red reflective band. You can't see if a pedestrian is deaf. Don't assume everyone can hear you approaching.

What action would you take when elderly people are crossing the road?

⊙ Wave them across so they know that you have seen them

⊙ Be patient and allow them to cross in their own time

⊙ Rev the engine to let them know that you are waiting

⊙ Tap the horn in case they are hard of hearing

⊙ **Be patient and allow them to cross in their own time**

Be aware that older people might take a long time to cross the road. They might also be hard of hearing and not hear you approaching. Don't hurry older people across the road by getting too close to them or revving your engine.

You see two elderly pedestrians about to cross the road ahead. You should

⊙ expect them to wait for you to pass

⊙ speed up to get past them quickly

⊙ stop and wave them across the road

⊙ be careful, they may misjudge your speed

⊙ **be careful, they may misjudge your speed**

Older people may have impaired hearing, vision, concentration and judgement. They may also walk slowly and so could take a long time to cross the road.

You are coming up to a roundabout. A cyclist is signalling to turn right. What should you do?

⊙ Overtake on the right

⊙ Give a horn warning

⊙ Signal the cyclist to move across

⊙ Give the cyclist plenty of room

⊙ **Give the cyclist plenty of room**

If you're following a cyclist who's signalling to turn right at a roundabout leave plenty of room. Give them space and time to get into the correct lane.

6.16
*Mark **two** answers*

Which TWO should you allow extra room when overtaking?

- Motorcycles
- Tractors
- Bicycles
- Road-sweeping vehicles

- ⊙ **Motorcycles**
- ⊙ **Bicycles**

Don't pass riders too closely as this may cause them to lose balance. Always leave as much room as you would for a car, and don't cut in.

6.17
*Mark **one** answer*

Why should you look particularly for motorcyclists and cyclists at junctions?

- They may want to turn into the side road
- They may slow down to let you turn
- They are harder to see
- They might not see you turn

- ⊙ **They are harder to see**

Cyclists and motorcyclists are smaller than other vehicles and so are more difficult to see. They can easily become hidden from your view by cars parked near a junction.

6.18
*Mark **one** answer*

You are waiting to come out of a side road. Why should you watch carefully for motorcycles?

- Motorcycles are usually faster than cars
- Police patrols often use motorcycles
- Motorcycles are small and hard to see
- Motorcycles have right of way

- ⊙ **Motorcycles are small and hard to see**

If you're waiting to emerge from a side road watch out for motorcycles: they're small and can be difficult to see. Be especially careful if there are parked vehicles restricting your view, there might be a motorcycle approaching.

IF YOU DON'T KNOW, DON'T GO.

In daylight, an approaching motorcyclist is using a dipped headlight. Why?

- So that the rider can be seen more easily
- To stop the battery overcharging
- To improve the rider's vision
- The rider is inviting you to proceed

So that the rider can be seen more easily

A motorcycle can be lost from sight behind another vehicle. The use of the headlight helps to make it more conspicuous and therefore more easily seen.

Motorcyclists should wear bright clothing mainly because

- they must do so by law
- it helps keep them cool in summer
- the colours are popular
- drivers often do not see them

drivers often do not see them

Motorcycles are small vehicles and can be difficult to see. If the rider wears bright clothing it can make it easier for other road users to see them approaching, especially at junctions.

There is a slow-moving motorcyclist ahead of you. You are unsure what the rider is going to do. You should

- pass on the left
- pass on the right
- stay behind
- move closer

stay behind

If a motorcyclist is travelling slowly it may be that they are looking for a turning or entrance. Be patient and stay behind them in case they need to make a sudden change of direction.

6.22
*Mark **one** answer*

Motorcyclists will often look round over their right shoulder just before turning right. This is because

- they need to listen for following traffic
- motorcycles do not have mirrors
- looking around helps them balance as they turn
- they need to check for traffic in their blind area

- **they need to check for traffic in their blind area**

If you see a motorcyclist take a quick glance over their shoulder, this could mean they are about to change direction. Recognising a clue like this helps you to be prepared and take appropriate action, making you safer on the road.

6.23
*Mark **three** answers*

At road junctions which of the following are most vulnerable?

- Cyclists
- Motorcyclists
- Pedestrians
- Car drivers
- Lorry drivers

- **Cyclists**

- **Motorcyclists**

- **Pedestrians**

Pedestrians and riders on two wheels can be harder to see than other road users. Make sure you keep a look-out for them, especially at junctions. Good effective observation, coupled with appropriate action, can save lives.

6.24
*Mark **one** answer*

Motorcyclists are particularly vulnerable

- when moving off
- on dual carriageways
- when approaching junctions
- on motorways

- **when approaching junctions**

Another road user failing to see a motorcyclist is a major cause of collisions at junctions. Wherever streams of traffic join or cross there's the potential for this type of incident to occur.

165

6.25 Mark **two** answers

You are approaching a roundabout. There are horses just ahead of you. You should

- ⊙ be prepared to stop
- ⊙ treat them like any other vehicle
- ⊙ give them plenty of room
- ⊙ accelerate past as quickly as possible
- ⊙ sound your horn as a warning

⊙ **be prepared to stop**

⊙ **give them plenty of room**

Horse riders often keep to the outside of the roundabout even if they are turning right. Give them plenty of room and remember that they may have to cross lanes of traffic.

6.26 Mark **one** answer

As you approach a pelican crossing the lights change to green. Elderly people are halfway across. You should

- ⊙ wave them to cross as quickly as they can
- ⊙ rev your engine to make them hurry
- ⊙ flash your lights in case they have not heard you
- ⊙ wait because they will take longer to cross

⊙ **wait because they will take longer to cross**

Even if the lights turn to green, wait for them to clear the crossing. Allow them to cross the road in their own time, and don't try to hurry them by revving your engine.

6.27 Mark **one** answer

There are flashing amber lights under a school warning sign. What action should you take?

- ⊙ Reduce speed until you are clear of the area
- ⊙ Keep up your speed and sound the horn
- ⊙ Increase your speed to clear the area quickly
- ⊙ Wait at the lights until they change to green

⊙ **Reduce speed until you are clear of the area**

The flashing amber lights are switched on to warn you that children may be crossing near a school. Slow down and take extra care as you may have to stop.

6.28   Mark **one** answer

These road markings must be kept clear to allow

- school children to be dropped off
- for teachers to park
- school children to be picked up
- a clear view of the crossing area

⊙ **a clear view of the crossing area**

The markings are there to show that the area must be kept clear to allow an unrestricted view for

- approaching drivers and riders
- children wanting to cross the road.

6.29   Mark **one** answer

Where would you see this sign?

- Near a school crossing
- At a playground entrance
- On a school bus
- At a 'pedestrians only' area

⊙ **On a school bus**

Watch out for children crossing the road from the other side of the bus.

6.30   Mark **one** answer

You are following two cyclists. They approach a roundabout in the left-hand lane. In which direction should you expect the cyclists to go?

- Left
- Right
- Any direction
- Straight ahead

⊙ **Any direction**

Cyclists approaching a roundabout in the left-hand lane may be turning right but may not have been able to get into the correct lane due to the heavy traffic. They may also feel safer keeping to the left all the way round the roundabout. Be aware of them and give them plenty of room.

You are travelling behind a moped. You want to turn left just ahead. You should

- ⊙ overtake the moped before the junction
- ⊙ pull alongside the moped and stay level until just before the junction
- ⊙ sound your horn as a warning and pull in front of the moped
- ⊙ stay behind until the moped has passed the junction

⊙ **stay behind until the moped has passed the junction**

Passing the moped and turning into the junction could mean that you cut across the front of the rider. This might force them to slow down, stop or even lose control. Slow down and stay behind the moped until it has passed the junction and you can then turn safely.

You see a horse rider as you approach a roundabout. They are signalling right but keeping well to the left. You should

- ⊙ proceed as normal
- ⊙ keep close to them
- ⊙ cut in front of them
- ⊙ stay well back

⊙ **stay well back**

Allow the horse rider to enter and exit the roundabout in their own time. They may feel safer keeping to the left all the way around the roundabout. Don't get up close behind or alongside them. This is very likely to upset the horse and create a dangerous situation.

6.33
*Mark **one** answer*

How would you react to drivers who appear to be inexperienced?

- ⊙ Sound your horn to warn them of your presence
- ⊙ Be patient and prepare for them to react more slowly
- ⊙ Flash your headlights to indicate that it is safe for them to proceed
- ⊙ Overtake them as soon as possible

⊙ **Be patient and prepare for them to react more slowly**

Learners might not have confidence when they first start to drive. Allow them plenty of room and don't react adversely to their hesitation. We all learn from experience, but new drivers will have had less practice in dealing with all the situations that might occur.

6.34
*Mark **one** answer*

You are following a learner driver who stalls at a junction. You should

- ⊙ be patient as you expect them to make mistakes
- ⊙ stay very close behind and flash your headlights
- ⊙ start to rev your engine if they take too long to restart
- ⊙ immediately steer around them and drive on

⊙ **be patient as you expect them to make mistakes**

Learning is a process of practice and experience. Try to understand this and tolerate those who are at the beginning of this process.

6.35
*Mark **one** answer*

You are on a country road. What should you expect to see coming towards you on YOUR side of the road?

- ⊙ Motorcycles
- ⊙ Bicycles
- ⊙ Pedestrians
- ⊙ Horse riders

⊙ **Pedestrians**

On a quiet country road always be aware that there may be a hazard just around the next bend, such as a slow-moving vehicle or pedestrians. Pedestrians are advised to walk on the right-hand side of the road if there is no pavement, so they may be walking towards you on your side of the road.

You are turning left into a side road. Pedestrians are crossing the road near the junction. You must

- ⊙ wave them on
- ⊙ sound your horn
- ⊙ switch on your hazard lights
- ⊙ wait for them to cross

⊙ **wait for them to cross**

Check that it's clear before you turn into a junction. If there are pedestrians crossing they have priority, so let them cross in their own time.

You are following a car driven by an elderly driver. You should

- ⊙ expect the driver to drive badly
- ⊙ flash your lights and overtake
- ⊙ be aware that the driver's reactions may not be as fast as yours
- ⊙ stay very close behind but be careful

⊙ **be aware that the driver's reactions may not be as fast as yours**

You must show consideration to other road users. The reactions of older drivers may be slower and they might need more time to deal with a situation. Be tolerant and don't lose patience or show your annoyance.

6.38
*Mark **one** answer*

You are following a cyclist. You wish to turn left just ahead. You should

⊙ overtake the cyclist before the junction

⊙ pull alongside the cyclist and stay level until after the junction

⊙ hold back until the cyclist has passed the junction

⊙ go around the cyclist on the junction

⊙ **hold back until the cyclist has passed the junction**

Make allowances for cyclists. Allow them plenty of room. Don't try to overtake and then immediately turn left. Be patient and stay behind them until they have passed the junction.

6.39
*Mark **one** answer*

A horse rider is in the left-hand lane approaching a roundabout. You should expect the rider to

⊙ go in any direction

⊙ turn right

⊙ turn left

⊙ go ahead

⊙ **go in any direction**

Horses and their riders will move more slowly than other road users. They might not have time to cut across heavy traffic to take up positions in the offside lane. For this reason a horse and rider may approach a roundabout in the left-hand lane, even though they're turning right.

6.40
*Mark **one** answer*

Powered vehicles used by disabled people are small and hard to see. How do they give early warning when on a dual carriageway?

⊙ They will have a flashing red light

⊙ They will have a flashing green light

⊙ They will have a flashing blue light

⊙ They will have a flashing amber light.

⊙ **They will have a flashing amber light.**

Powered vehicles used by disabled people are small, low, hard to see and travel very slowly. On a dual carriageway a flashing amber light will warn other road users.

  *Mark **one** answer*

You should never attempt to overtake a cyclist

- ⊙ just before you turn left
- ⊙ on a left hand bend
- ⊙ on a one-way street
- ⊙ on a dual carriageway

⊙ **just before you turn left**

If you want to turn left and there's a cyclist in front of you, hold back. Wait until the cyclist has passed the junction and then turn left behind them.

---

  *Mark **one** answer*

Ahead of you there is a moving vehicle with a flashing amber beacon. This means it is

- ⊙ slow moving
- ⊙ broken down
- ⊙ a doctor's car
- ⊙ a school crossing patrol

⊙ **slow moving**

As you approach the vehicle, assess the situation. Due to its slow progress you will need to judge whether it is safe to overtake.

---

  *Mark **one** answer*

What does this sign mean?

- ⊙ Contraflow pedal cycle lane
- ⊙ With-flow pedal cycle lane
- ⊙ Pedal cycles and buses only
- ⊙ No pedal cycles or buses

⊙ **With-flow pedal cycle lane**

The picture of a cycle will also usually be painted on the road, sometimes with a different coloured surface. Leave these clear for cyclists and don't pass too closely when you overtake.

6.44
*Mark **one** answer*

You notice horse riders in front. What should you do FIRST?

- Pull out to the middle of the road
- Slow down and be ready to stop
- Accelerate around them
- Signal right

⊙ **Slow down and be ready to stop**

Be particularly careful when approaching horse riders – slow down and be prepared to stop. Always pass wide and slowly and look out for signals given by horse riders. Horses are unpredictable: always treat them as potential hazards and take great care when passing them.

6.45
*Mark **one** answer*

You must not stop on these road markings because you may obstruct

- children's view of the crossing area
- teachers' access to the school
- delivery vehicles' access to the school
- emergency vehicles' access to the school

⊙ **children's view of the crossing area**

These markings are found on the road outside schools. DO NOT stop (even to set down or pick up children) or park on them. The markings are to make sure that drivers, riders, children and other pedestrians have a clear view.

The left-hand pavement is closed due to street repairs. What should you do?

⊙ Watch out for pedestrians walking in the road

⊙ Use your right-hand mirror more often

⊙ Speed up to get past the roadworks quicker

⊙ Position close to the left-hand kerb

⊙ **Watch out for pedestrians walking in the road**

Where street repairs have closed off pavements, proceed carefully and slowly as pedestrians might have to walk in the road.

You are following a motorcyclist on an uneven road. You should

⊙ allow less room so you can be seen in their mirrors

⊙ overtake immediately

⊙ allow extra room in case they swerve to avoid potholes

⊙ allow the same room as normal because road surfaces do not affect motorcyclists

⊙ **allow extra room in case they swerve to avoid potholes**

Potholes and bumps in the road can unbalance a motorcyclist. For this reason the rider might swerve to avoid an uneven road surface. Watch out at places where this is likely to occur.

What does this sign tell you?

⊙ No cycling

⊙ Cycle route ahead

⊙ Cycle parking only

⊙ End of cycle route

⊙ **Cycle route ahead**

With people's concern today for the environment, cycle routes are being created in our towns and cities. These are usually defined by road markings and signs.

Respect the presence of cyclists on the road and give them plenty of room if you need to pass.

6.49

You are approaching this roundabout and see the cyclist signal right. Why is the cyclist keeping to the left?

- ⊙ It is a quicker route for the cyclist
- ⊙ The cyclist is going to turn left instead
- ⊙ The cyclist thinks The Highway Code does not apply to bicycles
- ⊙ The cyclist is slower and more vulnerable

⊙ **The cyclist is slower and more vulnerable**

Cycling in today's heavy traffic can be hazardous. Some cyclists may not feel happy about crossing the path of traffic to take up a position in an outside lane. Be aware of this and understand that, although in the left-hand lane, the cyclist might be turning right.

6.50

You are approaching this crossing. You should

- ⊙ prepare to slow down and stop
- ⊙ stop and wave the pedestrians across
- ⊙ speed up and pass by quickly
- ⊙ continue unless the pedestrians step out

⊙ **prepare to slow down and stop**

Be courteous and prepare to stop. Do not wave people across as this could be dangerous if another vehicle is approaching the crossing.

6.51

You see a pedestrian with a dog. The dog has a yellow or burgundy coat. This especially warns you that the pedestrian is

- ⊙ elderly
- ⊙ dog training
- ⊙ colour blind
- ⊙ deaf

⊙ **deaf**

Take extra care as the pedestrian may not be aware of vehicles approaching.

6.52

At toucan crossings

- ⊙ you only stop if someone is waiting to cross
- ⊙ cyclists are not permitted
- ⊙ there is a continuously flashing amber beacon
- ⊙ pedestrians and cyclists may cross

⊙ **pedestrians and cyclists may cross**

There are some crossings where cycle routes lead the cyclists to cross at the same place as pedestrians. These are called toucan crossings. Always look out for cyclists, as they're likely to be approaching faster than pedestrians.

6.53

Some junctions controlled by traffic lights have a marked area between two stop lines. What is this for?

- ⊙ To allow taxis to position in front of other traffic
- ⊙ To allow people with disabilities to cross the road
- ⊙ To allow cyclists and pedestrians to cross the road together
- ⊙ To allow cyclists to position in front of other traffic

⊙ **To allow cyclists to position in front of other traffic**

These are known as advanced stop lines. When the lights are red (or about to become red) you should stop at the first white line. However if you have crossed that line as the lights change you must stop at the second line even if it means you are in the area reserved for cyclists.

6.54
*Mark **one** answer*

At some traffic lights there are advance stop lines and a marked area. What are these for?

⊙ To allow cyclists to position in front of other traffic

⊙ To let pedestrians cross when the lights change

⊙ To prevent traffic from jumping the lights

⊙ To let passengers get off a bus which is queuing

⊙ **To allow cyclists to position in front of other traffic**

You should always stop at the first white line. Avoid going into the marked area which is reserved for cyclists only. However if you have crossed the first white line at the time the signal changes to red you must stop at the second line even if you are in the marked area.

6.55
*Mark **one** answer*

When you are overtaking a cyclist you should leave as much room as you would give to a car. What is the main reason for this?

⊙ The cyclist might speed up

⊙ The cyclist might get off the bike

⊙ The cyclist might swerve

⊙ The cyclist might have to make a left turn

⊙ **The cyclist might swerve**

Before overtaking assess the situation. Look well ahead to see if the cyclist will need to change direction. Be especially aware of the cyclist approaching parked vehicles as they will need to alter course. Do not pass too closely or cut in sharply.

6.56
*Mark **three** answers*

Which THREE should you do when passing sheep on a road?

⊙ Allow plenty of room

⊙ Go very slowly

⊙ Pass quickly but quietly

⊙ Be ready to stop

⊙ Briefly sound your horn

⊙ **Allow plenty of room**

⊙ **Go very slowly**

⊙ **Be ready to stop**

Slow down and be ready to stop if you see animals in the road ahead. Animals are easily frightened by noise and vehicles passing too close to them. Stop if signalled to do so by the person in charge.

At night you see a pedestrian wearing reflective clothing and carrying a bright red light. What does this mean?

- You are approaching roadworks
- You are approaching an organised walk
- You are approaching a slow-moving vehicle
- You are approaching a traffic danger spot

⊙ **You are approaching an organised walk**

The people on the walk should be keeping to the left, but don't assume this. Pass slowly, make sure you have time to do so safely. Be aware that the pedestrians have their backs to you and may not know that you're there.

You have just passed your test. How can you reduce your risk of being involved in a collision?

- By always staying close to the vehicle in front
- By never going over 40 mph
- By staying only in the left-hand lane on all roads
- By taking further training

⊙ **By taking further training**

New drivers and riders are often involved in a collision or incident early in their driving career. Due to a lack of experience they may not react to hazards as quickly as more experienced road users. Approved training courses are offered by driver and rider training schools. The Pass Plus scheme has been created by DSA for new drivers who would like to improve their basic skills and safely widen their driving experience.

You want to reverse into a side road. You are not sure that the area behind your car is clear. What should you do?

- Look through the rear window only
- Get out and check
- Check the mirrors only
- Carry on, assuming it is clear

⊙ **Get out and check**

If you cannot be sure whether there is anything behind you, it is always safest to check before reversing. There may be a small child or a low obstruction close behind your car. The shape and size of your vehicle can restrict visibility.

6.60
*Mark **one** answer*

You are about to reverse into a side road. A pedestrian wishes to cross behind you. You should

- ⊙ wave to the pedestrian to stop
- ⊙ give way to the pedestrian
- ⊙ wave to the pedestrian to cross
- ⊙ reverse before the pedestrian starts to cross

⊙ **give way to the pedestrian**

If you need to reverse into a side road try to find a place that's free from traffic and pedestrians. Look all around before and during the manoeuvre. Stop and give way to any pedestrians who want to cross behind you. Avoid waving them across, sounding the horn, flashing your lights or giving any misleading signals that could lead them into a dangerous situation.

6.61
*Mark **one** answer*

Who is especially in danger of not being seen as you reverse your car?

- ⊙ Motorcyclists
- ⊙ Car drivers
- ⊙ Cyclists
- ⊙ Children

⊙ **Children**

As you look through the rear of your vehicle you may not be able to see a small child. Be aware of this before you reverse. If there are children about, get out and check if it is clear before reversing.

6.62
*Mark **one** answer*

You are reversing around a corner when you notice a pedestrian walking behind you. What should you do?

- ⊙ Slow down and wave the pedestrian across
- ⊙ Continue reversing and steer round the pedestrian
- ⊙ Stop and give way
- ⊙ Continue reversing and sound your horn

⊙ **Stop and give way**

Wait until the pedestrian has passed, then look around again before you start to reverse. Don't forget that you may not be able to see a small child directly behind your vehicle. Be aware of the possibility of hidden dangers.

You want to turn right from a junction but your view is restricted by parked vehicles. What should you do?

⊙ Move out quickly, but be prepared to stop

⊙ Sound your horn and pull out if there is no reply

⊙ Stop, then move slowly forward until you have a clear view

⊙ Stop, get out and look along the main road to check

⊙ **Stop, then move slowly forward until you have a clear view**

If you want to turn right from a junction and your view is restricted, STOP. Ease forward until you can see – there might be something approaching.

IF YOU DON'T KNOW, DON'T GO.

You are at the front of a queue of traffic waiting to turn right into a side road. Why is it important to check your right mirror just before turning?

⊙ To look for pedestrians about to cross

⊙ To check for overtaking vehicles

⊙ To make sure the side road is clear

⊙ To check for emerging traffic

⊙ **To check for overtaking vehicles**

There could be a motorcyclist riding along the outside of the queue. Always check your mirror before turning as situations behind you can change in the time you have been waiting to turn.

What must a driver do at a pelican crossing when the amber light is flashing?

⊙ Signal the pedestrian to cross

⊙ Always wait for the green light before proceeding

⊙ Give way to any pedestrians on the crossing

⊙ Wait for the red-and-amber light before proceeding

⊙ **Give way to any pedestrians on the crossing**

The flashing amber light allows pedestrians already on the crossing to get to the other side before a green light shows to the traffic. Be aware that some pedestrians, such as older people and young children, need longer to cross. Let them do this at their own pace.

6.66
*Mark **two** answers*

You have stopped at a pelican crossing. A disabled person is crossing slowly in front of you. The lights have now changed to green. You should

- ⊙ allow the person to cross
- ⊙ drive in front of the person
- ⊙ drive behind the person
- ⊙ sound your horn
- ⊙ be patient
- ⊙ edge forward slowly

⊙ **allow the person to cross**

⊙ **be patient**

At a pelican crossing the green light means you may proceed as long as the crossing is clear. If someone hasn't finished crossing, be patient and wait for them.

6.67
*Mark **one** answer*

You are driving past a line of parked cars. You notice a ball bouncing out into the road ahead. What should you do?

- ⊙ Continue driving at the same speed and sound your horn
- ⊙ Continue driving at the same speed and flash your headlights
- ⊙ Slow down and be prepared to stop for children
- ⊙ Stop and wave the children across to fetch their ball

⊙ **Slow down and be prepared to stop for children**

Beware of children playing in the street and running out into the road. If a ball bounces out from the pavement, slow down and stop. Don't encourage anyone to retrieve it. Other road users may not see your signal and you might lead a child into a dangerous situation.

6.68
Mark **one** answer

You want to turn right from a main road into a side road. Just before turning you should

- ⊙ cancel your right-turn signal
- ⊙ select first gear
- ⊙ check for traffic overtaking on your right
- ⊙ stop and set the handbrake

⊙ **check for traffic overtaking on your right**

Motorcyclists often overtake queues of vehicles. Make one last check in your mirror and your blind spot to avoid turning across their path.

6.69
Mark **one** answer

You are driving in slow-moving queues of traffic. Just before changing lane you should

- ⊙ sound the horn
- ⊙ look for motorcyclists filtering through the traffic
- ⊙ give a 'slowing down' arm signal
- ⊙ change down to first gear

⊙ **look for motorcyclists filtering through the traffic**

In this situation motorcyclists could be passing you on either side. Always check before you change lanes or change direction.

6.70
Mark **one** answer

You are driving in town. There is a bus at the bus stop on the other side of the road. Why should you be careful?

- ⊙ The bus may have broken down
- ⊙ Pedestrians may come from behind the bus
- ⊙ The bus may move off suddenly
- ⊙ The bus may remain stationary

⊙ **Pedestrians may come from behind the bus**

If you see a bus ahead watch out for pedestrians. They may not be able to see you if they're crossing from behind the bus.

6.71   *Mark **one** answer*

How should you overtake horse riders?

⊙ Drive up close and overtake as soon as possible

⊙ Speed is not important but allow plenty of room

⊙ Use your horn just once to warn them

⊙ Drive slowly and leave plenty of room

⊙ **Drive slowly and leave plenty of room**

When you're on country roads be aware of particular dangers. Be prepared for farm animals, horses, pedestrians, farm vehicles and wild animals. Always be prepared to slow down or stop.

6.72   *Mark **one** answer*

You are driving on a main road. You intend to turn right into a side road. Just before turning you should

⊙ adjust your interior mirror

⊙ flash your headlamps

⊙ steer over to the left

⊙ check for traffic overtaking on your right

⊙ **check for traffic overtaking on your right**

A last check in the offside mirror and blind spot will allow you sight of any cyclist or motorcyclist overtaking as you wait to turn.

6.73   *Mark **one** answer*

Why should you allow extra room when overtaking a motorcyclist on a windy day?

⊙ The rider may turn off suddenly to get out of the wind

⊙ The rider may be blown across in front of you

⊙ The rider may stop suddenly

⊙ The rider may be travelling faster than normal

⊙ **The rider may be blown across in front of you**

If you're driving in high winds, be aware that the conditions might force a motorcyclist or cyclist to swerve or wobble. Take this into consideration if you're following or wish to overtake a two-wheeled vehicle.

Where in particular should you look out for motorcyclists?

⊙ In a filling station

⊙ At a road junction

⊙ Near a service area

⊙ When entering a car park

⊙ **At a road junction**

Always look out for motorcyclists, and cyclists, particularly at junctions. They are smaller and usually more difficult to see than other vehicles.

Where should you take particular care to look out for motorcyclists and cyclists?

⊙ On dual carriageways

⊙ At junctions

⊙ At zebra crossings

⊙ On one-way streets

⊙ **At junctions**

Motorcyclists and cyclists are often more difficult to see on the road. This is especially the case at junctions. You may not be able to see a motorcyclist approaching a junction if your view is blocked by other traffic. A motorcycle may be travelling as fast as a car, sometimes faster. Make sure that you judge speeds correctly before you emerge.

6.76
*Mark **one** answer*

The road outside this school is marked with yellow zigzag lines. What do these lines mean?

- You may park on the lines when dropping off schoolchildren
- You may park on the lines when picking schoolchildren up
- You must not wait or park your vehicle here at all
- You must stay with your vehicle if you park here

You must not wait or park your vehicle here at all

Parking here would block the view of the school entrance and would endanger the lives of children on their way to and from school.

6.77
*Mark **one** answer*

You are driving past parked cars. You notice a bicycle wheel sticking out between them. What should you do?

- Accelerate past quickly and sound your horn
- Slow down and wave the cyclist across
- Brake sharply and flash your headlights
- Slow down and be prepared to stop for a cyclist

Slow down and be prepared to stop for a cyclist

Scan the road as you drive. Try to anticipate hazards by being aware of the places where they are likely to occur. You'll then be able to react in good time, if necessary.

You are dazzled at night by a vehicle behind you. You should

- ⊙ set your mirror to anti-dazzle
- ⊙ set your mirror to dazzle the other driver
- ⊙ brake sharply to a stop
- ⊙ switch your rear lights on and off

⊙ **set your mirror to anti-dazzle**

The interior mirror of most vehicles can be set to the anti-dazzle position. You will still be able to see the lights of the traffic behind you, but the dazzle will be greatly reduced.

You are driving towards a zebra crossing. A person in a wheelchair is waiting to cross. What should you do?

- ⊙ Continue on your way
- ⊙ Wave to the person to cross
- ⊙ Wave to the person to wait
- ⊙ Be prepared to stop

⊙ **Be prepared to stop**

You should slow down and be prepared to stop as you would with an able-bodied person. Don't wave them across as other traffic may not stop.

Yellow zigzag lines on the road outside schools mean

- ⊙ sound your horn to alert other road users
- ⊙ stop to allow children to cross
- ⊙ you should not park or stop on these lines
- ⊙ you must not drive over these lines

⊙ **you should not park or stop on these lines**

Where there are yellow zigzag markings, you should not park, wait or stop, even to pick up or drop off children. A vehicle parked on the zigzag lines would obstruct children's view of the road and other drivers' view of the pavement. Where there is an upright sign there is mandatory prohibition of stopping during the times shown.

6.81
*Mark **one** answer*

What do these road markings outside a school mean?

⊙ You may park here if you are a teacher

⊙ Sound your horn before parking

⊙ When parking, use your hazard warning lights

⊙ You should not wait or park your vehicle here

⊙ **You should not wait or park your vehicle here**

These markings are used outside schools so that children can see and be seen clearly when crossing the road. Parking here would block people's view of the school entrance. This could endanger the lives of children on their way to and from school.

OTHER TYPES OF VEHICLE

This section covers

- Motorcycles
- Lorries
- Buses
- Trams

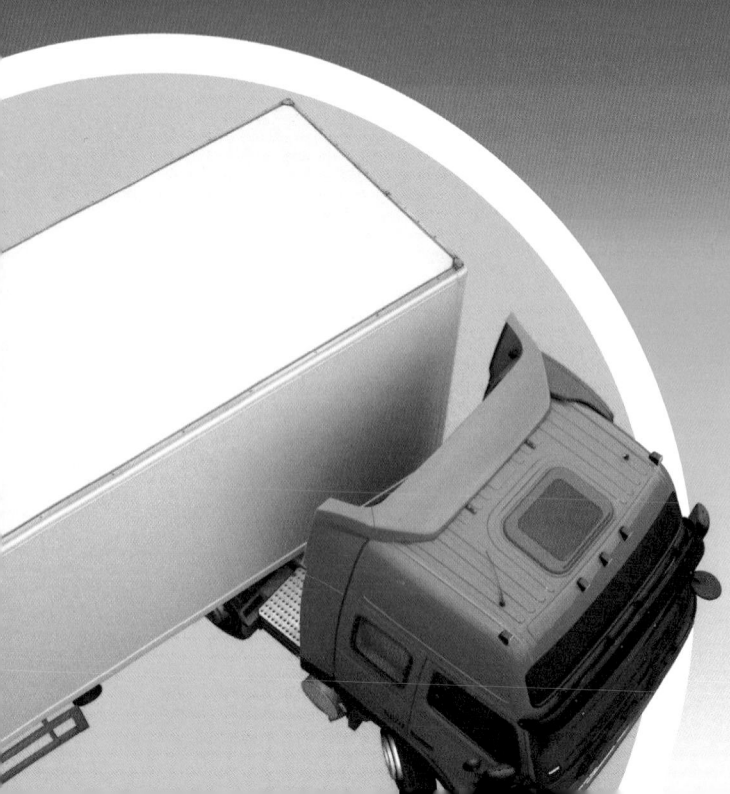

7.1

*Mark **one** answer*

You are about to overtake a slow-moving motorcyclist. Which one of these signs would make you take special care?

In windy weather, watch out for motorcyclists and also cyclists as they can be blown sideways into your path. When you pass them, leave plenty of room and check their position in your mirror before pulling back in.

7.2

*Mark **one** answer*

You are waiting to emerge left from a minor road. A large vehicle is approaching from the right. You have time to turn, but you should wait. Why?

- The large vehicle can easily hide an overtaking vehicle
- The large vehicle can turn suddenly
- The large vehicle is difficult to steer in a straight line
- The large vehicle can easily hide vehicles from the left

- **The large vehicle can easily hide an overtaking vehicle**

Large vehicles can hide other vehicles that are overtaking, especially motorcycles which may be filtering past queuing traffic. You need to be aware of the possibility of hidden vehicles and not assume that it is safe to emerge.

You are following a long vehicle. It approaches a crossroads and signals left, but moves out to the right. You should

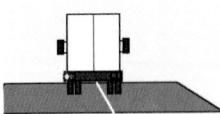

- ⊙ get closer in order to pass it quickly
- ⊙ stay well back and give it room
- ⊙ assume the signal is wrong and it is really turning right
- ⊙ overtake as it starts to slow down

⊙ **stay well back and give it room**

A lorry may swing out to the right as it approaches a left turn. This is to allow the rear wheels to clear the kerb as it turns. Don't try to filter through if you see a gap on the nearside.

You are following a long vehicle approaching a crossroads. The driver signals right but moves close to the left-hand kerb. What should you do?

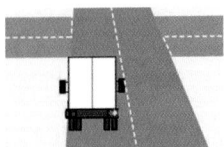

- ⊙ Warn the driver of the wrong signal
- ⊙ Wait behind the long vehicle
- ⊙ Report the driver to the police
- ⊙ Overtake on the right-hand side

⊙ **Wait behind the long vehicle**

When a long vehicle is going to turn right it may need to keep close to the left-hand kerb. This is to prevent the rear end of the trailer cutting the corner. You need to be aware of how long vehicles behave in such situations. Don't overtake the lorry because it could turn as you're alongside. Stay behind and wait for it to turn.

7.5
*Mark **one** answer*

You are approaching a mini-roundabout. The long vehicle in front is signalling left but positioned over to the right. You should

- ⊙ sound your horn
- ⊙ overtake on the left
- ⊙ follow the same course as the lorry
- ⊙ keep well back

⊙ **keep well back**

At mini-roundabouts there isn't much room for a long vehicle to manoeuvre. It will have to swing out wide so that it can complete the turn safely. Keep well back and don't try to move up alongside it.

7.6
*Mark **one** answer*

Before overtaking a large vehicle you should keep well back. Why is this?

- ⊙ To give acceleration space to overtake quickly on blind bends
- ⊙ To get the best view of the road ahead
- ⊙ To leave a gap in case the vehicle stops and rolls back
- ⊙ To offer other drivers a safe gap if they want to overtake you

⊙ **To get the best view of the road ahead**

When following a large vehicle keep well back. If you're too close you won't be able to see the road ahead and the driver of the long vehicle might not be able to see you in their mirrors.

You are travelling behind a bus that pulls up at a bus stop. What should you do?

- Accelerate past the bus sounding your horn
- Watch carefully for pedestrians
- Be ready to give way to the bus
- Pull in closely behind the bus

⊙ **Watch carefully for pedestrians**

⊙ **Be ready to give way to the bus**

There might be pedestrians crossing from in front of the bus. Look out for them if you intend to pass. Consider staying back and waiting.

How many people are waiting to get on the bus? Check the queue if you can. The bus might move off straight away if there is no one waiting to get on.

If a bus is signalling to pull out, give it priority as long as it is safe to do so.

You are following a large lorry on a wet road. Spray makes it difficult to see. You should

- drop back until you can see better
- put your headlights on full beam
- keep close to the lorry, away from the spray
- speed up and overtake quickly

⊙ **drop back until you can see better**

Large vehicles may throw up a lot of spray when the roads are wet. This will make it difficult for you to see ahead. Dropping back further will

- move you out of the spray and allow you to see further
- increase your separation distance. It takes longer to stop when the roads are wet and you need to allow more room.

Don't

- follow the vehicle in front too closely
- overtake, unless you can see and are sure that the way ahead is clear.

7.9

*Mark **one** answer*

You are following a large articulated vehicle. It is going to turn left into a narrow road. What action should you take?

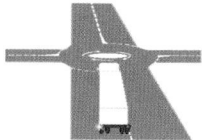

⊙ Move out and overtake on the right

⊙ Pass on the left as the vehicle moves out

⊙ Be prepared to stop behind

⊙ Overtake quickly before the lorry moves out

⊙ **Be prepared to stop behind**

Lorries are larger and longer than other vehicles and this can affect their position when approaching junctions. When turning left they may move out to the right so that they don't cut in and mount the kerb with the rear wheels.

7.10

*Mark **one** answer*

You keep well back while waiting to overtake a large vehicle. A car fills the gap. You should

⊙ sound your horn

⊙ drop back further

⊙ flash your headlights

⊙ start to overtake

⊙ **drop back further**

It's very frustrating when your separation distance is shortened by another vehicle. React positively, stay calm and drop further back.

You are following a long lorry. The driver signals to turn left into a narrow road. What should you do?

- ⊙ Overtake on the left before the lorry reaches the junction
- ⊙ Overtake on the right as soon as the lorry slows down
- ⊙ Do not overtake unless you can see there is no oncoming traffic
- ⊙ Do not overtake, stay well back and be prepared to stop.

⊙ **Do not overtake, stay well back and be prepared to stop.**

When turning into narrow roads articulated and long vehicles will need more room. Initially they will need to swing out in the opposite direction to which they intend to turn. They could mask another vehicle turning out of the same junction. DON'T be tempted to overtake them or pass on the inside.

When you approach a bus signalling to move off from a bus stop you should

- ⊙ get past before it moves
- ⊙ allow it to pull away, if it is safe to do so
- ⊙ flash your headlights as you approach
- ⊙ signal left and wave the bus on

⊙ **allow it to pull away, if it is safe to do so**

Try to give way to buses if you can do so safely, especially when they signal to pull away from bus stops. Look out for people who've stepped off the bus or are running to catch it, and may try to cross the road without looking. Don't try to accelerate past before it moves away or flash your lights as other road users may be misled by this signal.

7.13

*Mark **one** answer*

You wish to overtake a long, slow-moving vehicle on a busy road. You should

- follow it closely and keep moving out to see the road ahead
- flash your headlights for the oncoming traffic to give way
- stay behind until the driver waves you past
- keep well back until you can see that it is clear

⊙ **keep well back until you can see that it is clear**

If you want to overtake a long vehicle, stay well back so that you can get a better view of the road ahead. The closer you get the less you will be able to see of the road ahead. Be patient, overtaking calls for sound judgement. DON'T take a gamble, only overtake when you are certain that you can complete the manoeuvre safely.

7.14

*Mark **one** answer*

Which of these is LEAST likely to be affected by crosswinds?

- Cyclists
- Motorcyclists
- High-sided vehicles
- Cars

⊙ **Cars**

Although cars are the least likely to be affected, crosswinds can take anyone by surprise. This is most likely to happen, after overtaking a large vehicle, when passing gaps between hedges or buildings, and on exposed sections of road.

7.15

*Mark **one** answer*

What should you do as you approach this lorry?

- Slow down and be prepared to wait
- Make the lorry wait for you
- Flash your lights at the lorry
- Move to the right-hand side of the road

⊙ **Slow down and be prepared to wait**

When turning, long vehicles need much more room on the road than other vehicles. At junctions they may take up the whole of the road space, so be patient and allow them the room they need.

You are following a large vehicle approaching crossroads. The driver signals to turn left. What should you do?

- ☉ Overtake if you can leave plenty of room
- ☉ Overtake only if there are no oncoming vehicles
- ☉ Do not overtake until the vehicle begins to turn.
- ☉ Do not overtake when at or approaching a junction.

☉ **Do not overtake when at or approaching a junction.**

Hold back and wait until the vehicle has turned before proceeding. Do not overtake because the vehicle turning left could hide a vehicle emerging from the same junction.

Powered vehicles, such as wheelchairs or scooters, used by disabled people have a maximum speed of

- ☉ 8 mph
- ☉ 12 mph
- ☉ 16 mph
- ☉ 20 mph

☉ **8 mph**

These are small battery powered vehicles and include wheelchairs and mobility scooters. Some are designed for use on the pavement only and have an upper speed limit of 4 mph (6 km/h). Others can go on the road as well and have a speed limit of 8 mph (12 km/h). They are now very common and are generally used by the elderly, disabled or infirm. Take great care as they are extremely vulnerable because of their low speed and small size.

Why is it more difficult to overtake a large vehicle than a car?

- ☉ It takes longer to pass one
- ☉ They may suddenly pull up
- ☉ Their brakes are not as good
- ☉ They climb hills more slowly

☉ **It takes longer to pass one**

Depending on relevant speed, it will usually take you longer to pass a lorry than other vehicles. Some hazards to watch for include oncoming traffic, junctions ahead, bends or dips which could restrict your view, and signs or road markings that prohibit overtaking. Make sure you can see that it's safe to complete the manoeuvre before you start to overtake.

7.19
*Mark **one** answer*

In front of you is a class 3 powered vehicle (powered wheelchair) driven by a disabled person. These vehicles have a maximum speed of

- ◉ 8 mph (12 km/h)
- ◉ 18 mph (29 km/h)
- ◉ 28 mph (45 km/h)
- ◉ 38 mph (61 km/h)

◉ **8 mph (12 km/h)**

These vehicles are battery powered and very vulnerable due to their slow speed, small size and low height. Some are designed for pavement and road use and have a maximum speed of 8 mph (12 km/h). Others are for pavement use only and are restricted to 4 mph (6 km/h). Take extra care and be patient if you are following one. Allow plenty of room when overtaking and do not go past unless you can do so safely.

7.20
*Mark **one** answer*

It is very windy. You are behind a motorcyclist who is overtaking a high-sided vehicle. What should you do?

- ◉ Overtake the motorcyclist immediately
- ◉ Keep well back
- ◉ Stay level with the motorcyclist
- ◉ Keep close to the motorcyclist

◉ **Keep well back**

Motorcyclists are affected more by windy weather than other vehicles. In windy conditions, high-sided vehicles cause air turbulence. You should keep well back as the motorcyclist could be blown off course.

7.21
*Mark **one** answer*

It is very windy. You are about to overtake a motorcyclist. You should

- ◉ overtake slowly
- ◉ allow extra room
- ◉ sound your horn
- ◉ keep close as you pass

◉ **allow extra room**

Crosswinds can blow a motorcyclist or cyclist across the lane. Passing too close could also cause a draught, unbalancing the rider.

You are driving in town. Ahead of you a bus is at a bus stop. Which TWO of the following should you do?

- Be prepared to give way if the bus suddenly moves off
- Continue at the same speed but sound your horn as a warning
- Watch carefully for the sudden appearance of pedestrians
- Pass the bus as quickly as you possibly can

- **Be prepared to give way if the bus suddenly moves off**

- **Watch carefully for the sudden appearance of pedestrians**

As you approach, look out for any signal the driver might make. If you pass the vehicle watch out for pedestrians attempting to cross the road from the other side of the bus. They will be hidden from view until the last moment.

You are driving along this road. What should you be prepared to do?

- Sound your horn and continue
- Slow down and give way
- Report the driver to the police
- Squeeze through the gap

- **Slow down and give way**

Sometimes large vehicles may need more space than other road users. If a vehicle needs more time and space to turn be prepared to stop and wait.

As a driver why should you be more careful where trams operate?

- Because they do not have a horn
- Because they do not stop for cars
- Because they do not have lights
- Because they cannot steer to avoid you

- **Because they cannot steer to avoid you**

You should take extra care when you first encounter trams. You will have to get used to dealing with a different traffic system.

Be aware that they can accelerate and travel very quickly and that they cannot change direction to avoid obstructions.

7.25

*Mark **one** answer*

You are towing a caravan. Which is the safest type of rear-view mirror to use?

- ⊙ Interior wide-angle mirror
- ⊙ Extended-arm side mirrors
- ⊙ Ordinary door mirrors
- ⊙ Ordinary interior mirror

⊙ **Extended-arm side mirrors**

Towing a large trailer or caravan can greatly reduce your view of the road behind. You need to use the correct equipment to make sure you can see clearly behind and down both sides of the caravan or trailer.

7.26

*Mark **two** answers*

You are driving in heavy traffic on a wet road. Spray makes it difficult to be seen. You should use your

- ⊙ full beam headlights
- ⊙ rear fog lights if visibility is less than 100 metres (328 feet)
- ⊙ rear fog lights if visibility is more than 100 metres (328 feet)
- ⊙ dipped headlights
- ⊙ sidelights only

⊙ **rear fog lights if visibility is less than 100 metres (328 feet)**

⊙ **dipped headlights**

You must ensure that you can be seen by others on the road. Use your dipped headlights during the day if the visibility is bad. If you use your rear fog lights, don't forget to turn them off when the visibility improves.

7.27

*Mark **one** answer*

It is a very windy day and you are about to overtake a cyclist. What should you do?

- ⊙ Overtake very closely
- ⊙ Keep close as you pass
- ⊙ Sound your horn repeatedly
- ⊙ Allow extra room

⊙ **Allow extra room**

Cyclists, and motorcyclists, are very vulnerable in crosswinds. They can easily be blown well off course and veer into your path. Always allow plenty of room when overtaking them. Passing too close could cause a draught and unbalance the rider.

section **eight**
VEHICLE HANDLING

This section covers
- Weather conditions
- Road conditions
- Time of the day
- Speed
- Traffic calming

Give way to oncoming vehicles

8.1
*Mark **three** answers*

In which THREE of these situations may you overtake another vehicle on the left?

- ⊙ When you are in a one-way street
- ⊙ When approaching a motorway slip road where you will be turning off
- ⊙ When the vehicle in front is signalling to turn right
- ⊙ When a slower vehicle is travelling in the right-hand lane of a dual carriageway
- ⊙ In slow-moving traffic queues when traffic in the right-hand lane is moving more slowly

- ⊙ **When you are in a one-way street**

- ⊙ **When the vehicle in front is signalling to turn right**

- ⊙ **In slow-moving traffic queues when traffic in the right-hand lane is moving more slowly**

At certain times of the day, traffic might be heavy. If traffic is moving slowly in queues and vehicles in the right-hand lane are moving more slowly, you may overtake on the left. Don't keep changing lanes to try and beat the queue.

8.2
*Mark **one** answer*

You are travelling in very heavy rain. Your overall stopping distance is likely to be

- ⊙ doubled
- ⊙ halved
- ⊙ up to ten times greater
- ⊙ no different

- ⊙ **doubled**

As well as visibility being reduced, the road will be extremely wet. This will reduce the grip the tyres have on the road and increase the distance it takes to stop. Double your separation distance.

Which TWO of the following are correct?
When overtaking at night you should

- wait until a bend so that you can see the oncoming headlights
- sound your horn twice before moving out
- be careful because you can see less
- beware of bends in the road ahead
- put headlights on full beam

⊙ **be careful because you can see less**

⊙ **beware of bends in the road ahead**

Only overtake the vehicle in front if it's really necessary. At night the risks are increased due to the poor visibility. Don't overtake if there's a possibility of

- road junctions
- bends ahead
- the brow of a bridge or hill, except on a dual carriageway
- pedestrian crossings
- double white lines ahead
- vehicles changing direction
- any other potential hazard.

When may you wait in a box junction?

- When you are stationary in a queue of traffic
- When approaching a pelican crossing
- When approaching a zebra crossing
- When oncoming traffic prevents you turning right

⊙ **When oncoming traffic prevents you turning right**

The purpose of a box junction is to keep the junction clear by preventing vehicles from stopping in the path of crossing traffic.

You must not enter a box junction unless your exit is clear. But, you may enter the box and wait if you want to turn right and are only prevented from doing so by oncoming traffic.

8.5

Mark **one** answer

Which of these plates normally appear with this road sign?

⊙
```
Humps for
½ mile
```

Road humps are used to slow down the traffic. They are found in places where there are often pedestrians, such as

* in shopping areas
* near schools
* in residential areas.

Watch out for people close to the kerb or crossing the road.

⊙
```
Humps for
½ mile
```

⊙
```
Hump Bridge
```

⊙
```
Low Bridge
```

⊙
```
Soft Verge
```

8.6

Mark **one** answer

Traffic calming measures are used to

⊙ stop road rage

⊙ help overtaking

⊙ slow traffic down

⊙ help parking

⊙ **slow traffic down**

Traffic calming measures are used to make the roads safer for vulnerable road users, such as cyclists, pedestrians and children. These can be designed as chicanes, road humps or other obstacles that encourage drivers and riders to slow down.

You are on a motorway in fog. The left-hand edge of the motorway can be identified by reflective studs. What colour are they?

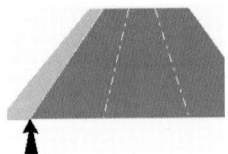

- ⊙ Green
- ⊙ Amber
- ⊙ Red
- ⊙ White

⊙ **Red**

Be especially careful if you're on a motorway in fog. Reflective studs are used to help you in poor visibility. Different colours are used so that you'll know which lane you are in. These are

- red on the left-hand side of the road
- white between lanes
- amber on the right-hand edge of the carriageway
- green between the carriageway and slip roads.

A rumble device is designed to

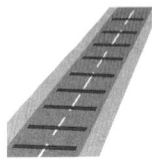

- ⊙ give directions
- ⊙ prevent cattle escaping
- ⊙ alert you to low tyre pressure
- ⊙ alert you to a hazard
- ⊙ encourage you to reduce speed

⊙ **alert you to a hazard**

⊙ **encourage you to reduce speed**

A rumble device usually consists of raised markings or strips across the road. It gives an audible, visual and tactile warning of a hazard. These strips are found in places where traffic has constantly ignored warning or restriction signs. They are there for a good reason. Slow down and be ready to deal with a hazard.

8.9 *Mark **one** answer*

You have to make a journey in foggy conditions. You should

- ⊙ follow other vehicles' tail lights closely
- ⊙ avoid using dipped headlights
- ⊙ leave plenty of time for your journey
- ⊙ keep two seconds behind other vehicles

⊙ **leave plenty of time for your journey**

If you're planning to make a journey when it's foggy, listen to the weather reports on the radio or television. Don't travel if visibility is very poor or your trip isn't necessary.

If you do travel, leave plenty of time for your journey. If someone is expecting you at the other end, let them know that you'll be taking longer than normal to arrive.

8.10 *Mark **one** answer*

You are overtaking a car at night. You must be sure that

- ⊙ you flash your headlights before overtaking
- ⊙ you select a higher gear
- ⊙ you have switched your lights to full beam before overtaking
- ⊙ you do not dazzle other road users

⊙ **you do not dazzle other road users**

To prevent your lights from dazzling the driver of the car in front, wait until you've overtaken before switching to full beam.

8.11 *Mark **one** answer*

You are on a road which has speed humps. A driver in front is travelling slower than you. You should

- ⊙ sound your horn
- ⊙ overtake as soon as you can
- ⊙ flash your headlights
- ⊙ slow down and stay behind

⊙ **slow down and stay behind**

Be patient and stay behind the car in front. Normally you should not overtake other vehicles in traffic-calmed areas. If you overtake here your speed may exceed that which is safe along that road, defeating the purpose of the traffic calming measures.

*Mark **one** answer*

You see these markings on the road. Why are they there?

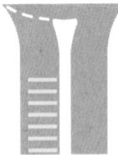

- To show a safe distance between vehicles
- To keep the area clear of traffic
- To make you aware of your speed
- To warn you to change direction

⊙ **To make you aware of your speed**

These lines may be painted on the road on the approach to a roundabout, village or a particular hazard. The lines are raised and painted yellow and their purpose is to make you aware of your speed. Reduce your speed in good time so that you avoid having to brake harshly over the last few metres before reaching the junction.

---

*Mark **three** answers*

Areas reserved for trams may have

- metal studs around them
- white line markings
- zigzag markings
- a different coloured surface
- yellow hatch markings
- a different surface texture

⊙ **white line markings**

⊙ **a different coloured surface**

⊙ **a different surface texture**

Trams can run on roads used by other vehicles and pedestrians. The part of the road used by the trams is known as the reserved area and this should be kept clear. It has a coloured surface and is usually edged with white road markings. It might also have a different surface texture.

---

*Mark **one** answer*

You see a vehicle coming towards you on a single-track road. You should

- go back to the main road
- do an emergency stop
- stop at a passing place
- put on your hazard warning lights

⊙ **stop at a passing place**

You must take extra care when on single track roads. You may not be able to see around bends due to high hedges or fences. Proceed with caution and expect to meet oncoming vehicles around the next bend. If you do, pull into or opposite a passing place.

8.15
*Mark **one** answer*

The road is wet. Why might a motorcyclist steer round drain covers on a bend?

⊙ To avoid puncturing the tyres on the edge of the drain covers

⊙ To prevent the motorcycle sliding on the metal drain covers

⊙ To help judge the bend using the drain covers as marker points

⊙ To avoid splashing pedestrians on the pavement

⊙ **To prevent the motorcycle sliding on the metal drain covers**

Other drivers or riders may have to change course due to the size or characteristics of their vehicle. Understanding this will help you to anticipate their actions.
Motorcyclists and cyclists will be checking the road ahead for uneven or slippery surfaces, especially in wet weather. They may need to move across their lane to avoid surface hazards such as potholes and drain covers.

8.16
*Mark **one** answer*

After this hazard you should test your brakes. Why is this?

⊙ You will be on a slippery road

⊙ Your brakes will be soaking wet

⊙ You will be going down a long hill

⊙ You will have just crossed a long bridge

⊙ **Your brakes will be soaking wet**

A ford is a crossing over a stream that's shallow enough to go through. After you've gone through a ford or deep puddle the water will affect your brakes. To dry them out apply a light brake pressure while moving slowly. Don't travel at normal speeds until you are sure your brakes are working properly again.

8.17
*Mark **one** answer*

Why should you always reduce your speed when travelling in fog?

⊙ The brakes do not work as well

⊙ You will be dazzled by other headlights

⊙ The engine will take longer to warm up

⊙ It is more difficult to see events ahead

⊙ **It is more difficult to see events ahead**

You won't be able to see as far ahead in fog as you can on a clear day. You will need to reduce your speed so that, if a hazard looms out of the fog, you have the time and space to take avoiding action.

Travelling in fog is hazardous. If you can, try and delay your journey until it has cleared.

Hills can affect the performance of your vehicle. Which TWO apply when driving up steep hills?

- ⊙ Higher gears will pull better
- ⊙ You will slow down sooner
- ⊙ Overtaking will be easier
- ⊙ The engine will work harder
- ⊙ The steering will feel heavier

⊙ **You will slow down sooner**

⊙ **The engine will work harder**

The engine will need more power to pull the vehicle up the hill. When approaching a steep hill you should select a lower gear to help maintain your speed. You should do this without hesitation, so that you don't lose too much speed before engaging the lower gear.

You are driving on the motorway in windy conditions. When passing high-sided vehicles you should

- ⊙ increase your speed
- ⊙ be wary of a sudden gust
- ⊙ drive alongside very closely
- ⊙ expect normal conditions

⊙ **be wary of a sudden gust**

The draught caused by other vehicles could be strong enough to push you out of your lane. Keep both hands on the steering wheel to maintain full control.

To correct a rear-wheel skid you should

- ⊙ not steer at all
- ⊙ steer away from it
- ⊙ steer into it
- ⊙ apply your handbrake

⊙ **steer into it**

Prevention is better than cure, so it's important that you take every precaution to avoid a skid from starting.

If you feel the rear wheels of your vehicle beginning to skid, try to steer in the same direction to recover control. Don't brake suddenly – this will only make the situation worse.

8.21
*Mark **one** answer*

You are driving in fog. Why should you keep well back from the vehicle in front?

- ⊙ In case it changes direction suddenly
- ⊙ In case its fog lights dazzle you
- ⊙ In case it stops suddenly
- ⊙ In case its brake lights dazzle you

⊙ **In case it stops suddenly**

If you're following another road user in fog stay well back. The driver in front won't be able to see hazards until they're close and might brake suddenly. Another reason why it is important to maintain a good separation distance in fog is that the road surface is likely to be wet and slippery.

8.22
*Mark **one** answer*

You should switch your rear fog lights on when visibility drops below

- ⊙ your overall stopping distance
- ⊙ ten car lengths
- ⊙ 200 metres (656 feet)
- ⊙ 100 metres (328 feet)

⊙ **100 metres (328 feet)**

If visibility falls below 100 metres (328 feet) in fog, switching on your rear fog lights will help following road users to see you. Don't forget to turn them off once visibility improves: their brightness might be mistaken for brake lights and they could dazzle other drivers.

8.23
*Mark **one** answer*

Whilst driving, the fog clears and you can see more clearly. You must remember to

- ⊙ switch off the fog lights
- ⊙ reduce your speed
- ⊙ switch off the demister
- ⊙ close any open windows

⊙ **switch off the fog lights**

Bright rear fog lights might be mistaken for brake lights and could be misleading for the traffic behind.

You have to park on the road in fog. You should

- ⊙ leave sidelights on
- ⊙ leave dipped headlights and fog lights on
- ⊙ leave dipped headlights on
- ⊙ leave main beam headlights on

⊙ **leave sidelights on**

If you have to park your vehicle in foggy conditions it's important that it can be seen by other road users. Try to find a place to park off the road. If this isn't possible leave it facing in the same direction as the traffic. Make sure that your lights are clean and that you leave your sidelights on.

On a foggy day you unavoidably have to park your car on the road. You should

- ⊙ leave your headlights on
- ⊙ leave your fog lights on
- ⊙ leave your sidelights on
- ⊙ leave your hazard lights on

⊙ **leave your sidelights on**

Ensure that your vehicle can be seen by other traffic. If possible, park your car off the road in a car park or driveway to avoid the extra risk to other road users.

You are travelling at night. You are dazzled by headlights coming towards you. You should

- ⊙ pull down your sun visor
- ⊙ slow down or stop
- ⊙ switch on your main beam headlights
- ⊙ put your hand over your eyes

⊙ **slow down or stop**

You will have additional hazards to deal with at night. Visibility may be very limited and the lights of oncoming vehicles can often dazzle you. When this happens don't close your eyes, swerve or flash your headlights, as this will also distract other drivers. It may help to focus on the left kerb, verge or lane line.

8.27
*Mark **one** answer*

Front fog lights may be used ONLY if

- visibility is seriously reduced
- they are fitted above the bumper
- they are not as bright as the headlights
- an audible warning device is used

⊙ **visibility is seriously reduced**

Your vehicle should have a warning light on the dashboard which illuminates when the fog lights are being used. You need to be familiar with the layout of your dashboard so you are aware if they have been switched on in error, or you have forgotten to switch them off.

8.28
*Mark **one** answer*

Front fog lights may be used ONLY if

- your headlights are not working
- they are operated with rear fog lights
- they were fitted by the vehicle manufacturer
- visibility is seriously reduced

⊙ **visibility is seriously reduced**

It is illegal to use fog lights unless visibility is seriously reduced, which is generally when you cannot see for more than 100 metres (328 feet). Check that they have been switched off when conditions improve.

8.29
*Mark **one** answer*

You are driving with your front fog lights switched on. Earlier fog has now cleared. What should you do?

- Leave them on if other drivers have their lights on
- Switch them off as long as visibility remains good
- Flash them to warn oncoming traffic that it is foggy
- Drive with them on instead of your headlights

⊙ **Switch them off as long as visibility remains good**

Switch off your fog lights if the weather improves, but be prepared to use them again if visibility reduces to less than 100 metres (328 feet).

8.30

Mark one answer

Front fog lights should be used ONLY when

- ⊙ travelling in very light rain
- ⊙ visibility is seriously reduced
- ⊙ daylight is fading
- ⊙ driving after midnight

⊙ **visibility is seriously reduced**

Fog lights will help others see you, but remember, they must only be used if visibility is seriously reduced to less than 100 metres (328 feet).

8.31

Mark three answers

You forget to switch off your rear fog lights when the fog has cleared. This may

- ⊙ dazzle other road users
- ⊙ reduce battery life
- ⊙ cause brake lights to be less clear
- ⊙ be breaking the law
- ⊙ seriously affect engine power

⊙ **dazzle other road users**

⊙ **cause brake lights to be less clear**

⊙ **be breaking the law**

Don't forget to switch off your fog lights when the weather improves. You could be prosecuted for driving with them on in good visibility. The high intensity of the rear fog lights can look like brake lights, and on a high speed road this can cause other road users to brake unnecessarily.

8.32

Mark one answer

You have been driving in thick fog which has now cleared. You must switch OFF your rear fog lights because

- ⊙ they use a lot of power from the battery
- ⊙ they make your brake lights less clear
- ⊙ they will cause dazzle in your rear view mirrors
- ⊙ they may not be properly adjusted

⊙ **they make your brake lights less clear**

It is essential that the traffic behind is given a clear warning when you brake. In good visibility, your rear fog lights can make it hard for others to see your brake lights. Make sure you switch off your fog lights when the visibility improves.

8.33   Mark **one** answer

Front fog lights should be used

- ⊙ when visibility is reduced to 100 metres (328 feet)
- ⊙ as a warning to oncoming traffic
- ⊙ when driving during the hours of darkness
- ⊙ in any conditions and at any time

⊙ **when visibility is reduced to 100 metres (328 feet)**

When visibility is seriously reduced, switch on your fog lights if you have them fitted. It is essential not only that you can see ahead, but also that other road users are able to see you.

8.34   Mark **one** answer

Using rear fog lights in clear daylight will

- ⊙ be useful when towing a trailer
- ⊙ give extra protection
- ⊙ dazzle other drivers
- ⊙ make following drivers keep back

⊙ **dazzle other drivers**

Rear fog lights shine brighter than normal rear lights so that they show up in reduced visibility. When the weather is clear they could dazzle the driver behind, so switch them off.

8.35   Mark **one** answer

Using front fog lights in clear daylight will

- ⊙ flatten the battery
- ⊙ dazzle other drivers
- ⊙ improve your visibility
- ⊙ increase your awareness

⊙ **dazzle other drivers**

Fog lights can be brighter than normal dipped headlights. If the weather has improved turn them off to avoid dazzling other road users.

8.36   Mark **one** answer

You may use front fog lights with headlights ONLY when visibility is reduced to less than

- ⊙ 100 metres (328 feet)
- ⊙ 200 metres (656 feet)
- ⊙ 300 metres (984 feet)
- ⊙ 400 metres (1312 feet)

⊙ **100 metres (328 feet)**

It is an offence to use fog lights if the visibility is better than 100 metres (328 feet). Switch front fog lights off if the fog clears to avoid dazzling other road users, but be aware that the fog may be patchy.

Chains can be fitted to your wheels to help prevent

- ⊙ damage to the road surface
- ⊙ wear to the tyres
- ⊙ skidding in deep snow
- ⊙ the brakes locking

⊙ **skidding in deep snow**

Snow chains can be fitted to your tyres during snowy conditions. They can help you to move off from rest or to keep moving in deep snow. You will still need to adjust your driving according to the road conditions at the time.

How can you use the engine of your vehicle to control your speed?

- ⊙ By changing to a lower gear
- ⊙ By selecting reverse gear
- ⊙ By changing to a higher gear
- ⊙ By selecting neutral

⊙ **By changing to a lower gear**

You should brake and slow down before selecting a lower gear. The gear can then be used to keep the speed low and help you control the vehicle. This is particularly helpful on long downhill stretches, where brake fade can occur if the brakes overheat.

Why could keeping the clutch down or selecting neutral for long periods of time be dangerous?

- ⊙ Fuel spillage will occur
- ⊙ Engine damage may be caused
- ⊙ You will have less steering and braking control
- ⊙ It will wear tyres out more quickly

⊙ **You will have less steering and braking control**

Letting your vehicle roll or coast in neutral reduces your control over steering and braking. This can be dangerous on downhill slopes where your vehicle could pick up speed very quickly.

214

8.40

You are driving on an icy road. What distance should you drive from the car in front?

- four times the normal distance
- six times the normal distance
- eight times the normal distance
- ten times the normal distance

- **ten times the normal distance**

Don't travel in icy or snowy weather unless your journey is necessary.

Drive extremely carefully when roads are or may be icy. Stopping distances can be ten times greater than on dry roads.

8.41

You are on a well-lit motorway at night. You must

- use only your sidelights
- always use your headlights
- always use rear fog lights
- use headlights only in bad weather

- **always use your headlights**

If you're driving on a motorway at night or in poor visibility, you must always use your headlights, even if the road is well-lit. The other road users in front must be able to see you in their mirrors.

8.42

You are on a motorway at night with other vehicles just ahead of you. Which lights should you have on?

- Front fog lights
- Main beam headlights
- Sidelights only
- Dipped headlights

- **Dipped headlights**

If you're driving behind other traffic at night on the motorway, leave a two-second time gap and use dipped headlights. Full beam will dazzle the other drivers. Your headlights' beam should fall short of the vehicle in front.

8.43 — Mark **three** answers

Which THREE of the following will affect your stopping distance?

- How fast you are going
- The tyres on your vehicle
- The time of day
- The weather
- The street lighting

⊙ **How fast you are going**

⊙ **The tyres on your vehicle**

⊙ **The weather**

There are several factors that can affect the distance it takes to stop your vehicle.

Adjust your driving to take account of how the weather conditions could affect your tyres' grip on the road.

8.44 — Mark **one** answer

You are on a motorway at night. You MUST have your headlights switched on unless

- there are vehicles close in front of you
- you are travelling below 50 mph
- the motorway is lit
- your vehicle is broken down on the hard shoulder

⊙ **your vehicle is broken down on the hard shoulder**

Always use your headlights at night on a motorway unless you have stopped on the hard shoulder. If you break down and have to stop on the hard shoulder, switch off the headlights but leave the sidelights on so that other road users can see your vehicle.

8.45 — Mark **one** answer

You will feel the effects of engine braking when you

- only use the handbrake
- only use neutral
- change to a lower gear
- change to a higher gear

⊙ **change to a lower gear**

When going downhill, prolonged use of the brakes can cause them to overheat and lose their effectiveness. Changing to a lower gear will assist your braking.

8.46

*Mark **one** answer*

Daytime visibility is poor but not seriously reduced. You should switch on

- ⊙ headlights and fog lights
- ⊙ front fog lights
- ⊙ dipped headlights
- ⊙ rear fog lights

⊙ **dipped headlights**

Only use your fog lights when visibility is seriously reduced. Use dipped headlights in poor conditions.

8.47

*Mark **one** answer*

Why are vehicles fitted with rear fog lights?

- ⊙ To be seen when driving at high speed
- ⊙ To use if broken down in a dangerous position
- ⊙ To make them more visible in thick fog
- ⊙ To warn drivers following closely to drop back

⊙ **To make them more visible in thick fog**

Rear fog lights make it easier to spot a vehicle ahead in foggy conditions. Avoid the temptation to use other vehicles' lights as a guide, as they may give you a false sense of security.

8.48

*Mark **one** answer*

While you are driving in fog, it becomes necessary to use front fog lights. You should

- ⊙ only turn them on in heavy traffic conditions
- ⊙ remember not to use them on motorways
- ⊙ only use them on dual carriageways
- ⊙ remember to switch them off as visibility improves

⊙ **remember to switch them off as visibility improves**

It is an offence to have your fog lights on in conditions other than seriously reduced visibility, ie. less than 100 metres (328 feet).

When snow is falling heavily you should

- only drive with your hazard lights on
- not drive unless you have a mobile phone
- only drive when your journey is short
- not drive unless it is essential

- **not drive unless it is essential**

Consider if the increased risk is worth it. If the weather conditions are bad and your journey isn't essential, then stay at home.

You are driving down a long steep hill. You suddenly notice your brakes are not working as well as normal. What is the usual cause of this?

- The brakes overheating
- Air in the brake fluid
- Oil on the brakes
- Badly adjusted brakes

- **The brakes overheating**

This is more likely to happen on vehicles fitted with drum brakes but can apply to disc brakes as well. Using a lower gear will assist the braking and help you to keep control of your vehicle.

You have to make a journey in fog. What are the TWO most important things you should do before you set out?

- Top up the radiator with anti-freeze
- Make sure that you have a warning triangle in the vehicle
- Check that your lights are working
- Check the battery
- Make sure that the windows are clean

- **Check that your lights are working**

- **Make sure that the windows are clean**

Don't drive in fog unless you really have to. Adjust your driving to the conditions. You should always be able to pull up within the distance you can see ahead.

8.52

*Mark **one** answer*

You have just driven out of fog. Visibility is now good. You MUST

- ⊙ switch off all your fog lights
- ⊙ keep your rear fog lights on
- ⊙ keep your front fog lights on
- ⊙ leave fog lights on in case fog returns

⊙ **switch off all your fog lights**

You MUST turn off your fog lights if visibility is over 100 metres (328 feet). However, be prepared for the fact that the fog may be patchy.

8.53

*Mark **one** answer*

You may drive with front fog lights switched on

- ⊙ when visibility is less than 100 metres (328 feet)
- ⊙ at any time to be noticed
- ⊙ instead of headlights on high speed roads
- ⊙ when dazzled by the lights of oncoming vehicles

⊙ **when visibility is less than 100 metres (328 feet)**

Only use front fog lights if the distance you are able to see is less than 100 metres (328 feet). Turn off your fog lights as the visibility improves.

8.54

*Mark **two** answers*

Why is it dangerous to leave rear fog lights on when they are not needed?

- ⊙ Brake lights are less clear
- ⊙ Following drivers can be dazzled
- ⊙ Electrical systems could be overloaded
- ⊙ Direction indicators may not work properly
- ⊙ The battery could fail

⊙ **Brake lights are less clear**

⊙ **Following drivers can be dazzled**

If your rear fog lights are left on when it isn't foggy, the glare they cause makes it difficult for road users behind to know whether you are braking or you have just forgotten to turn off your rear fog lights. This can be a particular problem on wet roads and on motorways. If you leave your rear fog lights on at night, road users behind you are likely to be dazzled and this could put them at risk.

8.55 — Mark **one** answer

Holding the clutch pedal down or rolling in neutral for too long while driving will

- use more fuel
- cause the engine to overheat
- reduce your control
- improve tyre wear

⊙ **reduce your control**

Holding the clutch down or staying in neutral for too long will cause your vehicle to freewheel. This is known as 'coasting' and it is dangerous as it reduces your control of the vehicle.

8.56 — Mark **one** answer

You are driving down a steep hill. Why could keeping the clutch down or rolling in neutral for too long be dangerous?

- Fuel consumption will be higher
- Your vehicle will pick up speed
- It will damage the engine
- It will wear tyres out more quickly

⊙ **Your vehicle will pick up speed**

Driving in neutral or with the clutch down for long periods is known as 'coasting'. There will be no engine braking and your vehicle will pick up speed on downhill slopes. Coasting can be very dangerous because it reduces steering and braking control.

8.57 — Mark **two** answers

What are TWO main reasons why coasting downhill is wrong?

- Fuel consumption will be higher
- The vehicle will get faster
- It puts more wear and tear on the tyres
- You have less braking and steering control
- It damages the engine

⊙ **The vehicle will get faster**

⊙ **You have less braking and steering control**

Coasting is when you allow the vehicle to freewheel in neutral or with the clutch pedal depressed. Doing this gives you less control over the vehicle. It's especially important not to let your vehicle coast when approaching hazards such as junctions and bends and when travelling downhill.

8.58 *Mark **four** answers*

Which FOUR of the following may apply when dealing with this hazard?

- It could be more difficult in winter
- Use a low gear and drive slowly
- Use a high gear to prevent wheelspin
- Test your brakes afterwards
- Always switch on fog lamps
- There may be a depth gauge

- **It could be more difficult in winter**
- **Use a low gear and drive slowly**
- **Test your brakes afterwards**
- **There may be a depth gauge**

During the winter the stream is likely to flood. It is also possible that in extremely cold weather it could ice over. Assess the situation carefully before you drive through. If you drive a vehicle with low suspension you may have to find a different route.

8.59 *Mark **one** answer*

Why is travelling in neutral for long distances (known as coasting) wrong?

- It will cause the car to skid
- It will make the engine stall
- The engine will run faster
- There is no engine braking

- **There is no engine braking**

Try to look ahead and read the road. Plan your approach to junctions and select the correct gear in good time. This will give you the control you need to deal with any hazards that occur.

You'll coast a little every time you change gear. This can't be avoided, but it should be kept to a minimum.

8.60 *Mark **one** answer*

When MUST you use dipped headlights during the day?

- All the time
- Along narrow streets
- In poor visibility
- When parking

- **In poor visibility**

You MUST use dipped headlights and/or fog lights in fog when visibility is seriously reduced to 100 metres (328 feet) or less.

You should use dipped headlights, but NOT fog lights, when visibility is poor, such as in heavy rain.

You are braking on a wet road. Your vehicle begins to skid. It does not have anti-lock brakes. What is the FIRST thing you should do?

⊙ Quickly pull up the handbrake

⊙ Release the footbrake

⊙ Push harder on the brake pedal

⊙ Gently use the accelerator

⊙ **Release the footbrake**

If the skid has been caused by braking too hard for the conditions, release the brake. You may then need to reapply and release the brake again. You may need to do this a number of times. This will allow the wheels to turn and so limit the skid. Skids are much easier to get into than they are to get out of. Prevention is better than cure. Stay alert to the road and weather conditions. Drive so that you can stop within the distance you can see to be clear.

Using rear fog lights on a clear dry night will

⊙ reduce glare from the road surface

⊙ make your brake lights less visible

⊙ give a better view of the road ahead

⊙ dazzle following drivers

⊙ help your indicators to be seen more clearly

⊙ **make your brake lights less visible**

⊙ **dazzle following drivers**

You should not use rear fog lights unless visibility is seriously reduced. A warning light will show on the dashboard to indicate when your rear fog lights are on. You should know the meaning of all the lights on your dashboard and check them before you move off and as you drive.

section **nine**

MOTORWAY RULES

This section covers

- Speed limits
- Lane discipline
- Stopping
- Lighting
- Parking

9.1　　　　　　　　*Mark **one** answer*

When joining a motorway you must always

⊙　use the hard shoulder

⊙　stop at the end of the acceleration lane

⊙　come to a stop before joining the motorway

⊙　give way to traffic already on the motorway

⊙　**give way to traffic already on the motorway**

You should give way to traffic already on the motorway. Where possible they may move over to let you in but don't force your way into the traffic stream. The traffic may be travelling at high speed so you should match your speed to fit in.

9.2　　　　　　　　*Mark **one** answer*

What is the national speed limit for cars and motorcycles in the centre lane of a three-lane motorway?

⊙　40 mph

⊙　50 mph

⊙　60 mph

⊙　70 mph

⊙　**70 mph**

Unless shown otherwise, the speed limit on a motorway applies to all the lanes. Look out for any signs of speed limit changes due to roadworks or traffic flow control.

9.3　　　　　　　　*Mark **one** answer*

What is the national speed limit on motorways for cars and motorcycles?

⊙　30 mph

⊙　50 mph

⊙　60 mph

⊙　70 mph

⊙　**70 mph**

Travelling at the national speed limit doesn't allow you to hog the right-hand lane. Always use the left-hand lane whenever possible. When leaving a motorway get into the left-hand lane well before your exit. Reduce your speed on the slip road and look out for sharp bends or curves and traffic queuing at roundabouts.

The left-hand lane on a three-lane motorway is for use by

- any vehicle
- large vehicles only
- emergency vehicles only
- slow vehicles only

⊙ **any vehicle**

On a motorway all traffic should use the left-hand lane unless overtaking. Use the centre or right-hand lanes if you need to overtake. If you're overtaking a number of slower vehicles move back to the left-hand lane when you're safely past. Check your mirrors frequently and don't stay in the middle or right-hand lane if the left-hand lane is free.

Which of these IS NOT allowed to travel in the right-hand lane of a three-lane motorway?

- A small delivery van
- A motorcycle
- A vehicle towing a trailer
- A motorcycle and side-car

⊙ **A vehicle towing a trailer**

A vehicle with a trailer is restricted to 60 mph. For this reason it isn't allowed in the right-hand lane as it might hold up the faster-moving traffic that wishes to overtake in that lane.

You break down on a motorway. You need to call for help. Why may it be better to use an emergency roadside telephone rather than a mobile phone?

- It connects you to a local garage
- Using a mobile phone will distract other drivers
- It allows easy location by the emergency services
- Mobile phones do not work on motorways

⊙ **It allows easy location by the emergency services**

On a motorway it is best to use a roadside emergency telephone so that the emergency services are able to locate you easily. The nearest telephone is shown by an arrow on marker posts at the edge of the hard shoulder. If you use a mobile, they will need to know your exact location. Before you call, find out the number on the nearest marker post. This number will identify your exact location.

9.7

*Mark **one** answer*

After a breakdown you need to rejoin the main carriageway of a motorway from the hard shoulder. You should

- ⊙ move out onto the carriageway then build up your speed
- ⊙ move out onto the carriageway using your hazard lights
- ⊙ gain speed on the hard shoulder before moving out onto the carriageway
- ⊙ wait on the hard shoulder until someone flashes their headlights at you

⊙ **gain speed on the hard shoulder before moving out onto the carriageway**

Wait for a safe gap in the traffic before you move out. Indicate your intention and use the hard shoulder to gain speed but don't force your way into the traffic.

9.8

*Mark **one** answer*

A crawler lane on a motorway is found

- ⊙ on a steep gradient
- ⊙ before a service area
- ⊙ before a junction
- ⊙ along the hard shoulder

⊙ **on a steep gradient**

Slow-moving, large vehicles might slow down the progress of other traffic. On a steep gradient this extra lane is provided for these slow-moving vehicles to allow the faster-moving traffic to flow more easily.

What do these motorway signs show?

- They are countdown markers to a bridge
- They are distance markers to the next telephone
- They are countdown markers to the next exit
- They warn of a police control ahead

⊙ **They are countdown markers to the next exit**

The exit from a motorway is indicated by countdown markers. These are positioned 90 metres (100 yards) apart, the first being 270 metres (300 yards) from the start of the slip road. Move into the left-hand lane well before you reach the start of the slip road.

On a motorway the amber reflective studs can be found between

- the hard shoulder and the carriageway
- the acceleration lane and the carriageway
- the central reservation and the carriageway
- each pair of the lanes

⊙ **the central reservation and the carriageway**

On motorways reflective studs are located into the road to help you in the dark and in conditions of poor visibility. Amber-coloured studs are found on the right-hand edge of the main carriageway, next to the central reservation.

9.11

*Mark **one** answer*

What colour are the reflective studs between the lanes on a motorway?

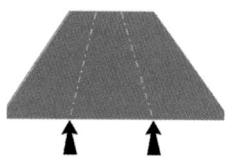

- ⊙ Green
- ⊙ Amber
- ⊙ White
- ⊙ Red

⊙ **White**

White studs are found between the lanes on motorways. The light from your headlights is reflected back and this is especially useful in bad weather, when visibility is restricted.

9.12

*Mark **one** answer*

What colour are the reflective studs between a motorway and its slip road?

- ⊙ Amber
- ⊙ White
- ⊙ Green
- ⊙ Red

⊙ **Green**

The studs between the carriageway and the hard shoulder are normally red. These change to green where there is a slip road. They will help you identify slip roads when visibility is poor or when it is dark.

9.13

*Mark **one** answer*

You have broken down on a motorway. To find the nearest emergency telephone you should always walk

- ⊙ with the traffic flow
- ⊙ facing oncoming traffic
- ⊙ in the direction shown on the marker posts
- ⊙ in the direction of the nearest exit

⊙ **in the direction shown on the marker posts**

Along the hard shoulder there are marker posts at 100-metre intervals. These will direct you to the nearest emergency telephone.

9.14

Mark *one* answer

You are joining a motorway. Why is it important to make full use of the slip road?

- Because there is space available to turn round if you need to
- To allow you direct access to the overtaking lanes
- To build up a speed similar to traffic on the motorway
- Because you can continue on the hard shoulder

⊙ **To build up a speed similar to traffic on the motorway**

Try to join the motorway without affecting the progress of the traffic already travelling on it. Always give way to traffic already on the motorway. At busy times you may have to slow down to merge into slow-moving traffic.

9.15

Mark *one* answer

How should you use the emergency telephone on a motorway?

- Stay close to the carriageway
- Face the oncoming traffic
- Keep your back to the traffic
- Stand on the hard shoulder

⊙ **Face the oncoming traffic**

Traffic is passing you at speed. If the draught from a large lorry catches you by surprise it could blow you off balance and even onto the carriageway. By facing the oncoming traffic you can see approaching lorries and so be prepared for their draught. You are also in a position to see other hazards approaching.

9.16

Mark *one* answer

You are on a motorway. What colour are the reflective studs on the left of the carriageway?

- Green
- Red
- White
- Amber

⊙ **Red**

Red studs are placed between the edge of the carriageway and the hard shoulder. Where slip roads leave or join the motorway the studs are green.

9.17   *Mark **one** answer*

On a three-lane motorway which lane should you normally use?

- ⊙ Left
- ⊙ Right
- ⊙ Centre
- ⊙ Either the right or centre

⊙ **Left**

On a three-lane motorway you should travel in the left-hand lane unless you're overtaking. This applies regardless of the speed at which you're travelling.

9.18   *Mark **one** answer*

When going through a contraflow system on a motorway you should

- ⊙ ensure that you do not exceed 30 mph
- ⊙ keep a good distance from the vehicle ahead
- ⊙ switch lanes to keep the traffic flowing
- ⊙ stay close to the vehicle ahead to reduce queues

⊙ **keep a good distance from the vehicle ahead**

There's likely to be a speed restriction in force. Keep to this. Don't

- switch lanes
- get too close to traffic in front of you.

Be aware there will be no permanent barrier between you and the oncoming traffic.

9.19

You are on a three-lane motorway. There are red reflective studs on your left and white ones to your right. Where are you?

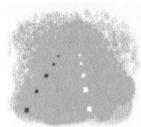

- ⊙ In the right-hand lane
- ⊙ In the middle lane
- ⊙ On the hard shoulder
- ⊙ In the left-hand lane

⊙ **In the left-hand lane**

The colours of the reflective studs on the motorway and their locations are

- red – between the hard shoulder and the carriageway
- white – lane markings
- amber – between the edge of the carriageway and the central reservation
- green – along slip road exits and entrances
- bright green/yellow – roadworks and contraflow systems.

9.20

You are approaching roadworks on a motorway. What should you do?

- ⊙ Speed up to clear the area quickly
- ⊙ Always use the hard shoulder
- ⊙ Obey all speed limits
- ⊙ Stay very close to the vehicle in front

⊙ **Obey all speed limits**

Collisions can often happen at roadworks. Be aware of the speed limits, slow down in good time and keep your distance from the vehicle in front.

9.21

Which FOUR of these must NOT use motorways?

- ⊙ Learner car drivers
- ⊙ Motorcycles over 50cc
- ⊙ Double-deck buses
- ⊙ Farm tractors
- ⊙ Horse riders
- ⊙ Cyclists

⊙ **Learner car drivers**

⊙ **Farm tractors**

⊙ **Horse riders**

⊙ **Cyclists**

In addition, motorways MUST NOT be used by pedestrians, motorcycles under 50 cc, certain slow-moving vehicles without permission, and invalid carriages weighing less than 254 kg (560 lbs).

9.22

*Mark **four** answers*

Which FOUR of these must NOT use motorways?

- Learner car drivers
- Motorcycles over 50cc
- Double-deck buses
- Farm tractors
- Learner motorcyclists
- Cyclists

- **Learner car drivers**
- **Farm tractors**
- **Learner motorcyclists**
- **Cyclists**

Learner car drivers and motorcyclists are not allowed on the motorway until they have passed their practical test.

Motorways have rules that you need to know before you venture out for the first time. When you've passed your practical test it's a good idea to have some lessons on motorways. Check with your instructor about this.

9.23

*Mark **one** answer*

Immediately after joining a motorway you should normally

- try to overtake
- re-adjust your mirrors
- position your vehicle in the centre lane
- keep in the left-hand lane

- **keep in the left-hand lane**

Stay in the left-hand lane long enough to get used to the higher speeds of motorway traffic.

9.24

*Mark **one** answer*

What is the right-hand lane used for on a three-lane motorway?

- Emergency vehicles only
- Overtaking
- Vehicles towing trailers
- Coaches only

- **Overtaking**

You should keep to the left and only use the right-hand lane if you're passing slower-moving traffic.

*Mark **one** answer*

What should you use the hard shoulder of a motorway for?

- ◉ Stopping in an emergency
- ◉ Leaving the motorway
- ◉ Stopping when you are tired
- ◉ Joining the motorway

◉ **Stopping in an emergency**

Don't use the hard shoulder for stopping unless it is an emergency. If you want to stop for any other reason go to the next exit or service station.

---

*Mark **one** answer*

You are in the right-hand lane on a motorway. You see these overhead signs. This means

- ◉ move to the left and reduce your speed to 50 mph
- ◉ there are roadworks 50 metres (55 yards) ahead
- ◉ use the hard shoulder until you have passed the hazard
- ◉ leave the motorway at the next exit

◉ **move to the left and reduce your speed to 50 mph**

You MUST obey this sign. There might not be any visible signs of a problem ahead. However, there might be queuing traffic or another hazard which you cannot yet see.

9.27
*Mark **one** answer*

You are allowed to stop on a motorway when you

- need to walk and get fresh air
- wish to pick up hitchhikers
- are told to do so by flashing red lights
- need to use a mobile telephone

⊙ **are told to do so by flashing red lights**

You MUST stop if there are red lights flashing above every lane on the motorway. However, if any of the other lanes do not show flashing red lights or a red cross you may move into that lane and continue if it is safe to do so.

9.28
*Mark **one** answer*

You are travelling along the left-hand lane of a three-lane motorway. Traffic is joining from a slip road. You should

- race the other vehicles
- move to another lane
- maintain a steady speed
- switch on your hazard flashers

⊙ **move to another lane**

You should move to another lane if it is safe to do so. This can greatly assist the flow of traffic joining the motorway, especially at peak times.

9.29
*Mark **one** answer*

A basic rule when on motorways is

- use the lane that has least traffic
- keep to the left-hand lane unless overtaking
- overtake on the side that is clearest
- try to keep above 50 mph to prevent congestion

⊙ **keep to the left-hand lane unless overtaking**

You should normally travel in the left-hand lane unless you are overtaking a slower-moving vehicle. When you are past that vehicle move back into the left-hand lane as soon as it's safe to do so. Don't cut across in front of the vehicle that you're overtaking.

On motorways you should never overtake on the left unless

- you can see well ahead that the hard shoulder is clear
- the traffic in the right-hand lane is signalling right
- you warn drivers behind by signalling left
- there is a queue of slow-moving traffic to your right that is moving more slowly than you are

⊙ **there is a queue of slow-moving traffic to your right that is moving more slowly than you are**

Only overtake on the left if traffic is moving slowly in queues and the traffic on your right is moving more slowly than the traffic in your lane.

Motorway emergency telephones are usually linked to the police. In some areas they are now linked to

- the Highways Agency Control Centre
- the Driver Vehicle Licensing Agency
- the Driving Standards Agency
- the local Vehicle Registration Office

⊙ **the Highways Agency Control Centre**

In some areas motorway telephones are now linked to a Highways Agency Control Centre, instead of the police. Highways Agency Traffic Officers work in partnership with the police and assist at motorway emergencies and incidents. They are recognised by a high-visibility orange and yellow jacket and high-visibility vehicle with yellow and black chequered markings.

An Emergency Refuge Area is an area

- on a motorway for use in cases of emergency or breakdown
- for use if you think you will be involved in a road rage incident
- on a motorway for a police patrol to park and watch traffic
- for construction and road workers to store emergency equipment

⊙ **on a motorway for use in cases of emergency or breakdown**

Emergency Refuge Areas may be found at the side of the hard shoulder about 500 metres apart. If you break down you should use them rather than the hard shoulder if you are able. When re-joining the motorway you must remember to take extra care especially when the hard shoulder is being used as a running lane within an Active Traffic Management area. Try to match your speed to that of traffic in the lane you are joining.

9.33 *Mark one answer*

What is an Emergency Refuge Area on a motorway for?

- ⊙ An area to park in when you want to use a mobile phone
- ⊙ To use in cases of emergency or breakdown
- ⊙ For an emergency recovery vehicle to park in a contra-flow system
- ⊙ To drive in when there is queuing traffic ahead

⊙ **To use in cases of emergency or breakdown**

In cases of breakdown or emergency try to get your vehicle into an Emergency Refuge Area. This is safer than just stopping on the hard shoulder as it gives you greater distance from the main carriageway. If you are able to re-join the motorway you must take extra care, especially when the hard shoulder is being used as a running lane.

9.34 NI EXEMPT *Mark one answer*

Highways Agency Traffic Officers

- ⊙ will not be able to assist at a breakdown or emergency
- ⊙ are not able to stop and direct anyone on a motorway
- ⊙ will tow a broken down vehicle and it's passengers home
- ⊙ are able to stop and direct anyone on a motorway

⊙ **are able to stop and direct anyone on a motorway**

Highways Agency Traffic Officers (HATOs) are able to stop and direct traffic on most motorways and some 'A' class roads. They work in partnership with the police at motorway incidents and provide a highly-trained and visible service. Their role is to help keep traffic moving and make your journey as safe and reliable as possible. They are recognised by an orange and yellow jacket and their vehicle has yellow and black markings.

You are on a motorway. A red cross is displayed above the hard shoulder. What does this mean?

- ⊙ Pull up in this lane to answer your mobile phone
- ⊙ Use this lane as a running lane
- ⊙ This lane can be used if you need a rest
- ⊙ You should not travel in this lane

⊙ **You should not travel in this lane**

Active Traffic Management schemes are being introduced on motorways. Within these areas at certain times the hard shoulder will be used as a running lane. A red cross above the hard shoulder shows that this lane should NOT be used, except for emergencies and breakdowns.

You are on a motorway in an Active Traffic Management (ATM) area. A mandatory speed limit is displayed above the hard shoulder. What does this mean?

- ⊙ You should not travel in this lane
- ⊙ The hard shoulder can be used as a running lane
- ⊙ You can park on the hard shoulder if you feel tired
- ⊙ You can pull up in this lane to answer a mobile phone

⊙ **The hard shoulder can be used as a running lane**

A mandatory speed limit sign above the hard shoulder shows that it can be used as a running lane between junctions. You must stay within the speed limit. Look out for vehicles that may have broken down and could be blocking the hard shoulder.

9.37   NI EXEMPT   Mark *one* answer

The aim of an Active Traffic Management scheme on a motorway is to

- prevent overtaking
- reduce rest stops
- prevent tailgating
- reduce congestion

⊙ **reduce congestion**

Active Traffic Management schemes are intended to reduce congestion and make journey times more reliable. In these areas the hard shoulder may be used as a running lane to ease congestion at peak times or in the event of an incident. It may appear that you could travel faster for a short distance, but keeping traffic flow at a constant speed may improve your journey time.

9.38   NI EXEMPT   Mark *one* answer

You are in an Active Traffic Management area on a motorway. When the Actively Managed mode is operating

- speed limits are only advisory
- the national speed limit will apply
- the speed limit is always 30 mph
- all speed limit signals are set

⊙ **all speed limit signals are set**

When an Active Traffic Management (ATM) scheme is operating on a motorway you MUST follow the mandatory instructions shown on the gantries above each lane. This includes the hard shoulder.

9.39   NI EXEMPT   Mark *one* answer

You are travelling on a motorway. A red cross is shown above the hard shoulder. What does this mean?

- Use this lane as a rest area
- Use this as a normal running lane
- Do not use this lane to travel in
- National speed limit applies in this lane

⊙ **Do not use this lane to travel in**

When a red cross is shown above the hard shoulder it should only be used for breakdowns or emergencies. Within Active Traffic Management (ATM) areas the hard shoulder may sometimes be used as a running lane. Speed limit signs directly above the hard shoulder will show that it's open.

9.40

*Mark **one** answer*

Why can it be an advantage for traffic speed to stay constant over a longer distance?

- ⊙ You will do more stop-start driving
- ⊙ You will use far more fuel
- ⊙ You will be able to use more direct routes
- ⊙ Your overall journey time will normally improve

⊙ **Your overall journey time will normally improve**

When traffic travels at a constant speed over a longer distance, journey times normally improve. You may feel that you could travel faster for short periods but this won't generally improve your overall journey time. Signs will show the maximum speed at which you should travel.

9.41   NI EXEMPT

*Mark **one** answer*

You should not normally travel on the hard shoulder of a motorway. When can you use it?

- ⊙ When taking the next exit
- ⊙ When traffic is stopped
- ⊙ When signs direct you to
- ⊙ When traffic is slow moving

⊙ **When signs direct you to**

Normally you should only use the hard shoulder for emergencies and breakdowns, and at roadworks when signs direct you to do so. Active Traffic Management (ATM) areas are being introduced to ease traffic congestion. In these areas the hard shoulder may be used as a running lane when speed limit signs are shown directly above.

9.42

*Mark **one** answer*

For what reason may you use the right-hand lane of a motorway?

- ⊙ For keeping out of the way of lorries
- ⊙ For travelling at more than 70 mph
- ⊙ For turning right
- ⊙ For overtaking other vehicles

⊙ **For overtaking other vehicles**

The right-hand lane of the motorway is for overtaking.

Sometimes you may be directed into a right-hand lane as a result of roadworks or a traffic incident. This will be indicated by signs or officers directing the traffic.

9.43
*Mark **one** answer*

On a motorway what is used to reduce traffic bunching?

- Variable speed limits
- Contraflow systems
- National speed limits
- Lane closures

⊙ **Variable speed limits**

Congestion can be reduced by keeping traffic at a constant speed. At busy times maximum speed limits are displayed on overhead gantries. These can be varied quickly depending on the amount of traffic. By keeping to a constant speed on busy sections of motorway overall journey times are normally improved.

9.44
*Mark **three** answers*

When should you stop on a motorway?

- If you have to read a map
- When you are tired and need a rest
- If red lights show above every lane
- When told to by the police
- If your mobile phone rings
- When signalled by a Highways Agency Traffic Officer

⊙ **If red lights show above every lane**

⊙ **When told to by the police**

⊙ **When signalled by a Highways Agency Traffic Officer**

There are some occasions when you may have to stop on the carriageway of a motorway. These include when being signalled by the police or a Highways Agency Traffic Officer, when flashing red lights show above every lane and in traffic jams.

9.45
*Mark **one** answer*

When may you stop on a motorway?

- If you have to read a map
- When you are tired and need a rest
- If your mobile phone rings
- In an emergency or breakdown

⊙ **In an emergency or breakdown**

You should not normally stop on a motorway but there may be occasions when you need to do so. If you are unfortunate enough to break down make every effort to pull up on the hard shoulder.

You are travelling on a motorway. Unless signs show a lower speed limit you must NOT exceed

- ⊙ 50 mph
- ⊙ 60 mph
- ⊙ 70 mph
- ⊙ 80 mph

⊙ **70 mph**

The national speed limit for a car or motorcycle on the motorway is 70 mph. Lower speed limits may be in force, for example at roadworks, so look out for the signs. Variable speed limits operate in some areas to control very busy stretches of motorway. The speed limit may change depending on the volume of traffic.

Motorway emergency telephones are usually linked to the police. In some areas they are now linked to

- ⊙ the local ambulance service
- ⊙ an Highways Agency control centre
- ⊙ the local fire brigade
- ⊙ a breakdown service control centre

⊙ **an Highways Agency control centre**

The controller will ask you

- the make and colour of your vehicle
- whether you are a member of an emergency breakdown service
- the number shown on the emergency telephone casing
- whether you are travelling alone.

You are on a motorway. There are red flashing lights above every lane. You must

- ⊙ pull onto the hard shoulder
- ⊙ slow down and watch for further signals
- ⊙ leave at the next exit
- ⊙ stop and wait

⊙ **stop and wait**

Red flashing lights above every lane mean you must not go on any further. You'll also see a red cross illuminated. Stop and wait. Don't

- change lanes
- continue
- pull onto the hard shoulder (unless in an emergency).

9.49   NI EXEMPT   *Mark one answer*

You are on a three-lane motorway. A red cross is shown above the hard shoulder and mandatory speed limits above all other lanes. This means

- ⊙ the hard shoulder can be used as a rest area if you feel tired
- ⊙ the hard shoulder is for emergency or breakdown use only
- ⊙ the hard shoulder can be used as a normal running lane
- ⊙ the hard shoulder has a speed limit of 50 mph

⊙ **the hard shoulder is for emergency or breakdown use only**

A red cross above the hard shoulder shows it is closed as a running lane and should only be used for emergencies or breakdowns. At busy times within an Active Traffic Management (ATM) area the hard shoulder may be used as a running lane. This will be shown by a mandatory speed limit on the gantry above.

9.50   NI EXEMPT   *Mark one answer*

You are on a three-lane motorway and see this sign. It means you can use

- ⊙ any lane except the hard shoulder
- ⊙ the hard shoulder only
- ⊙ the three right hand lanes only
- ⊙ all the lanes including the hard shoulder

⊙ **all the lanes including the hard shoulder**

Mandatory speed limit signs above all lanes including the hard shoulder, show that you are in an Active Traffic Management (ATM) area. In this case you can use the hard shoulder as a running lane. You must stay within the speed limit shown. Look out for any vehicles that may have broken down and be blocking the hard shoulder.

You are travelling on a motorway. You decide you need a rest. You should

⊙ stop on the hard shoulder

⊙ pull in at the nearest service area

⊙ pull up on a slip road

⊙ park on the central reservation

⊙ **pull in at the nearest service area**

If you feel tired stop at the nearest service area. If it's too far away leave the motorway at the next exit and find a safe place to stop. You must not stop on the carriageway or hard shoulder of a motorway except in an emergency, in a traffic queue, when signalled to do so by a police or enforcement officer, or by traffic signals. Plan your journey so that you have regular rest stops.

You are on a motorway. You become tired and decide you need to rest. What should you do?

⊙ Stop on the hard shoulder

⊙ Pull up on a slip road

⊙ Park on the central reservation

⊙ Leave at the next exit

⊙ **Leave at the next exit**

Ideally you should plan your journey so that you have regular rest stops. If you do become tired leave at the next exit, or pull in at a service area if this is sooner.

You are towing a trailer on a motorway. What is your maximum speed limit?

⊙ 40 mph

⊙ 50 mph

⊙ 60 mph

⊙ 70 mph

⊙ **60 mph**

Don't forget that you're towing a trailer. If you're towing a small, light, trailer, it won't reduce your vehicle's performance by very much. However, strong winds or buffeting from large vehicles might cause the trailer to snake from side to side. Be aware of your speed and don't exceed the lower limit imposed.

9.54
*Mark **one** answer*

The left-hand lane of a motorway should be used for

- breakdowns and emergencies only
- overtaking slower traffic in the other lanes
- slow vehicles only
- normal driving

⊙ **normal driving**

You should keep to the left-hand lane whenever possible. Only use the other lanes for overtaking or when directed by signals. Using other lanes when the left-hand lane is empty can frustrate drivers behind you.

9.55
*Mark **one** answer*

You are driving on a motorway. You have to slow down quickly due to a hazard. You should

- switch on your hazard lights
- switch on your headlights
- sound your horn
- flash your headlights

⊙ **switch on your hazard lights**

Using your hazard lights, as well as brake lights, will give following traffic an extra warning of the problem ahead. Only use them for long enough to ensure that your warning has been seen.

9.56
*Mark **one** answer*

You get a puncture on the motorway. You manage to get your vehicle onto the hard shoulder. You should

- change the wheel yourself immediately
- use the emergency telephone and call for assistance
- try to wave down another vehicle for help
- only change the wheel if you have a passenger to help you

⊙ **use the emergency telephone and call for assistance**

Due to the danger from passing traffic you should park as far to the left as you can and leave the vehicle by the nearside door.

Do not attempt even simple repairs. Instead walk to an emergency telephone on your side of the road and phone for assistance. While waiting for assistance to arrive wait near your car, keeping well away from the carriageway and hard shoulder.

*Mark **one** answer*

You are driving on a motorway. By mistake, you go past the exit that you wanted to take. You should

- carefully reverse on the hard shoulder
- carry on to the next exit
- carefully reverse in the left-hand lane
- make a U-turn at the next gap in the central reservation

⊙ **carry on to the next exit**

It is against the law to reverse, cross the central reservation or drive against the traffic flow on a motorway. If you have missed your exit ask yourself if your concentration is fading. It could be that you need to take a rest break before completing your journey.

*Mark **one** answer*

You are driving at 70 mph on a three-lane motorway. There is no traffic ahead. Which lane should you use?

- Any lane
- Middle lane
- Right lane
- Left lane

⊙ **Left lane**

If the left-hand lane is free you should use it, regardless of the speed you're travelling.

*Mark **one** answer*

Your vehicle has broken down on a motorway. You are not able to stop on the hard shoulder. What should you do?

- Switch on your hazard warning lights
- Stop following traffic and ask for help
- Attempt to repair your vehicle quickly
- Stand behind your vehicle to warn others

⊙ **Switch on your hazard warning lights**

If you can't get your vehicle onto the hard shoulder, use your hazard warning lights to warn others. Leave your vehicle only when you can safely get clear of the carriageway. Do not try to repair the vehicle or attempt to place any warning device on the carriageway.

9.60
*Mark **one** answer*

Why is it particularly important to carry out a check on your vehicle before making a long motorway journey?

- You will have to do more harsh braking on motorways
- Motorway service stations do not deal with breakdowns
- The road surface will wear down the tyres faster
- Continuous high speeds may increase the risk of your vehicle breaking down

- **Continuous high speeds may increase the risk of your vehicle breaking down**

Before you start your journey make sure that your vehicle can cope with the demands of high-speed driving. You should check a number of things, the main ones being oil, water and tyres. You also need to plan rest stops if you're going a long way.

9.61
*Mark **one** answer*

You are driving on a motorway. The car ahead shows its hazard lights for a short time. This tells you that

- the driver wants you to overtake
- the other car is going to change lanes
- traffic ahead is slowing or stopping suddenly
- there is a police speed check ahead

- **traffic ahead is slowing or stopping suddenly**

If the vehicle in front shows its hazard lights there may be an incident or queuing traffic ahead. As well as keeping a safe distance, look beyond it to help you get an early warning of any hazards and a picture of the situation ahead.

9.62
*Mark **one** answer*

You are intending to leave the motorway at the next exit. Before you reach the exit you should normally position your vehicle

- in the middle lane
- in the left-hand lane
- on the hard shoulder
- in any lane

- **in the left-hand lane**

You'll see the first advance direction sign one mile from the exit. If you're travelling at 60 mph in the right-hand lane you'll only have about 50 seconds before you reach the countdown markers. There will be another sign at the half-mile point. Move in to the left-hand lane in good time. Don't cut across traffic at the last moment and don't risk missing your exit.

As a provisional licence holder you should not drive a car

- ⊙ over 30 mph
- ⊙ at night
- ⊙ on the motorway
- ⊙ with passengers in rear seats

⊙ **on the motorway**

When you've passed your practical test ask your instructor to take you for a lesson on the motorway. You'll need to get used to the speed of traffic and how to deal with multiple lanes. The Pass Plus scheme has been created for new drivers, and includes motorway driving. Ask your ADI for details.

Your vehicle breaks down on the hard shoulder of a motorway. You decide to use your mobile phone to call for help. You should

- ⊙ stand at the rear of the vehicle while making the call
- ⊙ try to repair the vehicle yourself
- ⊙ get out of the vehicle by the right-hand door
- ⊙ check your location from the marker posts on the left

⊙ **check your location from the marker posts on the left**

The emergency services need to know your exact location so they can reach you as quickly as possible. Look for a number on the nearest marker post beside the hard shoulder. Give this number when you call the emergency services as it will help them to locate you. Be ready to describe where you are, for example, by reference to the last junction or service station you passed.

You are on a three-lane motorway towing a trailer. You may use the right-hand lane when

- ⊙ there are lane closures
- ⊙ there is slow moving traffic
- ⊙ you can maintain a high speed
- ⊙ large vehicles are in the left and centre lanes

⊙ **there are lane closures**

If you are towing a caravan or trailer you must not use the right-hand lane on a motorway with three or more lanes, except in certain circumstances, such as lane closures.

9.66
*Mark **one** answer*

You are on a motorway. There is a contraflow system ahead. What would you expect to find?

- ⊙ Temporary traffic lights
- ⊙ Lower speed limits
- ⊙ Wider lanes than normal
- ⊙ Speed humps

⊙ **Lower speed limits**

When approaching a contraflow system reduce speed in good time and obey all speed limits. You may be travelling in a narrower lane than normal with no permanent barrier between you and the oncoming traffic. Be aware that the hard shoulder may be used for traffic and the road ahead could be obstructed by slow-moving or broken down vehicles.

9.67
*Mark **one** answer*

On a motorway you may only stop on the hard shoulder

- ⊙ in an emergency
- ⊙ if you feel tired and need to rest
- ⊙ if you miss the exit that you wanted
- ⊙ to pick up a hitchhiker

⊙ **in an emergency**

You should only stop on the hard shoulder in a genuine emergency. DON'T stop on it to have a rest or picnic, pick up hitchhikers, answer a mobile phone or check a map. If you miss your intended exit carry on to the next, never reverse along the hard shoulder.

section **ten**
RULES OF THE ROAD

This section covers
- Speed limits
- Lane discipline
- Parking
- Lighting

10.1   *Mark **one** answer*

What is the meaning of this sign?

- Local speed limit applies
- No waiting on the carriageway
- National speed limit applies
- No entry to vehicular traffic

⊙ **National speed limit applies**

This sign doesn't tell you the speed limit in figures. You should know the speed limit for the type of road that you're on. Study your copy of The Highway Code.

10.2   *Mark **one** answer*

What is the national speed limit for cars and motorcycles on a dual carriageway?

- 30 mph
- 50 mph
- 60 mph
- 70 mph

⊙ **70 mph**

Ensure that you know the speed limit for the road that you're on. The speed limit on a dual carriageway or motorway is 70 mph for cars and motorcycles, unless there are signs to indicate otherwise. The speed limits for different types of vehicles are listed in The Highway Code.

10.3   *Mark **one** answer*

There are no speed limit signs on the road. How is a 30 mph limit indicated?

- By hazard warning lines
- By street lighting
- By pedestrian islands
- By double or single yellow lines

⊙ **By street lighting**

There is usually a 30 mph speed limit where there are street lights unless there are signs showing another limit.

Where you see street lights but no speed limit signs the limit is usually

- 30 mph
- 40 mph
- 50 mph
- 60 mph

⊙ **30 mph**

The presence of street lights generally shows that there is a 30 mph speed limit, unless signs tell you otherwise.

What does this sign mean?

- Minimum speed 30 mph
- End of maximum speed
- End of minimum speed
- Maximum speed 30 mph

⊙ **End of minimum speed**

A red slash through this sign indicates that the restriction has ended. In this case the restriction was a minimum speed limit of 30 mph.

There is a tractor ahead of you. You wish to overtake but you are NOT sure if it is safe to do so. You should

- follow another overtaking vehicle through
- sound your horn to the slow vehicle to pull over
- speed through but flash your lights to oncoming traffic
- not overtake if you are in doubt

⊙ **not overtake if you are in doubt**

Never overtake if you're not sure whether it's safe. Can you see far enough down the road to ensure that you can complete the manoeuvre safely? If the answer is no, DON'T GO.

10.7
*Mark **three** answers*

Which three of the following are most likely to take an unusual course at roundabouts?

- Horse riders
- Milk floats
- Delivery vans
- Long vehicles
- Estate cars
- Cyclists

- **Horse riders**
- **Long vehicles**
- **Cyclists**

Long vehicles might have to take a slightly different position when approaching the roundabout or going around it. This is to stop the rear of the vehicle cutting in and mounting the kerb.

Horse riders and cyclists might stay in the left-hand lane although they are turning right. Be aware of this and allow them room.

10.8
*Mark **one** answer*

On a clearway you must not stop

- at any time
- when it is busy
- in the rush hour
- during daylight hours

- **at any time**

Clearways are in place so that traffic can flow without the obstruction of parked vehicles. Just one parked vehicle will cause an obstruction for all other traffic. You MUST NOT stop where a clearway is in force, not even to pick up or set down passengers.

10.9
*Mark **one** answer*

What is the meaning of this sign?

- No entry
- Waiting restrictions
- National speed limit
- School crossing patrol

- **Waiting restrictions**

This sign indicates that there are waiting restrictions. It is normally accompanied by details of when restrictions are in force.

Details of most signs which are in common use are shown in The Highway Code and a more comprehensive selection is available in Know Your Traffic Signs.

You can park on the right-hand side of a road at night

- ⊙ in a one-way street
- ⊙ with your sidelights on
- ⊙ more than 10 metres (32 feet) from a junction
- ⊙ under a lamp-post

⊙ **in a one-way street**

Red rear reflectors show up when headlights shine on them. These are useful when you are parked at night but will only reflect if you park in the same direction as the traffic flow. Normally you should park on the left, but if you're in a one-way street you may also park on the right-hand side.

On a three-lane dual carriageway the right-hand lane can be used for

- ⊙ overtaking only, never turning right
- ⊙ overtaking or turning right
- ⊙ fast-moving traffic only
- ⊙ turning right only, never overtaking

⊙ **overtaking or turning right**

You should normally use the left-hand lane on any dual carriageway unless you are overtaking or turning right.

When overtaking on a dual carriageway, look for vehicles ahead that are turning right. They're likely to be slowing or stopped. You need to see them in good time so that you can take appropriate action.

You are approaching a busy junction. There are several lanes with road markings. At the last moment you realise that you are in the wrong lane. You should

- ⊙ continue in that lane
- ⊙ force your way across
- ⊙ stop until the area has cleared
- ⊙ use clear arm signals to cut across

⊙ **continue in that lane**

There are times where road markings can be obscured by queuing traffic, or you might be unsure which lane you need to be in.

If you realise that you're in the wrong lane, don't cut across lanes or bully other drivers to let you in. Follow the lane you're in and find somewhere safe to turn around if you need to.

10.13 *Mark **one** answer*

Where may you overtake on a one-way street?

- Only on the left-hand side
- Overtaking is not allowed
- Only on the right-hand side
- Either on the right or the left

⊙ **Either on the right or the left**

You can overtake other traffic on either side when travelling in a one-way street. Make full use of your mirrors and ensure that it's clear all around before you attempt to overtake. Look for signs and road markings and use the most suitable lane for your destination.

10.14 *Mark **one** answer*

When going straight ahead at a roundabout you should

- indicate left before leaving the roundabout
- not indicate at any time
- indicate right when approaching the roundabout
- indicate left when approaching the roundabout

⊙ **indicate left before leaving the roundabout**

When you want to go straight on at a roundabout, don't signal as you approach it, but indicate left just after you pass the exit before the one you wish to take.

10.15 *Mark **one** answer*

Which vehicle might have to use a different course to normal at roundabouts?

- Sports car
- Van
- Estate car
- Long vehicle

⊙ **Long vehicle**

A long vehicle may have to straddle lanes either on or approaching a roundabout so that the rear wheels don't cut in over the kerb.

If you're following a long vehicle, stay well back and give it plenty of room.

You may only enter a box junction when

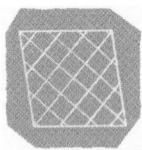

- there are less than two vehicles in front of you
- the traffic lights show green
- your exit road is clear
- you need to turn left

⊙ **your exit road is clear**

Yellow box junctions are marked on the road to prevent the road becoming blocked. Don't enter one unless your exit road is clear. You may only wait in the yellow box if your exit road is clear but oncoming traffic is preventing you from completing the turn.

You may wait in a yellow box junction when

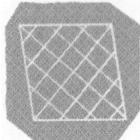

- oncoming traffic is preventing you from turning right
- you are in a queue of traffic turning left
- you are in a queue of traffic to go ahead
- you are on a roundabout

⊙ **oncoming traffic is preventing you from turning right**

The purpose of this road marking is to keep the junction clear of queuing traffic. You may only wait in the marked area when you're turning right and your exit lane is clear but you can't complete the turn because of oncoming traffic.

You MUST stop when signalled to do so by which THREE of these?

- A police officer
- A pedestrian
- A school crossing patrol
- A bus driver
- A red traffic light

⊙ **A police officer**

⊙ **A school crossing patrol**

⊙ **A red traffic light**

Looking well ahead and 'reading' the road will help you to anticipate hazards. This will enable you to stop safely at traffic lights or if ordered to do so by an authorised person.

10.19

*Mark **one** answer*

Someone is waiting to cross at a zebra crossing. They are standing on the pavement. You should normally

- go on quickly before they step onto the crossing
- stop before you reach the zigzag lines and let them cross
- stop, let them cross, wait patiently
- ignore them as they are still on the pavement

⊙ **stop, let them cross, wait patiently**

By standing on the pavement, the pedestrian is showing an intention to cross. If you are looking well down the road you will give yourself enough time to slow down and stop safely. Don't forget to check your mirrors before slowing down.

10.20

*Mark **one** answer*

At toucan crossings, apart from pedestrians you should be aware of

- emergency vehicles emerging
- buses pulling out
- trams crossing in front
- cyclists riding across

⊙ **cyclists riding across**

The use of cycles is being encouraged and more toucan crossings are being installed. These crossings enable pedestrians and cyclists to cross the path of other traffic. Watch out as cyclists will approach the crossing faster than pedestrians.

10.21

*Mark **two** answers*

Who can use a toucan crossing?

- Trains
- Cyclists
- Buses
- Pedestrians
- Trams

⊙ **Cyclists**

⊙ **Pedestrians**

Toucan crossings are similar to pelican crossings but there is no flashing amber phase. Cyclists share the crossing with pedestrians and are allowed to cycle across when the green cycle symbol is shown.

At a pelican crossing, what does a flashing amber light mean?

⊙ You must not move off until the lights stop flashing

⊙ You must give way to pedestrians still on the crossing

⊙ You can move off, even if pedestrians are still on the crossing

⊙ You must stop because the lights are about to change to red

⊙ **You must give way to pedestrians still on the crossing**

If there is no-one on the crossing when the amber light is flashing, you may proceed over the crossing. You don't need to wait for the green light to show.

You are waiting at a pelican crossing. The red light changes to flashing amber. This means you must

⊙ wait for pedestrians on the crossing to clear

⊙ move off immediately without any hesitation

⊙ wait for the green light before moving off

⊙ get ready and go when the continuous amber light shows

⊙ **wait for pedestrians on the crossing to clear**

This light allows time for the pedestrians already on the crossing to get to the other side in their own time, without being rushed. Don't rev your engine or start to move off while they are still crossing.

10.24

*Mark **one** answer*

When can you park on the left opposite these road markings?

- If the line nearest to you is broken
- When there are no yellow lines
- To pick up or set down passengers
- During daylight hours only

⊙ **To pick up or set down passengers**

You MUST NOT park or stop on a road marked with double white lines (even where one of the lines is broken) except to pick up or set down passengers.

10.25

*Mark **one** answer*

You are intending to turn right at a crossroads. An oncoming driver is also turning right. It will normally be safer to

- keep the other vehicle to your RIGHT and turn behind it (offside to offside)
- keep the other vehicle to your LEFT and turn in front of it (nearside to nearside)
- carry on and turn at the next junction instead
- hold back and wait for the other driver to turn first

⊙ **keep the other vehicle to your RIGHT and turn behind it (offside to offside)**

At some junctions the layout may make it difficult to turn offside to offside. If this is the case, be prepared to pass nearside to nearside, but take extra care as your view ahead will be obscured by the vehicle turning in front of you.

10.26

*Mark **one** answer*

You are on a road that has no traffic signs. There are street lights. What is the speed limit?

- 20 mph
- 30 mph
- 40 mph
- 60 mph

⊙ **30 mph**

If you aren't sure of the speed limit a good indication is the presence of street lights. If there is street lighting the speed limit will be 30 mph unless otherwise indicated.

You are going along a street with parked vehicles on the left-hand side. For which THREE reasons should you keep your speed down?

- So that oncoming traffic can see you more clearly
- You may set off car alarms
- Vehicles may be pulling out
- Drivers' doors may open
- Children may run out from between the vehicles

- ⊙ **Vehicles may be pulling out**

- ⊙ **Drivers' doors may open**

- ⊙ **Children may run out from between the vehicles**

Travel slowly and carefully where there are parked vehicles in a built-up area.

Beware of

- vehicles pulling out, especially bicycles and other motorcycles
- pedestrians, especially children, who may run out from between cars
- drivers opening their doors.

You meet an obstruction on your side of the road. You should

- carry on, you have priority
- give way to oncoming traffic
- wave oncoming vehicles through
- accelerate to get past first

- ⊙ **give way to oncoming traffic**

Take care if you have to pass a parked vehicle on your side of the road. Give way to oncoming traffic if there isn't enough room for you both to continue safely.

You are on a two-lane dual carriageway. For which TWO of the following would you use the right-hand lane?

- Turning right
- Normal progress
- Staying at the minimum allowed speed
- Constant high speed
- Overtaking slower traffic
- Mending punctures

- ⊙ **Turning right**

- ⊙ **Overtaking slower traffic**

Normally you should travel in the left-hand lane and only use the right-hand lane for overtaking or turning right. Move back into the left lane as soon as it's safe but don't cut in across the path of the vehicle you've just passed.

10.30 Mark **one** answer

Who has priority at an unmarked crossroads?

- The larger vehicle
- No one has priority
- The faster vehicle
- The smaller vehicle

⊙ **No one has priority**

Practise good observation in all directions before you emerge or make a turn. Proceed only when you're sure it's safe to do so.

10.31 NI EXEMPT Mark **one** answer

What is the nearest you may park to a junction?

- 10 metres (32 feet)
- 12 metres (39 feet)
- 15 metres (49 feet)
- 20 metres (66 feet)

⊙ **10 metres (32 feet)**

Don't park within 10 metres (32 feet) of a junction (unless in an authorised parking place). This is to allow drivers emerging from, or turning into, the junction a clear view of the road they are joining. It also allows them to see hazards such as pedestrians or cyclists at the junction.

10.32 NI EXEMPT Mark **three** answers

In which THREE places must you NOT park?

- Near the brow of a hill
- At or near a bus stop
- Where there is no pavement
- Within 10 metres (32 feet) of a junction
- On a 40 mph road

⊙ **Near the brow of a hill**

⊙ **At or near a bus stop**

⊙ **Within 10 metres (32 feet) of a junction**

Other traffic will have to pull out to pass you. They may have to use the other side of the road, and if you park near the brow of a hill, they may not be able to see oncoming traffic. It's important not to park at or near a bus stop as this could inconvenience passengers, and may put them at risk as they get on or off the bus. Parking near a junction could restrict the view for emerging vehicles.

You are waiting at a level crossing. A train has passed but the lights keep flashing. You must

- ⊙ carry on waiting
- ⊙ phone the signal operator
- ⊙ edge over the stop line and look for trains
- ⊙ park and investigate

⊙ **carry on waiting**

If the lights at a level crossing continue to flash after a train has passed, you should still wait as there might be another train coming. Time seems to pass slowly when you're held up in a queue. Be patient and wait until the lights stop flashing.

At a crossroads there are no signs or road markings. Two vehicles approach. Which has priority?

- ⊙ Neither of the vehicles
- ⊙ The vehicle travelling the fastest
- ⊙ Oncoming vehicles turning right
- ⊙ Vehicles approaching from the right

⊙ **Neither of the vehicles**

At a crossroads where there are no 'give way' signs or road markings be very careful. No vehicle has priority, even if the sizes of the roads are different.

What does this sign tell you?

- ⊙ That it is a no-through road
- ⊙ End of traffic calming zone
- ⊙ Free parking zone ends
- ⊙ No waiting zone ends

⊙ **No waiting zone ends**

The blue and red circular sign on its own means that waiting restrictions are in force. This sign shows that you are leaving the controlled zone and waiting restrictions no longer apply.

10.36
*Mark **one** answer*

You are entering an area of roadworks. There is a temporary speed limit displayed. You should

- not exceed the speed limit
- obey the limit only during rush hour
- ignore the displayed limit
- obey the limit except at night

○ **not exceed the speed limit**

Where there are extra hazards such as roadworks, it's often necessary to slow traffic down by imposing a temporary speed limit. These speed limits aren't advisory, they must be obeyed.

10.37
*Mark **two** answers*

In which TWO places should you NOT park?

- Near a school entrance
- Near a police station
- In a side road
- At a bus stop
- In a one-way street

○ **Near a school entrance**

○ **At a bus stop**

It may be tempting to park where you shouldn't while you run a quick errand. Careless parking is a selfish act and could endanger other road users.

10.38
*Mark **one** answer*

You are travelling on a well-lit road at night in a built-up area. By using dipped headlights you will be able to

- see further along the road
- go at a much faster speed
- switch to main beam quickly
- be easily seen by others

○ **be easily seen by others**

You may be difficult to see when you're travelling at night, even on a well lit road. If you use dipped headlights rather than sidelights other road users will see you more easily.

The dual carriageway you are turning right onto has a very narrow central reservation. What should you do?

- ◉ Proceed to the central reservation and wait
- ◉ Wait until the road is clear in both directions
- ◉ Stop in the first lane so that other vehicles give way
- ◉ Emerge slightly to show your intentions

◉ **Wait until the road is clear in both directions**

When the central reservation is narrow you should treat a dual carriageway as one road. Wait until the road is clear in both directions before emerging to turn right. If you try to treat it as two separate roads and wait in the middle, you are likely to cause an obstruction and possibly a collision.

What is the national speed limit on a single carriageway road for cars and motorcycles?

- ◉ 30 mph
- ◉ 50 mph
- ◉ 60 mph
- ◉ 70 mph

◉ **60 mph**

Exceeding the speed limit is dangerous and can result in you receiving penalty points on your licence. It isn't worth it. You should know the speed limit for the road that you're on by observing the road signs. Different speed limits apply if you are towing a trailer.

You park at night on a road with a 40 mph speed limit. You should park

- ◉ facing the traffic
- ◉ with parking lights on
- ◉ with dipped headlights on
- ◉ near a street light

◉ **with parking lights on**

You MUST use parking lights when parking at night on a road or lay-by with a speed limit greater than 30 mph. You MUST also park in the direction of the traffic flow and not close to a junction.

10.42
*Mark **one** answer*

You will see these red and white markers when approaching

- ⊙ the end of a motorway
- ⊙ a concealed level crossing
- ⊙ a concealed speed limit sign
- ⊙ the end of a dual carriageway

⊙ **a concealed level crossing**

If there is a bend just before the level crossing you may not be able to see the level crossing barriers or waiting traffic. These signs give you an early warning that you may find these hazards just around the bend.

10.43   NI EXEMPT   *Mark **one** answer*

You are travelling on a motorway. You MUST stop when signalled to do so by which of these?

- ⊙ Flashing amber lights above your lane
- ⊙ A Highways Agency Traffic Officer
- ⊙ Pedestrians on the hard shoulder
- ⊙ A driver who has broken down

⊙ **A Highways Agency Traffic Officer**

You will find Highways Agency Traffic Officers on many of Britain's motorways. They work in partnership with the police, helping to keep traffic moving and to make your journey as safe as possible. It is an offence not to comply with the directions given by a Traffic Officer.

10.44
*Mark **one** answer*

At a busy unmarked crossroads, which of the following has priority?

- ⊙ Vehicles going straight ahead
- ⊙ Vehicles turning right
- ⊙ None of the vehicles
- ⊙ The vehicles that arrived first

⊙ **None of the vehicles**

If there are no road signs or markings do not assume that you have priority. Remember that other drivers may assume they have the right to go. No type of vehicle has priority but it's courteous to give way to large vehicles. Also look out in particular for cyclists and motorcyclists.

You are going straight ahead at a roundabout. How should you signal?

- ⊙ Signal right on the approach and then left to leave the roundabout
- ⊙ Signal left after you leave the roundabout and enter the new road
- ⊙ Signal right on the approach to the roundabout and keep the signal on
- ⊙ Signal left just after you pass the exit before the one you will take

⊙ **Signal left just after you pass the exit before the one you will take**

To go straight ahead at a roundabout you should normally approach in the left-hand lane. You will not normally need to signal, but look out for the road markings. At some roundabouts the left lane on approach is marked as 'left turn only', so make sure you use the correct lane to go ahead. Signal before you leave as other road users need to know your intentions.

You may drive over a footpath

- ⊙ to overtake slow-moving traffic
- ⊙ when the pavement is very wide
- ⊙ if no pedestrians are near
- ⊙ to get into a property

⊙ **to get into a property**

It is against the law to drive on or over a footpath, except to gain access to a property. If you need to cross a pavement, watch for pedestrians in both directions.

A single carriageway road has this sign. What is the maximum permitted speed for a car towing a trailer?

- ⊙ 30 mph
- ⊙ 40 mph
- ⊙ 50 mph
- ⊙ 60 mph

⊙ **50 mph**

When towing trailers, speed limits are also lower on dual carriageways and motorways. These speed limits apply to vehicles pulling all sorts of trailers including caravans, horse boxes etc.

10.48   *Mark **one** answer*

You are towing a small caravan on a dual carriageway. You must not exceed

- 50 mph
- 40 mph
- 70 mph
- 60 mph

⊙ **60 mph**

The speed limit is reduced for vehicles towing caravans and trailers, to lessen the risk of the outfit becoming unstable. Due to the increased weight and size of the vehicle and caravan combination, you should plan well ahead. Be extra-careful in windy weather, as strong winds could cause a caravan or large trailer to snake from side to side.

10.49   *Mark **one** answer*

You want to park and you see this sign. On the days and times shown you should

- park in a bay and not pay
- park on yellow lines and pay
- park on yellow lines and not pay
- park in a bay and pay

⊙ **park in a bay and pay**

Parking restrictions apply in a variety of places and situations. Make sure you know the rules and understand where and when restrictions apply. Controlled parking areas will be indicated by signs and road markings. Parking in the wrong place could cause an obstruction and danger to other traffic. It can also result in a fine.

10.50

You are driving along a road that has a cycle lane. The lane is marked by a solid white line. This means that during its period of operation

- ⊙ the lane may be used for parking your car
- ⊙ you may drive in that lane at any time
- ⊙ the lane may be used when necessary
- ⊙ you must not drive in that lane

⊙ **you must not drive in that lane**

Leave the lane free for cyclists. At other times, when the lane is not in operation, you should still be aware that there may be cyclists about. Give them room and don't pass too closely.

10.51

A cycle lane is marked by a solid white line. You must not drive or park in it

- ⊙ at any time
- ⊙ during the rush hour
- ⊙ if a cyclist is using it
- ⊙ during its period of operation

⊙ **during its period of operation**

The cycle lanes are there for a reason. Keep them free and allow cyclists to use them.

It is illegal to drive or park in a cycle lane, marked by a solid white line, during its hours of operation. Parking in a cycle lane will obstruct cyclists and they may move into the path of traffic on the main carriageway as they ride around the obstruction. This could be hazardous for both the cyclist and other road users.

10.52

While driving, you intend to turn left into a minor road. On the approach you should

- ⊙ keep just left of the middle of the road
- ⊙ keep in the middle of the road
- ⊙ swing out wide just before turning
- ⊙ keep well to the left of the road

⊙ **keep well to the left of the road**

Don't swing out into the centre of the road in order to make the turn. This could endanger oncoming traffic and may cause other road users to misunderstand your intentions.

10.53

You are waiting at a level crossing. The red warning lights continue to flash after a train has passed by. What should you do?

- Get out and investigate
- Telephone the signal operator
- Continue to wait
- Drive across carefully

⊙ **Continue to wait**

At a level crossing flashing red lights mean you must stop. If the train passes but the lights keep flashing, wait. There may be another train coming.

10.54

You are driving over a level crossing. The warning lights come on and a bell rings. What should you do?

- Get everyone out of the vehicle immediately
- Stop and reverse back to clear the crossing
- Keep going and clear the crossing
- Stop immediately and use your hazard warning lights

⊙ **Keep going and clear the crossing**

Keep going, don't stop on the crossing. If the amber warning lights come on as you're approaching the crossing, you MUST stop unless it is unsafe to do so. Red flashing lights together with an audible signal mean you MUST stop.

10.55 *Mark **one** answer*

You are on a busy main road and find that you are travelling in the wrong direction. What should you do?

- Turn into a side road on the right and reverse into the main road
- Make a U-turn in the main road
- Make a 'three-point' turn in the main road
- Turn round in a side road

⊙ **Turn round in a side road**

Don't turn round in a busy street or reverse from a side road into a main road. Find a quiet side road and choose a place where you won't obstruct an entrance or exit. Look out for pedestrians and cyclists as well as other traffic.

10.56 *Mark **one** answer*

You may remove your seat belt when carrying out a manoeuvre that involves

- reversing
- a hill start
- an emergency stop
- driving slowly

⊙ **reversing**

Don't forget to put your seat belt back on when you've finished reversing.

10.57 *Mark **one** answer*

You must not reverse

- for longer than necessary
- for more than a car's length
- into a side road
- in a built-up area

⊙ **for longer than necessary**

You may decide to turn your vehicle around by reversing into an opening or side road. When you reverse, always look behind and all around and watch for pedestrians. Don't reverse from a side road into a main road. You MUST NOT reverse further than is necessary.

10.58

*Mark **one** answer*

When you are NOT sure that it is safe to reverse your vehicle you should

- ⊙ use your horn
- ⊙ rev your engine
- ⊙ get out and check
- ⊙ reverse slowly

⊙ **get out and check**

If you can't see all around your vehicle get out and have a look. You could also ask someone reliable outside the vehicle to guide you. A small child could easily be hidden directly behind you. Don't take risks.

10.59

*Mark **one** answer*

When may you reverse from a side road into a main road?

- ⊙ Only if both roads are clear of traffic
- ⊙ Not at any time
- ⊙ At any time
- ⊙ Only if the main road is clear of traffic

⊙ **Not at any time**

Don't reverse into a main road from a side road. The main road is likely to be busy and the traffic on it moving quickly. Cut down the risks by reversing into a quiet side road.

10.60

*Mark **one** answer*

You want to turn right at a box junction. There is oncoming traffic. You should

- ⊙ wait in the box junction if your exit is clear
- ⊙ wait before the junction until it is clear of all traffic
- ⊙ drive on, you cannot turn right at a box junction
- ⊙ drive slowly into the box junction when signalled by oncoming traffic

⊙ **wait in the box junction if your exit is clear**

You can move into the box junction to wait as long as your exit is clear. The oncoming traffic will stop when the traffic lights change, allowing you to proceed.

You are reversing your vehicle into a side road. When would the greatest hazard to passing traffic occur?

⊙ After you've completed the manoeuvre

⊙ Just before you actually begin to manoeuvre

⊙ After you've entered the side road

⊙ When the front of your vehicle swings out

⊙ **When the front of your vehicle swings out**

Always check road and traffic conditions in all directions before reversing into a side road. Keep a good look-out throughout the manoeuvre. Act on what you see and wait if necessary.

Where is the safest place to park your vehicle at night?

⊙ In a garage

⊙ On a busy road

⊙ In a quiet car park

⊙ Near a red route

⊙ **In a garage**

If you have a garage, use it. Your vehicle is less likely to be a victim of car crime if it's in a garage. Also in winter the windows will be free from ice and snow.

You are driving on an urban clearway. You may stop only to

⊙ set down and pick up passengers

⊙ use a mobile telephone

⊙ ask for directions

⊙ load or unload goods

⊙ **set down and pick up passengers**

Urban clearways may be in built-up areas and their times of operation will be clearly signed. You should stop only for as long as is reasonable to pick up or set down passengers. You should ensure that you are not causing an obstruction for other traffic.

10.64

*Mark **one** answer*

You are looking for somewhere to park your vehicle. The area is full EXCEPT for spaces marked 'disabled use'. You can

- ◉ use these spaces when elsewhere is full
- ◉ park if you stay with your vehicle
- ◉ use these spaces, disabled or not
- ◉ not park there unless permitted

◉ **not park there unless permitted**

It is illegal to park in a parking space reserved for disabled users.

These spaces are provided for people with limited mobility, who may need extra space to get in and out of their vehicle.

10.65

*Mark **one** answer*

Your vehicle is parked on the road at night. When must you use sidelights?

- ◉ Where there are continuous white lines in the middle of the road
- ◉ Where the speed limit exceeds 30 mph
- ◉ Where you are facing oncoming traffic
- ◉ Where you are near a bus stop

◉ **Where the speed limit exceeds 30 mph**

When parking at night, park in the direction of the traffic. This will enable other road users to see the reflectors on the rear of your vehicle. You MUST use your sidelights when parking on a road, or in a lay-by on a road, where the speed limit is over 30 mph.

10.66

*Mark **one** answer*

You are on a road that is only wide enough for one vehicle. There is a car coming towards you. What should you do?

- ◉ Pull into a passing place on your right
- ◉ Force the other driver to reverse
- ◉ Pull into a passing place if your vehicle is wider
- ◉ Pull into a passing place on your left

◉ **Pull into a passing place on your left**

Pull into the nearest passing place on the left if you meet another vehicle in a narrow road. If the nearest passing place is on the right, wait opposite it.

You are driving at night with full beam headlights on. A vehicle is overtaking you. You should dip your lights

- some time after the vehicle has passed you
- before the vehicle starts to pass you
- only if the other driver dips their headlights
- as soon as the vehicle passes you

⊙ **as soon as the vehicle passes you**

On full beam your lights could dazzle the driver in front. Make sure that your light beam falls short of the vehicle in front.

When may you drive a motor car in this bus lane?

- Outside its hours of operation
- To get to the front of a traffic queue
- You may not use it at any time
- To overtake slow-moving traffic

⊙ **Outside its hours of operation**

Some bus lanes only operate during peak hours and other vehicles may use them outside these hours. Make sure you check the sign for the hours of operation before driving in a bus lane.

Signals are normally given by direction indicators and

- brake lights
- side lights
- fog lights
- interior lights

⊙ **brake lights**

Your brake lights will give an indication to traffic behind that you're slowing down. Good anticipation will allow you time to check your mirrors before slowing.

10.70
*Mark **one** answer*

You are parked in a busy high street. What is the safest way to turn your vehicle around so you can go the opposite way?

- Find a quiet side road to turn round in
- Drive into a side road and reverse into the main road
- Get someone to stop the traffic
- Do a U-turn

Find a quiet side road to turn round in

Make sure you carry out the manoeuvre without causing a hazard to other vehicles. Choose a place to turn which is safe and convenient for you and for other road users.

10.71
*Mark **one** answer*

To help keep your vehicle secure at night, where should you park?

- Near a police station
- In a quiet road
- On a red route
- In a well-lit area

In a well-lit area

Whenever possible park in an area which will be well lit at night.

10.72
*Mark **one** answer*

You are in the right-hand lane of a dual carriageway. You see signs showing that the right-hand lane is closed 800 yards ahead. You should

- keep in that lane until you reach the queue
- move to the left immediately
- wait and see which lane is moving faster
- move to the left in good time

move to the left in good time

Keep a look-out for traffic signs. If you're directed to change lanes, do so in good time. Don't

- push your way into traffic in another lane
- leave changing lanes until the last moment.

You are driving on a road that has a cycle lane. The lane is marked by a broken white line. This means that

- ⊙ you should not drive in the lane unless it is unavoidable
- ⊙ you should not park in the lane unless it is unavoidable
- ⊙ cyclists can travel in both directions in that lane
- ⊙ the lane must be used by motorcyclists in heavy traffic

⊙ **you should not drive in the lane unless it is unavoidable**

⊙ **you should not park in the lane unless it is unavoidable**

Where signs or road markings show lanes are for cyclists only, leave them free. Do not drive or park in a cycle lane unless it is unavoidable.

What MUST you have to park in a disabled space?

- ⊙ A Blue Badge
- ⊙ A wheelchair
- ⊙ An advanced driver certificate
- ⊙ An adapted vehicle

⊙ **A Blue Badge**

Don't park in a space reserved for disabled people unless you or your passenger are a disabled badge holder. The badge must be displayed in your vehicle in the bottom left-hand corner of the windscreen.

10.75
*Mark **three** answers*

On which THREE occasions MUST you stop your vehicle?

- When in an incident where damage or injury is caused
- At a red traffic light
- When signalled to do so by a police or traffic officer
- At a junction with double broken white lines
- At a pelican crossing when the amber light is flashing and no pedestrians are crossing

- **When in an incident where damage or injury is caused**

- **At a red traffic light**

- **When signalled to do so by a police or traffic officer**

Situations when you MUST stop include the following. When signalled to do so by a police or traffic officer, traffic warden, school crossing patrol or red traffic light. You must also stop if you are involved in an incident which causes damage or injury to any other person, vehicle, animal or property.

section **eleven**

ROAD AND TRAFFIC SIGNS

This section covers
- Road signs
- Speed limits
- Road markings
- Regulations

11.1
*Mark **one** answer*

You MUST obey signs giving orders. These signs are mostly in

- green rectangles
- red triangles
- blue rectangles
- red circles

⊙ **red circles**

There are three basic types of traffic sign, those that warn, inform or give orders. Generally, triangular signs warn, rectangular ones give information or directions, and circular signs usually give orders. An exception is the eight-sided 'STOP' sign.

11.2
*Mark **one** answer*

Traffic signs giving orders are generally which shape?

Road signs in the shape of a circle give orders. Those with a red circle are mostly prohibitive. The 'stop' sign is octagonal to give it greater prominence. Signs giving orders MUST always be obeyed.

11.3
*Mark **one** answer*

Which type of sign tells you NOT to do something?

 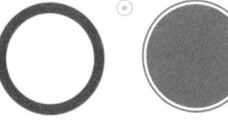

Signs in the shape of a circle give orders. A sign with a red circle means that you aren't allowed to do something. Study Know Your Traffic Signs to ensure that you understand what the different traffic signs mean.

What does this sign mean?

⊙ Maximum speed limit with traffic calming

⊙ Minimum speed limit with traffic calming

⊙ '20 cars only' parking zone

⊙ Only 20 cars allowed at any one time

⊙ **Maximum speed limit with traffic calming**

If you're in places where there are likely to be pedestrians such as outside schools, near parks, residential areas and shopping areas, you should be extra-cautious and keep your speed down.

Many local authorities have taken measures to slow traffic down by creating traffic calming measures such as speed humps. They are there for a reason; slow down.

Which sign means no motor vehicles are allowed?

⊙

You would generally see this sign at the approach to a pedestrian-only zone.

11.6 *Mark **one** answer*

Which of these signs means no motor vehicles?

If you are driving a motor vehicle or riding a motorcycle you MUST NOT travel past this sign. This area has been designated for use by pedestrians.

11.7 *Mark **one** answer*

What does this sign mean?

⊙ New speed limit 20 mph

⊙ No vehicles over 30 tonnes

⊙ Minimum speed limit 30 mph

⊙ End of 20 mph zone

⊙ **End of 20 mph zone**

Where you see this sign the 20 mph restriction ends. Check all around for possible hazards and only increase your speed if it's safe to do so.

*Mark **one** answer*

What does this sign mean?

- No overtaking
- No motor vehicles
- Clearway (no stopping)
- Cars and motorcycles only

⊙ **No motor vehicles**

A sign will indicate which types of vehicles are prohibited from certain roads. Make sure that you know which signs apply to the vehicle you're using.

*Mark **one** answer*

What does this sign mean?

- No parking
- No road markings
- No through road
- No entry

⊙ **No entry**

'No entry' signs are used in places such as one-way streets to prevent vehicles driving against the traffic. To ignore one would be dangerous, both for yourself and other road users, as well as being against the law.

11.10 — Mark **one** answer

What does this sign mean?

- Bend to the right
- Road on the right closed
- No traffic from the right
- No right turn

⊙ **No right turn**

The 'no right turn' sign may be used to warn road users that there is a 'no entry' prohibition on a road to the right ahead.

11.11 — Mark **one** answer

Which sign means 'no entry'?

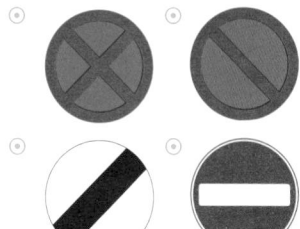

Look out for traffic signs. Disobeying or not seeing a sign could be dangerous. It may also be an offence for which you could be prosecuted.

11.12 — Mark **one** answer

What does this sign mean?

- Route for trams only
- Route for buses only
- Parking for buses only
- Parking for trams only

⊙ **Route for trams only**

Avoid blocking tram routes. Trams are fixed on their route and can't manoeuvre around other vehicles and pedestrians. Modern trams travel quickly and are quiet so you might not hear them approaching.

Which type of vehicle does this sign apply to?

- ⊙ Wide vehicles
- ⊙ Long vehicles
- ⊙ High vehicles
- ⊙ Heavy vehicles

⊙ **High vehicles**

The triangular shapes above and below the dimensions indicate a height restriction that applies to the road ahead.

Which sign means NO motor vehicles allowed?

This sign is used to enable pedestrians to walk free from traffic. It's often found in shopping areas.

11.15
*Mark **one** answer*

What does this sign mean?

⊙ **No overtaking**

Road signs that prohibit overtaking are placed in locations where passing the vehicle in front is dangerous. If you see this sign don't attempt to overtake. The sign is there for a reason and you must obey it.

- ◎ You have priority
- ◎ No motor vehicles
- ◎ Two-way traffic
- ◎ No overtaking

11.16
*Mark **one** answer*

What does this sign mean?

⊙ **Do not overtake**

If you're behind a slow-moving vehicle be patient. Wait until the restriction no longer applies and you can overtake safely.

- ◎ Keep in one lane
- ◎ Give way to oncoming traffic
- ◎ Do not overtake
- ◎ Form two lanes

11.17
*Mark **one** answer*

Which sign means no overtaking?

◎  ◎

  ◎

⊙

This sign indicates that overtaking here is not allowed and you could face prosecution if you ignore this prohibition.

What does this sign mean?

⊙ **Waiting restrictions apply**

There will be a plate or additional sign to tell you when the restrictions apply.

- ⊙ Waiting restrictions apply
- ⊙ Waiting permitted
- ⊙ National speed limit applies
- ⊙ Clearway (no stopping)

What does this sign mean?

⊙ **End of restricted parking area**

Even though you have left the restricted area, make sure that you park where you won't endanger other road users or cause an obstruction.

- ⊙ End of restricted speed area
- ⊙ End of restricted parking area
- ⊙ End of clearway
- ⊙ End of cycle route

11.20
*Mark **one** answer*

Which sign means 'no stopping'?

Stopping where this clearway restriction applies is likely to cause congestion. Allow the traffic to flow by obeying the signs.

11.21
*Mark **one** answer*

What does this sign mean?

- ⊙ Roundabout
- ⊙ Crossroads
- ⊙ No stopping
- ⊙ No entry

⊙ **No stopping**

This sign is in place to ensure a clear route for traffic. Don't stop except in an emergency.

11.22
*Mark **one** answer*

You see this sign ahead. It means

- ⊙ national speed limit applies
- ⊙ waiting restrictions apply
- ⊙ no stopping
- ⊙ no entry

⊙ **no stopping**

Clearways are stretches of road where you aren't allowed to stop unless in an emergency. You'll see this sign. Stopping where these restrictions apply may be dangerous and likely to cause an obstruction. Restrictions might apply for several miles and this may be indicated on the sign.

What does this sign mean?

- ⊙ Distance to parking place ahead
- ⊙ Distance to public telephone ahead
- ⊙ Distance to public house ahead
- ⊙ Distance to passing place ahead

⊙ **Distance to parking place ahead**

If you intend to stop and rest, this sign allows you time to reduce speed and pull over safely.

What does this sign mean?

- ⊙ Vehicles may not park on the verge or footway
- ⊙ Vehicles may park on the left-hand side of the road only
- ⊙ Vehicles may park fully on the verge or footway
- ⊙ Vehicles may park on the right-hand side of the road only

⊙ **Vehicles may park fully on the verge or footway**

In order to keep roads free from parked cars, there are some areas where you're allowed to park on the verge. Only do this where you see the sign. Parking on verges or footways anywhere else could lead to a fine.

11.25   *Mark **one** answer*

What does this traffic sign mean?

- No overtaking allowed
- Give priority to oncoming traffic
- Two way traffic
- One-way traffic only

⊙ **Give priority to oncoming traffic**

Priority signs are normally shown where the road is narrow and there isn't enough room for two vehicles to pass. These can be at narrow bridges, road works and where there's a width restriction.

Make sure that you know who has priority, don't force your way through. Show courtesy and consideration to other road users.

11.26   *Mark **one** answer*

What is the meaning of this traffic sign?

- End of two-way road
- Give priority to vehicles coming towards you
- You have priority over vehicles coming towards you
- Bus lane ahead

⊙ **You have priority over vehicles coming towards you**

Don't force your way through. Show courtesy and consideration to other road users. Although you have priority, make sure oncoming traffic is going to give way before you continue.

What does this sign mean?

- No overtaking
- You are entering a one-way street
- Two-way traffic ahead
- You have priority over vehicles from the opposite direction

- **You have priority over vehicles from the opposite direction**

Don't force your way through if oncoming vehicles fail to give way. If necessary, slow down and give way to avoid confrontation or a collision.

What shape is a STOP sign at a junction?

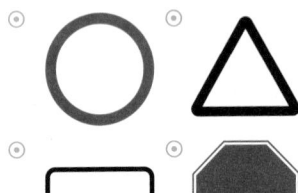

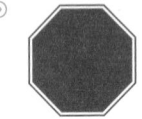

To make it easy to recognise, the 'stop' sign is the only sign of this shape. You must stop and take effective observation before proceeding.

11.29
*Mark **one** answer*

At a junction you see this sign partly covered by snow. What does it mean?

- ⊙ Cross roads
- ⊙ Give way
- ⊙ Stop
- ⊙ Turn right

⊙ **Stop**

The STOP sign is the only road sign that is octagonal. This is so that it can be recognised and obeyed even if it is obscured, for example by snow.

11.30
*Mark **one** answer*

What does this sign mean?

- ⊙ Service area 30 miles ahead
- ⊙ Maximum speed 30 mph
- ⊙ Minimum speed 30 mph
- ⊙ Lay-by 30 miles ahead

⊙ **Minimum speed 30 mph**

This sign is shown where slow-moving vehicles would impede the flow of traffic, for example in tunnels. However, if you need to slow down or even stop to avoid an incident or potential collision, you should do so.

*Mark **one** answer*

What does this sign mean?

- ⊙ Give way to oncoming vehicles
- ⊙ Approaching traffic passes you on both sides
- ⊙ Turn off at the next available junction
- ⊙ Pass either side to get to the same destination

⊙ **Pass either side to get to the same destination**

These signs are often seen in one-way streets that have more than one lane. When you see this sign, use the route that's the most convenient and doesn't require a late change of direction.

*Mark **one** answer*

What does this sign mean?

- ⊙ Route for trams
- ⊙ Give way to trams
- ⊙ Route for buses
- ⊙ Give way to buses

⊙ **Route for trams**

Take extra care when you encounter trams. Look out for road markings and signs that alert you to them. Modern trams are very quiet and you may not hear them approaching.

11.33   *Mark **one** answer*

What does a circular traffic sign with a blue background do?

- ⊙ Give warning of a motorway ahead
- ⊙ Give directions to a car park
- ⊙ Give motorway information
- ⊙ Give an instruction

⊙ **Give an instruction**

Signs with blue circles give a positive instruction. These are often found in urban areas and include signs for mini-roundabouts and directional arrows.

11.34   *Mark **one** answer*

Where would you see a contraflow bus and cycle lane?

- ⊙ On a dual carriageway
- ⊙ On a roundabout
- ⊙ On an urban motorway
- ⊙ On a one-way street

⊙ **On a one-way street**

In a contraflow lane the traffic permitted to use it travels in the opposite direction to traffic in the other lanes on the road.

11.35   *Mark **one** answer*

What does this sign mean?

- ⊙ Bus station on the right
- ⊙ Contraflow bus lane
- ⊙ With-flow bus lane
- ⊙ Give way to buses

⊙ **Contraflow bus lane**

There will also be markings on the road surface to indicate the bus lane. You must not use this lane for parking or overtaking.

What does a sign with a brown background show?

- ⊙ Tourist directions
- ⊙ Primary roads
- ⊙ Motorway routes
- ⊙ Minor routes

⊙ **Tourist directions**

Signs with a brown background give directions to places of interest. They will often be seen on a motorway directing you along the easiest route to the attraction.

This sign means

- ⊙ tourist attraction
- ⊙ beware of trains
- ⊙ level crossing
- ⊙ beware of trams

⊙ **tourist attraction**

These signs indicate places of interest and are designed to guide you by the easiest route. They are particularly useful if you are unfamiliar with the area.

What are triangular signs for?

- ⊙ To give warnings
- ⊙ To give information
- ⊙ To give orders
- ⊙ To give directions

⊙ **To give warnings**

This type of sign will warn you of hazards ahead.

Make sure you look at each sign that you pass on the road, so that you do not miss any vital instructions or information.

11.39
*Mark **one** answer*

What does this sign mean?

- ◉ Turn left ahead
- ◉ T-junction
- ◉ No through road
- ◉ Give way

◉ **T-junction**

This type of sign will warn you of hazards ahead. Make sure you look at each sign and road markings that you pass, so that you do not miss any vital instructions or information. This particular sign shows there is a T-junction with priority over vehicles from the right.

11.40
*Mark **one** answer*

What does this sign mean?

- ◉ Multi-exit roundabout
- ◉ Risk of ice
- ◉ Six roads converge
- ◉ Place of historical interest

◉ **Risk of ice**

It will take up to ten times longer to stop when it's icy. Where there is a risk of icy conditions you need to be aware of this and take extra care. If you think the road may be icy, don't brake or steer harshly as your tyres could lose their grip on the road.

What does this sign mean?

- ⊙ Crossroads
- ⊙ Level crossing with gate
- ⊙ Level crossing without gate
- ⊙ Ahead only

⊙ **Crossroads**

The priority through the junction is shown by the broader line. You need to be aware of the hazard posed by traffic crossing or pulling out onto a major road.

What does this sign mean?

- ⊙ Ring road
- ⊙ Mini-roundabout
- ⊙ No vehicles
- ⊙ Roundabout

⊙ **Roundabout**

As you approach a roundabout look well ahead and check all signs. Decide which exit you wish to take and move into the correct position as you approach the roundabout, signalling as required.

11.43 *Mark **four** answers*

Which FOUR of these would be indicated by a triangular road sign?

- Road narrows
- Ahead only
- Low bridge
- Minimum speed
- Children crossing
- T-junction

- ⊙ **Road narrows**
- ⊙ **Low bridge**
- ⊙ **Children crossing**
- ⊙ **T-junction**

Warning signs are there to make you aware of potential hazards on the road ahead. Act on the signs so you are prepared and can take whatever action is necessary.

11.44 *Mark **one** answer*

What does this sign mean?

- Cyclists must dismount
- Cycles are not allowed
- Cycle route ahead
- Cycle in single file

- ⊙ **Cycle route ahead**

Where there's a cycle route ahead, a sign will show a bicycle in a red warning triangle. Watch out for children on bicycles and cyclists rejoining the main road.

Which sign means that pedestrians may be walking along the road?

When you pass pedestrians in the road, leave plenty of room. You might have to use the right-hand side of the road, so look well ahead, as well as in your mirrors, before pulling out. Take great care if there is a bend in the road obscuring your view ahead.

Which of these signs means there is a double bend ahead?

Triangular signs give you a warning of hazards ahead. They are there to give you time to prepare for the hazard, for example by adjusting your speed.

What does this sign mean?

⊙ **Give way to trams**

Obey the 'give way' signs. Trams are unable to steer around you if you misjudge when it is safe to enter the junction.

- ⊙ Wait at the barriers
- ⊙ Wait at the crossroads
- ⊙ Give way to trams
- ⊙ Give way to farm vehicles

11.48   *Mark **one** answer*

What does this sign mean?

⊙ Humpback bridge
⊙ Humps in the road
⊙ Entrance to tunnel
⊙ Soft verges

⊙ **Humps in the road**

These have been put in place to slow the traffic down. They're usually found in residential areas. Slow down to an appropriate speed.

11.49   *Mark **one** answer*

Which of these signs means the end of a dual carriageway?

⊙

If you're overtaking make sure you move back safely into the left-hand lane before you reach the end of the dual carriageway.

11.50   *Mark **one** answer*

What does this sign mean?

⊙ End of dual carriageway
⊙ Tall bridge
⊙ Road narrows
⊙ End of narrow bridge

⊙ **End of dual carriageway**

Don't leave moving into the left-hand lane until the last moment. Plan ahead and don't rely on other traffic letting you in.

What does this sign mean?

⊙ Crosswinds

⊙ Road noise

⊙ Airport

⊙ Adverse camber

⊙ **Crosswinds**

A warning sign with a picture of a windsock will indicate there may be strong crosswinds. This sign is often found on exposed roads.

What does this traffic sign mean?

⊙ Slippery road ahead

⊙ Tyres liable to punctures ahead

⊙ Danger ahead

⊙ Service area ahead

⊙ **Danger ahead**

This sign is there to alert you to the likelihood of danger ahead. It may be accompanied by a plate indicating the type of hazard. Be ready to reduce your speed and take avoiding action.

11.53
*Mark **one** answer*

You are about to overtake when you see this sign. You should

Hidden dip

- ⊙ overtake the other driver as quickly as possible
- ⊙ move to the right to get a better view
- ⊙ switch your headlights on before overtaking
- ⊙ hold back until you can see clearly ahead

⊙ **hold back until you can see clearly ahead**

You won't be able to see any hazards that might be hidden in the dip. As well as oncoming traffic the dip may conceal

- cyclists
- horse riders
- parked vehicles
- pedestrians

in the road.

11.54
*Mark **one** answer*

What does this sign mean?

- ⊙ Level crossing with gate or barrier
- ⊙ Gated road ahead
- ⊙ Level crossing without gate or barrier
- ⊙ Cattle grid ahead

⊙ **Level crossing with gate or barrier**

Some crossings have gates but no attendant or signals. You should stop, look both ways, listen and make sure that there is no train approaching. If there is a telephone, contact the signal operator to make sure that it's safe to cross.

*Mark **one** answer*

What does this sign mean?

- No trams ahead
- Oncoming trams
- Trams crossing ahead
- Trams only

⊙ **Trams crossing ahead**

This sign warns you to beware of trams. If you don't usually drive in a town where there are trams, remember to look out for them at junctions and look for tram rails, signs and signals.

*Mark **one** answer*

What does this sign mean?

- Adverse camber
- Steep hill downwards
- Uneven road
- Steep hill upwards

⊙ **Steep hill downwards**

This sign will give you an early warning that the road ahead will slope downhill. Prepare to alter your speed and gear. Looking at the sign from left to right will show you whether the road slopes uphill or downhill.

11.57

*Mark **one** answer*

What does this sign mean?

- ⊙ Uneven road surface
- ⊙ Bridge over the road
- ⊙ Road ahead ends
- ⊙ Water across the road

⊙ **Water across the road**

This sign is found where a shallow stream crosses the road. Heavy rainfall could increase the flow of water. If the water looks too deep or the stream has spread over a large distance, stop and find another route.

11.58

*Mark **one** answer*

What does this sign mean?

- ⊙ Turn left for parking area
- ⊙ No through road on the left
- ⊙ No entry for traffic turning left
- ⊙ Turn left for ferry terminal

⊙ **No through road on the left**

If you intend to take a left turn, this sign shows you that you can't get through to another route using the left-turn junction ahead.

11.59 *Mark **one** answer*

What does this sign mean?

- ⊙ T-junction
- ⊙ No through road
- ⊙ Telephone box ahead
- ⊙ Toilet ahead

⊙ **No through road**

You will not be able to find a through route to another road. Use this road only for access.

11.60 *Mark **one** answer*

Which sign means 'no through road'?

⊙

This sign is found at the entrance to a road that can only be used for access.

11.61 *Mark **one** answer*

Which is the sign for a ring road?

⊙

Ring roads are designed to relieve congestion in towns and city centres.

11.62   *Mark **one** answer*

What does this sign mean?

⊙ The right-hand lane ahead is narrow

⊙ Right-hand lane for buses only

⊙ Right-hand lane for turning right

⊙ The right-hand lane is closed

⊙ **The right-hand lane is closed**

Yellow and black temporary signs may be used to inform you of roadworks or lane restrictions. Look well ahead. If you have to change lanes, do so in good time.

11.63   *Mark **one** answer*

What does this sign mean?

⊙ Change to the left lane

⊙ Leave at the next exit

⊙ Contraflow system

⊙ One-way street

⊙ **Contraflow system**

If you use the right-hand lane in a contraflow system, you'll be travelling with no permanent barrier between you and the oncoming traffic. Observe speed limits and keep a good distance from the vehicle ahead.

What does this sign mean?

⊙ Leave motorway at next exit

⊙ Lane for heavy and slow vehicles

⊙ All lorries use the hard shoulder

⊙ Rest area for lorries

⊙ **Lane for heavy and slow vehicles**

Where there's a long, steep, uphill gradient on a motorway, a crawler lane may be provided. This helps the traffic to flow by diverting the slower heavy vehicles into a dedicated lane on the left.

A red traffic light means

⊙ you should stop unless turning left

⊙ stop, if you are able to brake safely

⊙ you must stop and wait behind the stop line

⊙ proceed with caution

⊙ **you must stop and wait behind the stop line**

Make sure you learn and understand the sequence of traffic lights. Whatever light appears you will then know what light is going to appear next and be able to take the appropriate action. For example if amber is showing on its own you'll know that red will appear next, giving you ample time to slow and stop safely.

11.66   *Mark **one** answer*

At traffic lights, amber on its own means

⊙ **stop at the stop line**

When amber is showing on its own red will appear next. The amber light means STOP, unless you have already crossed the stop line or you are so close to it that pulling up might cause a collision.

⊙ prepare to go

⊙ go if the way is clear

⊙ go if no pedestrians are crossing

⊙ stop at the stop line

11.67   *Mark **one** answer*

You are at a junction controlled by traffic lights. When should you NOT proceed at green?

⊙ **When your exit from the junction is blocked**

As you approach the lights look into the road you wish to take. Only proceed if your exit road is clear. If the road is blocked hold back, even if you have to wait for the next green signal.

⊙ When pedestrians are waiting to cross

⊙ When your exit from the junction is blocked

⊙ When you think the lights may be about to change

⊙ When you intend to turn right

11.68

*Mark **one** answer*

You are in the left-hand lane at traffic lights. You are waiting to turn left. At which of these traffic lights must you NOT move on?

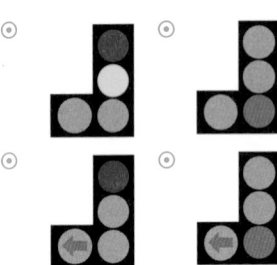

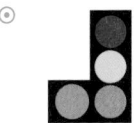

At some junctions there may be a separate signal for different lanes. These are called 'filter' lights. They're designed to help traffic flow at major junctions. Make sure that you're in the correct lane and proceed if the way is clear and the green light shows for your lane.

11.69

*Mark **one** answer*

What does this sign mean?

⊙ Traffic lights out of order

⊙ Amber signal out of order

⊙ Temporary traffic lights ahead

⊙ New traffic lights ahead

⊙ **Traffic lights out of order**

Where traffic lights are out of order you might see this sign. Proceed with caution as nobody has priority at the junction.

11.70

*Mark **one** answer*

When traffic lights are out of order, who has priority?

⊙ Traffic going straight on

⊙ Traffic turning right

⊙ Nobody

⊙ Traffic turning left

⊙ **Nobody**

When traffic lights are out of order you should treat the junction as an unmarked crossroads. Be cautious as you may need to give way or stop. Keep a look out for traffic attempting to cross the junction at speed.

11.71
*Mark **three** answers*

These flashing red lights mean STOP. In which THREE of the following places could you find them?

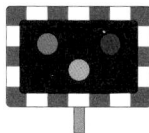

- ⊙ Pelican crossings
- ⊙ Lifting bridges
- ⊙ Zebra crossings
- ⊙ Level crossings
- ⊙ Motorway exits
- ⊙ Fire stations

- ⊙ **Lifting bridges**
- ⊙ **Level crossings**
- ⊙ **Fire stations**

You must always stop when the red lights are flashing, whether or not the way seems to be clear.

11.72
*Mark **one** answer*

What do these zigzag lines at pedestrian crossings mean?

- ⊙ No parking at any time
- ⊙ Parking allowed only for a short time
- ⊙ Slow down to 20 mph
- ⊙ Sounding horns is not allowed

- ⊙ **No parking at any time**

The approach to, and exit from, a pedestrian crossing is marked with zigzag lines. You must not park on them or overtake the leading vehicle when approaching the crossing. Parking here would block the view for pedestrians and the approaching traffic.

When may you cross a double solid white line in the middle of the road?

- ⊙ To pass traffic that is queuing back at a junction
- ⊙ To pass a car signalling to turn left ahead
- ⊙ To pass a road maintenance vehicle travelling at 10 mph or less
- ⊙ To pass a vehicle that is towing a trailer

⊙ **To pass a road maintenance vehicle travelling at 10 mph or less**

You may cross the solid white line to pass a stationary vehicle, pedal cycle, horse or road maintenance vehicle if they are travelling at 10 mph or less. You may also cross the solid line to enter into a side road or access a property.

What does this road marking mean?

- ⊙ Do not cross the line
- ⊙ No stopping allowed
- ⊙ You are approaching a hazard
- ⊙ No overtaking allowed

⊙ **You are approaching a hazard**

Road markings will warn you of a hazard ahead. A single, broken line along the centre of the road, with long markings and short gaps, is a hazard warning line. Don't cross it unless you can see that the road is clear well ahead.

11.75
*Mark **one** answer*

Where would you see this road marking?

- At traffic lights
- On road humps
- Near a level crossing
- At a box junction

⊙ **On road humps**

Due to the dark colour of the road, changes in level aren't easily seen. White triangles painted on the road surface give you an indication of where there are road humps.

11.76
*Mark **one** answer*

Which is a hazard warning line?

You need to know the difference between the normal centre line and a hazard warning line. If there is a hazard ahead, the markings are longer and the gaps shorter. This gives you advanced warning of an unspecified hazard ahead.

At this junction there is a stop sign with a solid white line on the road surface. Why is there a stop sign here?

- ⊙ Speed on the major road is de-restricted
- ⊙ It is a busy junction
- ⊙ Visibility along the major road is restricted
- ⊙ There are hazard warning lines in the centre of the road

⊙ **Visibility along the major road is restricted**

If your view is restricted at a road junction you must stop. There may also be a 'stop' sign. Don't emerge until you're sure there's no traffic approaching.

IF YOU DON'T KNOW, DON'T GO.

You see this line across the road at the entrance to a roundabout. What does it mean?

- ⊙ Give way to traffic from the right
- ⊙ Traffic from the left has right of way
- ⊙ You have right of way
- ⊙ Stop at the line

⊙ **Give way to traffic from the right**

Slow down as you approach the roundabout and check for traffic from the right. If you need to stop and give way, stay behind the broken line until it is safe to emerge onto the roundabout.

11.79 — Mark **one** answer

How will a police officer in a patrol vehicle normally get you to stop?

- Flash the headlights, indicate left and point to the left
- Wait until you stop, then approach you
- Use the siren, overtake, cut in front and stop
- Pull alongside you, use the siren and wave you to stop

⊙ **Flash the headlights, indicate left and point to the left**

You must obey signals given by the police. If a police officer in a patrol vehicle wants you to pull over they will indicate this without causing danger to you or other traffic.

11.80 — Mark **one** answer

You approach a junction. The traffic lights are not working. A police officer gives this signal. You should

- turn left only
- turn right only
- stop level with the officer's arm
- stop at the stop line

⊙ **stop at the stop line**

If a police officer or traffic warden is directing traffic you must obey them. They will use the arm signals shown in The Highway Code. Learn what these mean and act accordingly.

The driver of the car in front is giving this arm signal. What does it mean?

- The driver is slowing down
- The driver intends to turn right
- The driver wishes to overtake
- The driver intends to turn left

⊙ **The driver intends to turn left**

There might be an occasion where another driver uses an arm signal. This may be because the vehicle's indicators are obscured by other traffic. In order for such signals to be effective all drivers should know the meaning of them. Be aware that the 'left turn' signal might look similar to the 'slowing down' signal.

Where would you see these road markings?

- At a level crossing
- On a motorway slip road
- At a pedestrian crossing
- On a single-track road

⊙ **On a motorway slip road**

When driving on a motorway or slip road, you must not enter into an area marked with chevrons and bordered by a solid white line for any reason, except in an emergency.

11.83 *Mark **one** answer*

What does this motorway sign mean?

- ⊙ Change to the lane on your left
- ⊙ Leave the motorway at the next exit
- ⊙ Change to the opposite carriageway
- ⊙ Pull up on the hard shoulder

⊙ **Change to the lane on your left**

On the motorway, signs sometimes show temporary warnings due to traffic or weather conditions. They may be used to indicate

- lane closures
- temporary speed limits
- weather warnings.

11.84 *Mark **one** answer*

What does this motorway sign mean?

- ⊙ Temporary minimum speed 50 mph
- ⊙ No services for 50 miles
- ⊙ Obstruction 50 metres (164 feet) ahead
- ⊙ Temporary maximum speed 50 mph

⊙ **Temporary maximum speed 50 mph**

Look out for signs above your lane or on the central reservation. These will give you important information or warnings about the road ahead. Due to the high speed of motorway traffic these signs may light up some distance from any hazard. Don't ignore the signs just because the road looks clear to you.

11.85 *Mark **one** answer*

What does this sign mean?

- ⊙ Through traffic to use left lane
- ⊙ Right-hand lane T-junction only
- ⊙ Right-hand lane closed ahead
- ⊙ 11 tonne weight limit

⊙ **Right-hand lane closed ahead**

You should move into the lanes as directed by the sign. Here the right-hand lane is closed and the left-hand and centre lanes are available. Merging in turn is recommended when it's safe and traffic is going slowly, for example at road works or a road traffic incident. When vehicles are travelling at speed this is not advisable and you should move into the appropriate lane in good time.

On a motorway this sign means

- move over onto the hard shoulder
- overtaking on the left only
- leave the motorway at the next exit
- move to the lane on your left

⊙ **move to the lane on your left**

It is important to know and obey temporary signs on the motorway: they are there for a reason. You may not be able to see the hazard straight away, as the signs give warnings well in advance, due to the speed of traffic on the motorway.

What does '25' mean on this motorway sign?

- The distance to the nearest town
- The route number of the road
- The number of the next junction
- The speed limit on the slip road

⊙ **The number of the next junction**

Before you set out on your journey use a road map to plan your route. When you see advance warning of your junction, make sure you get into the correct lane in plenty of time. Last-minute harsh braking and cutting across lanes at speed is extremely hazardous.

The right-hand lane of a three-lane motorway is

- for lorries only
- an overtaking lane
- the right-turn lane
- an acceleration lane

⊙ **an overtaking lane**

You should stay in the left-hand lane of a motorway unless overtaking. The right-hand lane of a motorway is an overtaking lane and not a 'fast lane'.

After overtaking, move back to the left when it is safe to do so.

11.89 *Mark **one** answer*

Where can you find reflective amber studs on a motorway?

○ Separating the slip road from the motorway

○ On the left-hand edge of the road

○ On the right-hand edge of the road

○ Separating the lanes

⊙ **On the right-hand edge of the road**

At night or in poor visibility reflective studs on the road help you to judge your position on the carriageway.

11.90 *Mark **one** answer*

Where on a motorway would you find green reflective studs?

○ Separating driving lanes

○ Between the hard shoulder and the carriageway

○ At slip road entrances and exits

○ Between the carriageway and the central reservation

⊙ **At slip road entrances and exits**

Knowing the colours of the reflective studs on the road will help you judge your position, especially at night, in foggy conditions or when visibility is poor.

11.91 *Mark **one** answer*

You are travelling along a motorway. You see this sign. You should

○ leave the motorway at the next exit

○ turn left immediately

○ change lane

○ move onto the hard shoulder

⊙ **leave the motorway at the next exit**

You'll see this sign if the motorway is closed ahead. Pull into the nearside lane as soon as it is safe to do so. Don't leave it to the last moment.

What does this sign mean?

- ⊙ No motor vehicles
- ⊙ End of motorway
- ⊙ No through road
- ⊙ End of bus lane

⊙ **End of motorway**

When you leave the motorway make sure that you check your speedometer. You may be going faster than you realise. Slow down and look out for speed limit signs.

Which of these signs means that the national speed limit applies?

You should know the speed limit for the road on which you are travelling, and the vehicle that you are driving. The different speed limits are shown in The Highway Code.

What is the maximum speed on a single carriageway road?

- ⊙ 50 mph
- ⊙ 60 mph
- ⊙ 40 mph
- ⊙ 70 mph

⊙ **60 mph**

If you're travelling on a dual carriageway that becomes a single carriageway road, reduce your speed gradually so that you aren't exceeding the limit as you enter. There might not be a sign to remind you of the limit, so make sure you know what the speed limits are for different types of roads and vehicles.

11.95 *Mark **one** answer*

What does this sign mean?

◉ End of motorway
◉ End of restriction
◉ Lane ends ahead
◉ Free recovery ends

⊙ **End of restriction**

Temporary restrictions on motorways are shown on signs which have flashing amber lights. At the end of the restriction you will see this sign without any flashing lights.

11.96 *Mark **one** answer*

This sign is advising you to

◉ follow the route diversion
◉ follow the signs to the picnic area
◉ give way to pedestrians
◉ give way to cyclists

⊙ **follow the route diversion**

When a diversion route has been put in place, drivers are advised to follow a symbol which may be a triangle, square, circle or diamond shape on a yellow background.

*Mark **one** answer*

Why would this temporary speed limit sign be shown?

- ⊙ To warn of the end of the motorway
- ⊙ To warn you of a low bridge
- ⊙ To warn you of a junction ahead
- ⊙ To warn of road works ahead

⊙ **To warn of road works ahead**

In the interests of road safety, temporary speed limits are imposed at all major road works. Signs like this, giving advanced warning of the speed limit, are normally placed about three quarters of a mile ahead of where the speed limit comes into force.

*Mark **one** answer*

This traffic sign means there is

- ⊙ a compulsory maximum speed limit
- ⊙ an advisory maximum speed limit
- ⊙ a compulsory minimum speed limit
- ⊙ an advised separation distance

⊙ **a compulsory maximum speed limit**

The sign gives you an early warning of a speed restriction. If you are travelling at a higher speed, slow down in good time. You could come across queuing traffic due to roadworks or a temporary obstruction.

11.99
*Mark **one** answer*

You see this sign at a crossroads. You should

⊙ maintain the same speed

⊙ carry on with great care

⊙ find another route

⊙ telephone the police

⊙ **carry on with great care**

When traffic lights are out of order treat the junction as an unmarked crossroad. Be very careful as no one has priority and be prepared to stop.

11.100
*Mark **one** answer*

You are signalling to turn right in busy traffic. How would you confirm your intention safely?

⊙ Sound the horn

⊙ Give an arm signal

⊙ Flash your headlights

⊙ Position over the centre line

⊙ **Give an arm signal**

In some situations you may feel your indicators cannot be seen by other road users. If you think you need to make your intention more clearly seen, give the arm signal shown in The Highway Code.

11.101
*Mark **one** answer*

What does this sign mean?

⊙ Motorcycles only

⊙ No cars

⊙ Cars only

⊙ No motorcycles

⊙ **No motorcycles**

You must comply with all traffic signs and be especially aware of those signs which apply specifically to the type of vehicle you are using.

You are on a motorway. You see this sign on a lorry that has stopped in the right-hand lane. You should

⊙ move into the right-hand lane

⊙ stop behind the flashing lights

⊙ pass the lorry on the left

⊙ leave the motorway at the next exit

⊙ **pass the lorry on the left**

Sometimes work is carried out on the motorway without closing the lanes. When this happens, signs are mounted on the back of lorries to warn other road users of roadworks ahead.

You are on a motorway. Red flashing lights appear above your lane only. What should you do?

⊙ Continue in that lane and look for further information

⊙ Move into another lane in good time

⊙ Pull onto the hard shoulder

⊙ Stop and wait for an instruction to proceed

⊙ **Move into another lane in good time**

Flashing red lights above your lane show that your lane is closed. You should move into another lane as soon as you can do so safely.

11.104 *Mark **one** answer*

A red traffic light means

- you must stop behind the white stop line
- you may go straight on if there is no other traffic
- you may turn left if it is safe to do so
- you must slow down and prepare to stop if traffic has started to cross

⊙ **you must stop behind the white stop line**

The white line is generally positioned so that pedestrians have room to cross in front of waiting traffic. Don't move off while pedestrians are crossing, even if the lights change to green.

11.105 *Mark **one** answer*

The driver of this car is giving an arm signal. What are they about to do?

- Turn to the right
- Turn to the left
- Go straight ahead
- Let pedestrians cross

⊙ **Turn to the left**

In some situations drivers may need to give arm signals, in addition to indicators, to make their intentions clear. For arm signals to be effective, all road users should know their meaning.

11.106 *Mark **one** answer*

When may you sound the horn?

- To give you right of way
- To attract a friend's attention
- To warn others of your presence
- To make slower drivers move over

⊙ **To warn others of your presence**

Never sound the horn aggressively. You MUST NOT sound it when driving in a built-up area between 11.30 pm and 7.00 am or when you are stationary, an exception to this is when another road user poses a danger. Do not scare animals by sounding your horn.

You must not use your horn when you are stationary

- unless a moving vehicle may cause you danger
- at any time whatsoever
- unless it is used only briefly
- except for signalling that you have just arrived

- **unless a moving vehicle may cause you danger**

When stationary only sound your horn if you think there is a risk of danger from another road user. Don't use it just to attract someone's attention. This causes unnecessary noise and could be misleading.

What does this sign mean?

- You can park on the days and times shown
- No parking on the days and times shown
- No parking at all from Monday to Friday
- End of the urban clearway restrictions

- **No parking on the days and times shown**

Urban clearways are provided to keep traffic flowing at busy times. You may stop only briefly to set down or pick up passengers. Times of operation will vary from place to place so always check the signs.

What does this sign mean?

- Quayside or river bank
- Steep hill downwards
- Uneven road surface
- Road liable to flooding

- **Quayside or river bank**

You should be careful in these locations as the road surface is likely to be wet and slippery. There may be a steep drop to the water, and there may not be a barrier along the edge of the road.

11.110   *Mark **one** answer*

Which sign means you have priority over oncoming vehicles?

Even though you have priority, be prepared to give way if other drivers don't. This will help to avoid congestion, confrontation or even a collision.

11.111   *Mark **one** answer*

A white line like this along the centre of the road is a

- bus lane marking
- hazard warning
- give way marking
- lane marking

⊙ **hazard warning**

The centre of the road is usually marked by a broken white line, with lines that are shorter than the gaps. When the lines become longer than the gaps this is a hazard warning line. Look well ahead for these, especially when you are planning to overtake or turn off.

*Mark **one** answer*

What is the reason for the yellow criss-cross lines painted on the road here?

- ⊙ To mark out an area for trams only
- ⊙ To prevent queuing traffic from blocking the junction on the left
- ⊙ To mark the entrance lane to a car park
- ⊙ To warn you of the tram lines crossing the road

⊙ **To prevent queuing traffic from blocking the junction on the left**

Yellow 'box junctions' like this are often used where it's busy. Their purpose is to keep the junction clear for crossing traffic. Don't enter the painted area unless your exit is clear. The exception to this is when you are turning right and are only prevented from doing so by oncoming traffic or by other vehicles waiting to turn right.

*Mark **one** answer*

What is the reason for the area marked in red and white along the centre of this road?

- ⊙ It is to separate traffic flowing in opposite directions
- ⊙ It marks an area to be used by overtaking motorcyclists
- ⊙ It is a temporary marking to warn of the roadworks
- ⊙ It is separating the two sides of the dual carriageway

⊙ **It is to separate traffic flowing in opposite directions**

Areas of 'hatched markings' such as these are to separate traffic streams which could be a danger to each other. They are often seen on bends or where the road becomes narrow. If the area is bordered by a solid white line, you must not enter it except in an emergency.

11.114
*Mark **one** answer*

Other drivers may sometimes flash their headlights at you. In which situation are they allowed to do this?

- ⊙ To warn of a radar speed trap ahead
- ⊙ To show that they are giving way to you
- ⊙ To warn you of their presence
- ⊙ To let you know there is a fault with your vehicle

⊙ **To warn you of their presence**

If other drivers flash their headlights this isn't a signal to show priority. The flashing of headlights has the same meaning as sounding the horn, it's a warning of their presence.

11.115
*Mark **one** answer*

In some narrow residential streets you may find a speed limit of

- ⊙ 20 mph
- ⊙ 25 mph
- ⊙ 35 mph
- ⊙ 40 mph

⊙ **20 mph**

In some built-up areas, you may find the speed limit reduced to 20 mph. Driving at a slower speed will help give you the time and space to see and deal safely with hazards such as pedestrians and parked cars.

11.116
*Mark **one** answer*

At a junction you see this signal. It means

- ⊙ cars must stop
- ⊙ trams must stop
- ⊙ both trams and cars must stop
- ⊙ both trams and cars can continue

⊙ **trams must stop**

The white light shows that trams must stop, but the green light shows that other vehicles may go if the way is clear. You may not live in an area where there are trams but you should still learn the signs. You never know when you may go to a town with trams.

Where would you find these road markings?

- At a railway crossing
- At a junction
- On a motorway
- On a pedestrian crossing

⊙ **At a junction**

These markings show the direction in which the traffic should go at a mini-roundabout.

There is a police car following you. The police officer flashes the headlights and points to the left. What should you do?

- Turn left at the next junction
- Pull up on the left
- Stop immediately
- Move over to the left

⊙ **Pull up on the left**

You must pull up on the left as soon as it's safe to do so and switch off your engine.

You see this amber traffic light ahead. Which light or lights, will come on next?

- Red alone
- Red and amber together
- Green and amber together
- Green alone

⊙ **Red alone**

At junctions controlled by traffic lights you must stop behind the white line until the lights change to green. Red and amber lights showing together also mean stop.

You may proceed when the light is green unless your exit road is blocked or pedestrians are crossing in front of you.

If you're approaching traffic lights that are visible from a distance and the light has been green for some time they are likely to change. Be ready to slow down and stop.

11.120   *Mark **one** answer*

This broken white line painted in the centre of the road means

⊙ oncoming vehicles have priority over you

⊙ you should give priority to oncoming vehicles

⊙ there is a hazard ahead of you

⊙ the area is a national speed limit zone

⊙ **there is a hazard ahead of you**

A long white line with short gaps means that you are approaching a hazard. If you do need to cross it, make sure that the road is clear well ahead.

11.121   *Mark **one** answer*

You see this signal overhead on the motorway. What does it mean?

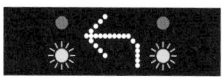

⊙ Leave the motorway at the next exit

⊙ All vehicles use the hard shoulder

⊙ Sharp bend to the left ahead

⊙ Stop, all lanes ahead closed

⊙ **Leave the motorway at the next exit**

You will see this sign if there has been an incident ahead and the motorway is closed. You MUST obey the sign. Make sure that you prepare to leave as soon as you see the warning sign.

Don't pull over at the last moment or cut across other traffic.

What is the purpose of these yellow criss-cross lines on the road?

- ⊙ To make you more aware of the traffic lights
- ⊙ To guide you into position as you turn
- ⊙ To prevent the junction becoming blocked
- ⊙ To show you where to stop when the lights change

⊙ **To prevent the junction becoming blocked**

You MUST NOT enter a box junction until your exit road or lane is clear. The exception to this is if you want to turn right and are only prevented from doing so by oncoming traffic or by other vehicles waiting to turn right.

What MUST you do when you see this sign?

- ⊙ Stop, only if traffic is approaching
- ⊙ Stop, even if the road is clear
- ⊙ Stop, only if children are waiting to cross
- ⊙ Stop, only if a red light is showing

⊙ **Stop, even if the road is clear**

STOP signs are situated at junctions where visibility is restricted or there is heavy traffic. They MUST be obeyed. You MUST stop.

Take good all-round observation before moving off.

11.124 *Mark **one** answer*

Which shape is used for a 'give way' sign?

Other warning signs are the same shape and colour, but the 'give way' sign triangle points downwards. When you see this sign you MUST give way to traffic on the road which you are about to enter.

11.125 *Mark **one** answer*

What does this sign mean?

- ⊙ Buses turning
- ⊙ Ring road
- ⊙ Mini-roundabout
- ⊙ Keep right

⊙ **Mini-roundabout**

When you see this sign, look out for any direction signs and judge whether you need to signal your intentions. Do this in good time so that other road users approaching the roundabout know what you're planning to do.

11.126 *Mark **one** answer*

What does this sign mean?

- ⊙ Two-way traffic straight ahead
- ⊙ Two-way traffic crosses a one-way road
- ⊙ Two-way traffic over a bridge
- ⊙ Two-way traffic crosses a two-way road

⊙ **Two-way traffic crosses a one-way road**

Be prepared for traffic approaching from junctions on either side of you. Try to avoid unnecessary changing of lanes just before the junction.

What does this sign mean?

- Two-way traffic ahead across a one-way road
- Traffic approaching you has priority
- Two-way traffic straight ahead
- Motorway contraflow system ahead

⊙ **Two-way traffic straight ahead**

This sign may be at the end of a dual carriageway or a one-way street. It is there to warn you of oncoming traffic.

What does this sign mean?

- Hump-back bridge
- Traffic calming hump
- Low bridge
- Uneven road

⊙ **Hump-back bridge**

You will need to slow down. At humpback bridges your view ahead will be restricted and the road will often be narrow on the bridge. If the bridge is very steep or your view is restricted sound your horn to warn others of your approach. Going too fast over the bridge is highly dangerous to other road users and could even cause your wheels to leave the road, with a resulting loss of control.

11.129
*Mark **one** answer*

Which of the following signs informs you that you are coming to a 'no through road'?

This sign is found at the entrance to a road that can only be used for access.

11.130
*Mark **one** answer*

What does this sign mean?

- ⊙ Direction to park-and-ride car park
- ⊙ No parking for buses or coaches
- ⊙ Directions to bus and coach park
- ⊙ Parking area for cars and coaches

⊙ **Direction to park-and-ride car park**

To ease the congestion in town centres, some cities and towns provide park-and-ride schemes. These allow you to park in a designated area and ride by bus into the centre.

Park-and-ride schemes are usually cheaper and easier than car parking in the town centre.

You are approaching traffic lights. Red and amber are showing. This means

⊙ pass the lights if the road is clear

⊙ there is a fault with the lights – take care

⊙ wait for the green light before you cross the stop line

⊙ the lights are about to change to red

⊙ **wait for the green light before you cross the stop line**

Be aware that other traffic might still be clearing the junction. Make sure the way is clear before continuing.

This marking appears on the road just before a

⊙ 'no entry' sign

⊙ 'give way' sign

⊙ 'stop' sign

⊙ 'no through road' sign

⊙ **'give way' sign**

Where you see this road marking you should give way to traffic on the main road. It might not be used at junctions where there is relatively little traffic. However, if there is a double broken line across the junction the 'give way' rules still apply.

At a railway level crossing the red light signal continues to flash after a train has gone by. What should you do?

⊙ Phone the signal operator

⊙ Alert drivers behind you

⊙ Wait

⊙ Proceed with caution

⊙ **Wait**

You MUST always obey red flashing stop lights. If a train passes but the lights continue to flash, another train will be passing soon. Cross only when the lights go off and the barriers open.

11.134   *Mark **one** answer*

You are in a tunnel and you see this sign. What does it mean?

- ⊙ Direction to emergency pedestrian exit
- ⊙ Beware of pedestrians, no footpath ahead
- ⊙ No access for pedestrians
- ⊙ Beware of pedestrians crossing ahead

⊙ **Direction to emergency pedestrian exit**

If you have to leave your vehicle in a tunnel and leave by an emergency exit, do so as quickly as you can. Follow the signs directing you to the nearest exit point. If there are several people using the exit, don't panic but try to leave in a calm and orderly manner.

11.135   *Mark **one** answer*

Which of these signs shows that you are entering a one-way system?

⊙

If the road has two lanes you can use either lane and overtake on either side. Use the lane that's more convenient for your destination unless signs or road markings indicate otherwise.

What does this sign mean?

- With-flow bus and cycle lane
- Contraflow bus and cycle lane
- No buses and cycles allowed
- No waiting for buses and cycles

⊙ **With-flow bus and cycle lane**

Buses and cycles can travel in this lane. In this case they will flow in the same direction as other traffic. If it's busy they may be passing you on the left, so watch out for them. Times on the sign will show its hours of operation. No times shown, or no sign at all, means it's 24 hours. In some areas other vehicles, such as taxis and motorcycles, are allowed to use bus lanes. The sign will show these.

Which of these signs warns you of a zebra crossing?

⊙

Look well ahead and check the pavements and surrounding areas for pedestrians. Look for anyone walking towards the crossing. Check your mirrors for traffic behind, in case you have to slow down or stop.

11.138

*Mark **one** answer*

What does this sign mean?

- ◉ No footpath
- ◉ No pedestrians
- ◉ Zebra crossing
- ◉ School crossing

◉ **Zebra crossing**

You need to be aware of the various signs that relate to pedestrians. Some of the signs look similar but have very different meanings. Make sure you know what they all mean and be ready for any potential hazard.

11.139

*Mark **one** answer*

What does this sign mean?

- ◉ School crossing patrol
- ◉ No pedestrians allowed
- ◉ Pedestrian zone – no vehicles
- ◉ Zebra crossing ahead

◉ **Zebra crossing ahead**

Look well ahead and be ready to stop for any pedestrians crossing, or about to cross, the road. Also check the pavements for anyone who looks like they might step or run into the road.

11.140

*Mark **one** answer*

Which sign means there will be two-way traffic crossing your route ahead?

◉

This sign is found in or at the end of a one-way system. It warns you that traffic will be crossing your path from both directions.

Which arm signal tells you that the car you are following is going to pull up?

There may be occasions when drivers need to give an arm signal to confirm an indicator. This could include in bright sunshine, at a complex road layout, when stopping at a pedestrian crossing or when turning right just after passing a parked vehicle. You should understand what each arm signal means. If you give arm signals, make them clear, correct and decisive.

Which of these signs means turn left ahead?

Blue circles tell you what you must do and this sign gives a clear instruction to turn left ahead. You should be looking out for signs at all times and know what they mean.

Which sign shows that traffic can only travel in one direction on the road you're on?

This sign means that traffic can only travel in one direction. The others show different priorities on a two-way road.

11.144   *Mark **one** answer*

You have just driven past this sign. You should be aware that

- ⊙ it is a single track road
- ⊙ you cannot stop on this road
- ⊙ there is only one lane in use
- ⊙ all traffic is going one way

⊙ **all traffic is going one way**

In a one-way system traffic may be passing you on either side. Always be aware of all traffic signs and understand their meaning. Look well ahead and react to them in good time.

11.145   *Mark **one** answer*

You are approaching a red traffic light. What will the signal show next?

- ⊙ Red and amber
- ⊙ Green alone
- ⊙ Amber alone
- ⊙ Green and amber

⊙ **Red and amber**

If you know which light is going to show next you can plan your approach accordingly. This can help prevent excessive braking or hesitation at the junction.

What does this sign mean?

⊙ **Tunnel ahead**

When approaching a tunnel switch on your dipped headlights. Be aware that your eyes might need to adjust to the sudden darkness. You may need to reduce your speed.

⊙ Low bridge ahead

⊙ Tunnel ahead

⊙ Ancient monument ahead

⊙ Traffic danger spot ahead

You are approaching a zebra crossing where pedestrians are waiting. Which arm signal might you give?

A 'slowing down' signal will indicate your intentions to oncoming and following vehicles. Be aware that pedestrians might start to cross as soon as they see this signal.

11.148

*Mark **one** answer*

The white line along the side of the road

- ⊙ shows the edge of the carriageway
- ⊙ shows the approach to a hazard
- ⊙ means no parking
- ⊙ means no overtaking

⊙ **shows the edge of the carriageway**

A continuous white line is used on many roads to indicate the edge of the carriageway. This can be useful when visibility is restricted. The line is discontinued at junctions, lay-bys and entrances and exits from private drives.

11.149

*Mark **one** answer*

You see this white arrow on the road ahead. It means

- ⊙ entrance on the left
- ⊙ all vehicles turn left
- ⊙ keep left of the hatched markings
- ⊙ road bending to the left

⊙ **keep left of the hatched markings**

Don't attempt to overtake here, as there might be unseen hazards over the brow of the hill. Keep to the left.

341

How should you give an arm signal to turn left?

There may be occasions where other road users are unable to see your indicator, such as in bright sunlight or at a busy, complicated junction. In these cases a hand signal will help others to understand your intentions.

You are waiting at a T-junction. A vehicle is coming from the right with the left signal flashing. What should you do?

- Move out and accelerate hard
- Wait until the vehicle starts to turn in
- Pull out before the vehicle reaches the junction
- Move out slowly

⊙ **Wait until the vehicle starts to turn in**

Other road users may give misleading signals. When you're waiting at a junction don't emerge until you're sure of their intentions.

11.152
*Mark **one** answer*

When may you use hazard warning lights when driving?

- ⊙ Instead of sounding the horn in a built-up area between 11.30 pm and 7 am
- ⊙ On a motorway or unrestricted dual carriageway, to warn of a hazard ahead
- ⊙ On rural routes, after a warning sign of animals
- ⊙ On the approach to toucan crossings where cyclists are waiting to cross

⊙ **On a motorway or unrestricted dual carriageway, to warn of a hazard ahead**

When there's queuing traffic ahead and you have to slow down or even stop, showing your hazard warning lights will alert following traffic to the hazard. Don't forget to switch them off as the queue forms behind you.

11.153
*Mark **one** answer*

You are driving on a motorway. There is a slow-moving vehicle ahead. On the back you see this sign. You should

- ⊙ pass on the right
- ⊙ pass on the left
- ⊙ leave at the next exit
- ⊙ drive no further

⊙ **pass on the left**

If a vehicle displaying this sign is in your lane you will have to pass it on the left. Use your mirrors and signal. When it's safe move into the lane on your left. You should always look well ahead so that you can spot any hazards early, giving yourself time to react safely.

11.154
*Mark **one** answer*

You should NOT normally stop on these markings near schools

- ⊙ except when picking up children
- ⊙ under any circumstances
- ⊙ unless there is nowhere else available
- ⊙ except to set down children

⊙ **under any circumstances**

At schools you should not stop on yellow zigzag lines for any length of time, not even to set down or pick up children or other passengers.

11.155
*Mark **one** answer*

Why should you make sure that your indicators are cancelled after turning?

- ⊙ To avoid flattening the battery
- ⊙ To avoid misleading other road users
- ⊙ To avoid dazzling other road users
- ⊙ To avoid damage to the indicator relay

⊙ **To avoid misleading other road users**

Leaving your indicators on could confuse other road users and may even lead to a crash. Be aware that if you haven't taken a sharp turn your indicators may not self-cancel and you will need to turn them off manually.

11.156
*Mark **one** answer*

You are driving in busy traffic. You want to pull up on the left just after a junction on the left. When should you signal?

- ⊙ As you are passing or just after the junction
- ⊙ Just before you reach the junction
- ⊙ Well before you reach the junction
- ⊙ It would be better not to signal at all

⊙ **As you are passing or just after the junction**

You need to signal to let other drivers know your intentions. However, if you indicate too early they may think you are turning left into the junction. Correct timing of the signal is very important to avoid misleading others.

section **twelve**
DOCUMENTS

This section covers
- Licences
- Insurance
- MOT certificate

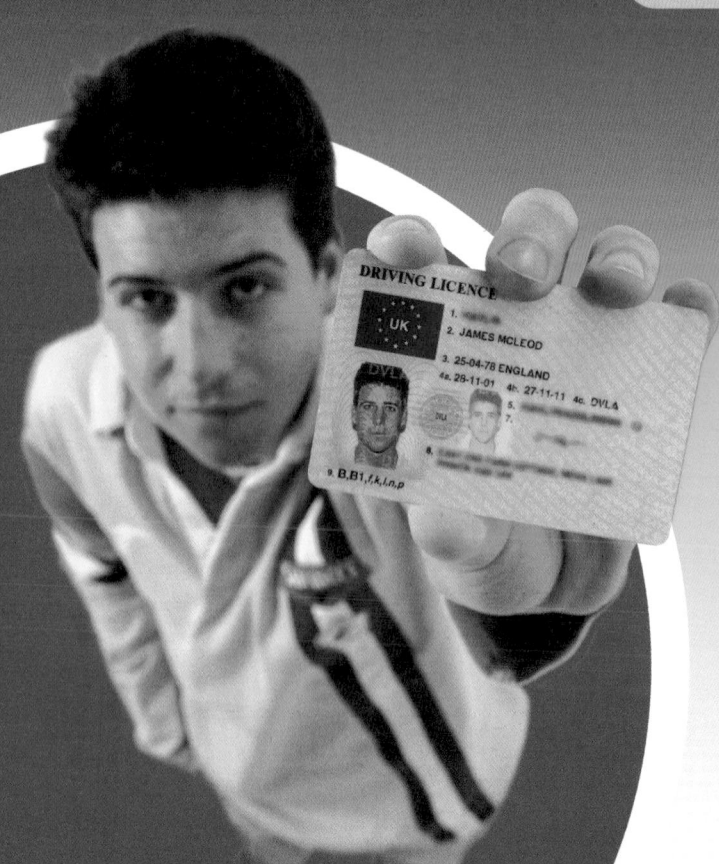

12.1

An MOT certificate is normally valid for

- three years after the date it was issued
- 10,000 miles
- one year after the date it was issued
- 30,000 miles

⊙ **one year after the date it was issued**

Make a note of the date that your MOT certificate expires. Some garages remind you that your vehicle is due an MOT but not all do. You may take your vehicle for MOT up to to one month in advance and have the certificate post-dated.

12.2

A cover note is a document issued before you receive your

- driving licence
- insurance certificate
- registration document
- MOT certificate

⊙ **insurance certificate**

Sometimes an insurance company will issue a temporary insurance certificate called a cover note. It gives you the same insurance cover as your certificate, but lasts for a limited period, usually one month.

12.3

You have just passed your practical test. You do not hold a full licence in another category. Within two years you get six penalty points on your licence. What will you have to do?

- Retake only your theory test
- Retake your theory and practical tests
- Retake only your practical test
- Reapply for your full licence immediately
- Reapply for your provisional licence

⊙ **Retake your theory and practical tests**

⊙ **Reapply for your provisional licence**

If you accumulate six or more penalty points within two years of gaining your first full licence it will be revoked. The six or more points include any gained due to offences you committed before passing your test. If this happens you may only drive as a learner until you pass both the theory and practical tests again.

How long will a Statutory Off-Road Notification (SORN) last for?

- ⊙ 12 months
- ⊙ 24 months
- ⊙ 3 years
- ⊙ 10 years

⊙ **12 months**

A SORN declaration allows you to keep a vehicle off-road and untaxed for 12 months. If you want to keep your vehicle off-road beyond that you must send a further SORN form to DVLA, or DVA in Northern Ireland. If the vehicle is sold SORN will end and the new owner becomes responsible immediately.

What is a Statutory Off-Road Notification (SORN) declaration?

- ⊙ A notification to tell VOSA that a vehicle does not have a current MOT
- ⊙ Information kept by the police about the owner of the vehicle
- ⊙ A notification to tell DVLA that a vehicle is not being used on the road
- ⊙ Information held by insurance companies to check the vehicle is insured

⊙ **A notification to tell DVLA that a vehicle is not being used on the road**

If you want to keep a vehicle off the public road you must declare SORN. It is an offence not to do so. You then won't have to pay road tax. If you don't renew the SORN declaration or re-license the vehicle, you will incur a penalty.

A Statutory Off-Road Notification (SORN) declaration is

- ⊙ to tell DVLA that your vehicle is being used on the road but the MOT has expired
- ⊙ to tell DVLA that you no longer own the vehicle
- ⊙ to tell DVLA that your vehicle is not being used on the road
- ⊙ to tell DVLA that you are buying a personal number plate

⊙ **to tell DVLA that your vehicle is not being used on the road**

This will enable you to keep a vehicle off the public road for 12 months without having to pay road tax. You must send a further SORN declaration after 12 months.

12.7

Mark **one** answer

A Statutory Off-Road Notification (SORN) is valid

- for as long as the vehicle has an MOT
- for 12 months only
- only if the vehicle is more than 3 years old
- provided the vehicle is insured

⊙ **for 12 months only**

If you want to keep a vehicle off the public road you must declare SORN. It is an offence not to do so. You then won't have to pay road tax for that vehicle. You will incur a penalty after 12 months if you don't renew the SORN declaration, or re-license the vehicle. If you sell the vehicle the SORN declaration ends and the new owner should declare SORN or re-license the vehicle.

12.8

Mark **one** answer

A Statutory Off-Road Notification (SORN) will last

- for the life of the vehicle
- for as long as you own the vehicle
- for 12 months only
- until the vehicle warranty expires

⊙ **for 12 months only**

If you are keeping a vehicle, or vehicles, off-road and don't want to pay road tax you must declare SORN. You must still do this even if the vehicle is incapable of being used, for example it may be under restoration or being stored. After twelve months you must send another SORN declaration or re-license your vehicle. You will be fined if you don't do this. The SORN will end if you sell the vehicle and the new owner will be responsible immediately.

12.9

Mark **one** answer

What is the maximum specified fine for driving without insurance?

- £50
- £500
- £1000
- £5000

⊙ **£5000**

It is a serious offence to drive without insurance. As well as a heavy fine you may be disqualified or incur penalty points.

Mark one answer

Who is legally responsible for ensuring that a Vehicle Registration Certificate (V5C) is updated?

- The registered vehicle keeper
- The vehicle manufacturer
- Your insurance company
- The licensing authority

⊙ **The registered vehicle keeper**

It is your legal responsibility to keep the details of your Vehicle Registration Certificate (V5C) up to date. You should tell the licensing authority of any changes. These include your name, address, or vehicle details. If you don't do this you may have problems when you sell your vehicle.

Mark one answer

For which of these MUST you show your insurance certificate?

- When making a SORN declaration
- When buying or selling a vehicle
- When a police officer asks you for it
- When having an MOT inspection

⊙ **When a police officer asks you for it**

You MUST be able to produce your valid insurance certificate when requested by a police officer. If you can't do this immediately you may be asked to take it to a police station. Other documents you may be asked to produce are your driving licence and MOT certificate.

Mark one answer

You must have valid insurance before you can

- make a SORN declaration
- buy or sell a vehicle
- apply for a driving licence
- obtain a tax disc

⊙ **obtain a tax disc**

You MUST have valid insurance before you can apply for a tax disc. Your vehicle will also need to have a valid MOT certificate, if applicable. You can apply for a tax disc online, at certain post offices or by post. It is illegal and can be dangerous to drive without valid insurance or an MOT.

12.13
*Mark **one** answer*

Your vehicle needs a current MOT certificate. Until you have one you will NOT be able to

- ⊙ renew your driving licence
- ⊙ change your insurance company
- ⊙ renew your road tax disc
- ⊙ notify a change of address

⊙ **renew your road tax disc**

If your vehicle is required to have an MOT certificate you will need to make sure this is current before you are able to renew your tax disc (also known as vehicle excise duty). You can renew the tax disc online, by phone or by post.

12.14
*Mark **three** answers*

Which THREE of these do you need before you can use a vehicle on the road legally?

- ⊙ A valid driving licence
- ⊙ A valid tax disc clearly displayed
- ⊙ Proof of your identity
- ⊙ Proper insurance cover
- ⊙ Breakdown cover
- ⊙ A vehicle handbook

⊙ **A valid driving licence**

⊙ **A valid tax disc clearly displayed**

⊙ **Proper insurance cover**

Using a vehicle on the road illegally carries a heavy fine and can lead to penalty points on your licence. Things you MUST have include a valid driving licence, a current valid tax disc, and proper insurance cover.

12.15
*Mark **one** answer*

When you apply to renew your Vehicle Excise Duty (tax disc) you must have

- ⊙ valid insurance
- ⊙ the old tax disc
- ⊙ the handbook
- ⊙ a valid driving licence

⊙ **valid insurance**

Tax discs can be renewed at post offices, vehicle registration offices, online, or by post. When applying make sure you have all the relevant valid documents, including MOT where applicable.

*Mark **one** answer*

A police officer asks to see your documents. You do not have them with you. You may be asked to take them to a police station within

⊙ 5 days

⊙ 7 days

⊙ 14 days

⊙ 21 days

⊙ **7 days**

You don't have to carry the documents for your vehicle around with you. If a police officer asks to see them and you don't have them with you, you may be asked to produce them at a police station within seven days.

---

*Mark **one** answer*

When you apply to renew your vehicle excise licence (tax disc) what must you have?

⊙ Valid insurance

⊙ The old tax disc

⊙ The vehicle handbook

⊙ A valid driving licence

⊙ **Valid insurance**

Tax discs can be renewed online, at most post offices, your nearest vehicle registration office or by post to the licensing authority. Make sure you have or take all the relevant documents with your application.

---

*Mark **one** answer*

When should you update your Vehicle Registration Certificate?

⊙ When you pass your driving test

⊙ When you move house

⊙ When your vehicle needs an MOT

⊙ When you have a collision

⊙ **When you move house**

As the registered keeper of a vehicle it is up to you to inform DVLA (DVA in Northern Ireland) of any changes in your vehicle or personal details, for example, change of name or address. You do this by completing the relevant section of the Registration Certificate and sending it to them.

12.19
*Mark **one** answer*

To drive on the road learners MUST

- ⊙ have NO penalty points on their licence
- ⊙ have taken professional instruction
- ⊙ have a signed, valid provisional licence
- ⊙ apply for a driving test within 12 months

⊙ **have a signed, valid provisional licence**

Before you drive on the road you MUST have a valid provisional licence, for the category of vehicle that you're driving. It must show your signature; it isn't valid without it.

12.20
*Mark **one** answer*

Before driving anyone else's motor vehicle you should make sure that

- ⊙ the vehicle owner has third party insurance cover
- ⊙ your own vehicle has insurance cover
- ⊙ the vehicle is insured for your use
- ⊙ the owner has left the insurance documents in the vehicle

⊙ **the vehicle is insured for your use**

Driving a vehicle without insurance cover is illegal. If you cause injury to anyone or damage to property, it could be very expensive and you could also be subject to a criminal prosecution. You can arrange insurance cover with an insurance company, a broker and some motor manufacturers or dealers.

12.21
*Mark **one** answer*

Your car needs an MOT certificate. If you drive without one this could invalidate your

- ⊙ vehicle service record
- ⊙ insurance
- ⊙ road tax disc
- ⊙ vehicle registration document

⊙ **insurance**

If your vehicle requires an MOT certificate, it's illegal to drive it without one. The only exceptions are that you may drive to a pre-arranged MOT test appointment, or to a garage for repairs required for the test. As well as being illegal, the vehicle may also be unsafe for use on the road and could endanger you, any passengers, and other road users.

How old must you be to supervise a learner driver?

- 18 years old
- 19 years old
- 20 years old
- 21 years old

- **21 years old**

As well as being at least 21 years old you must hold a full EC/EEA driving licence for the category of vehicle being driven and have held that licence for at least three years.

A newly qualified driver must

- display green 'L' plates
- not exceed 40 mph for 12 months
- be accompanied on a motorway
- have valid motor insurance

- **have valid motor insurance**

It is your responsibility to make sure you are properly insured for the vehicle you are driving.

You have third party insurance. What does this cover?

- Damage to your own vehicle
- Damage to your vehicle by fire
- Injury to another person
- Damage to someone's property
- Damage to other vehicles
- Injury to yourself

- **Injury to another person**
- **Damage to someone's property**
- **Damage to other vehicles**

Third party insurance doesn't cover damage to your own vehicle or injury to yourself. If you have a crash and your vehicle is damaged you might have to carry out the repairs at your own expense.

12.25
Mark one answer

Vehicle excise duty is often called 'Road Tax' or 'The Tax Disc'. You must

- ⊙ keep it with your registration document
- ⊙ display it clearly on your vehicle
- ⊙ keep it concealed safely in your vehicle
- ⊙ carry it on you at all times

⊙ **display it clearly on your vehicle**

The tax disc should be displayed at the bottom of the windscreen on the nearside (left-hand side). This allows it to be easily seen from the kerbside. It must be current, and you can't transfer the disc from vehicle to vehicle.

12.26
Mark one answer

Your vehicle needs a current MOT certificate. You do not have one. Until you do have one you will not be able to renew your

- ⊙ driving licence
- ⊙ vehicle insurance
- ⊙ road tax disc
- ⊙ vehicle registration document

⊙ **road tax disc**

When you renew your road tax disc you need to produce a current, valid MOT certificate for your vehicle.

12.27
Mark three answers

Which THREE pieces of information are found on a vehicle registration document?

- ⊙ Registered keeper
- ⊙ Make of the vehicle
- ⊙ Service history details
- ⊙ Date of the MOT
- ⊙ Type of insurance cover
- ⊙ Engine size

⊙ **Registered keeper**

⊙ **Make of the vehicle**

⊙ **Engine size**

Every vehicle used on the road has a registration certificate. This is issued by the Driver and Vehicle Licensing Agency (DVLA) or Driver and Vehicle Agency (DVA) in Northern Ireland. The document shows vehicle details including date of first registration, registration number, previous keeper, registered keeper, make of vehicle, engine size and chassis number, year of manufacture and colour.

12.28

Mark **three** answers

You have a duty to contact the licensing authority when

- you go abroad on holiday
- you change your vehicle
- you change your name
- your job status is changed
- your permanent address changes
- your job involves travelling abroad

- ⊙ **you change your vehicle**
- ⊙ **you change your name**
- ⊙ **your permanent address changes**

The licensing authority need to keep their records up to date. They send out a reminder when your road tax is due and need your current address to send this to you. Every vehicle in the country is registered, so it's possible to trace its history.

12.29

Mark **three** answers

You must notify the licensing authority when

- your health affects your driving
- your eyesight does not meet a set standard
- you intend lending your vehicle
- your vehicle requires an MOT certificate
- you change your vehicle

- ⊙ **your health affects your driving**
- ⊙ **your eyesight does not meet a set standard**
- ⊙ **you change your vehicle**

The Driver and Vehicle Licensing Agency (DVLA) hold the records of all vehicles and drivers in Great Britain (DVA in Northern Ireland). They need to know of any change in circumstances so that they can keep their records up to date. Your health might affect your ability to drive safely. Don't risk endangering your own safety or that of other road users.

12.30   NI EXEMPT   *Mark **one** answer*

The cost of your insurance may reduce if you

- are under 25 years old
- do not wear glasses
- pass the driving test first time
- take the Pass Plus scheme

⊙ **take the Pass Plus scheme**

The cost of insurance varies with your age and how long you have been driving. Usually, the younger you are the more expensive it is, especially if you are under 25 years of age.

The Pass Plus scheme provides additional training to newly qualified drivers. Pass Plus is recognised by many insurance companies and taking this extra training could give you reduced insurance premiums, as well as improving your skills and experience.

12.31   NI EXEMPT   *Mark **one** answer*

Which of the following may reduce the cost of your insurance?

- Having a valid MOT certificate
- Taking a Pass Plus course
- Driving a powerful car
- Having penalty points on your licence

⊙ **Taking a Pass Plus course**

The aim of the Pass Plus course is to build up your skills and experience. It is recognised by some insurance companies, who reward people completing the scheme with cheaper insurance premiums.

12.32   *Mark **two** answers*

To supervise a learner driver you must

- have held a full licence for at least 3 years
- be at least 21 years old
- be an approved driving instructor
- hold an advanced driving certificate

⊙ **have held a full licence for at least 3 years**

⊙ **be at least 21 years old**

Don't just take someone's word that they are qualified to supervise you. The person who sits alongside you while you are learning should be a responsible adult and an experienced driver.

When is it legal to drive a car over three years old without an MOT certificate?

- ⊙ Up to seven days after the old certificate has run out
- ⊙ When driving to an MOT centre to arrange an appointment
- ⊙ Just after buying a second-hand car with no MOT
- ⊙ When driving to an appointment at an MOT centre

⊙ **When driving to an appointment at an MOT centre**

Any car over three years old MUST have a valid MOT certificate before it can be used on the road. Exceptionally, you may drive to a pre-arranged test appointment or to a garage for repairs required for the test. However you should check this with your insurance company. Driving an unroadworthy vehicle may invalidate your insurance.

Motor cars must first have an MOT test certificate when they are

- ⊙ one year old
- ⊙ three years old
- ⊙ five years old
- ⊙ seven years old

⊙ **three years old**

The vehicle you drive MUST be roadworthy and in good condition. If it's over three years old it MUST have a valid MOT test certificate. The MOT test ensures that a vehicle meets minimum legal standards in terms of safety, components and environmental impact at the time it is tested.

The Pass Plus scheme has been created for new drivers. What is its main purpose?

- ⊙ To allow you to drive faster
- ⊙ To allow you to carry passengers
- ⊙ To improve your basic skills
- ⊙ To let you drive on motorways

⊙ **To improve your basic skills**

New drivers are far more vulnerable on the road and more likely to be involved in incidents and collisions. The Pass Plus scheme has been designed to improve new drivers' basic skills and help widen their driving experience.

12.36 — Mark *two answers*

Your vehicle is insured third party only. This covers

- damage to your vehicle
- damage to other vehicles
- injury to yourself
- injury to others
- all damage and injury

- **damage to other vehicles**

- **injury to others**

This type of insurance cover is usually cheaper than comprehensive. However, it does not cover any damage to your own vehicle or property. It only covers damage and injury to others.

12.37 — Mark *one answer*

What is the legal minimum insurance cover you must have to drive on public roads?

- Third party, fire and theft
- Comprehensive
- Third party only
- Personal injury cover

- **Third party only**

The minimum insurance required by law is third party cover. This covers others involved in a collision but not damage to your vehicle. Basic third party insurance won't cover theft or fire damage. Check with your insurance company for advice on the best cover for you and make sure that you read the policy carefully.

12.38 — Mark *one answer*

You claim on your insurance to have your car repaired. Your policy has an excess of £100. What does this mean?

- The insurance company will pay the first £100 of any claim
- You will be paid £100 if you do not claim within one year
- Your vehicle is insured for a value of £100 if it is stolen
- You will have to pay the first £100 of the cost of repair to your car

- **You will have to pay the first £100 of the cost of repair to your car**

Having an excess on your policy will help to keep down the premium, but if you make a claim you will have to pay the excess yourself, in this case £100.

The Pass Plus scheme is designed to

⊙ give you a discount on your MOT
⊙ improve your basic driving skills
⊙ increase your mechanical knowledge
⊙ allow you to drive anyone else's vehicle

⊙ **improve your basic driving skills**

After passing your practical driving test you can take further training. This is known as the Pass Plus scheme. It is designed to improve your basic driving skills and involves a series of modules including night time and motorway driving. The sort of things you may not have covered whilst learning.

By taking part in the Pass Plus scheme you will

⊙ never get any points on your licence
⊙ be able to service your own car
⊙ allow you to drive anyone else's vehicle
⊙ improve your basic driving skills

⊙ **improve your basic driving skills**

The Pass Plus scheme can be taken after you've passed your practical driving test. Ask your ADI for details. It is designed to improve your basic driving skills. By successfully completing the course you may get a discount on your insurance.

The Pass Plus scheme is aimed at all newly qualified drivers. It enables them to

⊙ widen their driving experience
⊙ supervise a learner driver
⊙ increase their insurance premiums
⊙ avoid mechanical breakdowns

⊙ **widen their driving experience**

The Pass Plus scheme was created by DSA for newly qualified drivers. It aims to widen their driving experience and improve basic skills. After passing the practical driving test additional professional training can be taken with an Approved Driving Instructor (ADI). Some insurance companies also offer discounts to holders of a Pass Plus certificate. You will find more information in Drive On magazine.

12.42 NI EXEMPT *Mark **two** answers*

New drivers can take further training after passing the practical test. A Pass Plus course will help to

- ⊙ improve your basic skills
- ⊙ widen your experience
- ⊙ increase your insurance premiums
- ⊙ get cheaper road tax

⊙ **improve your basic skills**

⊙ **widen your experience**

Novice drivers are in much more danger than experienced drivers. They can often be involved in collisions soon after passing their test, sometimes with tragic results. The Pass Plus scheme gives structured training to help new drivers improve basic skills and widen their experience. Approved Driving Instructors (ADIs) will be able to advise of the benefits.

12.43 NI EXEMPT *Mark **one** answer*

The Pass Plus Scheme is operated by DSA for newly qualified drivers. It is intended to

- ⊙ improve your basic skills
- ⊙ reduce the cost of your driving licence
- ⊙ prevent you from paying congestion charges
- ⊙ allow you to supervise a learner driver

⊙ **improve your basic skills**

The Pass Plus scheme provides a wide range of driving experience accompanied by a qualified instructor. There is no test and when completed you may get a reduction in insurance costs. It can help to improve basic skills, reduce the risk of having a collision and make you a safer driver.

12.44 *Mark **one** answer*

For which of these must you show your motor insurance certificate?

- ⊙ When you are taking your driving test
- ⊙ When buying or selling a vehicle
- ⊙ When a police officer asks you for it
- ⊙ When having an MOT inspection

⊙ **When a police officer asks you for it**

When you take out motor insurance you'll be issued with a certificate. This contains details explaining who and what is insured. If a police officer asks to see your insurance certificate you must produce it at the time or at a police station within a specified period. You also need to have current valid insurance when renewing your vehicle excise duty (road tax).

Which THREE of these do you need before you can drive legally?

- A valid driving licence
- A valid tax disc displayed on your vehicle
- A vehicle service record
- Proper insurance cover
- Breakdown cover
- A vehicle handbook

- **A valid driving licence**

- **A valid tax disc displayed on your vehicle**

- **Proper insurance cover**

Make sure that you have a valid driving licence and proper insurance cover before driving any vehicle. These are legal requirements, as is displaying a valid tax disc in the vehicle.

A friend wants to help you learn to drive. They must be

- at least 21 and have held a full licence for at least one year
- over 18 and hold an advanced driver's certificate
- over 18 and have fully comprehensive insurance
- at least 21 and have held a full licence for at least three years

- **at least 21 and have held a full licence for at least three years**

Helping someone to drive is a responsible task. Before learning to drive you're advised to find a qualified Approved Driving Instructor (ADI) to teach you. This will ensure that you're taught the correct procedures from the start.

Your motor insurance policy has an excess of £100. What does this mean?

- The insurance company will pay the first £100 of any claim
- You will be paid £100 if you do not have a crash
- Your vehicle is insured for a value of £100 if it is stolen
- You will have to pay the first £100 of any claim

- **You will have to pay the first £100 of any claim**

This is a method used by insurance companies to keep annual premiums down. Generally, the higher the excess you choose to pay, the lower the annual premium you will be charged.

section **thirteen**
ACCIDENTS

This section covers

- First aid
- Warning devices
- Reporting procedures
- Safety regulations

13.1
*Mark **one** answer*

You see a car on the hard shoulder of a motorway with a HELP pennant displayed. This means the driver is most likely to be

- ⊙ a disabled person
- ⊙ first aid trained
- ⊙ a foreign visitor
- ⊙ a rescue patrol person

⊙ **a disabled person**

If a disabled driver's vehicle breaks down and they are unable to walk to an emergency phone, they are advised to stay in their car and switch on the hazard warning lights. They may also display a 'Help' pennant in their vehicle.

13.2
*Mark **two** answers*

For which TWO should you use hazard warning lights?

- ⊙ When you slow down quickly on a motorway because of a hazard ahead
- ⊙ When you have broken down
- ⊙ When you wish to stop on double yellow lines
- ⊙ When you need to park on the pavement

⊙ **When you slow down quickly on a motorway because of a hazard ahead**

⊙ **When you have broken down**

Hazard warning lights are fitted to all modern cars and some motorcycles. They should only be used to warn other road users of a hazard ahead.

13.3
*Mark **one** answer*

When are you allowed to use hazard warning lights?

- ⊙ When stopped and temporarily obstructing traffic
- ⊙ When travelling during darkness without headlights
- ⊙ When parked for shopping on double yellow lines
- ⊙ When travelling slowly because you are lost

⊙ **When stopped and temporarily obstructing traffic**

You must not use hazard warning lights when moving, except when slowing suddenly on a motorway or unrestricted dual carriageway to warn the traffic behind.

Never use hazard warning lights to excuse dangerous or illegal parking.

*Mark **one** answer*

You are going through a congested tunnel and have to stop. What should you do?

- ⦿ Pull up very close to the vehicle in front to save space
- ⦿ Ignore any message signs as they are never up to date
- ⦿ Keep a safe distance from the vehicle in front
- ⦿ Make a U-turn and find another route

⦿ **Keep a safe distance from the vehicle in front**

It's important to keep a safe distance from the vehicle in front at all times. This still applies in congested tunnels even if you are moving very slowly or have stopped. If the vehicle in front breaks down you may need room to manoeuvre past it.

---

*Mark **one** answer*

On the motorway, the hard shoulder should be used

- ⦿ to answer a mobile phone
- ⦿ when an emergency arises
- ⦿ for a short rest when tired
- ⦿ to check a road atlas

⦿ **when an emergency arises**

Pull onto the hard shoulder and use the emergency telephone to report your problem. This lets the emergency services know your exact location so they can send help. Never cross the carriageway to use the telephone on the other side.

---

*Mark **one** answer*

You arrive at the scene of a crash. Someone is bleeding badly from an arm wound. There is nothing embedded in it. What should you do?

- ⦿ Apply pressure over the wound and keep the arm down
- ⦿ Dab the wound
- ⦿ Get them a drink
- ⦿ Apply pressure over the wound and raise the arm

⦿ **Apply pressure over the wound and raise the arm**

If possible, lay the casualty down. Check for anything that may be in the wound. Apply firm pressure to the wound using clean material, without pressing on anything which might be in it. Raising the arm above the level of the heart will also help to stem the flow of blood.

13.7
*Mark **one** answer*

You are at an incident where a casualty is unconscious. Their breathing should be checked. This should be done for at least

- ⊙ 2 seconds
- ⊙ 10 seconds
- ⊙ 1 minute
- ⊙ 2 minutes

⊙ **10 seconds**

Once the airway is open, check breathing. Listen and feel for breath. Do this by placing your cheek over their mouth and nose, and look to see if the chest rises. This should be done for up to 10 seconds.

13.8
*Mark **one** answer*

Following a collision someone has suffered a burn. The burn needs to be cooled. What is the shortest time it should be cooled for?

- ⊙ 5 minutes
- ⊙ 10 minutes
- ⊙ 15 minutes
- ⊙ 20 minutes

⊙ **10 minutes**

Check the casualty for shock and if possible try to cool the burn for at least ten minutes. Use a clean, cold non-toxic liquid preferably water.

13.9
*Mark **one** answer*

After a collision someone has suffered a burn. The burn needs to be cooled. What is the shortest time it should be cooled for?

- ⊙ 30 seconds
- ⊙ 60 seconds
- ⊙ 5 minutes
- ⊙ 10 minutes

⊙ **10 minutes**

It's important to cool a burn for at least ten minutes. Use a clean, cold non-toxic liquid preferably water. Bear in mind the person may also be in shock.

A casualty is not breathing normally. Chest compressions should be given. At what rate?

- ⊙ 50 per minute
- ⊙ 100 per minute
- ⊙ 200 per minute
- ⊙ 250 per minute

⊙ **100 per minute**

If a casualty is not breathing normally chest compressions may be needed to maintain circulation. Place two hands on the centre of the chest and press down about 4-5 centimetres, at the rate of 100 per minute.

A person has been injured. They may be suffering from shock. What are the warning signs to look for?

- ⊙ Flushed complexion
- ⊙ Warm dry skin
- ⊙ Slow pulse
- ⊙ Pale grey skin

⊙ **Pale grey skin**

The effects of shock may not be immediately obvious. Warning signs are rapid pulse, sweating, pale grey skin and rapid shallow breathing.

You suspect that an injured person may be suffering from shock. What are the warning signs to look for?

- ⊙ Warm dry skin
- ⊙ Sweating
- ⊙ Slow pulse
- ⊙ Skin rash

⊙ **Sweating**

Sometimes you may not realise that someone is in shock. The signs to look for are rapid pulse, sweating, pale grey skin and rapid shallow breathing.

13.13
*Mark **one** answer*

An injured person has been placed in the recovery position. They are unconscious but breathing normally. What else should be done?

- Press firmly between the shoulders
- Place their arms by their side
- Give them a hot sweet drink
- Check the airway is clear

⊙ **Check the airway is clear**

After a casualty has been placed in the recovery position, their airway should be checked to make sure it's clear. Don't leave them alone until medical help arrives. Where possible do NOT move a casualty unless there's further danger.

13.14
*Mark **one** answer*

An injured motorcyclist is lying unconscious in the road. You should always

- remove the safety helmet
- seek medical assistance
- move the person off the road
- remove the leather jacket

⊙ **seek medical assistance**

If someone has been injured, the sooner proper medical attention is given the better. Send someone to phone for help or go yourself. An injured person should only be moved if they're in further danger. An injured motorcyclist's helmet should NOT be removed unless it is essential.

13.15
*Mark **one** answer*

You are on a motorway. A large box falls onto the road from a lorry. The lorry does not stop. You should

- go to the next emergency telephone and report the hazard
- catch up with the lorry and try to get the driver's attention
- stop close to the box until the police arrive
- pull over to the hard shoulder, then remove the box

⊙ **go to the next emergency telephone and report the hazard**

Lorry drivers can be unaware of objects falling from their vehicles. If you see something fall onto a motorway look to see if the driver pulls over. If they don't stop, do not attempt to retrieve it yourself. Pull on to the hard shoulder near an emergency telephone and report the hazard. You will be connected to the police or a Highways Agency control centre.

13.16

Mark **one** answer

You are going through a long tunnel. What will warn you of congestion or an incident ahead?

- ⊙ Hazard warning lines
- ⊙ Other drivers flashing their lights
- ⊙ Variable message signs
- ⊙ Areas marked with hatch markings

⊙ **Variable message signs**

Follow the instructions given by the signs or by tunnel officials.

In congested tunnels a minor incident can soon turn into a major one with serious or even fatal results.

13.17

Mark **one** answer

An adult casualty is not breathing. To maintain circulation, compressions should be given. What is the correct depth to press?

- ⊙ 1 to 2 centimetres
- ⊙ 4 to 5 centimetres
- ⊙ 10 to 15 centimetres
- ⊙ 15 to 20 centimetres

⊙ **4 to 5 centimetres**

An adult casualty is not breathing normally. To maintain circulation place two hands on the centre of the chest. Then press down 4 to 5 centimetres at a rate of 100 times per minute.

13.18

Mark **two** answers

You are the first to arrive at the scene of a crash. Which TWO of these should you do?

- ⊙ Leave as soon as another motorist arrives
- ⊙ Make sure engines are switched off
- ⊙ Drag all casualties away from the vehicles
- ⊙ Call the emergency services promptly

⊙ **Make sure engines are switched off**

⊙ **Call the emergency services promptly**

At a crash scene you can help in practical ways, even if you aren't trained in first aid. Make sure you do not put yourself or anyone else in danger. The safest way to warn other traffic is by switching on your hazard warning lights.

13.19
Mark one answer

At the scene of a traffic incident you should

⊙ not put yourself at risk

⊙ go to those casualties who are screaming

⊙ pull everybody out of their vehicles

⊙ leave vehicle engines switched on

⊙ **not put yourself at risk**

It's important that people at the scene of a collision do not create further risk to themselves or others. If the incident is on a motorway or major road, traffic will be approaching at speed. Do not put yourself at risk when trying to help casualties or warning other road users.

13.20
Mark three answers

You are the first person to arrive at an incident where people are badly injured. Which THREE should you do?

⊙ Switch on your own hazard warning lights

⊙ Make sure that someone telephones for an ambulance

⊙ Try and get people who are injured to drink something

⊙ Move the people who are injured clear of their vehicles

⊙ Get people who are not injured clear of the scene

⊙ **Switch on your own hazard warning lights**

⊙ **Make sure that someone telephones for an ambulance**

⊙ **Get people who are not injured clear of the scene**

If you're the first to arrive at a crash scene the first concerns are the risk of further collision and fire. Ensuring that vehicle engines are switched off will reduce the risk of fire. Use hazard warning lights so that other traffic knows there's a need for caution. Make sure the emergency services are contacted, don't assume this has already been done.

13.21
Mark one answer

You arrive at the scene of a motorcycle crash. The rider is injured. When should the helmet be removed?

⊙ Only when it is essential

⊙ Always straight away

⊙ Only when the motorcyclist asks

⊙ Always, unless they are in shock

⊙ **Only when it is essential**

DO NOT remove a motorcyclist's helmet unless it is essential. Remember they may be suffering from shock. Don't give them anything to eat or drink but do reassure them confidently.

*Mark **three** answers*

You arrive at a serious motorcycle crash. The motorcyclist is unconscious and bleeding. Your THREE main priorities should be to

- ⊙ try to stop the bleeding
- ⊙ make a list of witnesses
- ⊙ check their breathing
- ⊙ take the numbers of other vehicles
- ⊙ sweep up any loose debris
- ⊙ check their airways

- ⊙ **try to stop the bleeding**
- ⊙ **check their breathing**
- ⊙ **check their airways**

Further collisions and fire are the main dangers immediately after a crash. If possible get others to assist you and make the area safe. Help those involved and remember DR ABC; Danger, Response, Airway, Breathing, Compressions. This will help when dealing with any injuries.

*Mark **one** answer*

You arrive at an incident. A motorcyclist is unconscious. Your FIRST priority is the casualty's

- ⊙ breathing
- ⊙ bleeding
- ⊙ broken bones
- ⊙ bruising

- ⊙ **breathing**

At the scene of an incident always be aware of danger from further collisions or fire. The first priority when dealing with an unconscious person is to ensure they can breathe. This may involve clearing their airway if you can see an obstruction, or if they're having difficulty breathing.

*Mark **three** answers*

At an incident a casualty is unconscious. Which THREE of these should you check urgently?

- ⊙ Circulation
- ⊙ Airway
- ⊙ Shock
- ⊙ Breathing
- ⊙ Broken bones

- ⊙ **Circulation**
- ⊙ **Airway**
- ⊙ **Breathing**

Remember DR ABC. An unconscious casualty may have difficulty breathing. Check that their airway is clear by tilting the head back gently and unblock it if necessary. Then make sure they are breathing. If there is bleeding, stem the flow by placing clean material over any wounds but without pressing on any objects in the wound. Compressions may need to be given to maintain circulation.

13.25   *Mark **three** answers*

You arrive at the scene of an incident. It has just happened and someone is unconscious. Which THREE of these should be given urgent priority to help them?

- ⊙ Clear the airway and keep it open
- ⊙ Try to get them to drink water
- ⊙ Check that they are breathing
- ⊙ Look for any witnesses
- ⊙ Stop any heavy bleeding
- ⊙ Take the numbers of vehicles involved

- ⊙ **Clear the airway and keep it open**
- ⊙ **Check that they are breathing**
- ⊙ **Stop any heavy bleeding**

Make sure that the emergency services are called immediately. Once first aid has been given, stay with the casualty.

13.26   *Mark **three** answers*

At an incident someone is unconscious. Your THREE main priorities should be to

- ⊙ sweep up the broken glass
- ⊙ take the names of witnesses
- ⊙ count the number of vehicles involved
- ⊙ check the airway is clear
- ⊙ make sure they are breathing
- ⊙ stop any heavy bleeding

- ⊙ **check the airway is clear**
- ⊙ **make sure they are breathing**
- ⊙ **stop any heavy bleeding**

Remember this procedure by saying DR ABC. This stands for Danger, Response, Airway, Breathing, Compressions.

You have stopped at an incident to give help. Which THREE things should you do?

- ⊙ Keep injured people warm and comfortable
- ⊙ Keep injured people calm by talking to them reassuringly
- ⊙ Keep injured people on the move by walking them around
- ⊙ Give injured people a warm drink
- ⊙ Make sure that injured people are not left alone

⊙ **Keep injured people warm and comfortable**

⊙ **Keep injured people calm by talking to them reassuringly**

⊙ **Make sure that injured people are not left alone**

There are a number of things you can do to help, even without expert training. Be aware of further danger and fire, make sure the area is safe. People may be in shock. Don't give them anything to eat or drink. Keep them warm and comfortable and reassure them. Don't move injured people unless there is a risk of further danger.

You arrive at an incident. It has just happened and someone is injured. Which THREE should be given urgent priority?

- ⊙ Stop any severe bleeding
- ⊙ Give them a warm drink
- ⊙ Check they are breathing
- ⊙ Take numbers of vehicles involved
- ⊙ Look for witnesses
- ⊙ Clear their airway and keep it open

⊙ **Stop any severe bleeding**

⊙ **Check they are breathing**

⊙ **Clear their airway and keep it open**

The first priority with a casualty is to make sure their airway is clear and they are breathing. Any wounds should be checked for objects and then bleeding stemmed using clean material. Ensure the emergency services are called, they are the experts. If you're not first aid trained consider getting training. It might save a life.

13.29
*Mark **one** answer*

Which of the following should you NOT do at the scene of a collision?

- ⊙ Warn other traffic by switching on your hazard warning lights
- ⊙ Call the emergency services immediately
- ⊙ Offer someone a cigarette to calm them down
- ⊙ Ask drivers to switch off their engines

⊙ **Offer someone a cigarette to calm them down**

Keeping casualties or witnesses calm is important, but never offer a cigarette because of the risk of fire. Bear in mind they may be in shock. Don't offer an injured person anything to eat or drink. They may have internal injuries or need surgery.

13.30
*Mark **two** answers*

There has been a collision. A driver is suffering from shock. What TWO of these should you do?

- ⊙ Give them a drink
- ⊙ Reassure them
- ⊙ Not leave them alone
- ⊙ Offer them a cigarette
- ⊙ Ask who caused the incident

⊙ **Reassure them**

⊙ **Not leave them alone**

Be aware they could have an injury that is not immediately obvious. Ensure the emergency services are called. Reassure and stay with them until the experts arrive.

13.31
*Mark **one** answer*

You have to treat someone for shock at the scene of an incident. You should

- ⊙ reassure them constantly
- ⊙ walk them around to calm them down
- ⊙ give them something cold to drink
- ⊙ cool them down as soon as possible

⊙ **reassure them constantly**

Stay with the casualty and talk to them quietly and firmly to calm and reassure them. Avoid moving them unnecessarily in case they are injured. Keep them warm, but don't give them anything to eat or drink.

You arrive at the scene of a motorcycle crash. No other vehicle is involved. The rider is unconscious and lying in the middle of the road. The FIRST thing you should do is

- ⊙ move the rider out of the road
- ⊙ warn other traffic
- ⊙ clear the road of debris
- ⊙ give the rider reassurance

⊙ **warn other traffic**

The motorcyclist is in an extremely vulnerable position, exposed to further danger from traffic. Approaching vehicles need advance warning in order to slow down and safely take avoiding action or stop. Don't put yourself or anyone else at risk. Use the hazard warning lights on your vehicle to alert other road users to the danger.

At an incident a small child is not breathing. To restore normal breathing you should breathe into their mouth

- ⊙ sharply
- ⊙ gently
- ⊙ heavily
- ⊙ rapidly

⊙ **gently**

If a young child has stopped breathing, first check that the airway is clear. Then give compressions to the chest using one hand (two fingers for an infant) and begin mouth to mouth resuscitation. Breathe very gently and continue the procedure until they can breathe without help.

At an incident a casualty is not breathing. To start the process to restore normal breathing you should

- ⊙ tilt their head forward
- ⊙ clear the airway
- ⊙ turn them on their side
- ⊙ tilt their head back gently
- ⊙ pinch the nostrils together
- ⊙ put their arms across their chest

⊙ **clear the airway**

⊙ **tilt their head back gently**

⊙ **pinch the nostrils together**

It's important to ensure that the airways are clear before you start mouth to mouth resuscitation. Gently tilt their head back and use your finger to check for and remove any obvious obstruction in the mouth.

13.35   *Mark **one** answer*

You arrive at an incident. There has been an engine fire and someone's hands and arms have been burnt. You should NOT

- douse the burn thoroughly with clean cool non-toxic liquid
- lay the casualty down on the ground
- remove anything sticking to the burn
- reassure them confidently and repeatedly

- **remove anything sticking to the burn**

This could cause further damage and infection to the wound. Your first priority is to cool the burn with a clean, cool, non-toxic liquid, preferably water. Don't forget the casualty may be in shock.

13.36   *Mark **one** answer*

You arrive at an incident where someone is suffering from severe burns. You should

- apply lotions to the injury
- burst any blisters
- remove anything stuck to the burns
- douse the burns with clean cool non-toxic liquid

- **douse the burns with clean cool non-toxic liquid**

Use a liquid that is clean, cold and non-toxic, preferably water. Its coolness will help take the heat out of the burn and relieve the pain. Keep the wound doused for at least ten minutes. If blisters appear don't attempt to burst them as this could lead to infection.

13.37   *Mark **two** answers*

You arrive at an incident. A pedestrian has a severe bleeding leg wound. It is not broken and there is nothing in the wound. What TWO of these should you do?

- Dab the wound to stop bleeding
- Keep both legs flat on the ground
- Apply firm pressure to the wound
- Raise the leg to lessen bleeding
- Fetch them a warm drink

- **Apply firm pressure to the wound**

- **Raise the leg to lessen bleeding**

First check for anything that may be in the wound such as glass. If there's nothing in it apply a pad of clean cloth or bandage. Raising the leg will lessen the flow of blood. Don't tie anything tightly round the leg. This will restrict circulation and can result in long-term injury.

At an incident a casualty is unconscious but still breathing. You should only move them if

- ⊙ an ambulance is on its way
- ⊙ bystanders advise you to
- ⊙ there is further danger
- ⊙ bystanders will help you to

⊙ **there is further danger**

Do not move a casualty unless there is further danger, for example, from other traffic or fire. They may have unseen or internal injuries. Moving them unnecessarily could cause further injury. Do NOT remove a motorcyclists helmet unless it's essential.

At a collision you suspect a casualty has back injuries. The area is safe. You should

- ⊙ offer them a drink
- ⊙ not move them
- ⊙ raise their legs
- ⊙ not call an ambulance

⊙ **not move them**

Talk to the casualty and keep them calm. Do not attempt to move them as this could cause further injury. Call an ambulance at the first opportunity.

At an incident it is important to look after any casualties. When the area is safe, you should

- ⊙ get them out of the vehicle
- ⊙ give them a drink
- ⊙ give them something to eat
- ⊙ keep them in the vehicle

⊙ **keep them in the vehicle**

When the area is safe and there's no danger from other traffic or fire it's better not to move casualties. Moving them may cause further injury.

13.41 — Mark **one** answer

A tanker is involved in a collision. Which sign shows that it is carrying dangerous goods?

LONG VEHICLE

There will be an orange label on the side and rear of the tanker. Look at this carefully and report what it says when you phone the emergency services. Details of hazard warning plates are given in The Highway Code.

13.42 — Mark **three** answers

You are involved in a collision. Because of this which THREE of these documents may the police ask you to produce?

- Vehicle registration document
- Driving licence
- Theory test certificate
- Insurance certificate
- MOT test certificate
- Vehicle service record

- **Driving licence**
- **Insurance certificate**
- **MOT test certificate**

You MUST stop if you have been involved in a collision which results in injury or damage. The police may ask to see your documents at the time or later at a police station.

13.43 — Mark **one** answer

After a collision someone is unconscious in their vehicle. When should you call the emergency services?

- Only as a last resort
- As soon as possible
- After you have woken them up
- After checking for broken bones

- **As soon as possible**

It is important to make sure that emergency services arrive on the scene as soon as possible. When a person is unconscious, they could have serious injuries that are not immediately obvious.

13.44

*Mark **one** answer*

A casualty has an injured arm. They can move it freely but it is bleeding. Why should you get them to keep it in a raised position?

- ⊙ Because it will ease the pain
- ⊙ It will help them to be seen more easily
- ⊙ To stop them touching other people
- ⊙ It will help to reduce the blood flow

⊙ **It will help to reduce the blood flow**

If a casualty is bleeding heavily, raise the limb to a higher position. This will help to reduce the blood flow. Before raising the limb you should make sure that it is not broken.

13.45

*Mark **one** answer*

You are going through a tunnel. What systems are provided to warn of any incidents, collisions or congestion?

- ⊙ Double white centre lines
- ⊙ Variable message signs
- ⊙ Chevron 'distance markers'
- ⊙ Rumble strips

⊙ **Variable message signs**

Take notice of any instructions given on variable message signs or by tunnel officials. They will warn you of any incidents or congestion ahead and advise you what to do.

13.46

*Mark **one** answer*

A collision has just happened. An injured person is lying in a busy road. What is the FIRST thing you should do to help?

- ⊙ Treat the person for shock
- ⊙ Warn other traffic
- ⊙ Place them in the recovery position
- ⊙ Make sure the injured person is kept warm

⊙ **Warn other traffic**

The most immediate danger is further collisions and fire. You could warn other traffic by displaying an advance warning triangle or sign (but not on a motorway), switching on hazard warning lights or by any other means that does not put you or others at risk.

13.47 — Mark **two** answers

At an incident a casualty has stopped breathing. You should

- remove anything that is blocking the mouth
- keep the head tilted forwards as far as possible
- raise the legs to help with circulation
- try to give the casualty something to drink
- tilt the head back gently to clear the airway

- **remove anything that is blocking the mouth**
- **tilt the head back gently to clear the airway**

Unblocking the airway and gently tilting the head back will help the casualty to breathe. They will then be in the correct position if mouth-to-mouth resuscitation is required. Don't move a casualty unless there's further danger.

13.48 — Mark **four** answers

You are at the scene of an incident. Someone is suffering from shock. You should

- reassure them constantly
- offer them a cigarette
- keep them warm
- avoid moving them if possible
- avoid leaving them alone
- give them a warm drink

- **reassure them constantly**
- **keep them warm**
- **avoid moving them if possible**
- **avoid leaving them alone**

The signs of shock may not be immediately obvious. Prompt treatment can help to minimise the effects. Lay the casualty down, loosen tight clothing, call an ambulance and check their breathing and pulse.

13.49 — Mark **one** answer

There has been a collision. A motorcyclist is lying injured and unconscious. Unless it's essential, why should you usually NOT attempt to remove their helmet?

- Because they may not want you to
- This could result in more serious injury
- They will get too cold if you do this
- Because you could scratch the helmet

- **This could result in more serious injury**

When someone is injured, any movement which is not absolutely necessary should be avoided since it could make injuries worse. Unless it is essential, it's generally safer to leave a motorcyclist's helmet in place.

You have broken down on a two-way road. You have a warning triangle. You should place the warning triangle at least how far from your vehicle?

- ⊙ 5 metres (16 feet)
- ⊙ 25 metres (82 feet)
- ⊙ 45 metres (147 feet)
- ⊙ 100 metres (328 feet)

⊙ **45 metres (147 feet)**

Advance warning triangles fold flat and don't take up much room. Use it to warn other road users if your vehicle has broken down or there's been an incident. Place it at least 45 metres (147 feet) behind your vehicle or incident on the same side of the road or verge. Place it further back if the scene is hidden by, for example, a bend, hill or dip in the road. Don't use them on motorways.

You break down on a level crossing. The lights have not yet begun to flash. Which THREE things should you do?

- ⊙ Telephone the signal operator
- ⊙ Leave your vehicle and get everyone clear
- ⊙ Walk down the track and signal the next train
- ⊙ Move the vehicle if a signal operator tells you to
- ⊙ Tell drivers behind what has happened

⊙ **Telephone the signal operator**

⊙ **Leave your vehicle and get everyone clear**

⊙ **Move the vehicle if a signal operator tells you to**

If your vehicle breaks down on a level crossing, your first priority is to get everyone out of the vehicle and clear of the crossing. Then use the railway telephone, if there is one, to tell the signal operator. If you have time before the train arrives, move the vehicle clear of the crossing, but only do this if alarm signals are not on.

13.52 · Mark **two** answers

Your tyre bursts while you are driving. Which TWO things should you do?

- ⊙ Pull on the handbrake
- ⊙ Brake as quickly as possible
- ⊙ Pull up slowly at the side of the road
- ⊙ Hold the steering wheel firmly to keep control
- ⊙ Continue on at a normal speed

⊙ **Pull up slowly at the side of the road**

⊙ **Hold the steering wheel firmly to keep control**

A tyre bursting can lead to a loss of control, especially if you're travelling at high speed. Using the correct procedure should help you to stop the vehicle safely.

13.53 · Mark **two** answers

Which TWO things should you do when a front tyre bursts?

- ⊙ Apply the handbrake to stop the vehicle
- ⊙ Brake firmly and quickly
- ⊙ Let the vehicle roll to a stop
- ⊙ Hold the steering wheel lightly
- ⊙ Grip the steering wheel firmly

⊙ **Let the vehicle roll to a stop**

⊙ **Grip the steering wheel firmly**

Try not to react by applying the brakes harshly. This could lead to further loss of steering control. Indicate your intention to pull up at the side of the road and roll to a stop.

13.54 · Mark **one** answer

Your vehicle has a puncture on a motorway. What should you do?

- ⊙ Drive slowly to the next service area to get assistance
- ⊙ Pull up on the hard shoulder. Change the wheel as quickly as possible
- ⊙ Pull up on the hard shoulder. Use the emergency phone to get assistance
- ⊙ Switch on your hazard lights. Stop in your lane

⊙ **Pull up on the hard shoulder. Use the emergency phone to get assistance**

Pull up on the hard shoulder and make your way to the nearest emergency telephone to call for assistance.

Do not attempt to repair your vehicle while it is on the hard shoulder because of the risk posed by traffic passing at high speeds.

You have stalled in the middle of a level crossing and cannot restart the engine. The warning bell starts to ring. You should

- ⊙ get out and clear of the crossing
- ⊙ run down the track to warn the signal operator
- ⊙ carry on trying to restart the engine
- ⊙ push the vehicle clear of the crossing

⊙ **get out and clear of the crossing**

Try to stay calm, especially if you have passengers on board. If you can't restart your engine before the warning bells ring, leave the vehicle and get yourself and any passengers well clear of the crossing.

You are on a motorway. When can you use hazard warning lights?

- ⊙ When a vehicle is following too closely
- ⊙ When you slow down quickly because of danger ahead
- ⊙ When you are towing another vehicle
- ⊙ When driving on the hard shoulder
- ⊙ When you have broken down on the hard shoulder

⊙ **When you slow down quickly because of danger ahead**

⊙ **When you have broken down on the hard shoulder**

Hazard warning lights will warn the traffic travelling behind you that there is a hazard ahead.

You have broken down on a motorway. When you use the emergency telephone you will be asked

- ⊙ for the number on the telephone that you are using
- ⊙ for your driving licence details
- ⊙ for the name of your vehicle insurance company
- ⊙ for details of yourself and your vehicle
- ⊙ whether you belong to a motoring organisation

⊙ **for the number on the telephone that you are using**

⊙ **for details of yourself and your vehicle**

⊙ **whether you belong to a motoring organisation**

Have these details ready before you use the emergency telephone and be sure to give the correct information. For your own safety always face the traffic when you speak on a roadside telephone.

13.58   *Mark **one** answer*

Before driving through a tunnel what should you do?

- Switch your radio off
- Remove any sunglasses
- Close your sunroof
- Switch on windscreen wipers

⊙ **Remove any sunglasses**

If you are wearing sunglasses you should remove them before driving into a tunnel. If you don't, your vision will be restricted, even in tunnels that appear to be well-lit.

13.59   *Mark **one** answer*

You are driving through a tunnel and the traffic is flowing normally. What should you do?

- Use parking lights
- Use front spot lights
- Use dipped headlights
- Use rear fog lights

⊙ **Use dipped headlights**

Before entering a tunnel you should switch on your dipped headlights, as this will allow you to see and be seen. In many tunnels it is a legal requirement.

Don't wear sunglasses while driving in a tunnel. You may wish to tune your radio into a local channel.

13.60   *Mark **one** answer*

You are driving through a tunnel. Your vehicle breaks down. What should you do?

- Switch on hazard warning lights
- Remain in your vehicle
- Wait for the police to find you
- Rely on CCTV cameras seeing you

⊙ **Switch on hazard warning lights**

If your vehicle breaks down in a tunnel it could present a danger to other traffic. First switch on your hazard warning lights and then call for help from an emergency telephone point.

Don't rely on being found by the police or being seen by a CCTV camera. The longer the vehicle stays in an exposed position, the more danger it poses to other drivers.

When driving through a tunnel you should

- Look out for variable message signs
- Use your air conditioning system
- Switch on your rear fog lights
- Always use your windscreen wipers

⊙ **Look out for variable message signs**

A minor incident in a tunnel can quickly turn into a major disaster. Variable message signs are provided to warn of any incidents or congestion. Follow their advice.

What TWO safeguards could you take against fire risk to your vehicle?

- Keep water levels above maximum
- Carry a fire extinguisher
- Avoid driving with a full tank of petrol
- Use unleaded petrol
- Check out any strong smell of petrol
- Use low octane fuel

⊙ **Carry a fire extinguisher**

⊙ **Check out any strong smell of petrol**

The fuel in your vehicle can be a dangerous fire hazard. Never

- use a naked flame near the vehicle if you can smell fuel
- smoke when refuelling your vehicle.

You are on the motorway. Luggage falls from your vehicle. What should you do?

- Stop at the next emergency telephone and contact the police
- Stop on the motorway and put on hazard lights while you pick it up
- Walk back up the motorway to pick it up
- Pull up on the hard shoulder and wave traffic down

⊙ **Stop at the next emergency telephone and contact the police**

If any object falls onto the motorway carriageway from your vehicle pull over onto the hard shoulder near an emergency telephone and phone for assistance. You will be connected to the police or a Highways Agency control centre. Don't stop on the carriageway or attempt to retrieve anything.

13.64
*Mark **one** answer*

While driving, a warning light on your vehicle's instrument panel comes on. You should

- ⊙ continue if the engine sounds all right
- ⊙ hope that it is just a temporary electrical fault
- ⊙ deal with the problem when there is more time
- ⊙ check out the problem quickly and safely

⊙ **check out the problem quickly and safely**

Make sure you know what the different warning lights mean. An illuminated warning light could mean that your car is unsafe to drive. Don't take risks. If you aren't sure about the problem get a qualified mechanic to check it.

13.65
*Mark **one** answer*

You have broken down on a two-way road. You have a warning triangle. It should be displayed

- ⊙ on the roof of your vehicle
- ⊙ at least 150 metres (492 feet) behind your vehicle
- ⊙ at least 45 metres (147 feet) behind your vehicle
- ⊙ just behind your vehicle

⊙ **at least 45 metres (147 feet) behind your vehicle**

If you need to display a warning triangle make sure that it can be clearly seen by other road users. Place it on the same side of the road as the broken down vehicle and away from any obstruction that would make it hard to see.

Your engine catches fire. What should you do first?

- Lift the bonnet and disconnect the battery
- Lift the bonnet and warn other traffic
- Call a breakdown service
- Call the fire brigade

◉ **Call the fire brigade**

If you suspect a fire in the engine compartment you should pull up as safely and as quickly as possible. DO NOT open the bonnet as this will fuel the fire further. Get any passengers out of the vehicle and dial 999 immediately to contact the fire brigade.

Your vehicle breaks down in a tunnel. What should you do?

- Stay in your vehicle and wait for the police
- Stand in the lane behind your vehicle to warn others
- Stand in front of your vehicle to warn oncoming drivers
- Switch on hazard lights then go and call for help immediately

◉ **Switch on hazard lights then go and call for help immediately**

A broken-down vehicle in a tunnel can cause serious congestion and danger to other road users. If your vehicle breaks down, get help without delay. Switch on your hazard warning lights, then go to an emergency telephone point to call for help.

Your vehicle catches fire while driving through a tunnel. It is still driveable. What should you do?

- Leave it where it is with the engine running
- Pull up, then walk to an emergency telephone point
- Park it away from the carriageway
- Drive it out of the tunnel if you can do so

◉ **Drive it out of the tunnel if you can do so**

If it's possible, and you can do so without causing further danger, it may be safer to drive a vehicle which is on fire out of a tunnel. The greatest danger in a tunnel fire is smoke and suffocation.

13.69
*Mark **one** answer*

You are driving through a tunnel. Your vehicle catches fire. What should you do?

- Continue through the tunnel if you can
- Turn your vehicle around immediately
- Reverse out of the tunnel
- Carry out an emergency stop

◉ **Continue through the tunnel if you can**

The main dangers in a tunnel fire are suffocation and smoke. If you can do so safely it's better to drive a burning vehicle out of a tunnel. If you can't do this, pull over, switch off the engine, use hazard warning lights and phone immediately for help. It may be possible to put out a small fire but if it seems large do NOT tackle it!

13.70
*Mark **two** answers*

You are in a tunnel. Your vehicle is on fire and you CANNOT drive it. What should you do?

- Stay in the vehicle and close the windows
- Switch on hazard warning lights
- Leave the engine running
- Try and put out the fire
- Switch off all of your lights
- Wait for other people to phone for help

◉ **Switch on hazard warning lights**

◉ **Try and put out the fire**

It's usually better to drive a burning vehicle out of a tunnel. If you can't do this pull over and stop at an emergency point if possible. Switch off the engine, use hazard warning lights, and leave the vehicle immediately. Call for help from the nearest emergency point. If you have an extinguisher it may help to put out a small fire but do NOT try to tackle a large one.

13.71
*Mark **one** answer*

When approaching a tunnel it is good advice to

- put on your sunglasses and use the sun visor
- check your tyre pressures
- change down to a lower gear
- make sure your radio is tuned to the frequency shown

◉ **make sure your radio is tuned to the frequency shown**

On the approach to tunnels a sign will usually show a local radio channel. It should give a warning of any incidents or congestion in the tunnel ahead. Many radios can be set to automatically pick up traffic announcements and local frequencies. If you have to tune the radio manually don't be distracted while doing so. Incidents in tunnels can lead to serious casualties. The greatest hazard is fire. Getting an advance warning of problems could save your life and others.

13.72

Your vehicle has broken down on an automatic railway level crossing. What should you do FIRST?

- ⊙ Get everyone out of the vehicle and clear of the crossing
- ⊙ Telephone your vehicle recovery service to move it
- ⊙ Walk along the track to give warning to any approaching trains
- ⊙ Try to push the vehicle clear of the crossing as soon as possible

⊙ **Get everyone out of the vehicle and clear of the crossing**

Firstly get yourself and anyone else well away from the crossing. If there's a railway phone use that to get instructions from the signal operator. Then if there's time move the vehicle clear of the crossing.

13.73

Which THREE of these items should you carry for use in the event of a collision?

- ⊙ Road map
- ⊙ Can of petrol
- ⊙ Jump leads
- ⊙ Fire extinguisher
- ⊙ First aid kit
- ⊙ Warning triangle

⊙ **Fire extinguisher**

⊙ **First aid kit**

⊙ **Warning triangle**

Used correctly, these items can provide invaluable help in the event of a collision or breakdown. They could even save a life.

13.74

You have a collision whilst your car is moving. What is the FIRST thing you must do?

- ⊙ Stop only if someone waves at you
- ⊙ Call the emergency services
- ⊙ Stop at the scene of the incident
- ⊙ Call your insurance company

⊙ **Stop at the scene of the incident**

If you are in a collision that causes damage or injury to any other person, vehicle, animal or property, by law you MUST STOP. Give your name, the vehicle owner's name and address, and the vehicle's registration number to anyone who has reasonable grounds for requiring them.

13.75 — Mark **four** answers

You are in collision with another moving vehicle. Someone is injured and your vehicle is damaged. Which FOUR of the following should you find out?

- ⊙ Whether the driver owns the other vehicle involved
- ⦿ The other driver's name, address and telephone number
- ⦿ The make and registration number of the other vehicle
- ⊙ The occupation of the other driver
- ⦿ The details of the other driver's vehicle insurance
- ⊙ Whether the other driver is licensed to drive

⊙ **Whether the driver owns the other vehicle involved**

⊙ **The other driver's name, address and telephone number**

⊙ **The make and registration number of the other vehicle**

⊙ **The details of the other driver's vehicle insurance**

Try to keep calm and don't rush. Ensure that you have all the details before you leave the scene. If possible take pictures and note the positions of all the vehicles involved.

13.76   NI EXEMPT   Mark **one** answer

You lose control of your car and damage a garden wall. No one is around. What must you do?

- ⊙ Report the incident to the police within 24 hours
- ⊙ Go back to tell the house owner the next day
- ⊙ Report the incident to your insurance company when you get home
- ⊙ Find someone in the area to tell them about it immediately

⊙ **Report the incident to the police within 24 hours**

If the property owner is not available at the time, you MUST inform the police of the incident. This should be done as soon as possible, and within 24 hours.

You are in a collision on a two-way road. You have a warning triangle with you. At what distance before the obstruction should you place the warning triangle?

- ⊙ 25 metres (82 feet)
- ⊙ 45 metres (147 feet)
- ⊙ 100 metres (328 feet)
- ⊙ 150 metres (492 feet)

⊙ **45 metres (147 feet)**

This is the minimum distance to place the triangle from the obstruction. If there's a bend or hump in the road place it so that approaching traffic has plenty of time to react to the warning and slow down. You may also need to use your hazard warning lights, especially in poor visibility or at night.

You have a collision while driving through a tunnel. You are not injured but your vehicle cannot be driven. What should you do FIRST?

- ⊙ Rely on other drivers phoning for the police
- ⊙ Switch off the engine and switch on hazard lights
- ⊙ Take the names of witnesses and other drivers
- ⊙ Sweep up any debris that is in the road

⊙ **Switch off the engine and switch on hazard lights**

If you are involved in a collision in a tunnel be aware of the danger this can cause to other traffic. The greatest danger is fire. Put on your hazard warning lights straight away and switch off your engine. Then call for help from an emergency telephone point.

You are driving through a tunnel. There has been a collision and the car in front is on fire and blocking the road. What should you do?

- ⊙ Overtake and continue as quickly as you can
- ⊙ Lock all the doors and windows
- ⊙ Switch on hazard warning lights
- ⊙ Stop, then reverse out of the tunnel

⊙ **Switch on hazard warning lights**

If the vehicle in front is on fire, you should pull over to the side and stop. Switch on your warning lights and switch off your engine. If you can locate a fire extinguisher use it to put out the fire, taking great care. Do NOT open the bonnet. Always call for help from the nearest emergency point and if possible give first aid to anyone who is injured.

section **fourteen**
VEHICLE LOADING

This section covers
- Stability
- Towing regulations

14.1 — Mark **two** answers

You are towing a small trailer on a busy three-lane motorway. All the lanes are open. You must

- not exceed 60 mph
- not overtake
- have a stabiliser fitted
- use only the left and centre lanes

- **not exceed 60 mph**
- **use only the left and centre lanes**

You should be aware of the motorway regulations for vehicles towing trailers. These state that a vehicle towing a trailer must not

- use the right-hand lane of a three-lane motorway unless directed to do so, for example, at roadworks or due to a lane closure
- exceed 60 mph.

14.2 — Mark **one** answer

If a trailer swerves or snakes when you are towing it you should

- ease off the accelerator and reduce your speed
- let go of the steering wheel and let it correct itself
- brake hard and hold the pedal down
- increase your speed as quickly as possible

- **ease off the accelerator and reduce your speed**

Strong winds or buffeting from large vehicles can cause a trailer or caravan to snake or swerve. If this happens, ease off the accelerator. Don't brake harshly, steer sharply or increase your speed.

14.3 — Mark **one** answer

How can you stop a caravan snaking from side to side?

- Turn the steering wheel slowly to each side
- Accelerate to increase your speed
- Stop as quickly as you can
- Slow down very gradually

- **Slow down very gradually**

Keep calm and don't brake harshly or you could lose control completely. Ease off the accelerator until the unit is brought back under control. The most dangerous time is on long downhill gradients.

On which TWO occasions might you inflate your tyres to more than the recommended normal pressure?

- When the roads are slippery
- When driving fast for a long distance
- When the tyre tread is worn below 2mm
- When carrying a heavy load
- When the weather is cold
- When the vehicle is fitted with anti-lock brakes

⊙ **When driving fast for a long distance**

⊙ **When carrying a heavy load**

Check the vehicle handbook. This should give you guidance on the correct tyre pressures for your vehicle and when you may need to adjust them. If you are carrying a heavy load you may need to adjust the headlights as well. Most cars have a switch on the dashboard to do this.

A heavy load on your roof rack will

- improve the road holding
- reduce the stopping distance
- make the steering lighter
- reduce stability

⊙ **reduce stability**

A heavy load on your roof rack will reduce the stability of the vehicle because it moves the centre of gravity away from that designed by the manufacturer. Be aware of this when you negotiate bends and corners.

If you change direction at speed, your vehicle and/or load could become unstable and you could lose control.

You are towing a caravan along a motorway. The caravan begins to swerve from side to side. What should you do?

- Ease off the accelerator slowly
- Steer sharply from side to side
- Do an emergency stop
- Speed up very quickly

⊙ **Ease off the accelerator slowly**

Try not to brake or steer heavily as this will only make matters worse and you could lose control altogether. Keep calm and regain control by easing off the accelerator.

14.7

Overloading your vehicle can seriously affect the

- gearbox
- steering
- handling
- battery life
- journey time

⊙ **steering**

⊙ **handling**

Any load will have an effect on the handling of your vehicle and this becomes worse as you increase the load. Any change in the centre of gravity or weight the vehicle is carrying will affect its braking and handling on bends.

You need to be aware of this when carrying passengers, heavy loads, fitting a roof rack or towing a trailer.

14.8

Who is responsible for making sure that a vehicle is not overloaded?

- The driver of the vehicle
- The owner of the items being carried
- The person who loaded the vehicle
- The licensing authority

⊙ **The driver of the vehicle**

Your vehicle must not be overloaded. Carrying heavy loads will affect control and handling characteristics. If your vehicle is overloaded and it causes a crash, you'll be held responsible.

14.9

You are planning to tow a caravan. Which of these will mostly help to aid the vehicle handling?

- A jockey wheel fitted to the towbar
- Power steering fitted to the towing vehicle
- Anti-lock brakes fitted to the towing vehicle
- A stabiliser fitted to the towbar

⊙ **A stabiliser fitted to the towbar**

Towing a caravan or trailer affects the way the tow vehicle handles. It is highly recommended that you take a caravan manoeuvring course. These are provided by various organisations for anyone wishing to tow a trailer.

Are passengers allowed to ride in a caravan that is being towed?

- Yes, if they are over fourteen
- No, not at any time
- Only if all the seats in the towing vehicle are full
- Only if a stabiliser is fitted

⊙ **No, not at any time**

Riding in a towed caravan is highly dangerous. The safety of the entire unit is dependent on the stability of the trailer. Moving passengers would make the caravan unstable and could cause loss of control.

A trailer must stay securely hitched up to the towing vehicle. What additional safety device can be fitted to the trailer braking system?

- Stabiliser
- Jockey wheel
- Corner steadies
- Breakaway cable

⊙ **Breakaway cable**

In the event of a towbar failure the cable activates the trailer brakes, then snaps. This allows the towing vehicle to get free of the trailer and out of danger.

Why would you fit a stabiliser before towing a caravan?

- It will help with stability when driving in crosswinds
- It will allow heavy items to be loaded behind the axle
- It will help you to raise and lower the jockey wheel
- It will allow you to tow without the breakaway cable

⊙ **It will help with stability when driving in crosswinds**

Fitting a stabiliser to your tow bar will help to reduce snaking by the caravan especially where there are crosswinds. However, this does not take away your responsibility to ensure that your vehicle/caravan combination is loaded correctly.

14.13

You wish to tow a trailer. Where would you find the maximum noseweight of your vehicle's tow ball?

- In the vehicle handbook
- In The Highway Code
- In your vehicle registration certificate
- In your licence documents

In the vehicle handbook

You must know how to load your trailer or caravan so that the hitch exerts a downward force onto the tow ball. This information can be found in your vehicle handbook or from your vehicle manufacturer's agent.

14.14

Any load that is carried on a roof rack should be

- securely fastened when driving
- loaded towards the rear of the vehicle
- visible in your exterior mirror
- covered with plastic sheeting

securely fastened when driving

The safest way to carry items on the roof is in a specially designed roof box. This will help to keep your luggage secure and dry, and also has less wind resistance than loads carried on a roof rack.

14.15

You are carrying a child in your car. They are under three years of age. Which of these is a suitable restraint?

- A child seat
- An adult holding a child
- An adult seat belt
- An adult lap belt

A child seat

It's your responsibility to ensure that all children in your car are secure. Suitable restraints include a child seat, baby seat, booster seat or booster cushion. It's essential that any restraint used should be suitable for the child's size and weight, and fitted to the manufacturers instructions.

annex one
CASE STUDIES

Some of the questions within the test will be presented as a case study.

You will be presented with a set of facts – the case study – which will appear on the left-hand side of the screen. The set of facts or scenario will be presented in a text format and may be accompanied by a supporting picture or diagram.

As you move within the case study and answer each question, you can be assured that the facts and the scenario content will not change, although you do have the opportunity to re-read the scenario throughout the case study should you wish to do so.

The questions will appear, one by one, on the right-hand side of the screen, and you will be asked to respond.

An example of the type of scenario and questions you will be asked is given below (answers to the questions can be found on page 507).

CASE STUDY 1

You decide to visit your friend who lives about 20 miles away.

The journey will take you on various roads including country lanes and A-roads.

You've been before so think you know the way. You also have a mobile phone with you, so will be able to ring for directions if you get lost.

During the journey you go the wrong way and need to turn round. Later on, you decide to ring your friend to make sure you are still travelling in the right direction.

1. To turn round after going the wrong way, you decide to make a U-turn in the road. Before doing this, what should you do?

Mark one answer

☐ Give an arm signal as well as using indicators

☐ Signal so that other road users can slow down for you

☐ Look over your shoulder for a final check

☐ Select a higher gear than normal

◀ Previous   ! Flag   👓 Review   Next ▶

CASE STUDY 1

You decide to visit your friend who lives about 20 miles away.

The journey will take you on various roads including country lanes and A-roads.

You've been before so think you know the way. You also have a mobile phone with you, so will be able to ring for directions if you get lost.

During the journey you go the wrong way and need to turn round. Later on, you decide to ring your friend to make sure you are still travelling in the right direction.

2. What should you do as you approach this bridge on your journey?

Mark three answers

☐ Move into the middle of the road to get a better view

☐ Slow down

☐ Consider using the horn

☐ Find another route

☐ Beware of pedestrians

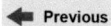 Previous   ! Flag    𝓞𝓞 Review    Next ➡

CASE STUDY 1

You decide to visit your friend who lives about 20 miles away.

The journey will take you on various roads including country lanes and A-roads.

You've been before so think you know the way. You also have a mobile phone with you, so will be able to ring for directions if you get lost.

During the journey you go the wrong way and need to turn round. Later on, you decide to ring your friend to make sure you are still travelling in the right direction.

3. During your journey, you ring your friend. What is the safest way for you to use your mobile phone?

Mark one answer

☐ Use hands-free equipment

☐ Find a suitable place to stop

☐ Travel slowly on a quiet road

☐ Direct your call through the operator

⬅ Previous   ! Flag    𝓞𝓞 Review   Next ➡

CASE STUDY 1

You decide to visit your friend who lives about 20 miles away.

The journey will take you on various roads including country lanes and A-roads.

You've been before so think you know the way. You also have a mobile phone with you, so will be able to ring for directions if you get lost.

During the journey you go the wrong way and need to turn round. Later on, you decide to ring your friend to make sure you are still travelling in the right direction.

4. You are travelling along a country road. A horse and rider are approaching. What should you do?

Mark two answers

☐ Increase your speed

☐ Sound your horn

☐ Flash your headlights

☐ Go slowly past

☐ Give plenty of room

☐ Rev your engine

← Previous   ! Flag   👓 Review   Next →

CASE STUDY 1

You decide to visit your friend who lives about 20 miles away.

The journey will take you on various roads including country lanes and A-roads.

You've been before so think you know the way. You also have a mobile phone with you, so will be able to ring for directions if you get lost.

During the journey you go the wrong way and need to turn round. Later on, you decide to ring your friend to make sure you are still travelling in the right direction.

5. Near the end of your journey, you come to a pedestrian crossing, with pedestrians who are hesitating to cross. Why should you never wave people across at pedestrian crossings?

Mark one answer

☐ There may be another vehicle coming

☐ They may not be looking

☐ It is safer for you to carry on

☐ They may not be ready to cross

← Previous   ! Flag   👓 Review   Next →

annex two
LIST OF TEST CENTRES

England

Aldershot
Barnstaple
Barrow
Basildon
Basingstoke
Bath
Berwick-upon-Tweed
Birkenhead
Birmingham
Blackpool
Bolton
Boston
Bournemouth
Bradford
Brighton
Bristol
Bury St Edmunds
Cambridge
Canterbury
Carlisle
Chatham
Chelmsford
Cheltenham
Chester
Chesterfield
Colchester
Coventry
Crawley
Derby
Doncaster
Dudley

Durham
Eastbourne
Exeter
Fareham
Gloucester
Grantham
Grimsby
Guildford
Harlow
Harrogate
Hastings
Hereford
Huddersfield
Hull
Ipswich
Isle of Wight
Isles of Scilly
King's Lynn
Leeds
Leicester
Lincoln
Liverpool
London
– Croydon
– Ilford
– Kingston
– Southgate
– Southwark
– Staines
– Uxbridge
Lowestoft
Luton

Manchester
Mansfield
Middlesbrough
Milton Keynes
Morpeth
Newcastle
Northampton
Norwich
Nottingham
Oldham
Oxford
Penzance
Peterborough
Plymouth
Portsmouth
Preston
Reading
Redditch
Runcorn
Salford
Salisbury
Scarborough
Scunthorpe
Sheffield
Shrewsbury
Sidcup
Slough
Solihull
Southampton
Southend-on-Sea
Southport
St Helens

Stevenage
Stockport
Stoke-on-Trent
Stratford-upon-Avon
Sunderland
Sutton Coldfield
Swindon
Taunton
Torquay
Truro
Watford
Weymouth
Wigan
Wolverhampton
Worcester
Workington
Worthing
Yeovil
York

Scotland
Aberdeen
Ayr
Clydebank
Dumfries
Dundee
Dunfermline
Edinburgh
Elgin
Fort William
Gairloch
Galashiels
Glasgow
Greenock
Helmsdale

Huntly
Inverness
Isle of Arran
Isle of Barra
Isle of Benbecula
Isle of Islay, Bowmore
Isle of Mull, Salen
Isle of Tiree
Kirkwall
Kyle of Lochalsh
Lerwick
Motherwell
Oban
Pitlochry
Portree
Stirling
Stornoway
Stranraer
Tarbert, Argyllshire
Tongue
Ullapool
Wick

Wales
Aberystwyth
Bangor
Builth Wells
Cardiff
Haverfordwest
Merthyr Tydfil
Newport
Rhyl
Swansea

Northern Ireland
Ballymena
Belfast
Londonderry
Newry
Omagh
Portadown

annex three
SERVICE STANDARDS

We judge our performance against the following standards (printed in our Business Plan) which we review each year

- 95% of calls to booking offices will make contact with our automated call-handling system without receiving an engaged tone
- after a call has gone through our automated call-handling system, we will answer 90% of all incoming calls to booking offices in no more than 20 seconds
- we will give 95% of candidates an appointment at their preferred centre within two weeks of their preferred date
- our online booking service will be available 99% of the time over 24 hours, 7 days a week.
- we will keep 99.5% of all theory test appointments
- we will answer 97% of all letters and e-mails within 10 working days
- we will pay 95% of all refunds within 15 days of receiving a valid claim.

Complaints guide - We aim to give our customers the best possible service. Please tell us when we have done well or if you're not satisfied.

Your comments can help us to improve the service we offer.

If you have any questions about your theory test, please contact us using the numbers below.

For DSA:
Tel 0300 200 1122, fax 0300 200 1177
Minicom 0300 200 1144
Welsh speakers 0300 200 1133

For DVA (Testing) in Northern Ireland:
Tel 0845 600 6700, fax 0870 010 4372

If you have any complaints about how your theory test was carried out, or any aspect of our customer service, please call the Customer Services section on 0300 200 1188. Alternatively you can write to the Customer Services Manager at the following address:

Customer Services
Driving Theory Test
PO Box 381
Manchester M50 3UW

If you're dissatisfied with the reply you can write to the Managing Director at the same address.

If you're still not satisfied, you can take up your complaint with:

The Chief Executive
Driving Standards Agency
The Axis building
112 Upper Parliament Street
Nottingham NG1 6LP

In Northern Ireland you should write to

The Chief Executive
Driver and Vehicle Agency (Testing)
Balmoral Road
Belfast BT12 6QL

None of this removes your right to take your complaint to your Member of Parliament, who may decide to raise your case personally with the DSA or DVA Chief Executive, the Minister or the Parliamentary Commissioner for Administration (the Ombudsman). Please refer to our leaflet *Customer Service - a guide to our service standards*.

DSA is a Trading Fund and we are required to cover our costs from the driving test fee.

We don't have a quota for test passes or fails and if you demonstrate the standard required, you'll pass your test.

Refunding fees and expenses - DSA will normally refund the test fee, or rearrange another test at no further cost to you, if

- we cancel your test
- you cancel and give us at least three clear working days notice
- you keep the test appointment but the test doesn't take place, or isn't finished, for a reason that isn't your fault.

We'll also repay you the expenses that you had to pay on the day of the test if we cancelled your test at short notice. We'll consider reasonable claims for

- the cost of travelling to and from the test centre

- any standard pay or earnings you lost through taking unpaid holiday leave (usually for half a day), after tax and national insurance contributions.

Please write to the address below and send a receipt showing travel costs and an employer's letter, which shows what earnings you lost. If you think you're entitled to fees and expenses write to:

Customer Services
Driving Theory Test
PO Box 381
Manchester M50 3UW

This reimbursement policy doesn't affect your existing legal rights.

DVA has a different reimbursement policy.

The OFFICIAL
HIGHWAY CODE

Contents

Introduction

This Highway Code applies to England, Scotland and Wales. *The Highway Code* is essential reading for everyone.

The most vulnerable road users are pedestrians, particularly children, older or disabled people, cyclists, motorcyclists and horse riders. It is important that all road users are aware of the Code and are considerate towards each other. This applies to pedestrians as much as to drivers and riders.

Many of the rules in the Code are legal requirements, and if you disobey these rules you are committing a criminal offence. You may be fined, given penalty points on your licence or be disqualified from driving. In the most serious cases you may be sent to prison. Such rules are identified by the use of the words '**MUST/MUST NOT**'. In addition, the rule includes an abbreviated reference to the legislation which creates the offence. An explanation of the abbreviations is on page 487.

Although failure to comply with the other rules of the Code will not, in itself, cause a person to be prosecuted, *The Highway Code* may be used in evidence in any court proceedings under the Traffic Acts (see page 487) to establish liability. This includes rules which use advisory wording such as 'should/should not' or 'do/do not'.

Knowing and applying the rules contained in *The Highway Code* could significantly reduce road casualties. Cutting the number of deaths and injuries that occur on our roads every day is a responsibility we all share. *The Highway Code* can help us discharge that responsibility. Further information on driving/riding techniques can be found in *The Official DSA Guide to Driving - the essential skills* and *The Official DSA Guide to Riding - the essential skills*.

Rules for pedestrians

General guidance

1 Pavements (including any path along the side of a road) should be used if provided. Where possible, avoid being next to the kerb with your back to the traffic. If you have to step into the road, look both ways first. Always show due care and consideration for others.

2 If there is no pavement, keep to the right-hand side of the road so that you can see oncoming traffic. You should take extra care and

- be prepared to walk in single file, especially on narrow roads or in poor light

- keep close to the side of the road.

It may be safer to cross the road well before a sharp right-hand bend so that oncoming traffic has a better chance of seeing you. Cross back after the bend.

3 Help other road users to see you. Wear or carry something light-coloured, bright or fluorescent in poor daylight conditions. When it is dark, use reflective materials (e.g. armbands, sashes, waistcoats, jackets, footwear), which can be seen by drivers using headlights up to three times as far away as non-reflective materials.

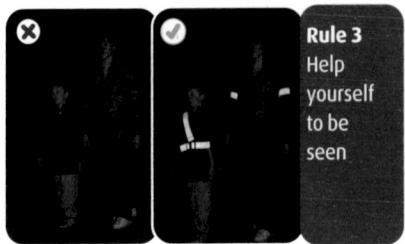

Rule 3
Help yourself to be seen

4 Young children should not be out alone on the pavement or road (see Rule 7). When taking children out, keep between them and the traffic and hold their hands firmly. Strap very young children into push-chairs or use reins. When pushing a young child in a buggy, do not push the buggy into the road when checking to see if it is clear to cross, particularly from between parked vehicles.

5 Organised walks. Large groups of people walking together should use a pavement if available; if one is not, they should keep to the left. Look-outs should be positioned at the front and back of the group, and they should wear fluorescent clothes in daylight and reflective clothes in the dark. At night, the look-out in front should show a white light and the one at the back a red light. People on the outside of large groups should also carry lights and wear reflective clothing.

6 Motorways. Pedestrians **MUST NOT** be on motorways or slip roads except in an emergency (see Rules 271 and 275).

Laws RTRA sect 17, MT(E&W)R 1982 as amended, reg 15(1)(b) & MT(S)R reg 13

Crossing the road
7 The Green Cross Code. The advice given below on crossing the road is for all pedestrians. Children should be taught the Code and should not be allowed out alone until they can understand and use it properly. The age when they can do this is different for each child. Many children cannot judge how fast vehicles are going or how far away they are. Children learn by example, so parents and carers should always use the Code in full when out with their children. They are responsible for deciding at what age children can use it safely by themselves.

A First find a safe place to cross and where there is space to reach the pavement on the other side. Where there is a crossing nearby, use it. It is safer to cross using a subway, a footbridge, an island, a zebra, pelican, toucan or puffin crossing, or where there is a crossing point controlled by a police officer, a school crossing patrol or a traffic warden.

Rule 7
Look all around and listen for traffic before crossing

Otherwise choose a place where you can see clearly in all directions. Try to avoid crossing between parked cars (see Rule 14), on a blind bend, or close to the brow of a hill. Move to a space where drivers and riders can see you clearly. Do not cross the road diagonally.

B Stop just before you get to the kerb, where you can see if anything is coming. Do not get too close to the traffic. If there's no pavement, keep back from the edge of the road but make sure you can still see approaching traffic.

C Look all around for traffic and listen. Traffic could come from any direction. Listen as well, because you can sometimes hear traffic before you see it.

D If traffic is coming, let it pass. Look all around again and listen. Do not cross until there is a safe gap in the traffic and you are certain that there is plenty of time. Remember, even if traffic is a long way off, it may be approaching very quickly.

E When it is safe, go straight across the road - do not run. Keep looking and listening for traffic while you cross, in case there is any traffic you did not see, or in case other traffic appears suddenly. Look out for cyclists and motorcyclists travelling between lanes of traffic. Do not walk diagonally across the road.

8 At a junction. When crossing the road, look out for traffic turning into the road, especially from behind you. If you have started crossing and traffic wants to turn into the road, you have priority and they should give way (see Rule 170).

9 Pedestrian Safety Barriers. Where there are barriers, cross the road only at the gaps provided for pedestrians. Do not climb over the barriers or walk between them and the road.

10 Tactile paving. Raised surfaces that can be felt underfoot provide warning and guidance to blind or partially sighted people. The most common surfaces are a series of raised studs, which are used at crossing points with a dropped kerb, or a series of rounded raised bars which are used at level crossings, at the top and bottom of steps and at some other hazards.

11 One-way streets. Check which way the traffic is moving. Do not cross until it is safe to do so without stopping. Bus and cycle lanes may operate in the opposite direction to the rest of the traffic.

12 Bus and cycle lanes. Take care when crossing these lanes as traffic may be moving faster than in the other lanes, or against the flow of traffic.

13 Routes shared with cyclists. Some cycle tracks run alongside footpaths or pavements, using a segregating feature to separate cyclists from people on foot. Segregated routes may also incorporate short lengths of tactile paving to help visually impaired people stay on the correct side. On the pedestrian side this will comprise a series of flat-topped bars running across the direction of travel (ladder pattern). On the cyclist side the same bars are orientated in the direction of travel (tramline pattern). Not all routes which are shared with cyclists are segregated. Take extra care where this is so (see Rule 62).

14 Parked vehicles. If you have to cross between parked vehicles, use the outside edges of the vehicles as if they were the kerb. Stop there and make sure you can see all around and that the traffic can see you. Make sure there is a gap between any parked vehicles on the other side, so you can reach the pavement. Never cross the road in front of, or behind, any vehicle with its engine running, especially a large vehicle, as the driver may not be able to see you.

15 Reversing vehicles. Never cross behind a vehicle which is reversing, showing white reversing lights or sounding a warning.

16 Moving vehicles. You **MUST NOT** get onto or hold onto a moving vehicle.
Law RTA 1988 sect 26

17 At night. Wear something reflective to make it easier for others to see you (see Rule 3). If there is no pedestrian crossing nearby, cross the road near a street light so that traffic can see you more easily.

Crossings
18 At all crossings. When using any type of crossing you should

- always check that the traffic has stopped before you start to cross or push a pram onto a crossing

- always cross between the studs or over the zebra markings. Do not cross at the side of the crossing or on the zig-zag lines, as it can be dangerous.

You **MUST NOT** loiter on any type of crossing.
Laws ZPPPCRGD reg 19 & RTRA sect 25(5)

19 Zebra crossings. Give traffic plenty of time to see you and to stop before you start to cross. Vehicles will need more time when the road is slippery. Wait until traffic has stopped from both directions or the road is clear before crossing. Remember that traffic does not have to stop until someone has moved onto the crossing. Keep looking both ways, and listening, in case a driver or rider has not seen you and attempts to overtake a vehicle that has stopped.

Rule 19
Zebra crossings have flashing beacons

20 Where there is an island in the middle of a zebra crossing, wait on the island and follow Rule 19 before you cross the second half of the road - it is a separate crossing.

Rule 20
Zebra crossings with a central island are two separate crossings

21 At traffic lights. There may be special signals for pedestrians. You should only start to cross the road when the green figure shows. If you have started to cross the road and the green figure goes out, you should still have time to reach the other side, but do not delay. If no pedestrian signals have been provided, watch carefully and do not cross until the traffic lights are red and the traffic has stopped. Keep looking and check for traffic that may be turning the corner. Remember that traffic lights may let traffic move in some lanes while traffic in other lanes has stopped.

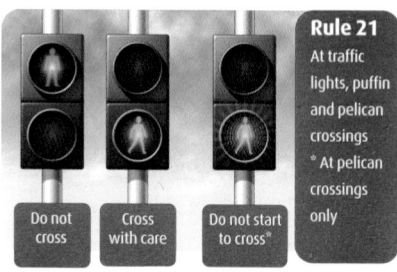

Rule 21
At traffic lights, puffin and pelican crossings
* At pelican crossings only

Do not cross | Cross with care | Do not start to cross*

22 Pelican crossings. These are signal-controlled crossings operated by pedestrians. Push the control button to activate the traffic signals. When the red figure shows, do not cross. When a steady green figure shows, check the traffic has stopped then cross with care. When the green figure begins to flash you should not start to cross. If you have already started you should have time to finish crossing safely.

23 Puffin crossings differ from pelican crossings as the red and green figures are above the control box on your side of the road and there is no flashing green figure phase. Press the button and wait for the green figure to show.

24 When the road is congested, traffic on your side of the road may be forced to stop even though their lights are green. Traffic may still be moving on the other side of the road, so press the button and wait for the signal to cross.

25 Toucan crossings are light-controlled crossings which allow cyclists and pedestrians to share crossing space and cross at the same time. They are push-button operated. Pedestrians and cyclists will see the green signal together. Cyclists are permitted to ride across.

Rule 25
Toucan crossings can be used by both cyclists and pedestrians

26 At some crossings there is a bleeping sound or voice signal to indicate to blind or partially sighted people when the steady green figure is showing, and there may be a tactile signal to help deafblind people.

27 Equestrian crossings are for horse riders. They have pavement barriers, wider crossing spaces, horse and rider figures in the light panels and either two sets of controls (one higher), or just one higher control panel.

Rule 27
Equestrian crossings are used by horse riders. There is often a parallel crossing

28 'Staggered' pelican or puffin crossings. When the crossings on each side of the central refuge are not in line they are two separate crossings. On reaching the central island, press the button again and wait for a steady green figure.

Rule 28
Staggered crossings (with an island in the middle) are two separate crossings

29 Crossings controlled by an authorised person. Do not cross the road unless you are signalled to do so by a police officer, traffic warden or school crossing patrol. Always cross in front of them.

30 Where there are no controlled crossing points available it is advisable to cross where there is an island in the middle of the road. Use the Green Cross Code (see Rule 7) to cross to the island and then stop and use it again to cross the second half of the road.

Situations needing extra care
31 Emergency vehicles. If an ambulance, fire engine, police or other emergency vehicle approaches using flashing blue lights, headlights and/or sirens, keep off the road.

32 Buses. Get on or off a bus only when it has stopped to allow you to do so. Watch out for cyclists when you are getting off. Never cross the road directly behind or in front of a bus. Wait until it has moved off and you can see clearly in both directions.

33 Tramways. These may run through pedestrian areas. Their path will be marked out by shallow kerbs, changes in the paving or other road surface, white lines or yellow dots. Cross at designated crossings where provided. Elsewhere treat trams as you would other road vehicles and look both ways along the track before crossing. Do not walk along the track as trams may come up behind you. Trams move quietly and cannot steer to avoid you.

34 Railway level crossings. You **MUST NOT** cross or pass a stop line when the red lights show, (including a red pedestrian figure). Also do not cross if an alarm is sounding or the barriers are being lowered. The tone of the alarm may change if another train is approaching. If there are no lights, alarms or barriers, stop, look both ways and listen before crossing. A tactile surface comprising rounded bars running across the direction of pedestrian travel may be installed on the footpath approaching a level crossing to warn visually impaired people of its presence. The tactile surface should extend across the full width of the footway and should be located at an appropriate distance from the barrier or projected line of the barrier.

Law TSRGD, reg 52

35 Street and pavement repairs. A pavement may be closed temporarily because it is not safe to use. Take extra care if you are directed to walk in or to cross the road.

Rules for users of powered wheelchairs and powered mobility scooters

(Called Invalid Carriages in law)

36 There is one class of manual wheelchair (called a Class 1 invalid carriage) and two classes of powered wheelchairs and powered mobility scooters. Manual wheelchairs and Class 2 vehicles are those with an upper speed limit of 4 mph (6 km/h) and are designed to be used on pavements. Class 3 vehicles are those with an upper speed limit of 8 mph (12 km/h) and are equipped to be used on the road as well as the pavement.

37 When you are on the road you should obey the guidance and rules for other vehicles; when on the pavement you should follow the guidance and rules for pedestrians.

On pavements

38 Pavements are safer than roads and should be used when available. You should give pedestrians priority and show consideration for other pavement users, particularly those with a hearing or visual impairment who may not be aware that you are there.

39 Powered wheelchairs and scooters **MUST NOT** travel faster than 4 mph (6 km/h) on pavements or in pedestrian areas. You may need to reduce your speed to adjust to other pavement users who may not be able to move out of your way quickly enough or where the pavement is too narrow.

Law UICHR 1988 reg 4

40 When moving off the pavement onto the road, you should take special care. Before moving off, always look round and make sure it's safe to join the traffic. Always try to use dropped kerbs when moving off the pavement, even if this means travelling further to locate one. If you have to climb or descend a kerb, always approach it at right angles and don't try to negotiate a kerb higher than the vehicle manufacturer's recommendations.

On the road

41 You should take care when travelling on the road as you may be travelling more slowly than other traffic (your machine is restricted to 8 mph (12 km/h) and may be less visible).

42 When on the road, Class 3 vehicles should travel in the direction of the traffic. Class 2 users should always use the pavement when it is available. When there is no pavement, you should use caution when on the road. Class 2 users should, where possible, travel in the direction of the traffic. If you are travelling at night when lights **MUST** be used, you should travel in the direction of the traffic to avoid confusing other road users.

Law UICHR 1988 reg 9

43 You **MUST** follow the same rules about using lights, indicators and horns as for other road vehicles, if your vehicle is fitted with them. At night, lights **MUST** be used. Be aware that other road users may not see you and you should make yourself more visible - even in the daytime and also at dusk - by, for instance, wearing a reflective jacket or reflective strips on the back of the vehicle.

Law UICHR 1988 reg 9

44 Take extra care at road junctions. When going straight ahead, check to make sure there are no vehicles about to cross your path from the left, the right, or overtaking you and turning left. There are several options for dealing with right turns, especially turning from a major road. If moving into the middle of the road is difficult or dangerous, you can

- stop on the left-hand side of the road and wait for a safe gap in the traffic
- negotiate the turn as a pedestrian, i.e. travel along the pavement and cross the road between pavements where it is safe to do so. Class 3 users should switch the vehicle to the lower speed limit when on pavements.

If the junction is too hazardous, it may be worth considering an alternative route. Similarly, when negotiating major roundabouts (i.e. with two or more lanes) it may be safer for you to use the pavement or find a route which avoids the roundabout altogether.

45 All normal parking restrictions should be observed. Your vehicle should not be left unattended if it causes an obstruction to other pedestrians - especially those in wheelchairs. Parking concessions provided under the Blue Badge scheme (see page 496) will apply to those vehicles displaying a valid badge.

46 These vehicles **MUST NOT** be used on motorways (See Rule 253). They should not be used on unrestricted dual carriageways where the speed limit exceeds 50 mph (80 km/h) but if they are used on these dual carriageways, they **MUST** have a flashing amber beacon. A flashing amber beacon should be used on all other dual carriageways (see Rule 220).

Laws RTRA sect 17(2) & (3), & RVLR reg 17(1) & 26

Rules about animals

Horse-drawn vehicles

47 Horse-drawn vehicles used on the highway should be operated and maintained in accordance with standards set out in the Department for Transport's Code of Practice for Horse-Drawn Vehicles. This Code lays down the requirements for a road driving assessment and includes a comprehensive list of safety checks to ensure that a carriage and its fittings are safe and in good working order.

The standards set out in the Road Driving Assessment may be required to be met by a Local Authority if an operator wishes to obtain a local authority licence to operate a passenger-carrying service (see page 496).

48 Safety equipment and clothing. All horse-drawn vehicles should have two red rear reflectors. It is safer not to drive at night but if you do, a light showing white to the front and red to the rear **MUST** be fitted.

Law RVLR 1989 reg 4

Horse riders

49 Safety equipment. Children under the age of 14 **MUST** wear a helmet which complies with the Regulations. It **MUST** be fastened securely. Other riders should also follow these requirements. These requirements do not apply to a child who is a follower of the Sikh religion while wearing a turban.

Laws H(PHYR) Act 1990, sect 1 & H(PHYR) Regulations 1992, reg 3

50 Other clothing. You should wear

- boots or shoes with hard soles and heels
- light-coloured or fluorescent clothing in daylight
- reflective clothing if you have to ride at night or in poor visibility.

Rule 50
Help yourself to be seen

51 At night. It is safer not to ride on the road at night or in poor visibility, but if you do, make sure you wear reflective clothing and your horse has reflective bands above the fetlock joints. A light which shows white to the front and red to the rear should be fitted, with a band, to the rider's right arm and/or leg/riding boot. If you are leading a horse at night, carry a light in your right hand, showing white to the front and red to the rear, and wear reflective clothing on both you and your horse. It is strongly recommended that a fluorescent/reflective tail guard is also worn by your horse.

Riding

52 Before you take a horse on to a road, you should

- ensure all tack fits well and is in good condition
- make sure you can control the horse.

Always ride with other, less nervous horses if you think that your horse will be nervous of traffic. Never ride a horse without both a saddle and bridle.

53 Before riding off or turning, look behind you to make sure it is safe, then give a clear arm signal.

When riding on the road you should

- keep to the left
- keep both hands on the reins unless you are signalling
- keep both feet in the stirrups
- not carry another person
- not carry anything which might affect your balance or get tangled up with the reins
- keep a horse you are leading to your left

- move in the direction of the traffic flow in a one-way street
- never ride more than two abreast, and ride in single file on narrow or busy roads and when riding round bends.

54 You **MUST NOT** take a horse onto a footpath or pavement, and you should not take a horse onto a cycle track. Use a bridleway where possible. Equestrian crossings may be provided for horse riders to cross the road and you should use these where available (see page 414). You should dismount at level crossings where a 'Horse Rider Dismount' sign is displayed.

Laws HA 1835 sect 72, R(S)A 1984, sect 129(5)

55 Avoid roundabouts wherever possible. If you use them you should

- keep to the left and watch out for vehicles crossing your path to leave or join the roundabout
- signal right when riding across exits to show you are not leaving
- signal left just before you leave the roundabout.

Other animals

56 Dogs. Do not let a dog out on the road on its own. Keep it on a short lead when walking on the pavement, road or path shared with cyclists or horse riders.

57 When in a vehicle make sure dogs or other animals are suitably restrained so they cannot distract you while you are driving or injure you, or themselves, if you stop quickly. A seat belt harness, pet carrier, dog cage or dog guard are ways of restraining animals in cars.

58 Animals being herded. These should be kept under control at all times. You should, if possible, send another person along the road in front to warn other road users, especially at a bend or the brow of a hill. It is safer not to move animals after dark, but if you do, then wear reflective clothing and ensure that lights are carried (white at the front and red at the rear of the herd).

Rules for cyclists

These rules are in addition to those in the following sections, which apply to all vehicles (except the motorway section on page 453). See also page 482 - You and your bicycle.

59 Clothing. You should wear

- a cycle helmet which conforms to current regulations, is the correct size and securely fastened
- appropriate clothes for cycling. Avoid clothes which may get tangled in the chain, or in a wheel or may obscure your lights
- light-coloured or fluorescent clothing which helps other road users to see you in daylight and poor light
- reflective clothing and/or accessories (belt, arm or ankle bands) in the dark.

Rule 59 Help yourself to be seen

60 At night your cycle **MUST** have white front and red rear lights lit. It **MUST** also be fitted with a red rear reflector (and amber pedal reflectors, if manufactured after 1/10/85). White front reflectors and spoke reflectors will also help you to be seen. Flashing lights are permitted but it is recommended that cyclists who are riding in areas without street lighting use a steady front lamp.

Law RVLR regs 13, 18 & 24

61 Cycle Routes and Other Facilities.
Use cycle routes, advanced stop lines, cycle boxes and toucan crossings unless at the time it is unsafe to do so. Use of these facilities is not compulsory and will depend on your experience and skills, but they can make your journey safer.

62 Cycle Tracks. These are normally located away from the road, but may occasionally be found alongside footpaths or pavements. Cyclists and pedestrians may be segregated or they may share the same space (unsegregated). When using segregated tracks you **MUST** keep to the side intended for cyclists as the pedestrian side remains a pavement or footpath. Take care when passing pedestrians, especially children, older or disabled people, and allow them plenty of room. Always be prepared to slow down and stop if necessary. Take care near road junctions as you may have difficulty seeing other road users, who might not notice you.

Law HA 1835 sect 72

63 Cycle Lanes. These are marked by a white line (which may be broken) along the carriageway (see Rule 140). When using a cycle lane, keep within the lane when practicable. When leaving a cycle lane check before pulling out that it is safe to do so and signal your intention clearly to other road users. Use of cycle lanes is not compulsory and will depend on your experience and skills, but they can make your journey safer.

64 You **MUST NOT** cycle on a pavement.

Laws HA 1835 sect 72 & R(S)A 1984, sect 129

65 Bus Lanes. Most bus lanes may be used by cyclists as indicated on signs. Watch out for people getting on or off a bus. Be very careful when overtaking a bus or leaving a bus lane as you will be entering a busier traffic flow. Do not pass between the kerb and a bus when it is at a stop.

66 You should

- keep both hands on the handlebars except when signalling or changing gear
- keep both feet on the pedals
- never ride more than two abreast, and ride in single file on narrow or busy roads and when riding round bends
- not ride close behind another vehicle
- not carry anything which will affect your balance or may get tangled up with your wheels or chain
- be considerate of other road users, particularly blind and partially sighted pedestrians. Let them know you are there when necessary, for example, by ringing your bell if you have one. It is recommended that a bell be fitted.

67 You should

- look all around before moving away from the kerb, turning or manoeuvring, to make sure it is safe to do so. Give a clear signal to show other road users what you intend to do (see page 467)
- look well ahead for obstructions in the road, such as drains, pot-holes and parked vehicles so that you do not have to swerve suddenly to avoid them. Leave plenty of room when passing parked vehicles and watch out for doors being opened or pedestrians stepping into your path
- be aware of traffic coming up behind you
- take extra care near road humps, narrowings and other traffic calming features
- take care when overtaking (see Rules 162-169).

68 You **MUST NOT**

- carry a passenger unless your cycle has been built or adapted to carry one
- hold onto a moving vehicle or trailer
- ride in a dangerous, careless or inconsiderate manner
- ride when under the influence of drink or drugs, including medicine.

Law RTA 1988 sects 24, 26, 28, 29 & 30 as amended by RTA 1991

69 You **MUST** obey all traffic signs and traffic light signals.

Laws RTA 1988 sect 36 & TSRGD reg 10(1)

70 When parking your cycle

- find a conspicuous location where it can be seen by passers-by
- use cycle stands or other cycle parking facilities wherever possible
- do not leave it where it would cause an obstruction or hazard to other road users
- secure it well so that it will not fall over and become an obstruction or hazard.

71 You **MUST NOT** cross the stop line when the traffic lights are red. Some junctions have an advanced stop line to enable you to wait and position yourself ahead of other traffic (see Rule 178).

Laws RTA 1988 sect 36 & TSRGD regs 10 & 36(1)

Road junctions

72 On the left. When approaching a junction on the left, watch out for vehicles turning in front of you, out of or into the side road. Just before you turn, check for undertaking cyclists or motorcyclists. Do not ride on the inside of vehicles signalling or slowing down to turn left.

73 Pay particular attention to long vehicles which need a lot of room to manoeuvre at corners. Be aware that drivers may not see you. They may have to move over to the right before turning left. Wait until they have completed the manoeuvre because the rear wheels come very close to the kerb while turning. Do not be tempted to ride in the space between them and the kerb.

74 **On the right.** If you are turning right, check the traffic to ensure it is safe, then signal and move to the centre of the road. Wait until there is a safe gap in the oncoming traffic and give a final look before completing the turn. It may be safer to wait on the left until there is a safe gap or to dismount and push your cycle across the road.

75 **Dual carriageways.** Remember that traffic on most dual carriageways moves quickly. When crossing wait for a safe gap and cross each carriageway in turn. Take extra care when crossing slip roads.

Roundabouts

76 Full details about the correct procedure at roundabouts are contained in Rules 184-190. Roundabouts can be hazardous and should be approached with care.

77 You may feel safer walking your cycle round on the pavement or verge. If you decide to ride round keeping to the left-hand lane you should

- be aware that drivers may not easily see you

- take extra care when cycling across exits. You may need to signal right to show you are not leaving the roundabout

- watch out for vehicles crossing your path to leave or join the roundabout.

78 Give plenty of room to long vehicles on the roundabout as they need more space to manoeuvre. Do not ride in the space they need to get round the roundabout. It may be safer to wait until they have cleared the roundabout.

Crossing the road

79 Do not ride across equestrian crossings, as they are for horse riders only. Do not ride across a pelican, puffin or zebra crossing. Dismount and wheel your cycle across.

80 **Toucan crossings.** These are light-controlled crossings which allow cyclists and pedestrians to share crossing space and cross at the same time. They are push-button operated. Pedestrians and cyclists will see the green signal together. Cyclists are permitted to ride across.

81 **Cycle-only crossings.** Cycle tracks on opposite sides of the road may be linked by signalled crossings. You may ride across but you **MUST NOT** cross until the green cycle symbol is showing.

Law TSRGD regs 33(2) & 36(1)

82 **Level crossings/Tramways.** Take extra care when crossing the tracks (See Rule 306). You should dismount at level crossings where a 'Cyclist Dismount' sign is displayed.

Rules for motorcyclists

These Rules are in addition to those in the following sections which apply to all vehicles. For motorcycle licence requirements see pages 482-483.

General

83 On all journeys, the rider and pillion passenger on a motorcycle, scooter or moped **MUST** wear a protective helmet.

This does not apply to a follower of the Sikh religion while wearing a turban. Helmets **MUST** comply with the Regulations and they **MUST** be fastened securely. Riders and passengers of motor tricycles and quadricycles, also called quadbikes, should also wear a protective helmet. Before each journey check that your helmet visor is clean and in good condition.

Laws RTA 1988 sects 16 & 17 & MC(PH)R as amended reg 4

84 It is also advisable to wear eye protectors, which **MUST** comply with the Regulations. Scratched or poorly fitting eye protectors can limit your view when riding, particularly in bright sunshine and the hours of darkness. Consider wearing ear protection. Strong boots, gloves and suitable clothing may help to protect you if you are involved in a collision.

Law RTA sect 18 & MC(EP)R as amended reg 4

85 You **MUST NOT** carry more than one pillion passenger who **MUST** sit astride the machine on a proper seat. They should face forward with both feet on the footrests. You **MUST NOT** carry a pillion passenger unless your motor cycle is designed to do so. Provisional licence holders **MUST NOT** carry a pillion passenger.

Laws RTA 1988 sect 23, MV(DL)R 1999 reg 16(6) & CUR 1986 reg 102

86 Daylight riding. Make yourself as visible as possible from the side as well as the front and rear. You could wear a light or brightly coloured helmet and fluorescent clothing or strips. Dipped headlights, even in good daylight, may also make you more conspicuous. However, be aware that other vehicle drivers may still not have seen you, or judged your distance or speed correctly, especially at junctions.

Rule 86
Help yourself to be seen

87 Riding in the dark. Wear reflective clothing or strips to improve your visibility in the dark. These reflect light from the headlamps of other vehicles, making you visible from a longer distance. See Rules 113-116 for lighting requirements.

88 Manoeuvring. You should be aware of what is behind and to the sides before manoeuvring. Look behind you; use mirrors if they are fitted. When in traffic queues look out for pedestrians crossing between vehicles and vehicles emerging from junctions or changing lanes. Position yourself so that drivers can see you in their mirrors. Additionally, when filtering in slow-moving traffic, take care and keep your speed low.
Remember: Observation - Signal - Manoeuvre

Rules for drivers and motorcyclists

89 **Vehicle condition.** You **MUST** ensure your vehicle and trailer comply with the full requirements of the Road Vehicles (Construction and Use) Regulations and Road Vehicles Lighting Regulations (see page 487).

Fitness to drive
90 Make sure that you are fit to drive. You **MUST** report to the Driver and Vehicle Licensing Agency (DVLA) any health condition likely to affect your driving.
Law RTA 1988 sect 94

91 Driving when you are tired greatly increases your risk of collision. To minimise this risk

- make sure you are fit to drive. Do not begin a journey if you are tired. Get a good night's sleep before embarking on a long journey

- avoid undertaking long journeys between midnight and 6 am, when natural alertness is at a minimum

- plan your journey to take sufficient breaks. A minimum break of at least 15 minutes after every two hours of driving is recommended

- if you feel at all sleepy, stop in a safe place. Do not stop on the hard shoulder of a motorway

- the most effective ways to counter sleepiness are to drink, for example, two cups of caffeinated coffee and to take a short nap (at least 15 minutes).

92 **Vision.** You **MUST** be able to read a vehicle number plate, in good daylight, from a distance of 20 metres (or 20.5 metres where the old style number plate is used). If you need to wear glasses (or contact lenses) to do this, you **MUST** wear them at all times while driving. The police have the power to require a driver to undertake an eyesight test.
Laws RTA 1988 sect 96 & MV(DL)R reg 40 & sch 8

93 Slow down, and if necessary stop, if you are dazzled by bright sunlight.

94 At night or in poor visibility, do not use tinted glasses, lenses or visors if they restrict your vision.

Alcohol and drugs
95 **Do not drink and drive** as it will seriously affect your judgement and abilities. You **MUST NOT** drive with a breath alcohol level higher than 35 microgrammes/100 millilitres of breath or a blood alcohol level of more than 80 milligrammes/100 millilitres of blood. Alcohol will

- give a false sense of confidence

- reduce co-ordination and slow down reactions

- affect judgement of speed, distance and risk

- reduce your driving ability, even if you're below the legal limit

- take time to leave your body; you may be unfit to drive in the evening after drinking at lunchtime, or in the morning after drinking the previous evening.

The best solution is not to drink at all when planning to drive because any amount of alcohol affects your ability to drive safely. If you are going to drink, arrange another means of transport.

Law RTA 1988 sects 4, 5 & 11(2)

96 You **MUST NOT** drive under the influence of drugs or medicine. Check the instructions or ask your doctor or pharmacist. Using illegal drugs is highly dangerous. Never take them if you intend to drive; the effects are unpredictable, but can be even more severe than alcohol and may result in fatal or serious road crashes.

Law RTA 1988 sect 4

97 Before setting off. You should ensure that

- you have planned your route and allowed sufficient time

- clothing and footwear do not prevent you using the controls in the correct manner

- you know where all the controls are and how to use them before you need them. Not all vehicles are the same; do not wait until it is too late to find out

- your mirrors and seat are adjusted correctly to ensure comfort, full control and maximum vision

- head restraints are properly adjusted to reduce the risk of neck and spine injuries in the event of a collision

- you have sufficient fuel before commencing your journey, especially if it includes motorway driving. It can be dangerous to lose power when driving in traffic

- ensure your vehicle is legal and roadworthy

- switch off your mobile phone.

Rule 97
Make sure head restraints are properly adjusted

98 Vehicle towing and loading.
As a driver

- you **MUST NOT** tow more than your licence permits. If you passed a car test after 1 Jan 1997 you are restricted on the weight of trailer you can tow

- you **MUST NOT** overload your vehicle or trailer. You should not tow a weight greater than that recommended by the manufacturer of your vehicle

- you **MUST** secure your load and it **MUST NOT** stick out dangerously. Make sure any heavy or sharp objects and any animals are secured safely. If there is a collision, they might hit someone inside the vehicle and cause serious injury

- you should properly distribute the weight in your caravan or trailer with heavy items mainly over the axle(s) and ensure a downward load on the tow ball. Manufacturer's recommended weight and tow ball load should not be exceeded. This should avoid the possibility of swerving or snaking and going out of control. If this does happen, ease off the accelerator and reduce speed gently to regain control

- carrying a load or pulling a trailer may require you to adjust the headlights.

	Front seat	Rear seat	Who is responsible?
Driver	Seat belt **MUST** be worn if fitted	-	**Driver**
Child under 3 years of age	Correct child restraint **MUST** be used	Correct child restraint **MUST** be used. If one is not available in a taxi, may travel unrestrained	**Driver**
Child from 3rd birthday up to 1.35 metres in height (or 12th birthday, whichever they reach first)	Correct child restraint **MUST** be used	Correct child restraint **MUST** be used where seat belts fitted. **MUST** use adult belt if correct child restraint is not available in a licensed taxi or private hire vehicle, or for reasons of unexpected necessity over a short distance, or if two occupied restraints prevent fitment of a third	**Driver**
Child over 1.35 metres (approx 4ft 5 ins) in height or 12 or 13 years	Seat belt **MUST** be worn if available	Seat belt **MUST** be worn if available	**Driver**
Adult passengers aged 14 and over	Seat belt **MUST** be worn if available	Seat belt **MUST** be worn if available	**Passenger**

In the event of a breakdown, be aware that towing a vehicle on a tow rope is potentially dangerous. You should consider professional recovery.

Laws CUR reg 100 & MV(DL)R reg 43

Seat belts and child restraints

99 You **MUST** wear a seat belt in cars, vans and other goods vehicles if one is fitted (see table below). Adults, and children aged 14 years and over, **MUST** use a seat belt or child restraint, where fitted, when seated in minibuses, buses and coaches. Exemptions are allowed for the holders of medical exemption certificates and those making deliveries or collections in goods vehicles when travelling less than 50 metres (approx 162 feet).

Laws RTA 1988 sects 14 & 15, MV(WSB)R, MV(WSBCFS)R & MV(WSB)(A)R

Seat belt requirements. This table summarises the main legal requirements for wearing seat belts in cars, vans and other goods vehicles.

100 The driver **MUST** ensure that all children under 14 years of age in cars, vans and other goods vehicles wear seat belts or sit in an approved child restraint where required (see table above). If a child is under 1.35 metres (approx 4 feet 5 inches) tall, a baby seat, child seat, booster seat or booster cushion **MUST** be used suitable for the child's weight and fitted to the manufacturer's instructions.

Laws RTA 1988 sects 14 & 15, MV(WSB)R, MV(WSBCFS)R & MV(WSB)(A)R

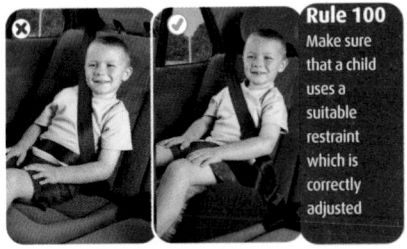

Rule 100
Make sure that a child uses a suitable restraint which is correctly adjusted

101   A rear-facing baby seat **MUST NOT** be fitted into a seat protected by an active frontal airbag, as in a crash it can cause serious injury or death to the child.

Laws RTA 1988 sects 14 & 15, MV(WSB)R, MV(WSBCFS)R & MV(WSB)(A)R

102   Children in cars, vans and other goods vehicles. Drivers who are carrying children in cars, vans and other goods vehicles should also ensure that

- children should get into the vehicle through the door nearest the kerb

- child restraints are properly fitted to manufacturer's instructions

- children do not sit behind the rear seats in an estate car or hatchback, unless a special child seat has been fitted

- the child safety door locks, where fitted, are used when children are in the vehicle

- children are kept under control.

General rules, techniques and advice for all drivers and riders

This section should be read by all drivers, motorcyclists, cyclists and horse riders. The rules in *The Highway Code* do not give you the right of way in any circumstance, but they advise you when you should give way to others. Always give way if it can help to avoid an incident.

Signals

103   Signals warn and inform other road users, including pedestrians (see page 469), of your intended actions. You should always

- give clear signals in plenty of time, having checked it is not misleading to signal at that time

- use them to advise other road users before changing course or direction, stopping or moving off

- cancel them after use

- make sure your signals will not confuse others. If, for instance, you want to stop after a side road, do not signal until you are passing the road. If you signal earlier it may give the impression that you intend to turn into the road. Your brake lights will warn traffic behind you that you are slowing down

- use an arm signal to emphasise or reinforce your signal if necessary. Remember that signalling does not give you priority.

104 You should also

- watch out for signals given by other road users and proceed only when you are satisfied that it is safe

- be aware that an indicator on another vehicle may not have been cancelled.

105 You **MUST** obey signals given by police officers, traffic officers, traffic wardens (see pages 470-471) and signs used by school crossing patrols.

Laws RTRA sect 28, RTA 1988 sect 35, TMA 2004 sect 6, & FTWO art 3

106 **Police stopping procedures.** If the police want to stop your vehicle they will, where possible, attract your attention by

- flashing blue lights, headlights or sounding their siren or horn, usually from behind

- directing you to pull over to the side by pointing and/or using the left indicator.

You **MUST** then pull over and stop as soon as it is safe to do so. Then switch off your engine.

Law RTA 1988 sect 163

Other stopping procedures

107 **Vehicle & Operator Services Agency Officers** have powers to stop vehicles on all roads, including motorways and trunk roads, in England and Wales. They will attract your attention by flashing amber lights

- either from the front requesting you to follow them to a safe place to stop

- or from behind directing you to pull over to the side by pointing and/or using the left indicator.

It is an offence not to comply with their directions. You **MUST** obey any signals given (See page 471).

Laws RTA 1988, sect 67, & PRA 2002, sect 41 & sched 5(8)

108 **Highways Agency Traffic Officers** have powers to stop vehicles on most motorways and some 'A' class roads, in England only. If HA traffic officers in uniform want to stop your vehicle on safety grounds (e.g. an insecure load) they will, where possible, attract your attention by

- flashing amber lights, usually from behind

- directing you to pull over to the side by pointing and/or using the left indicator.

You **MUST** then pull over and stop as soon as it is safe to do so. Then switch off your engine. It is an offence not to comply with their directions (see page 471).

Law RTA 1988, sects 35 &163 as amended by TMA 2004, sect 6

109 **Traffic light signals and traffic signs.** You **MUST** obey all traffic light signals (see page 468) and traffic signs giving orders, including temporary signals and signs (see pages 472-479). Make sure you know, understand and act on all other traffic and information signs and road markings (see pages 472-483).

Laws RTA 1988 sect 36 & TSRGD regs 10, 15, 16, 25, 26, 27, 28, 29, 36, 38 & 40

110 Flashing headlights. Only flash your headlights to let other road users know that you are there. Do not flash your headlights to convey any other message or intimidate other road users.

111 Never assume that flashing headlights is a signal inviting you to proceed. Use your own judgement and proceed carefully.

112 The horn. Use only while your vehicle is moving and you need to warn other road users of your presence. Never sound your horn aggressively. You **MUST NOT** use your horn

- while stationary on the road
- when driving in a built-up area between the hours of 11.30 pm and 7.00 am

except when another road user poses a danger.

Law CUR reg 99

Lighting requirements

113 You **MUST**

- ensure all sidelights and rear registration plate lights are lit between sunset and sunrise
- use headlights at night, except on a road which has lit street lighting. These roads are generally restricted to a speed limit of 30 mph (48 km/h) unless otherwise specified
- use headlights when visibility is seriously reduced (see Rule 226).

Night (the hours of darkness) is defined as the period between half an hour after sunset and half an hour before sunrise.

Laws RVLR regs 3, 24, & 25 (In Scotland - RTRA 1984 sect 82 (as amended by NRSWA, para 59 of sched 8))

114 You **MUST NOT**

- use any lights in a way which would dazzle or cause discomfort to other road users, including pedestrians, cyclists and horse riders
- use front or rear fog lights unless visibility is seriously reduced. You **MUST** switch them off when visibility improves to avoid dazzling other road users (see Rule 226).

In stationary queues of traffic, drivers should apply the parking brake and, once the following traffic has stopped, take their foot off the footbrake to deactivate the vehicle brake lights. This will minimise glare to road users behind until the traffic moves again.

Law RVLR reg 27

115 You should also

- use dipped headlights, or dim-dip if fitted, at night in built-up areas and in dull daytime weather, to ensure that you can be seen
- keep your headlights dipped when overtaking until you are level with the other vehicle and then change to main beam if necessary, unless this would dazzle oncoming road users
- slow down, and if necessary stop, if you are dazzled by oncoming headlights.

116 Hazard warning lights. These may be used when your vehicle is stationary, to warn that it is temporarily obstructing traffic. Never use them as an excuse for dangerous or illegal parking. You **MUST NOT** use hazard warning lights while driving or being towed unless you are on a motorway or unrestricted dual carriageway and you need to warn drivers behind you of a hazard or obstruction ahead. Only use them for long enough to ensure that your warning has been observed.

Law RVLR reg 27

Control of the vehicle

Braking

117 In normal circumstances. The safest way to brake is to do so early and lightly. Brake more firmly as you begin to stop. Ease the pressure off just before the vehicle comes to rest to avoid a jerky stop.

118 In an emergency. Brake immediately. Try to avoid braking so harshly that you lock your wheels. Locked wheels can lead to loss of control.

119 Skids. Skidding is usually caused by the driver braking, accelerating or steering too harshly or driving too fast for the road conditions. If skidding occurs, remove the cause by releasing the brake pedal fully or easing off the accelerator. Turn the steering wheel in the direction of the skid. For example, if the rear of the vehicle skids to the right, steer immediately to the right to recover.

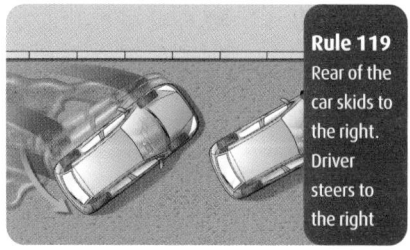

Rule 119
Rear of the car skids to the right. Driver steers to the right

120 ABS. If your vehicle is fitted with anti-lock brakes, you should follow the advice given in the vehicle handbook. However, in the case of an emergency, apply the footbrake firmly; do not release the pressure until the vehicle has slowed to the desired speed. The ABS should ensure that steering control will be retained, but do not assume that a vehicle with ABS will stop in a shorter distance.

121 Brakes affected by water. If you have driven through deep water your brakes may be less effective. Test them at the first safe opportunity by pushing gently on the brake pedal to make sure that they work. If they are not fully effective, gently apply light pressure while driving slowly. This will help to dry them out.

122 Coasting. This term describes a vehicle travelling in neutral or with the clutch pressed down. It can reduce driver control because

• engine braking is eliminated

• vehicle speed downhill will increase quickly

• increased use of the footbrake can reduce its effectiveness

• steering response will be affected, particularly on bends and corners

• it may be more difficult to select the appropriate gear when needed.

123 The Driver and the Environment.

You **MUST NOT** leave a parked vehicle unattended with the engine running or leave a vehicle engine running unnecessarily while that vehicle is stationary on a public road. Generally, if the vehicle is stationary and is likely to remain so for more than a couple of minutes, you should apply the parking brake and switch off the engine to reduce emissions and noise pollution. However it is permissible to leave the engine running if the vehicle is stationary in traffic or for diagnosing faults.

Law CUR regs 98 & 107.

Speed Limits

Type of vehicle	Built-up areas* mph (km/h)	Single carriage-ways mph (km/h)	Dual carriage-ways mph (km/h)	Motorways mph (km/h)
Cars & motorcycles (including car-derived vans up to 2 tonnes maximum laden weight)	30 (48)	60 (96)	70 (112)	70 (112)
Cars towing caravans or trailers (including car-derived vans and motorcycles)	30 (48)	50 (80)	60 (96)	60 (96)
Buses, coaches and minibuses (not exceeding 12 metres in overall length)	30 (48)	50 (80)	60 (96)	70 (112)
Goods vehicles (not exceeding 7.5 tonnes maximum laden weight)	30 (48)	50 (80)	60 (96)	70† (112)
Goods vehicles (exceeding 7.5 tonnes maximum laden weight)	30 (48)	40 (64)	50 (80)	60 (96)

* The 30 mph limit usually applies to all traffic on all roads with street lighting unless signs show otherwise. † 60 mph (96 km/h) if articulated or towing a trailer.

Typical Stopping Distances

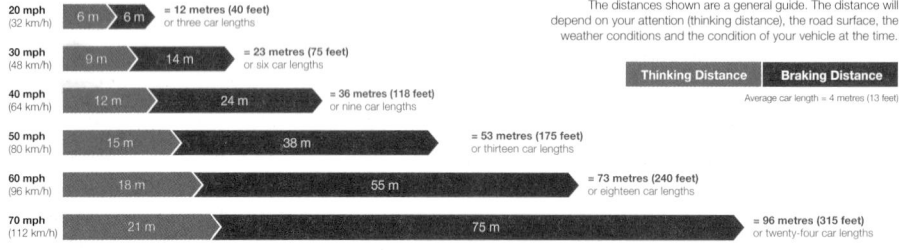

The distances shown are a general guide. The distance will depend on your attention (thinking distance), the road surface, the weather conditions and the condition of your vehicle at the time.

Thinking Distance | **Braking Distance**

Average car length = 4 metres (13 feet)

20 mph (32 km/h) 6 m | 6 m = 12 metres (40 feet) or three car lengths

30 mph (48 km/h) 9 m | 14 m = 23 metres (75 feet) or six car lengths

40 mph (64 km/h) 12 m | 24 m = 36 metres (118 feet) or nine car lengths

50 mph (80 km/h) 15 m | 38 m = 53 metres (175 feet) or thirteen car lengths

60 mph (96 km/h) 18 m | 55 m = 73 metres (240 feet) or eighteen car lengths

70 mph (112 km/h) 21 m | 75 m = 96 metres (315 feet) or twenty-four car lengths

Speed limits

124 You **MUST NOT** exceed the maximum speed limits for the road and for your vehicle (see the table above). The presence of street lights generally means that there is a 30 mph (48 km/h) speed limit unless otherwise specified.

Law RTRA sects 81, 86, 89 & sch 6

125 The speed limit is the absolute maximum and does not mean it is safe to drive at that speed irrespective of conditions. Driving at speeds too fast for the road and traffic conditions is dangerous. You should always reduce your speed when

- the road layout or condition presents hazards, such as bends

- sharing the road with pedestrians, cyclists and horse riders, particularly children, and motorcyclists

- weather conditions make it safer to do so

- driving at night as it is more difficult to see other road users.

126 Stopping distances. Drive at a speed that will allow you to stop well within the distance you can see to be clear. You should

- leave enough space between you and the vehicle in front so that you can pull up safely if it suddenly slows down or stops. The safe rule is never to get closer than the overall stopping distance (see Typical Stopping Distances diagram, shown on previous page)

- allow at least a two-second gap between you and the vehicle in front on roads carrying faster-moving traffic and in tunnels where visibility is reduced. The gap should be at least doubled on wet roads and increased still further on icy roads

- remember, large vehicles and motorcycles need a greater distance to stop. If driving a large vehicle in a tunnel, you should allow a four-second gap between you and the vehicle in front.

If you have to stop in a tunnel, leave at least a 5-metre gap between you and the vehicle in front.

Rule 126
Use a fixed point to help measure a two-second gap

Lines and lane markings on the road

Diagrams of all lines are shown on page 478.

127 A broken white line. This marks the centre of the road. When this line lengthens and the gaps shorten, it means that there is a hazard ahead. Do not cross it unless you can see the road is clear and wish to overtake or turn off.

128 Double white lines where the line nearest to you is broken. This means you may cross the lines to overtake if it is safe, provided you can complete the manoeuvre before reaching a solid white line on your side. White direction arrows on the road indicate that you need to get back onto your side of the road.

129 Double white lines where the line nearest you is solid. This means you **MUST NOT** cross or straddle it unless it is safe and you need to enter adjoining premises or a side road. You may cross the line if necessary, provided the road is clear, to pass a stationary vehicle, or overtake a pedal cycle, horse or road maintenance vehicle, if they are travelling at 10 mph (16 km/h) or less.

Laws RTA 1988 sect 36 & TSRGD regs 10 & 26

130 Areas of white diagonal stripes or chevrons painted on the road. These are to separate traffic lanes or to protect traffic turning right.

- If the area is bordered by a broken white line, you should not enter the area unless it is necessary and you can see that it is safe to do so.

- If the area is marked with chevrons and bordered by solid white lines you **MUST NOT** enter it except in an emergency.

Laws MT(E&W)R regs 5, 9, 10 & 16, MT(S)R regs 4, 8, 9 & 14, RTA sect 36 & TSRGD 10(1)

131 Lane dividers. These are short, broken white lines which are used on wide carriageways to divide them into lanes. You should keep between them.

132 Reflective road studs may be used with white lines.

- White studs mark the lanes or the middle of the road.

- Red studs mark the left edge of the road.

- Amber studs mark the central reservation of a dual carriageway or motorway.

- Green studs mark the edge of the main carriageway at lay-bys and slip roads.

- Green/yellow studs indicate temporary adjustments to lane layouts, e.g. where road works are taking place.

Rule 132
Reflective road studs mark the lanes and edges of the carriageway

Multi-lane carriageways

Lane discipline

133 If you need to change lane, first use your mirrors and if necessary take a quick sideways glance to make sure you will not force another road user to change course or speed. When it is safe to do so, signal to indicate your intentions to other road users and when clear, move over.

134 You should follow the signs and road markings and get into the lane as directed. In congested road conditions do not change lanes unnecessarily. Merging in turn is recommended but only if safe and appropriate when vehicles are travelling at a very low speed, e.g. when approaching road works or a road traffic incident. It is not recommended at high speed.

Single carriageway

135 Where a single carriageway has three lanes and the road markings or signs do not give priority to traffic in either direction

- use the middle lane only for overtaking or turning right. Remember, you have no more right to use the middle lane than a driver coming from the opposite direction

- do not use the right-hand lane.

136 Where a single carriageway has four or more lanes, use only the lanes that signs or markings indicate.

Dual carriageways

A dual carriageway is a road which has a central reservation to separate the carriageways.

137 On a two-lane dual carriageway you should stay in the left-hand lane. Use the right-hand lane for overtaking or turning right. After overtaking, move back to the left-hand lane when it is safe to do so.

138 On a three-lane dual carriageway, you may use the middle lane or the right-hand lane to overtake but return to the middle and then the left-hand lane when it is safe.

139 Climbing and crawler lanes. These are provided on some hills. Use this lane if you are driving a slow-moving vehicle or if there are vehicles behind you wishing to overtake. Be aware of the signs and road markings which indicate the lane is about to end.

140 Cycle lanes. These are shown by road markings and signs. You **MUST NOT** drive or park in a cycle lane marked by a solid white line during its times of operation. Do not drive or park in a cycle lane marked by a broken white line unless it is unavoidable. You **MUST NOT** park in any cycle lane whilst waiting restrictions apply.
Law RTRA sects 5 & 8

141 Bus lanes. These are shown by road markings and signs that indicate which (if any) other vehicles are permitted to use the bus lane. Unless otherwise indicated, you should not drive in a bus lane during its period of operation. You may enter a bus lane to stop, to load or unload where this is not prohibited.

142 High-occupancy vehicle lanes and other designated vehicle lanes. Lanes may be restricted for use by particular types of vehicle; these restrictions may apply some or all of the time. The operating times and vehicle types will be indicated on the accompanying traffic signs. You **MUST NOT** drive in such lanes during their times of operation unless signs indicate that your vehicle is permitted (see page 476).

Vehicles permitted to use designated lanes may or may not include cycles, buses, taxis, licensed private hire vehicles, motorcycles, heavy goods vehicles (HGVs) and high-occupancy vehicles (HOVs).

Where HOV lanes are in operation, they **MUST ONLY** be used by

- vehicles containing at least the minimum number of people indicated on the traffic signs

- any other vehicles, such as buses and motorcycles, as indicated on signs prior to the start of the lane, irrespective of the number of occupants.
Laws RTRA sects 5 & 8, & RTA 1988, sect 36

143 One-way streets. Traffic **MUST** travel in the direction indicated by signs. Buses and/or cycles may have a contraflow lane. Choose the correct lane for your exit as soon as you can. Do not change lanes suddenly. Unless road signs or markings indicate otherwise, you should use

- the left-hand lane when going left

- the right-hand lane when going right

- the most appropriate lane when going straight ahead. Remember - traffic could be passing on both sides.
Laws RTA 1988 sect 36 & RTRA sects 5 & 8

General advice

144 You **MUST NOT**

- drive dangerously

- drive without due care and attention

- drive without reasonable consideration for other road users.

Law RTA 1988 sects 2 & 3 as amended by RTA 1991

145 You **MUST NOT** drive on or over a pavement, footpath or bridleway except to gain lawful access to property, or in the case of an emergency.

Laws HA 1835 sect 72 & RTA 1988 sect 34

146 Adapt your driving to the appropriate type and condition of road you are on. In particular

- do not treat speed limits as a target. It is often not appropriate or safe to drive at the maximum speed limit

- take the road and traffic conditions into account. Be prepared for unexpected or difficult situations, for example, the road being blocked beyond a blind bend. Be prepared to adjust your speed as a precaution

- where there are junctions, be prepared for road users emerging

- in side roads and country lanes look out for unmarked junctions where nobody has priority

- be prepared to stop at traffic control systems, road works, pedestrian crossings or traffic lights as necessary

- try to anticipate what pedestrians and cyclists might do. If pedestrians, particularly children, are looking the other way, they may step out into the road without seeing you.

147 Be considerate. Be careful of and considerate towards all types of road users, especially those requiring extra care (see Rule 204). You should

- try to be understanding if other road users cause problems; they may be inexperienced or not know the area well

- be patient; remember that anyone can make a mistake

- not allow yourself to become agitated or involved if someone is behaving badly on the road. This will only make the situation worse. Pull over, calm down and, when you feel relaxed, continue your journey

- slow down and hold back if a road user pulls out into your path at a junction. Allow them to get clear. Do not over-react by driving too close behind to intimidate them.

- not throw anything out of a vehicle, for example, cigarette ends, cans, paper or carrier bags. This can endanger other road users, particularly motorcyclists and cyclists.

148 Safe driving and riding needs concentration. Avoid distractions when driving or riding such as

- loud music (this may mask other sounds)

- trying to read maps

- inserting a cassette or CD or tuning a radio

- arguing with your passengers or other road users

- eating and drinking

- smoking.

You **MUST NOT** smoke in public transport vehicles or in vehicles used for work purposes in certain prescribed circumstances. Separate regulations apply to England, Wales and Scotland.

Laws TSf(EV) regs 2007, TSfP(W) regs 2007 & TPSCP(S) regs 2006

Mobile phones and in-vehicle technology

149 You **MUST** exercise proper control of your vehicle at all times. You **MUST NOT** use a hand-held mobile phone, or similar device, when driving or when supervising a learner driver, except to call 999 or 112 in a genuine emergency when it is unsafe or impractical to stop. Never use a hand-held microphone when driving. Using hands-free equipment is also likely to distract your attention from the road. It is far safer not to use any telephone while you are driving or riding - find a safe place to stop first or use the voicemail facility and listen to messages later.

Laws RTA 1988 sects 2 & 3 & CUR regs 104 & 110

150 There is a danger of driver distraction being caused by in-vehicle systems such as satellite navigation systems, congestion warning systems, PCs, multi-media, etc. You **MUST** exercise proper control of your vehicle at all times. Do not rely on driver assistance systems such as cruise control or lane departure warnings. They are available to assist but you should not reduce your concentration levels. Do not be distracted by maps or screen-based information (such as navigation or vehicle management systems) while driving or riding. If necessary find a safe place to stop.

Laws RTA 1988 sects 2 & 3 & CUR reg 104

151 **In slow-moving traffic.** You should

- reduce the distance between you and the vehicle ahead to maintain traffic flow
- never get so close to the vehicle in front that you cannot stop safely
- leave enough space to be able to manoeuvre if the vehicle in front breaks down or an emergency vehicle needs to get past
- not change lanes to the left to overtake
- allow access into and from side roads, as blocking these will add to congestion
- be aware of cyclists and motorcyclists who may be passing on either side.

Rule 151
Do not block access to a side road

Driving in built-up areas

152 **Residential streets.** You should drive slowly and carefully on streets where there are likely to be pedestrians, cyclists and parked cars. In some areas a 20 mph (32 km/h) maximum speed limit may be in force. Look out for

- vehicles emerging from junctions or driveways
- vehicles moving off
- car doors opening
- pedestrians
- children running out from between parked cars
- cyclists and motorcyclists.

153 Traffic-calming measures. On some roads there are features such as road humps, chicanes and narrowings which are intended to slow you down. When you approach these features reduce your speed. Allow cyclists and motorcyclists room to pass through them. Maintain a reduced speed along the whole of the stretch of road within the calming measures. Give way to oncoming road users if directed to do so by signs. You should not overtake other moving road users while in these areas.

Rule 153
Chicanes may be used to slow traffic down

154 Country roads

Take extra care on country roads and reduce your speed at approaches to bends, which can be sharper than they appear, and at junctions and turnings, which may be partially hidden. Be prepared for pedestrians, horse riders, cyclists, slow-moving farm vehicles or mud on the road surface. Make sure you can stop within the distance you can see to be clear. You should also reduce your speed where country roads enter villages.

155 Single-track roads. These are only wide enough for one vehicle. They may have special passing places. If you see a vehicle coming towards you, or the driver behind wants to overtake, pull into a passing place on your left, or wait opposite a passing place on your right. Give way to road users coming uphill whenever you can. If necessary, reverse until you reach a passing place to let the other vehicle pass.

Slow down when passing pedestrians, cyclists and horse riders.

156 Do not park in passing places.

Vehicles prohibited from using roads and pavements

157 Certain motorised vehicles do not meet the construction and technical requirements for road vehicles and are generally not intended, not suitable and not legal for road, pavement, footpath, cycle path or bridleway use. These include most types of miniature motorcycles, also called mini motos, and motorised scooters, also called go peds, which are powered by electric or internal combustion engines. These types of vehicle **MUST NOT** be used on roads, pavements, footpaths or bridleways.
Laws RTA 1988 sects 34, 41a, 42, 47, 63 & 66, HA 1835, sect 72, & R(S)A sect 129

158 Certain models of motorcycles, motor tricycles and quadricycles, also called quad bikes, are suitable only for off-road use and do not meet legal standards for use on roads. Vehicles that do not meet these standards **MUST NOT** be used on roads. They **MUST NOT** be used on pavements, footpaths, cycle paths or bridleways either. You **MUST** make sure that any motorcycle, motor tricycle, quadricycle or any other motor vehicle meets legal standards and is properly registered, taxed and insured before using it on the roads. Even when registered, taxed and insured for the road, vehicles **MUST NOT** be used on pavements.
Laws RTA 1988 sects 34, 41a, 42, 47, 63, 66 & 156, HA 1835, sect 72, R(S)A sect 129, & VERA sects 1, 29, 31A, & 43A

Using the road

General rules

159 Before moving off you should

- use all mirrors to check the road is clear
- look round to check the blind spots (the areas you are unable to see in the mirrors)
- signal if necessary before moving out
- look round for a final check.

Move off only when it is safe to do so.

Rule 159
Check the blind spot before moving off

160 Once moving you should

- keep to the left, unless road signs or markings indicate otherwise. The exceptions are when you want to overtake, turn right or pass parked vehicles or pedestrians in the road
- keep well to the left on right-hand bends. This will improve your view of the road and help avoid the risk of colliding with traffic approaching from the opposite direction
- drive with both hands on the wheel where possible. This will help you to remain in full control of the vehicle at all times
- be aware of other road users, especially cycles and motorcycles who may be filtering through the traffic. These are more difficult to see than larger vehicles and their riders are particularly vulnerable. Give

them plenty of room, especially if you are driving a long vehicle or towing a trailer

- select a lower gear before you reach a long downhill slope. This will help to control your speed
- when towing, remember the extra length will affect overtaking and manoeuvring. The extra weight will also affect the braking and acceleration.

161 Mirrors. All mirrors should be used effectively throughout your journey. You should

- use your mirrors frequently so that you always know what is behind and to each side of you
- use them in good time before you signal or change direction or speed
- be aware that mirrors do not cover all areas and there will be blind spots. You will need to look round and check.

Remember: Mirrors - Signal - Manoeuvre

Overtaking

162 Before overtaking you should make sure

- the road is sufficiently clear ahead
- road users are not beginning to overtake you
- there is a suitable gap in front of the road user you plan to overtake.

163 **Overtake only** when it is safe and legal to do so. You should

- not get too close to the vehicle you intend to overtake

- use your mirrors, signal when it is safe to do so, take a quick sideways glance if necessary into the blind spot area and then start to move out

- not assume that you can simply follow a vehicle ahead which is overtaking; there may only be enough room for one vehicle

- move quickly past the vehicle you are overtaking, once you have started to overtake. Allow plenty of room. Move back to the left as soon as you can but do not cut in

- take extra care at night and in poor visibility when it is harder to judge speed and distance

- give way to oncoming vehicles before passing parked vehicles or other obstructions on your side of the road

- only overtake on the left if the vehicle in front is signalling to turn right, and there is room to do so

- stay in your lane if traffic is moving slowly in queues. If the queue on your right is moving more slowly than you are, you may pass on the left

- give motorcyclists, cyclists and horse riders at least as much room as you would when overtaking a car (see Rules 211-215).

Remember: Mirrors - Signal - Manoeuvre

Rule 163
Give vulnerable road users at least as much space as you would a car

164 **Large vehicles.** Overtaking these is more difficult. You should

- drop back. This will increase your ability to see ahead and should allow the driver of the large vehicle to see you in their mirrors. Getting too close to large vehicles, including agricultural vehicles such as a tractor with a trailer or other fixed equipment, will obscure your view of the road ahead and there may be another slow-moving vehicle in front

Rule 164
Do not cut in too quickly

- make sure that you have enough room to complete your overtaking manoeuvre before committing yourself. It takes longer to pass a large vehicle. If in doubt do not overtake

- not assume you can follow a vehicle ahead which is overtaking a long vehicle. If a problem develops, they may abort overtaking and pull back in.

165 You **MUST NOT** overtake

- if you would have to cross or straddle double white lines with a solid line nearest to you (but see Rule 129)

- if you would have to enter an area designed to divide traffic, if it is surrounded by a solid white line

- the nearest vehicle to a pedestrian crossing, especially when it has stopped to let pedestrians cross

- if you would have to enter a lane reserved for buses, trams or cycles during its hours of operation

- after a 'No Overtaking' sign and until you pass a sign cancelling the restriction.

Laws RTA 1988 sect 36, TSRGD regs 10, 22, 23 & 24, ZPPPCRGD reg 24

166 DO NOT overtake if there is any doubt, or where you cannot see far enough ahead to be sure it is safe. For example, when you are approaching

- a corner or bend

- a hump bridge

- the brow of a hill.

167 DO NOT overtake where you might come into conflict with other road users. For example

- approaching or at a road junction on either side of the road

- where the road narrows

- when approaching a school crossing patrol

- between the kerb and a bus or tram when it is at a stop

- where traffic is queuing at junctions or road works

- when you would force another road user to swerve or slow down

- at a level crossing

- when a road user is indicating right, even if you believe the signal should have been cancelled. Do not take a risk; wait for the signal to be cancelled

- stay behind if you are following a cyclist approaching a roundabout or junction, and you intend to turn left

- when a tram is standing at a kerbside tram stop and there is no clearly marked passing lane for other traffic.

168   Being overtaken. If a driver is trying to overtake you, maintain a steady course and speed, slowing down if necessary to let the vehicle pass. Never obstruct drivers who wish to pass. Speeding up or driving unpredictably while someone is overtaking you is dangerous. Drop back to maintain a two-second gap if someone overtakes and pulls into the gap in front of you.

169   Do not hold up a long queue of traffic, especially if you are driving a large or slow-moving vehicle. Check your mirrors frequently, and if necessary, pull in where it is safe and let traffic pass.

Road junctions

170 Take extra care at junctions. You should

- watch out for cyclists, motorcyclists, powered wheelchairs/mobility scooters and pedestrians as they are not always easy to see. Be aware that they may not have seen or heard you if you are approaching from behind

- watch out for pedestrians crossing a road into which you are turning. If they have started to cross they have priority, so give way

- watch out for long vehicles which may be turning at a junction ahead; they may have to use the whole width of the road to make the turn (see Rule 221)

- watch out for horse riders who may take a different line on the road from that which you would expect

- not assume, when waiting at a junction, that a vehicle coming from the right and signalling left will actually turn. Wait and make sure

- look all around before emerging. Do not cross or join a road until there is a gap large enough for you to do so safely.

171 You **MUST** stop behind the line at a junction with a 'Stop' sign and a solid white line across the road. Wait for a safe gap in the traffic before you move off.

Laws RTA 1988 sect 36 & TSRGD regs 10 & 16

172 The approach to a junction may have a 'Give Way' sign or a triangle marked on the road. You **MUST** give way to traffic on the main road when emerging from a junction with broken white lines across the road.

Laws RTA 1988 sect 36 & TSRGD regs 10(1), 16(1) & 25

173 Dual carriageways. When crossing or turning right, first assess whether the central reservation is deep enough to protect the full length of your vehicle.

- If it is, then you should treat each half of the carriageway as a separate road. Wait in the central reservation until there is a safe gap in the traffic on the second half of the road.

- If the central reservation is too shallow for the length of your vehicle, wait until you can cross both carriageways in one go.

Rule 170
Give way to pedestrians who have started to cross

Rule 173
Assess your vehicle's length and do not obstruct traffic

174   Box junctions. These have criss-cross yellow lines painted on the road (see page 480). You **MUST NOT** enter the box until your exit road or lane is clear. However, you may enter the box and wait when you want to turn right, and are only stopped from doing so by oncoming traffic, or by other vehicles waiting to turn right. At signalled roundabouts you **MUST NOT** enter the box unless you can cross over it completely without stopping.

Law TSRGD regs 10(1) & 29(2)

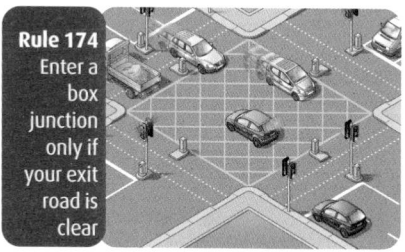

Rule 174
Enter a box junction only if your exit road is clear

Junctions controlled by traffic lights

175   You **MUST** stop behind the white 'Stop' line across your side of the road unless the light is green. If the amber light appears you may go on only if you have already crossed the stop line or are so close to it that to stop might cause a collision.

Laws RTA 1988 sect 36 & TSRGD regs 10 & 36

176   You **MUST NOT** move forward over the white line when the red light is showing. Only go forward when the traffic lights are green if there is room for you to clear the junction safely or you are taking up a position to turn right. If the traffic lights are not working, treat the situation as you would an unmarked junction and proceed with great care.

Laws RTA 1988 sect 36 & TSRGD regs 10 & 36

177   Green filter arrow. This indicates a filter lane only. Do not enter that lane unless you want to go in the direction of the arrow. You may proceed in the direction of the green arrow when it, or the full green light shows. Give other traffic, especially cyclists, time and room to move into the correct lane.

178   Advanced stop lines. Some signal-controlled junctions have advanced stop lines to allow cycles to be positioned ahead of other traffic. Motorists, including motorcyclists, **MUST** stop at the first white line reached if the lights are amber or red and should avoid blocking the way or encroaching on the marked area at other times, e.g. if the junction ahead is blocked. If your vehicle has proceeded over the first white line at the time that the signal goes red, you **MUST** stop at the second white line, even if your vehicle is in the marked area. Allow cyclists time and space to move off when the green signal shows.

Laws RTA 1988 sect 36 & TSRGD regs 10, 36(1) & 43(2)

Rule 178
Do not unnecessarily encroach on the cyclists' waiting area

Turning right

179 Well before you turn right you should

- use your mirrors to make sure you know the position and movement of traffic behind you
- give a right-turn signal
- take up a position just left of the middle of the road or in the space marked for traffic turning right
- leave room for other vehicles to pass on the left, if possible.

180 Wait until there is a safe gap between you and any oncoming vehicle. Watch out for cyclists, motorcyclists, pedestrians and other road users. Check your mirrors and blind spot again to make sure you are not being overtaken, then make the turn. Do not cut the corner. Take great care when turning into a main road; you will need to watch for traffic in both directions and wait for a safe gap.

Remember: Mirrors - Signal - Manoeuvre

Rule 180
Position your vehicle correctly to avoid obstructing traffic

181 When turning right at crossroads where an oncoming vehicle is also turning right, there is a choice of two methods

- turn right side to right side; keep the other vehicle on your right and turn behind it. This is generally the safer method as you have a clear view of any approaching traffic when completing your turn
- left side to left side, turning in front of each other. This can block your view of oncoming vehicles, so take extra care. Cyclists and motorcyclists in particular may be hidden from your view. Road layout, markings or how the other vehicle is positioned can determine which course should be taken.

Rule 181
Left - Turning right side to right side.
Right - Turning left side to left side

Turning left

182 Use your mirrors and give a left-turn signal well before you turn left. Do not overtake just before you turn left and watch out for traffic coming up on your left before you make the turn, especially if driving a large vehicle. Cyclists, motorcyclists and other road users in particular may be hidden from your view.

Rule 182
Do not cut in on cyclists

183 When turning

- keep as close to the left as is safe and practicable

- give way to any vehicles using a bus lane, cycle lane or tramway from either direction.

Roundabouts

184 On approaching a roundabout

take notice and act on all the information available to you, including traffic signs, traffic lights and lane markings which direct you into the correct lane. You should

- use **Mirrors - Signal - Manoeuvre** at all stages

- decide as early as possible which exit you need to take

- give an appropriate signal (see Rule 186). Time your signals so as not to confuse other road users

- get into the correct lane

- adjust your speed and position to fit in with traffic conditions

- be aware of the speed and position of all the road users around you.

185 When reaching the roundabout

you should

- give priority to traffic approaching from your right, unless directed otherwise by signs, road markings or traffic lights

- check whether road markings allow you to enter the roundabout without giving way. If so, proceed, but still look to the right before joining

- watch out for all other road users already on the roundabout; be aware they may not be signalling correctly or at all

- look forward before moving off to make sure traffic in front has moved off.

Rule 185
Follow the correct procedure at roundabouts

186 Signals and position.

When taking the first exit to the left, unless signs or markings indicate otherwise

- signal left and approach in the left-hand lane

- keep to the left on the roundabout and continue signalling left to leave.

When taking an exit to the right or going full circle, unless signs or markings indicate otherwise

- signal right and approach in the right-hand lane

- keep to the right on the roundabout until you need to change lanes to exit the roundabout

- signal left after you have passed the exit before the one you want.

When taking any intermediate exit, unless signs or markings indicate otherwise

- select the appropriate lane on approach to the roundabout

- you should not normally need to signal on approach

- stay in this lane until you need to alter course to exit the roundabout

- signal left after you have passed the exit before the one you want.

When there are more than three lanes at the entrance to a roundabout, use the most appropriate lane on approach and through it.

187 **In all cases watch out for** and give plenty of room to

- pedestrians who may be crossing the approach and exit roads
- traffic crossing in front of you on the roundabout, especially vehicles intending to leave by the next exit
- traffic which may be straddling lanes or positioned incorrectly
- motorcyclists
- cyclists and horse riders who may stay in the left-hand lane and signal right if they intend to continue round the roundabout. Allow them to do so
- long vehicles (including those towing trailers). These might have to take a different course or straddle lanes either approaching or on the roundabout because of their length. Watch out for their signals.

188 **Mini-roundabouts.** Approach these in the same way as normal roundabouts. All vehicles **MUST** pass round the central markings except large vehicles which are physically incapable of doing so. Remember, there is less space to manoeuvre and less time to signal. Avoid making U-turns at mini-roundabouts. Beware of others doing this. Laws RTA 1988 sect 36 & TSRGD regs 10(1) & 16(1)

189 At double mini-roundabouts treat each roundabout separately and give way to traffic from the right.

190 **Multiple roundabouts.** At some complex junctions, there may be a series of mini-roundabouts at each intersection. Treat each mini-roundabout separately and follow the normal rules.

Rule 190
Treat each roundabout separately

Pedestrian crossings

191 You **MUST NOT** park on a crossing or in the area covered by the zig-zag lines. You **MUST NOT** overtake the moving vehicle nearest the crossing or the vehicle nearest the crossing which has stopped to give way to pedestrians.

Laws ZPPPCRGD regs 18, 20 & 24, RTRA sect 25(5) & TSRGD regs 10, 27 & 28

192 In queuing traffic, you should keep the crossing clear.

Rule 192
Keep the crossing clear

193 You should take extra care where the view of either side of the crossing is blocked by queuing traffic or incorrectly parked vehicles. Pedestrians may be crossing between stationary vehicles.

194 Allow pedestrians plenty of time to cross and do not harass them by revving your engine or edging forward.

195 Zebra crossings. As you approach a zebra crossing

- look out for pedestrians waiting to cross and be ready to slow down or stop to let them cross

- you **MUST** give way when a pedestrian has moved onto a crossing

- allow more time for stopping on wet or icy roads

- do not wave or use your horn to invite pedestrians across; this could be dangerous if another vehicle is approaching

- be aware of pedestrians approaching from the side of the crossing.

A zebra crossing with a central island is two separate crossings (see pictures on page 413).

Law ZPPPCRGD reg 25

Signal-controlled crossings

196 Pelican crossings. These are signal-controlled crossings where flashing amber follows the red 'Stop' light. You **MUST** stop when the red light shows. When the amber light is flashing, you **MUST** give way to any pedestrians on the crossing. If the amber light is flashing and there are no pedestrians on the crossing, you may proceed with caution.

Laws ZPPPCRGD regs 23 & 26 & RTRA sect 25(5)

Rule 196 Allow pedestrians to cross when the amber light is flashing

197 Pelican crossings which go straight across the road are one crossing, even when there is a central island. You **MUST** wait for pedestrians who are crossing from the other side of the island.

Laws ZPPPCRGD reg 26 & RTRA sect 25(5)

198 Give way to anyone still crossing after the signal for vehicles has changed to green. This advice applies to all crossings.

199 Toucan, puffin and equestrian crossings. These are similar to pelican crossings, but there is no flashing amber phase; the light sequence for traffic at these three crossings is the same as at traffic lights. If the signal-controlled crossing is not working, proceed with extreme caution.

Reversing

200 Choose an appropriate place to manoeuvre. If you need to turn your vehicle around, wait until you find a safe place. Try not to reverse or turn round in a busy road; find a quiet side road or drive round a block of side streets.

201 Do not reverse from a side road into a main road. When using a driveway, reverse in and drive out if you can.

202 Look carefully before you start reversing. You should

- use all your mirrors
- check the 'blind spot' behind you (the part of the road you cannot see easily in the mirrors)
- check there are no pedestrians (particularly children), cyclists, other road users or obstructions in the road behind you.

Reverse slowly while

- checking all around
- looking mainly through the rear window
- being aware that the front of your vehicle will swing out as you turn.

Get someone to guide you if you cannot see clearly.

Rule 202
Check all round when reversing

203 You **MUST NOT** reverse your vehicle further than necessary.

Law CUR reg 106

Road users requiring extra care

204 The most vulnerable road users are pedestrians, cyclists, motorcyclists and horse riders. It is particularly important to be aware of children, older and disabled people, and learner and inexperienced drivers and riders.

Pedestrians

205 There is a risk of pedestrians, especially children, stepping unexpectedly into the road. You should drive with the safety of children in mind at a speed suitable for the conditions.

206 **Drive carefully and slowly** when

- in crowded shopping streets, Home Zones and Quiet Lanes (see Rule 218) or residential areas
- driving past bus and tram stops; pedestrians may emerge suddenly into the road
- passing parked vehicles, especially ice cream vans; children are more interested in ice cream than traffic and may run into the road unexpectedly
- needing to cross a pavement or cycle track; for example, to reach or leave a driveway. Give way to pedestrians and cyclists on the pavement
- reversing into a side road; look all around the vehicle and give way to any pedestrians who may be crossing the road
- turning at road junctions; give way to pedestrians who are already crossing the road into which you are turning

- the pavement is closed due to street repairs and pedestrians are directed to use the road

- approaching pedestrians on narrow rural roads without a footway or footpath. Always slow down and be prepared to stop if necessary, giving them plenty of room as you drive past.

Rule 206
Watch out for children in busy areas

207 Particularly vulnerable pedestrians. These include

- children and older pedestrians who may not be able to judge your speed and could step into the road in front of you. At 40 mph (64 km/h) your vehicle will probably kill any pedestrians it hits. At 20 mph (32 km/h) there is only a 1 in 20 chance of the pedestrian being killed. So kill your speed

- older pedestrians who may need more time to cross the road. Be patient and allow them to cross in their own time. Do not hurry them by revving your engine or edging forward

- people with disabilities. People with hearing impairments may not be aware of your vehicle approaching. Those with walking difficulties require more time

- blind or partially sighted people, who may be carrying a white cane or using a guide dog. They may not be able to see you approaching

- deafblind people who may be carrying a white cane with a red band or using a dog with a red and white harness. They may not see or hear instructions or signals.

208 Near schools. Drive slowly and be particularly aware of young cyclists and pedestrians. In some places, there may be a flashing amber signal below the 'School' warning sign which tells you that there may be children crossing the road ahead. Drive very slowly until you are clear of the area.

209 Drive carefully and slowly when passing a stationary bus showing a 'School Bus' sign (see page 481) as children may be getting on or off.

210 You **MUST** stop when a school crossing patrol shows a 'Stop for children' sign (see pages 469 and 470).
Law RTRA sect 28

Motorcyclists and cyclists

211 It is often difficult to see motorcyclists and cyclists, especially when they are coming up from behind, coming out of junctions, at roundabouts, overtaking you or filtering through traffic. Always look out for them before you emerge from a junction; they could be approaching faster than you think. When turning right across a line of slow-moving or stationary traffic, look out for cyclists or motorcyclists on the inside of the traffic you are crossing. Be especially careful when turning, and when changing direction or lane. Be sure to check mirrors and blind spots carefully.

Rule 211
Look out for motor cyclists and cyclists at junctions

212 When passing motorcyclists and cyclists, give them plenty of room (see Rules 162-167). If they look over their shoulder it could mean that they intend to pull out, turn right or change direction. Give them time and space to do so.

213 Motorcyclists and cyclists may suddenly need to avoid uneven road surfaces and obstacles such as drain covers or oily, wet or icy patches on the road. Give them plenty of room and pay particular attention to any sudden change of direction they may have to make.

Other road users

214 Animals. When passing animals, drive slowly. Give them plenty of room and be ready to stop. Do not scare animals by sounding your horn, revving your engine or accelerating rapidly once you have passed them. Look out for animals being led, driven or ridden on the road and take extra care. Keep your speed down at bends and on narrow country roads. If a road is blocked by a herd of animals, stop and switch off your engine until they have left the road. Watch out for animals on unfenced roads.

215 Horse riders and horse-drawn vehicles. Be particularly careful of horse riders and horse-drawn vehicles especially when overtaking. Always pass wide and slowly. Horse riders are often children, so

take extra care and remember riders may ride in double file when escorting a young or inexperienced horse or rider. Look out for horse riders' and horse drivers' signals and heed a request to slow down or stop. Take great care and treat all horses as a potential hazard; they can be unpredictable, despite the efforts of their rider/driver.

216 Older drivers. Their reactions may be slower than other drivers. Make allowance for this.

217 Learners and inexperienced drivers. They may not be so skilful at anticipating and responding to events. Be particularly patient with learner drivers and young drivers. Drivers who have recently passed their test may display a 'New driver' plate or sticker (see Annex 8 - Safety code for new drivers).

218 Home Zones and Quiet Lanes. These are places where people could be using the whole of the road for a range of activities such as children playing or for a community event. You should drive slowly and carefully and be prepared to stop to allow people extra time to make space for you to pass them in safety.

Other vehicles

219 Emergency and Incident Support vehicles. You should look and listen for ambulances, fire engines, police, doctors or other emergency vehicles using flashing blue, red or green lights and sirens or flashing headlights, or Highways Agency Traffic Officer and Incident Support vehicles using flashing amber lights. When one approaches do not panic. Consider the route of such a vehicle and take appropriate action to let it pass, while complying with all traffic signs. If necessary, pull to the side of the road and stop, but try to avoid stopping before the brow of a hill, a bend or narrow section of road. Do not endanger yourself, other road users or pedestrians and avoid mounting the kerb. Do not brake harshly on approach to a junction or roundabout, as a following vehicle may not have the same view as you.

220 Powered vehicles used by disabled people. These small vehicles travel at a maximum speed of 8 mph (12 km/h). On a dual carriageway where the speed limit exceeds 50 mph (80 km/h) they **MUST** have a flashing amber beacon, but on other roads you may not have that advance warning (see Rules 36-46 inclusive).

Law RVLR reg 17(1) & 26

221 Large vehicles. These may need extra road space to turn or to deal with a hazard that you are not able to see. If you are following a large vehicle, such as a bus or articulated lorry, be aware that the driver may not be able to see you in the mirrors. Be prepared to stop and wait if it needs room or time to turn.

Rule 221
Large vehicles need extra room

222 Large vehicles can block your view. Your ability to see and to plan ahead will be improved if you pull back to increase your separation distance. Be patient, as larger vehicles are subject to lower speed limits than cars and motorcycles. Many large vehicles may be fitted with speed limiting devices which will restrict speed to 56 mph (90 km/h) even on a motorway.

223 Buses, coaches and trams. Give priority to these vehicles when you can do so safely, especially when they signal to pull away from stops. Look out for people getting off a bus or tram and crossing the road.

224 Electric vehicles. Be careful of electric vehicles such as milk floats and trams. Trams move quickly but silently and cannot steer to avoid you.

225 Vehicles with flashing amber beacons. These warn of a slow-moving or stationary vehicle (such as a Traffic Officer vehicle, salt spreader, snow plough or recovery vehicle) or abnormal loads, so approach with caution. On unrestricted dual carriageways, motor vehicles first used on or after 1 January 1947 with a maximum speed of 25 mph (40 km/h) or less (such as tractors) **MUST** use a flashing amber beacon (also see Rule 220).

Law RVLR 1989, reg 17

Driving in adverse weather conditions

226 You **MUST** use headlights when visibility is seriously reduced, generally when you cannot see for more than 100 metres (328 feet). You may also use front or rear fog lights but you **MUST** switch them off when visibility improves (see Rule 236).

Law RVLR regs 25 & 27

227 **Wet weather.** In wet weather, stopping distances will be at least double those required for stopping on dry roads (see page 429). This is because your tyres have less grip on the road. In wet weather

- you should keep well back from the vehicle in front. This will increase your ability to see and plan ahead

- if the steering becomes unresponsive, it probably means that water is preventing the tyres from gripping the road. Ease off the accelerator and slow down gradually

- the rain and spray from vehicles may make it difficult to see and be seen

- be aware of the dangers of spilt diesel that will make the surface very slippery (see Annex 6)

- take extra care around pedestrians, cyclists, motorcyclists and horse riders.

Icy and snowy weather

228 In winter check the local weather forecast for warnings of icy or snowy weather. **DO NOT** drive in these conditions unless your journey is essential. If it is, take great care and allow more time for your journey.

Take an emergency kit of de-icer and ice scraper, torch, warm clothing and boots, first aid kit, jump leads and a shovel, together with a warm drink and emergency food in case you get stuck or your vehicle breaks down.

229 Before you set off

- you **MUST** be able to see, so clear all snow and ice from all your windows

- you **MUST** ensure that lights are clean and number plates are clearly visible and legible

- make sure the mirrors are clear and the windows are demisted thoroughly

- remove all snow that might fall off into the path of other road users

- check your planned route is clear of delays and that no further snowfalls or severe weather are predicted.

Laws CUR reg 30, RVLR reg 23, VERA Sect 43 & RV(DRM)R reg 11

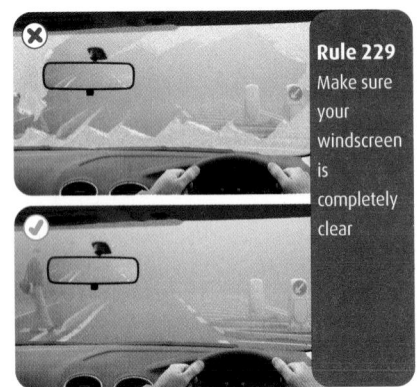

Rule 229
Make sure your windscreen is completely clear

230 **When driving** in icy or snowy weather

- drive with care, even if the roads have been treated
- keep well back from the road user in front as stopping distances can be ten times greater than on dry roads
- take care when overtaking vehicles spreading salt or other de-icer, particularly if you are riding a motorcycle or cycle
- watch out for snowploughs which may throw out snow on either side. Do not overtake them unless the lane you intend to use has been cleared
- be prepared for the road conditions to change over relatively short distances
- listen to travel bulletins and take note of variable message signs that may provide information about weather, road and traffic conditions ahead.

231 **Drive extremely carefully** when the roads are icy. Avoid sudden actions as these could cause loss of control. You should

- drive at a slow speed in as high a gear as possible; accelerate and brake very gently
- drive particularly slowly on bends where loss of control is more likely. Brake progressively on the straight before you reach a bend. Having slowed down, steer smoothly round the bend, avoiding sudden actions
- check your grip on the road surface when there is snow or ice by choosing a safe place to brake gently. If the steering feels unresponsive this may indicate ice and your vehicle losing its grip on the road.

When travelling on ice, tyres make virtually no noise.

Windy weather

232 High-sided vehicles are most affected by windy weather, but strong gusts can also blow a car, cyclist, motorcyclist or horse rider off course. This can happen on open stretches of road exposed to strong crosswinds, or when passing bridges or gaps in hedges.

233 In very windy weather your vehicle may be affected by turbulence created by large vehicles. Motorcyclists are particularly affected, so keep well back from them when they are overtaking a high-sided vehicle.

Fog

234 **Before entering fog** check your mirrors then slow down. If the word 'Fog' is shown on a roadside signal but the road is clear, be prepared for a bank of fog or drifting patchy fog ahead. Even if it seems to be clearing, you can suddenly find yourself in thick fog.

235 **When driving in fog** you should

- use your lights as required (see Rule 226)
- keep a safe distance behind the vehicle in front. Rear lights can give a false sense of security
- be able to pull up well within the distance you can see clearly. This is particularly important on motorways and dual carriageways, as vehicles are travelling faster
- use your windscreen wipers and demisters
- beware of other drivers not using headlights

- not accelerate to get away from a vehicle which is too close behind you

- check your mirrors before you slow down. Then use your brakes so that your brake lights warn drivers behind you that you are slowing down

- stop in the correct position at a junction with limited visibility and listen for traffic. When you are sure it is safe to emerge, do so positively and do not hesitate in a position that puts you directly in the path of approaching vehicles.

236 You **MUST NOT** use front or rear fog lights unless visibility is seriously reduced (see Rule 226) as they dazzle other road users and can obscure your brake lights. You **MUST** switch them off when visibility improves.

Law RVLR regs 25 & 27

237 Hot weather. Keep your vehicle well ventilated to avoid drowsiness. Be aware that the road surface may become soft or if it rains after a dry spell it may become slippery. These conditions could affect your steering and braking. If you are dazzled by bright sunlight, slow down and if necessary, stop.

Waiting and parking

238 You **MUST NOT** wait or park on yellow lines during the times of operation shown on nearby time plates (or zone entry signs if in a Controlled Parking Zone) - see pages 476 and 479. Double yellow lines indicate a prohibition of waiting at any time even if there are no upright signs. You **MUST NOT** wait or park, or stop to set down and pick up passengers, on school

entrance markings (see page 480) when upright signs indicate a prohibition of stopping.

Law RTRA sects 5 & 8

Parking

239 Use off-street parking areas, or bays marked out with white lines on the road as parking places, wherever possible.
If you have to stop on the roadside

- do not park facing against the traffic flow

- stop as close as you can to the side

- do not stop too close to a vehicle displaying a Blue Badge: remember, the occupant may need more room to get in or out

- you **MUST** switch off the engine, headlights and fog lights

- you **MUST** apply the handbrake before leaving the vehicle

- you **MUST** ensure you do not hit anyone when you open your door. Check for cyclists or other traffic

- it is safer for your passengers (especially children) to get out of the vehicle on the side next to the kerb

- put all valuables out of sight and make sure your vehicle is secure

- lock your vehicle.

Laws CUR reg 98, 105 & 107, RVLR reg 27 & RTA 1988 sect 42

Rule 239
Check before opening your door

240 You **MUST NOT** stop or park on

- the carriageway or the hard shoulder of a motorway except in an emergency (see Rule 270)

- a pedestrian crossing, including the area marked by the zig-zag lines (see Rule 191)

- a clearway (see page 471)

- taxi bays as indicated by upright signs and markings

- an urban clearway within its hours of operation, except to pick up or set down passengers (see page 471)

- a road marked with double white lines, even when a broken white line is on your side of the road, except to pick up or set down passengers, or to load or unload goods

- a tram or cycle lane during its period of operation

- a cycle track

- red lines, in the case of specially designated 'red routes', unless otherwise indicated by signs.

Any vehicle may enter a bus lane to stop, load or unload where this is not prohibited (see Rule 141).

Laws MT(E&W)R regs 7 & 9, MT(S)R regs 6 & 8, ZPPPCRGD regs 18 & 20, RTRA sects 5, 6 & 8, TSRGD regs 10, 26 & 27, RTA 1988 sects 21(1) & 36

241 You **MUST NOT** park in parking spaces reserved for specific users, such as Blue Badge holders, residents or motorcycles, unless entitled to do so.

Laws CSDPA sect 21 & RTRA sects 5 & 8

242 You **MUST NOT** leave your vehicle or trailer in a dangerous position or where it causes any unnecessary obstruction of the road.

Laws RTA 1988, sects 22 & CUR reg 103

243 **DO NOT** stop or park

- near a school entrance

- anywhere you would prevent access for Emergency Services

- at or near a bus or tram stop or taxi rank

- on the approach to a level crossing/tramway crossing

- opposite or within 10 metres (32 feet) of a junction, except in an authorised parking space

- near the brow of a hill or hump bridge

- opposite a traffic island or (if this would cause an obstruction) another parked vehicle

- where you would force other traffic to enter a tram lane

- where the kerb has been lowered to help wheelchair users and powered mobility vehicles

- in front of an entrance to a property

- on a bend

- where you would obstruct cyclists' use of cycle facilities

except when forced to do so by stationary traffic.

244 You **MUST NOT** park partially or wholly on the pavement in London, and should not do so elsewhere unless signs permit it. Parking on the pavement can obstruct and seriously inconvenience pedestrians, people in wheelchairs or with visual impairments and people with prams or pushchairs.

Law GL(GP)A sect 15

245 Controlled Parking Zones. The zone entry signs indicate the times when the waiting restrictions within the zone are in force. Parking may be allowed in some places at other times. Otherwise parking will be within separately signed and marked bays.

246 Goods vehicles. Vehicles with a maximum laden weight of over 7.5 tonnes (including any trailer) **MUST NOT** be parked on a verge, pavement or any land situated between carriageways, without police permission. The only exception is when parking is essential for loading and unloading, in which case the vehicle **MUST NOT** be left unattended.

Law RTA 1988 sect 19

247 Loading and unloading. Do not load or unload where there are yellow markings on the kerb and upright signs advise restrictions are in place (see pages 479-480). This may be permitted where parking is otherwise restricted. On red routes, specially marked and signed bays indicate where and when loading and unloading is permitted.

Law RTRA sects 5 & 8

Parking at night

248 You **MUST NOT** park on a road at night facing against the direction of the traffic flow unless in a recognised parking space.

Laws CUR reg 101 & RVLR reg 24

249 All vehicles **MUST** display parking lights when parked on a road or a lay-by on a road with a speed limit greater than 30 mph (48 km/h).

Law RVLR reg 24

250 Cars, goods vehicles not exceeding 1525 kg unladen weight, invalid carriages, motorcycles and pedal cycles may be parked without lights on a road (or lay-by) with a speed limit of 30 mph (48 km/h) or less if they are

- at least 10 metres (32 feet) away from any junction, close to the kerb and facing in the direction of the traffic flow

- in a recognised parking place or lay-by.

Other vehicles and trailers, and all vehicles with projecting loads, **MUST NOT** be left on a road at night without lights.

Laws RVLR reg 24 & CUR reg 82(7)

251 Parking in fog. It is especially dangerous to park on the road in fog. If it is unavoidable, leave your parking lights or sidelights on.

252 Parking on hills. If you park on a hill you should

- park close to the kerb and apply the handbrake firmly

- select a forward gear and turn your steering wheel away from the kerb when facing uphill

- select reverse gear and turn your steering wheel towards the kerb when facing downhill

- use 'park' if your car has an automatic gearbox.

Rule 252
Turn your wheels away from the kerb when parking facing uphill. Turn them towards the kerb when parking facing downhill

Decriminalised Parking Enforcement (DPE)

DPE is becoming increasingly common as more authorities take on this role. The local traffic authority assumes responsibility for enforcing many parking contraventions in place of the police.

Further details on DPE may be found at the following websites:

www.parking-appeals.gov.uk (outside London)

www.parkingandtrafficappeals.gov.uk (inside London)

Motorways

Many other Rules apply to motorway driving, either wholly or in part: Rules 46, 57, 83-126, 130-134, 139, 144, 146-151, 160, 161, 219, 221-222, 225, 226-237, 274-278, 280, and 281-290.

General

253 Prohibited vehicles. Motorways **MUST NOT** be used by pedestrians, holders of provisional motorcycle or car licences, riders of motorcycles under 50 cc, cyclists, horse riders, certain slow-moving vehicles and those carrying oversized loads (except by special permission), agricultural vehicles, and powered wheelchairs/powered mobility scooters (see Rules 36-46 incl).

Laws HA 1980 sects 16, 17 & sch 4, MT(E&W)R regs 3(d), 4 & 11, MT(E&W)(A)R, R(S)A sects 7, 8 & sch 3, RTRA sects 17(2) & (3), & MT(S)R reg 10

254 Traffic on motorways usually travels faster than on other roads, so you have less time to react. It is especially important to use your mirrors earlier and look much further ahead than you would on other roads.

Motorway signals

255 Motorway signals (see page 466) are used to warn you of a danger ahead. For example, there may be an incident, fog, a spillage or road workers on the carriageway which you may not immediately be able to see.

256 Signals situated on the central reservation apply to all lanes. On very busy stretches, signals may be overhead with a separate signal for each lane.

257 Amber flashing lights. These warn of a hazard ahead. The signal may show a temporary maximum speed limit, lanes that are closed or a message such as 'Fog'. Adjust your speed and look out for the danger until you pass a signal which is not flashing or one that gives the 'All clear' sign and you are sure it is safe to increase your speed.

258 Red flashing lights. If red lights on the overhead signals flash above your lane and a red 'X' is showing, you **MUST NOT** go beyond the signal in that lane. If red lights flash on a signal in the central reservation or at the side of the road, you **MUST NOT** go beyond the signal in any lane.

Laws RTA 1988 sect 36 & TSRGD regs 10 & 38

Driving on the motorway

259 Joining the motorway. When you join the motorway you will normally approach it from a road on the left (a slip road) or from an adjoining motorway. You should

- give priority to traffic already on the motorway
- check the traffic on the motorway and match your speed to fit safely into the traffic flow in the left-hand lane
- not cross solid white lines that separate lanes or use the hard shoulder
- stay on the slip road if it continues as an extra lane on the motorway
- remain in the left-hand lane long enough to adjust to the speed of traffic before considering overtaking.

On the motorway

260 When you can see well ahead and the road conditions are good, you should

- drive at a steady cruising speed which you and your vehicle can handle safely and is within the speed limit (see table on page 430)
- keep a safe distance from the vehicle in front and increase the gap on wet or icy roads, or in fog (see Rules 126 and 235).

261 You **MUST NOT** exceed 70 mph (112 km/h), or the maximum speed limit permitted for your vehicle (see page 430). If a lower speed limit is in force, either permanently or temporarily, at road works for example, you **MUST NOT** exceed the lower limit. On some motorways, mandatory motorway signals (which display the speed within a red ring) are used to vary the maximum speed limit to improve traffic flow. You **MUST NOT** exceed this speed limit.

Law RTRA sects 17, 86, 89 & sch 6

262 The monotony of driving on a motorway can make you feel sleepy. To minimise the risk, follow the advice in Rule 91.

263 You **MUST NOT** reverse, cross the central reservation, or drive against the traffic flow. If you have missed your exit, or have taken the wrong route, carry on to the next exit.

Laws MT(E&W)R regs 6, 8 & 10 & MT(S)R regs 4, 5, 7 & 9

Lane discipline

264 You should always drive in the left-hand lane when the road ahead is clear. If you are overtaking a number of slower-moving vehicles, you should return to the left-hand lane as soon as you are safely past. Slow-moving or speed-restricted vehicles should always remain in the left-hand lane of the carriageway unless overtaking. You **MUST NOT** drive on the hard shoulder except in an emergency or if directed to do so by the police, HA traffic officers in uniform or by signs.

Laws MT(E&W)R regs 5, 9 & 16(1)(a), MT(S)R regs 4, 8 & 14(1)(a), and RTA 1988, sects 35 & 186, as amended by TMA 2004 sect 6.

265 The right-hand lane of a motorway with three or more lanes **MUST NOT** be used (except in prescribed circumstances) if you are driving

- any vehicle drawing a trailer

- a goods vehicle with a maximum laden weight exceeding 3.5 tonnes but not exceeding 7.5 tonnes, which is required to be fitted with a speed limiter

- a goods vehicle with a maximum laden weight exceeding 7.5 tonnes

- a passenger vehicle with a maximum laden weight exceeding 7.5 tonnes constructed or adapted to carry more than eight seated passengers in addition to the driver

- a passenger vehicle with a maximum laden weight not exceeding 7.5 tonnes which is constructed or adapted to carry more than eight seated passengers in addition to the driver, which is required to be fitted with a speed limiter.

Laws MT(E&W)R reg 12, MT(E&W)AR (2004), MT(S)R reg 11 & MT(S)AR (2004)

266 Approaching a junction. Look well ahead for signals or signs. Direction signs may be placed over the road. If you need to change lanes, do so in good time. At some junctions a lane may lead directly off the motorway. Only get in that lane if you wish to go in the direction indicated on the overhead signs.

Overtaking

267 Do not overtake unless you are sure it is safe and legal to do so. Overtake only on the right. You should

- check your mirrors
- take time to judge the speeds correctly

- make sure that the lane you will be joining is sufficiently clear ahead and behind

- take a quick sideways glance into the blind spot area to verify the position of a vehicle that may have disappeared from your view in the mirror

- remember that traffic may be coming up behind you very quickly. Check all your mirrors carefully. Look out for motor cyclists. When it is safe to do so, signal in plenty of time, then move out

- ensure you do not cut in on the vehicle you have overtaken

- be especially careful at night and in poor visibility when it is harder to judge speed and distance.

268 Do not overtake on the left or move to a lane on your left to overtake. In congested conditions, where adjacent lanes of traffic are moving at similar speeds, traffic in left-hand lanes may sometimes be moving faster than traffic to the right. In these conditions you may keep up with the traffic in your lane even if this means passing traffic in the lane to your right. Do not weave in and out of lanes to overtake.

269 **Hard shoulder.** You **MUST NOT**

use the hard shoulder for overtaking. In areas where an Active Traffic Management (ATM) Scheme is in force, the hard shoulder may be used as a running lane. You will know when you can use this because a speed limit sign will be shown above all open lanes, including the hard shoulder. A red cross or blank sign above the hard shoulder means that you **MUST NOT** drive on the hard shoulder except in an emergency or breakdown. Emergency refuge areas have also been built into these areas for use in cases of emergency or breakdown.

Laws MT(E&W)R regs 5, 5A & 9, MT(S)R regs 4 & 8

Rule 269
Overhead gantry showing red cross over hard shoulder

Stopping

270 You **MUST NOT** stop on the

carriageway, hard shoulder, slip road, central reservation or verge except in an emergency, or when told to do so by the police, HA traffic officers in uniform, an emergency sign or by flashing red light signals. Do not stop on the hard shoulder to either make or receive mobile phone calls.

Laws MT(E&W)R regs 5A, 7, 9, 10 & 16, MT(S)R regs 6(1), 8, 9 & 14, PRA 2002 sect 41 & sched 5(8), & RTA 1988 Sects 35 & 163 as amended by TMA 2004, Sect 6

271 You **MUST NOT** pick up or set down

anyone, or walk on a motorway, except in an emergency.

Laws RTRA sect 17 & MT(E&W)R reg 15

Leaving the motorway

272 Unless signs indicate that a lane leads

directly off the motorway, you will normally leave the motorway by a slip road on your left. You should

- watch for the signs letting you know you are getting near your exit

- move into the left-hand lane well before reaching your exit

- signal left in good time and reduce your speed on the slip road as necessary.

273 On leaving the motorway or using a

link road between motorways, your speed may be higher than you realise - 50 mph may feel like 30 mph. Check your speedometer and adjust your speed accordingly. Some slip-roads and link roads have sharp bends, so you will need to slow down.

Breakdowns and incidents

Breakdowns

274 If your vehicle breaks down, think first

of all other road users and

- get your vehicle off the road if possible

- warn other traffic by using your hazard warning lights if your vehicle is causing an obstruction

- help other road users see you by wearing light-coloured or fluorescent clothing in daylight and reflective clothing at night or in poor visibility

- put a warning triangle on the road at least 45 metres (147 feet) behind your broken-down vehicle on the same side of the road, or use other permitted warning devices if you have them. Always take great care when placing or retrieving them, but never use them on motorways
- if possible, keep your sidelights on if it is dark or visibility is poor
- do not stand (or let anybody else stand) between your vehicle and oncoming traffic
- at night or in poor visibility do not stand where you will prevent other road users seeing your lights.

Additional rules for the motorway

275 If your vehicle develops a problem, leave the motorway at the next exit or pull into a service area. If you cannot do so, you should

- pull on to the hard shoulder and stop as far to the left as possible, with your wheels turned to the left
- try to stop near an emergency telephone (situated at approximately one-mile intervals along the hard shoulder)
- leave the vehicle by the left-hand door and ensure your passengers do the same. You **MUST** leave any animals in the vehicle or, in an emergency, keep them under proper control on the verge. Never attempt to place a warning triangle on a motorway
- do not put yourself in danger by attempting even simple repairs
- ensure that passengers keep away from the carriageway and hard shoulder, and that children are kept under control

- walk to an emergency telephone on your side of the carriageway (follow the arrows on the posts at the back of the hard shoulder) - the telephone is free of charge and connects directly to the Highways Agency or the police. Use these in preference to a mobile phone (see Rule 283). Always face the traffic when you speak on the phone
- give full details to the Highways Agency or the police; also inform them if you are a vulnerable motorist such as disabled, older or travelling alone
- return and wait near your vehicle (well away from the carriageway and hard shoulder)
- if you feel at risk from another person, return to your vehicle by a left-hand door and lock all doors. Leave your vehicle again as soon as you feel this danger has passed.

Laws MT(E&W)R reg 14 & MT(S)R reg 12

Rule 275
Keep well back from the hard shoulder

276 Before you rejoin the carriageway after a breakdown, build up speed on the hard shoulder and watch for a safe gap in the traffic. Be aware that other vehicles may be stationary on the hard shoulder.

277 If you cannot get your vehicle onto the hard shoulder

- do not attempt to place any warning device on the carriageway
- switch on your hazard warning lights
- leave your vehicle only when you can safely get clear of the carriageway.

278 Disabled drivers. If you have a disability which prevents you from following the above advice you should

- stay in your vehicle
- switch on your hazard warning lights
- display a 'Help' pennant or, if you have a car or mobile telephone, contact the emergency services and be prepared to advise them of your location.

Obstructions

279 If anything falls from your vehicle (or any other vehicle) on to the road, stop and retrieve it only if it is safe to do so.

280 Motorways. On a motorway do not try to remove the obstruction yourself. Stop at the next emergency telephone and call the Highways Agency or the police.

Incidents

281 Warning signs or flashing lights. If you see or hear emergency or incident support vehicles in the distance, be aware there may be an incident ahead (see Rule 219). Police Officers and Highways Agency Traffic Officers may be required to work in the carriageway, for example dealing with debris, collisions or conducting rolling road blocks. Police officers will use rear-facing

flashing red and blue lights and HA Traffic Officers will use rear-facing flashing red and amber lights in these situations. Watch out for such signals, slow down and be prepared to stop. You **MUST** follow any directions given by Police officers or Traffic officers as to whether you can safely pass the incident or blockage.

Laws RTA1988, sects 35 &163, and as amended by TMA 2004, sect 6

282 When passing the scene of an incident or crash do not be distracted or slow down unnecessarily (for example if an incident is on the other side of a dual carriageway). This may cause a collision or traffic congestion, but see Rule 283.

283 If you are involved in a crash or stop to give assistance

- use your hazard warning lights to warn other traffic
- ask drivers to switch off their engines and stop smoking
- arrange for the emergency services to be called immediately with full details of the incident location and any casualties (on a motorway, use the emergency telephone which allows easy location by the emergency services. If you use a mobile phone, first make sure you have identified your location from the marker posts on the side of the hard shoulder)
- move uninjured people away from the vehicles to safety; on a motorway this should, if possible, be well away from the traffic, the hard shoulder and the central reservation
- do not move injured people from their vehicles unless they are in immediate danger from fire or explosion

- do not remove a motorcyclist's helmet unless it is essential to do so

- be prepared to give first aid as shown on pages 493-494

- stay at the scene until emergency services arrive.

If you are involved in any other medical emergency on the motorway you should contact the emergency services in the same way.

Incidents involving dangerous goods

284 Vehicles carrying dangerous goods in packages will be marked with plain orange reflective plates. Road tankers and vehicles carrying tank containers of dangerous goods will have hazard warning plates (see page 481).

285 If an incident involves a vehicle containing dangerous goods, follow the advice in Rule 283 and, in particular

- switch off engines and **DO NOT SMOKE**

- keep well away from the vehicle and do not be tempted to try to rescue casualties as you yourself could become one

- call the emergency services and give as much information as possible about the labels and markings on the vehicle. **DO NOT** use a mobile phone close to a vehicle carrying flammable loads.

Documentation

286 If you are involved in a collision which causes damage or injury to any other person, vehicle, animal or property, you **MUST**

- stop

- give your own and the vehicle owner's

name and address, and the registration number of the vehicle, to anyone having reasonable grounds for requiring them

- if you do not give your name and address at the time of the collision, report it to the police as soon as reasonably practicable, and in any case within 24 hours.

Law RTA 1988 sect 170

287 If another person is injured and you do not produce your insurance certificate at the time of the crash to a police officer or to anyone having reasonable grounds to request it, you **MUST**

- report it to the police as soon as possible and in any case within 24 hours

- produce your insurance certificate for the police within seven days.

Law RTA 1988 sect 170

Road works

288 When the 'Road Works Ahead' sign is displayed, you will need to be more watchful and look for additional signs providing more specific instructions. Observe all signs - they are there for your safety and the safety of road workers.

- You **MUST NOT** exceed any temporary maximum speed limit.

- Use your mirrors and get into the correct lane for your vehicle in good time and as signs direct.

- Do not switch lanes to overtake queuing traffic.

- Take extra care near cyclists and motorcyclists as they are vulnerable to skidding on grit, mud or other debris at road works.

- Where lanes are restricted due to road works, merge in turn (see Rule 134).

- Do not drive through an area marked off by traffic cones.

- Watch out for traffic entering or leaving the works area, but do not be distracted by what is going on there. Concentrate on the road ahead, not the road works.

- Bear in mind that the road ahead may be obstructed by the works or by slow moving or stationary traffic.

- Keep a safe distance - there could be queues in front.

To obtain further information about road works see page 496.

Law RTRA sect 16

Additional rules for high-speed roads

289 Take special care on motorways and other high-speed dual carriageways.

- One or more lanes may be closed to traffic and a lower speed limit may apply.

- Works vehicles that are slow-moving or stationary with a large 'Keep Left' or 'Keep Right' sign on the back are sometimes used to close lanes for repairs, and a flashing light arrow may also be used to make the works vehicle more conspicuous from a distance and give earlier warning to drivers that they need to move over to the next lane.

- Check mirrors, slow down and change lanes if necessary.

- Keep a safe distance from the vehicle in front (see Rule 126).

290 Contraflow systems mean that you may be travelling in a narrower lane than normal and with no permanent barrier between you and oncoming traffic. The hard shoulder may be used for traffic, but be aware that there may be broken-down vehicles ahead of you. Keep a good distance from the vehicle ahead and observe any temporary speed limits.

Level crossings

291 A level crossing is where a road crosses a railway or tramway line. Approach and cross it with care. Never drive onto a crossing until the road is clear on the other side and do not get too close to the car in front. Never stop or park on, or near, a crossing.

292 Overhead electric lines. It is dangerous to touch overhead electric lines. You **MUST** obey the safe height warning road signs and you should not continue forward onto the railway if your vehicle touches any height barrier or bells. The clearance available is usually 5 metres (16 feet 6 inches) but may be lower.

Laws RTA 1988 sect 36, TSRGD 2002 reg 17(5)

293 Controlled crossings. Most crossings have traffic light signals with a steady amber light, twin flashing red stop lights (see pages 466 and 473) and an audible alarm for pedestrians. They may have full, half or no barriers.

- You **MUST** always obey the flashing red stop lights.

- You **MUST** stop behind the white line across the road.

- Keep going if you have already crossed the white line when the amber light comes on.

- Do not reverse onto or over a controlled crossing.

- You **MUST** wait if a train goes by and the red lights continue to flash. This means another train will bepassing soon.

- Only cross when the lights go off and barriers open.

- Never zig-zag around half-barriers, they lower automatically because a train is approaching.

- At crossings where there are no barriers, a train is approaching when the lights show.

Laws RTA 1988 sect 36 & TSRGD regs 10 & 40

Rule 293
Stop when the traffic lights show

294 Railway telephones. If you are driving a large or slow-moving vehicle, a long, low vehicle with a risk of grounding, or herding animals, a train could arrive before you are clear of the crossing. You **MUST** obey any sign instructing you to use the railway telephone to obtain permission to cross. You **MUST** also telephone when clear of the crossing if requested to do so.

Laws RTA 1988 sect 36 & TSRGD regs 10 & 16(1)

295 Crossings without traffic lights. Vehicles should stop and wait at the barrier or gate when it begins to close and not cross until the barrier or gate opens.

296 User-operated gates or barriers. Some crossings have 'Stop' signs and small red and green lights. You **MUST NOT** cross when the red light is showing, only cross if the green light is on. If crossing with a vehicle, you should

- open the gates or barriers on both sides of the crossing

- check that the green light is still on and cross quickly

- close the gates or barriers when you are clear of the crossing.

Laws RTA 1988 sect 36 & TSRGD regs 10 & 52(2)

297 If there are no lights, follow the procedure in Rule 296. Stop, look both ways and listen before you cross. If there is a railway telephone, always use it to contact the signal operator to make sure it is safe to cross. Inform the signal operator again when you are clear of the crossing.

298 Open crossings. These have no gates, barriers, attendant or traffic lights but will have a 'Give Way' sign. You should look both ways, listen and make sure there is no train coming before you cross.

299 Incidents and breakdowns. If your vehicle breaks down, or if you have an incident on a crossing you should

- get everyone out of the vehicle and clear of the crossing immediately

- use a railway telephone if available to tell the signal operator. Follow the instructions you are given

- move the vehicle clear of the crossing if there is time before a train arrives. If the alarm sounds, or the amber light comes on, leave the vehicle and get clear of the crossing immediately.

Tramways

300 You **MUST NOT** enter a road, lane or other route reserved for trams. Take extra care where trams run along the road. You should avoid driving directly on top of the rails and should take care where trams leave the main carriageway to enter the reserved route, to ensure you do not follow them. The width taken up by trams is often shown by tram lanes marked by white lines, yellow dots or by a different type of road surface. Diamond-shaped signs and white light signals give instructions to tram drivers only.

Law RTRA sects 5 & 8

301 Take extra care where the track crosses from one side of the road to the other and where the road narrows and the

tracks come close to the kerb. Tram drivers usually have their own traffic signals and may be permitted to move when you are not. Always give way to trams. Do not try to race or overtake them or pass them on the inside, unless they are at tram stops or stopped by tram signals and there is a designated tram lane for you to pass.

302 You **MUST NOT** park your vehicle where it would get in the way of trams or where it would force other drivers to do so. Do not stop on any part of a tram track, except in a designated bay where this has been provided alongside and clear of the track. When doing so, ensure that all parts of your vehicle are outside the delineated tram path. Remember that a tram cannot steer round an obstruction.

Law RTRA sects 5 & 8

303 Tram stops. Where the tram stops at a platform, either in the middle or at the side of the road, you **MUST** follow the route shown by the road signs and markings. At stops without platforms you **MUST NOT** drive between a tram and the left-hand kerb when a tram has stopped to pick up passengers. If there is no alternative route signed, do not overtake the tram - wait until it moves off.

Law RTRA sects 5 & 8

304 Look out for pedestrians, especially children, running to catch a tram approaching a stop.

305 Always give priority to trams, especially when they signal to pull away from stops, unless it would be unsafe to do so. Remember that they may be carrying large numbers of standing passengers who could be injured if the tram had to make an emergency stop. Look out for people getting off a bus or tram and crossing the road.

306 All road users, but particularly cyclists and motorcyclists, should take extra care when driving or riding close to or crossing the tracks, especially if the rails are wet. You should take particular care when crossing the rails at shallow angles, on bends and at junctions. It is safest to cross the tracks directly at right angles. Other road users should be aware that cyclists and motorcyclists may need more space to cross the tracks safely.

307 Overhead electric lines. Tramway overhead wires are normally 5.8 metres above any carriageway, but can be lower. You should ensure that you have sufficient clearance between the wire and your vehicle (including any load you are carrying) before driving under an overhead wire. Drivers of vehicles with extending cranes, booms, tipping apparatus or other types of variable height equipment should ensure that the equipment is fully lowered. Where overhead wires are set lower than 5.8 metres, these will be indicated by height clearance markings - similar to 'low bridge' signs. The height clearances on these plates should be carefully noted and observed.

If you are in any doubt as to whether your vehicle will pass safely under the wires, you should always contact the local police or the tramway operator. Never take a chance as this can be extremely hazardous.

Light signals controlling traffic

Traffic Light Signals

  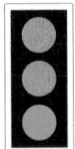  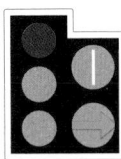

RED means 'Stop'. Wait behind the stop line on the carriageway

RED AND AMBER also means 'Stop'. Do not pass through or start until GREEN shows

GREEN means you may go on if the way is clear. Take special care if you intend to turn left or right and give way to pedestrians who are crossing

AMBER means 'Stop' at the stop line. You may go on only if the AMBER appears after you have crossed the stop line or are so close to it that to pull up might cause an accident

A GREEN ARROW may be provided in addition to the full green signal if movement in a certain direction is allowed before or after the full green phase. If the way is clear you may go but only in the direction shown by the arrow. You may do this whatever other lights may be showing. White light signals may be provided for trams

Flashing red lights

Alternately flashing red lights mean YOU MUST STOP

At level crossings, lifting bridges, airfields, fire stations, etc.

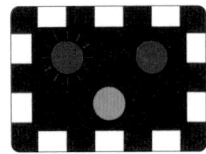

Motorway signals

You **MUST NOT** proceed further in this lane

Change lane

Reduced visibility ahead

Lane ahead closed

Temporary maximum speed advised and information message

Leave motorway at next exit

Temporary maximum speed advised

End of restriction

Lane control signals

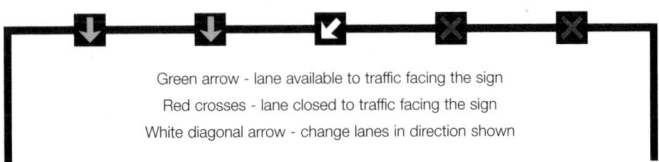

Green arrow - lane available to traffic facing the sign

Red crosses - lane closed to traffic facing the sign

White diagonal arrow - change lanes in direction shown

Signals to other road users

Direction indicator signals

I intend to move out to the right or turn right

I intend to move in to the left or turn left or stop on the left

Brake light signals

I am applying the brakes

Reversing light signals

I intend to reverse

These signals should not be used except for the purposes described.

Arm signals

For use when direction indicator signals are not used, or when necessary to reinforce direction indicator signals and stop lights. *Also for use by pedal cyclists and those in charge of horses.*

I intend to move in to the left or turn left

I intend to move out to the right or turn right

I intend to slow down or stop

Signals by authorised persons

Police officers

Stop

Traffic approaching
from the front

Traffic approaching from
both front and behind

Traffic approaching
from behind

To beckon traffic on

From the side

From the front

From behind*

Arm signals to persons controlling traffic

I want to go straight on

I want to turn left;
use either hand

I want to turn right

* In Wales, bilingual signs appear on emergency services vehicles and clothing

Vehicle and Operator Services Agency and Highways Agency Traffic Officers

Highways Agency Traffic Officer

VOSA Traffic Officer

These officers now have new powers to stop/direct vehicles and will be using hand signals and light signals similar to those used by police. You **MUST** obey any signals given (see Rules 107 and 108).

School Crossing Patrols

Not ready to cross pedestrians

Barrier to stop pedestrians crossing

Ready to cross pedestrians, vehicles must be prepared to stop

All vehicles must stop

Traffic signs

Signs giving orders

Signs with red circles are mostly prohibitive.
Plates below signs qualify their message.

Entry to
20 mph zone

End of
20 mph zone

Maximum
speed

National speed
limit applies

School crossing
patrol

Stop and
give way

Give way to
traffic on
major road

Manually operated temporary
STOP and GO signs

No entry for
vehicular traffic

No vehicles
except bicycles
being pushed

No cycling

No motor
vehicles

No buses
(over 8
passenger
seats)

No
overtaking

No
towed
caravans

No vehicles
carrying
explosives

No vehicle or
combination of
vehicles over
length shown

No vehicles
over
height shown

No vehicles
over
width shown

Give priority to
vehicles from
opposite
direction

No right turn

No left turn

No
U-turns

No goods vehicles
over maximum
gross weight
shown (in tonnes)
except for loading
and unloading

Note: Although *The Highway Code* shows many of the signs commonly in use, a comprehensive explanation of our signing system is given in the Department's booklet *Know Your Traffic Signs*, which is on sale at booksellers. The booklet also illustrates and explains the vast majority of signs the road user is likely to encounter. The signs illustrated in *The Highway Code* are not all drawn to the same scale. In Wales, bilingual versions of some signs are used including Welsh and English versions of place names. Some older designs of signs may still be seen on the roads.

No vehicles over maximum gross weight shown (in tonnes)

Parking restricted to permit holders

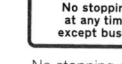

No stopping during period indicated except for buses

No stopping during times shown except for as long as necessary to set down or pick up passengers

No waiting

No stopping (Clearway)

Signs with blue circles but no red border mostly give positive instruction.

Ahead only

Turn left ahead (right if symbol reversed)

Turn left (right if symbol reversed)

Keep left (right if symbol reversed)

Vehicles may pass either side to reach same destination

Mini-roundabout (roundabout circulation - give way to vehicles from the immediate right)

Route to be used by pedal cycles only

Segregated pedal cycle and pedestrian route

Minimum speed

End of minimum speed

Buses and cycles only

Trams only

Pedestrian crossing point over tramway

One-way traffic (note: compare circular 'Ahead only' sign)

With-flow bus and cycle lane

Contra-flow bus lane

With-flow pedal cycle lane

Warning signs

Mostly triangular

Distance to
'STOP' line
ahead

Dual
carriageway
ends

Road narrows on
right (left if
symbol reversed)

Road
narrows on
both sides

Distance to
'Give Way'
line ahead

Crossroads

Junction on
bend ahead

T-junction with
priority over
vehicles from
the right

Staggered
junction

Traffic merging
from left ahead

The priority through route is indicated by the broader line.

Double bend first
to left (symbol
may be reversed)

Bend to right
(or left if symbol
reversed)

Roundabout

Uneven road

Plate below
some signs

Two-way
traffic crosses
one-way road

Two-way traffic
straight ahead

Opening or
swing bridge
ahead

Low-flying aircraft
or sudden
aircraft noise

Falling or
fallen rocks

Traffic signals
not in use

Traffic signals

Slippery road

Steep hill
downwards

Steep hill
upwards

Gradients may be shown as a ratio i.e. 20% = 1:5

Tunnel ahead

Trams
crossing
ahead

Level crossing
with barrier or
gate ahead

Level crossing
without barrier
or gate ahead

Level crossing
without barrier

Warning signs - continued

School crossing patrol ahead (some signs have amber lights which flash when crossings are in use)

Frail (or blind or disabled if shown) pedestrians likely to cross road ahead

Pedestrians in road ahead

Zebra crossing

Overhead electric cable; plate indicates maximum height of vehicles which can pass safely

Available width of headroom indicated

Sharp deviation of route to left (or right if chevrons reversed)

Light signals ahead at level crossing, airfield or bridge

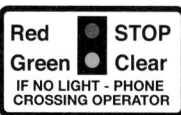

Miniature warning lights at level crossings

Cattle

Wild animals

Wild horses or ponies

Accompanied horses or ponies

Cycle route ahead

Risk of ice

Traffic queues likely ahead

Distance over which road humps extend

Other danger; plate indicates nature of danger

Soft verges

Side winds

Hump bridge

Worded warning sign

Quayside or river bank

Risk of grounding

Direction signs

Mostly rectangular

Signs on motorways - blue backgrounds

At a junction leading directly
into a motorway (junction
number may be shown
on a black background)

On approaches to
junctions (junction number
on black background)

Route confirmatory
sign after junction

Downward pointing arrows mean 'Get in lane'
The left-hand lane leads to a different destination from the other lanes.

The panel with the inclined arrow indicates the destinations which can be reached
by leaving the motorway at the next junction

Signs on primary routes - green backgrounds

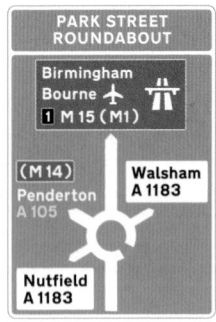

On approaches to junctions

At the junction

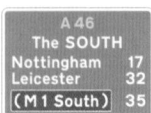

Route confirmatory
sign after junction

On approaches
to junctions

On approach to a junction
in Wales (bilingual)

Blue panels indicate that the motorway starts at the junction ahead.
Motorways shown in brackets can also be reached along the route indicated.
White panels indicate local or non-primary routes leading from the junction ahead.
Brown panels show the route to tourist attractions.
The name of the junction may be shown at the top of the sign.
The aircraft symbol indicates the route to an airport.
A symbol may be included to warn of a hazard or restriction along that route.

Green background signs - continued

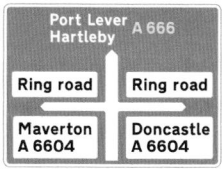

Primary route forming part of a ring road

Signs on non-primary and local routes - black borders

On approaches to junctions

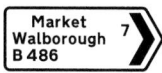

At the junction

Direction to toilets with access for the disabled

Green panels indicate that the primary route starts at the junction ahead.
Route numbers on a blue background show the direction to a motorway.
Route numbers on a green background show the direction to a primary route.

Other direction signs

Picnic site

Ancient monument in the care of English Heritage

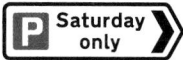

Direction to a car park

Tourist attraction

Direction to camping and caravan site

Advisory route for lorries

Route for pedal cycles forming part of a network

Recommended route for pedal cycles to place shown

Route for pedestrians

Symbols showing emergency diversion route for motorway and other main road traffic

Diversion route

Information signs

All rectangular

Entrance to controlled parking zone

Entrance to congestion charging zone

End of controlled parking zone

Advance warning of restriction or prohibition ahead

Parking place for solo motorcycles

With-flow bus lane ahead which pedal cycles and taxis may also use

Lane designated for use by high occupancy vehicles (HOV) - see rule 142

Vehicles permitted to use an HOV lane ahead

End of motorway

Start of motorway and point from which motorway regulations apply

Appropriate traffic lanes at junction ahead

Traffic on the main carriageway coming from right has priority over joining traffic

Additional traffic joining from left ahead. Traffic on main carriageway has priority over joining traffic from right hand lane of slip road

Traffic in right hand lane of slip road joining the main carriageway has prority over left hand lane

'Countdown' markers at exit from motorway (each bar represents 100 yards to the exit). Green-backed markers may be used on primary routes and white-backed markers with black bars on other routes. At approaches to concealed level crossings white-backed markers with red bars may be used. Although these will be erected at equal distances the bars do not represent 100 yard intervals.

Motorway service area sign showing the operator's name

Information signs - continued

Traffic has priority over
oncoming vehicles

Hospital ahead with
Accident and
Emergency facilities

Tourist
information
point

No through road
for vehicles

Recommended route
for pedal cycles

Home Zone Entry

Area in which
cameras are
used to enforce
traffic regulations

Bus lane on road at
junction ahead

Road works signs

Road works

Loose
chippings

Temporary hazard
at road works

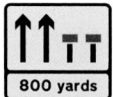

Temporary lane closure
(the number and position
of arrows and red bars
may be varied according
to lanes open and closed)

Slow-moving or
stationary works
vehicle blocking a
traffic lane. Pass in
the direction shown
by the arrow.

Mandatory
speed
limit ahead

Road works
1 mile ahead

End of road works and
any temporary restrictions
including speed limits

Signs used on the back of slow-moving or
stationary vehicles warning of a lane closed
ahead by a works vehicle. There are no
cones on the road.

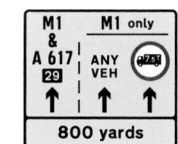

Lane restrictions at
road works ahead

One lane crossover
at contraflow
road works

Road markings

Across the carriageway

Stop line at signals or police control

Stop line at 'Stop' sign

Stop line for pedestrians at a level crossing

Give way to traffic on major road (can also be used at mini roundabouts)

Give way to traffic from the right at a roundabout

Give way to traffic from the right at a mini-roundabout

Along the carriageway

Edge line

Centre line
See Rule 127

Hazard warning line
See Rule 127

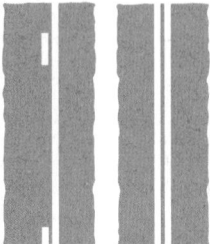

Double white lines
See Rules 128 and 129

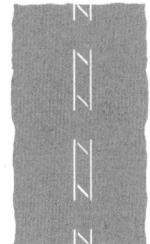

See Rule 130

Lane line See Rule 131

Along the edge of the carriageway

Waiting restrictions

Waiting restrictions indicated by yellow lines apply to the carriageway, pavement and verge. You may stop to load or unload (unless there are also loading restrictions as described below) or while passengers board or alight. Double yellow lines mean no waiting at any time, unless there are signs that specifically indicate seasonal restrictions. The times at which the restrictions apply for other road markings are shown on nearby plates or on entry signs to controlled parking zones. If no days are shown on the signs, the restrictions are in force every day including Sundays and Bank Holidays. White bay markings and upright signs (see below) indicate where parking is allowed.

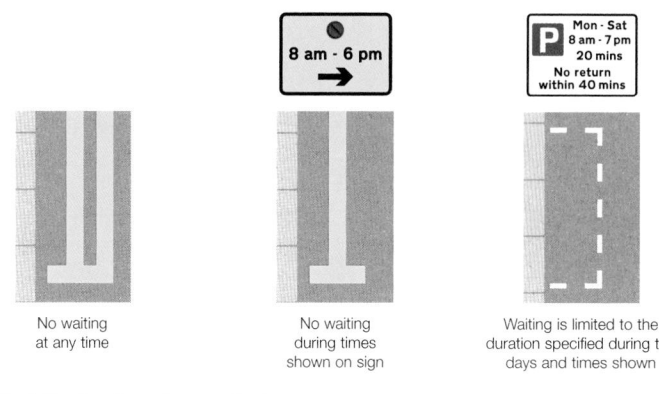

| No waiting at any time | No waiting during times shown on sign | Waiting is limited to the duration specified during the days and times shown |

Red Route stopping controls

Red lines are used on some roads instead of yellow lines. In London the double and single red lines used on Red Routes indicate that stopping to park, load/unload or to board and alight from a vehicle (except for a licensed taxi or if you hold a Blue Badge) is prohibited. The red lines apply to the carriageway, pavement and verge. The times that the red line prohibitions apply are shown on nearby signs, but the double red line ALWAYS means no stopping at any time. On Red Routes you may stop to park, load/unload in specially marked boxes and adjacent signs specify the times and purposes and duration allowed. A box MARKED IN RED indicates that it may only be available for the purpose specified for part of the day (eg between busy peak periods). A box MARKED IN WHITE means that it is available throughout the day.

RED AND SINGLE YELLOW LINES CAN ONLY GIVE A GUIDE TO THE RESTRICTIONS AND CONTROLS IN FORCE AND SIGNS, NEARBY OR AT A ZONE ENTRY, MUST BE CONSULTED.

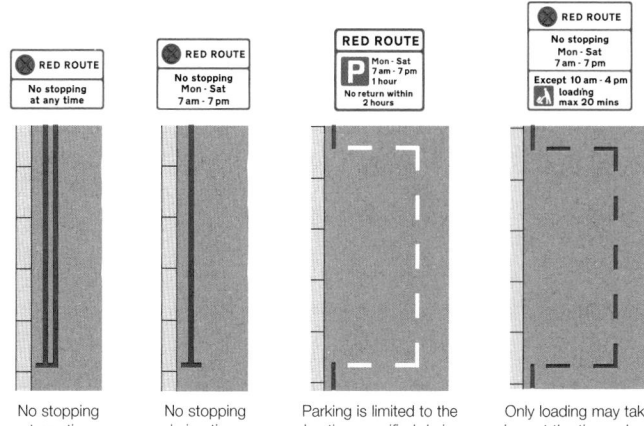

| No stopping at any time | No stopping during times shown on sign | Parking is limited to the duration specified during the days and times shown | Only loading may take place at the times shown for up to a maximum duration of 20 mins |

On the kerb or at the edge of the carriageway

Loading restrictions on roads other than Red Routes

Yellow marks on the kerb or at the edge of the carriageway indicate that loading or unloading is prohibited at the times shown on the nearby black and white plates. You may stop while passengers board or alight. If no days are indicated on the signs the restrictions are in force every day including Sundays and Bank Holidays.

ALWAYS CHECK THE TIMES SHOWN ON THE PLATES.

Lengths of road reserved for vehicles loading and unloading are indicated by a white 'bay' marking with the words 'Loading Only' and a sign with the white on blue 'trolley' symbol. This sign also shows whether loading and unloading is restricted to goods vehicles and the times at which the bay can be used. If no times or days are shown it may be used at any time. Vehicles may not park here if they are not loading or unloading.

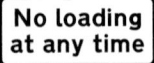

No loading or unloading
at any time

No loading or unloading
at the times shown

Loading bay

Other road markings

Keep entrance clear of stationary vehicles, even if picking up or setting down children

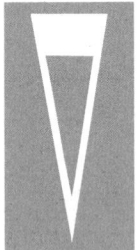

Warning of 'Give Way'
just ahead

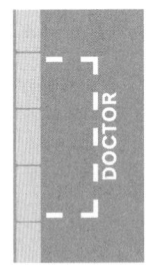

Parking space reserved
for vehicles named

See Rule 243

See Rule 141

Box junction - See Rule 174

Do not block that part of
the carriageway indicated

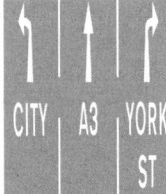

Indication of traffic lanes

Vehicle markings

Large goods vehicle rear markings

Motor vehicles over 7500 kilograms maximum gross weight and trailers over 3500 kilograms maximum gross weight

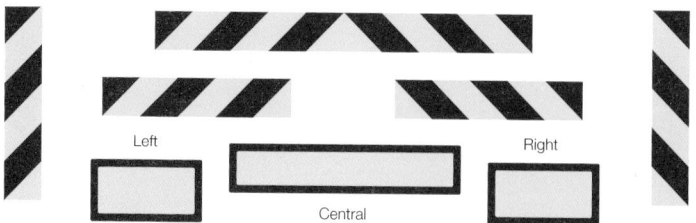

Left

Right

Central

The vertical markings are also required to be fitted to builders' skips placed in the road, commercial vehicles or combinations longer than 13 metres (optional on combinations between 11 and 13 metres)

Hazard warning plates

Certain tank vehicles carrying dangerous goods must display hazard information panels

The panel illustrated is for flammable liquid. Diamond symbols indicating other risks include:

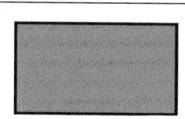

The above panel will be displayed by vehicles carrying certain dangerous goods in packages

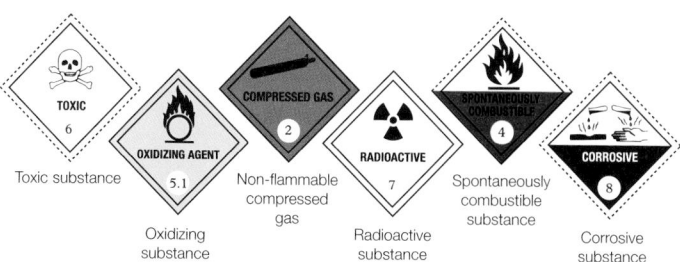

Toxic substance

Oxidizing substance

Non-flammable compressed gas

Radioactive substance

Spontaneously combustible substance

Corrosive substance

Projection markers

Side marker

End marker

Both required when load or equipment (eg crane jib) overhangs front or rear by more than two metres

Other

School bus (displayed in front or rear window of bus or coach)

Annexes

1. You and your bicycle

Make sure that you feel confident of your ability to ride safely on the road. Be sure that

- you choose the right size and type of cycle for comfort and safety
- lights and reflectors are kept clean and in good working order
- tyres are in good condition and inflated to the pressure shown on the tyre
- gears are working correctly
- the chain is properly adjusted and oiled
- the saddle and handlebars are adjusted to the correct height.

It is recommended that you fit a bell to your cycle.

You **MUST**

- ensure your brakes are efficient
- at night, use lit front and rear lights and have a red rear reflector.

Laws PCUR regs 6 & 10 & RVLR reg 18

Cycle training can help both children and adults, especially those adults returning to cycling to develop the skills needed to cycle safely on today's roads. A new national cycle training standard has been developed which the Government is promoting and making funding available for delivery in schools.

All cyclists should consider the benefits of undertaking cycle training. For information, contact your local authority.

2. Motorcycle licence requirements

If you have a provisional motorcycle licence, you **MUST** satisfactorily complete a Compulsory Basic Training (CBT) course. You can then ride on the public road, with L plates (in Wales either D plates, L plates or both can be used), for up to two years. To obtain your full motorcycle licence you **MUST** pass a motorcycle theory test and then a practical test.

Law MV(DL)R regs 16 & 68

If you have a full car licence you may ride motorcycles up to 125 cc and 11 kW power output, with L plates (and/or D plates in Wales), on public roads, but you **MUST** first satisfactorily complete a CBT course if you have not already done so.

Law MV(DL)R reg 43

If you have a full moped licence and wish to obtain full motorcycle entitlement, you will be required to take a motorcycle theory test if you did not take a separate theory test when you obtained your moped licence. You **MUST** then pass a practical motorcycle test. Note that if CBT was completed for the full moped licence there is no need to repeat it, but if the moped test was taken before 1/12/90 CBT will need to be completed before riding a motorcycle as a learner.

Law MV(DL)R regs 42(1) & 69(1)

Light motorcycle licence (A1): you take a test on a motorcycle of between 75 and 125 cc. If you pass you may ride a motorcycle up to 125 cc with power output up to 11 kW.

Standard motorcycle licence (A): if your test vehicle is between 120 and 125 cc and capable of more than 100 km/h you will be given a standard (A) licence. You will then be restricted to motorcycles of up to 25 kW for two years. After two years you may ride any size machine.

Direct or Accelerated Access enables riders over the age of 21, or those who reach 21 before their two-year restriction ends, to ride larger motorcycles sooner. To obtain a licence to do so they are required to

- have successfully completed a CBT course

- pass a theory test, if they are required to do so

- pass a practical test on a machine with power output of at least 35 kW.

To practise, they can ride larger motorcycles, with L plates (and/or D plates in Wales), on public roads, but only when accompanied by an approved instructor on another motorcycle in radio contact.

You **MUST NOT** carry a pillion passenger or pull a trailer until you have passed your test.

Law MV(DL)R reg 16

Moped licence requirements

A moped **MUST** have an engine capacity not exceeding 50 cc, not weigh more than 250 kg and be designed to have a maximum speed not exceeding 31 mph (50 km/h). From June 2003 all EC Type Approved mopeds have been restricted to 28 mph (45 km/h).

Law RTA 1988 (as amended) sect 108

To ride a moped, learners **MUST**

- be 16 or over

- have a provisional moped licence

- complete CBT training.

You **MUST** first pass the theory test for motorcycles and then the moped practical test to obtain your full moped licence. If you passed your driving test before 1 February 2001 you are qualified to ride a moped without L plates (and/or D plates in Wales), although it is recommended that you complete CBT before riding on the road. If you passed your driving test after this date you **MUST** complete CBT before riding a moped on the road.

Laws RTA 1988 sects 97(e) & 101 & MV(DL)R regs 38(4) & 43

Note. For motorcycle and moped riders wishing to upgrade, the following give exemption from taking the motorcycle theory test

- full A1 motorcycle licence

- full moped licence, if gained after 1/7/96.

Law MV(DL)R reg 42

3. Motor vehicle documentation and learner driver requirements

Documents

Driving licence. You **MUST** have a valid driving licence for the category of motor vehicle you are driving. You **MUST** inform the Driver and Vehicle Licensing Agency (DVLA) if you change your name and/or address.

Law RTA 1988 sects 87 & 99(4)

Holders of non-European Community licences who are now resident in the UK may only drive on that licence for a maximum of 12 months from the date they become resident in this country.

To ensure continuous driving entitlement

- a British provisional licence should be obtained and a driving test(s) passed before the 12-month period elapses, or

- in the case of a driver who holds a licence from a country which has been designated in law for licence exchange purposes, the driver should exchange the licence for a British one.

MOT. Cars and motorcycles **MUST** normally pass an MOT test three years from the date of the first registration and every year after that. You **MUST NOT** drive a motor vehicle without an MOT certificate when it should have one. Exceptionally, you may drive to a pre-arranged test appointment or to a garage for repairs required for the test. Driving an unroadworthy motor vehicle may invalidate your insurance.
Law RTA 1988 sects 45, 47, 49 & 53

Insurance. To use a motor vehicle on the road, you **MUST** have a valid insurance policy. This **MUST** at least cover you for injury or damage to a third party while using that motor vehicle. Before driving any motor vehicle, make sure that it has this cover for your use or that your own insurance provides adequate cover. You **MUST NOT** drive a motor vehicle without insurance. Also, be aware that even if a road traffic incident is not your fault, you may still be held liable by insurance companies.
Law RTA 1988 sect 143

Uninsured drivers can now be automatically detected by roadside cameras. Further to the penalties for uninsured driving listed on page 489, an offender's vehicle can now be seized by the police, taken away and crushed.
Law RTA 1988, sects 165a & 165b

The types of cover available are indicated below:

Third-party insurance - this is often the cheapest form of insurance, and is the minimum cover required by law. It covers anyone you might injure or whose property you might damage. It does not cover damage to your own motor vehicle or injury to yourself.

Third-party, Fire and Theft insurance - similar to third-party, but also covers you against your motor vehicle being stolen, or damaged by fire.

Comprehensive insurance - this is the most expensive but the best insurance. Apart from covering other persons and property against injury or damage, it also covers damage to your own motor vehicle, up to the market value of that vehicle, and personal injury to yourself.

Registration certificate. Registration certificates (also called harmonised registration certificates) are issued for all motor vehicles used on the road, describing them (make, model, etc.) and giving details of the registered keeper. You **MUST** notify the Driver and Vehicle Licensing Agency in Swansea as soon as possible when you buy or sell a motor vehicle, or if you change your name or address. For registration certificates issued after 27 March 1997, the buyer and seller are responsible for completing the registration certificates.

The seller is responsible for forwarding them to DVLA. The procedures are explained on the back of the registration certificates.

Law RV(R&L)R regs 21, 22, 23 & 24

Vehicle Excise Duty (VED).

All motor vehicles used or kept on public roads **MUST** display a valid Vehicle Excise Duty disc (tax disc) displayed at all times. Even motor vehicles exempt from duty **MUST** display a tax disc at all times.

Law VERA sects 29 & 33

Statutory Off-Road Notification (SORN).

This is a notification to the DVLA that a motor vehicle is not being used on the road. If you are the vehicle keeper and want to keep a motor vehicle untaxed and off the public road you **MUST** declare SORN - it is an offence not to do so. You then won't have to pay any road tax for that vehicle for a period of 12 months. You need to send a further declaration after that period if the vehicle is still off the public road. The SORN will end if you sell the vehicle and the new owner will become immediately responsible.

Law RV(RL)R 2002, reg 26 sched 4

Production of documents.

You **MUST** be able to produce your driving licence and counterpart, a valid insurance certificate and (if appropriate) a valid MOT certificate, when requested by a police officer. If you cannot do this you may be asked to take them to a police station within seven days.

Law RTA 1988 sects 164 & 165

Learner drivers

Learners driving a car **MUST** hold a valid provisional licence. They **MUST** be supervised by someone at least 21 years old who holds a full EC/EEA licence for that type of car (automatic or manual) and has held one for at least three years.

Laws MV(DL)R reg 16 & RTA 1988 sect 87

Vehicles.

Any vehicle driven by a learner **MUST** display red L plates. In Wales, either red D plates, red L plates, or both, can be used. Plates **MUST** conform to legal specifications and **MUST** be clearly visible to others from in front of the vehicle and from behind. Plates should be removed or covered when not being driven by a learner (except on driving school vehicles).

Law MV(DL)R reg 16 & sched 4

You **MUST** pass the theory test (if one is required) and then a practical driving test for the category of vehicle you wish to drive before driving unaccompanied.

Law MV(DL)R reg 40

4. The road user and the law

Road traffic law

The following list can be found abbreviated throughout the Code. It is not intended to be a comprehensive guide, but a guide to some of the important points of law. For the precise wording of the law, please refer to the various Acts and Regulations (as amended) indicated in the Code. Abbreviations are listed on the following page.

Most of the provisions apply on all roads throughout Great Britain, although there are some exceptions. The definition of a road in England and Wales is 'any highway and any other road to which the public has access and includes bridges over which a road passes' (RTA 1988 sect 192(1)). In Scotland, there is a similar definition which is extended to include any way over which the public have a right of passage (R(S)A 1984 sect 151(1)).

It is important to note that references to 'road' therefore generally include footpaths, bridleways and cycle tracks, and many roadways and driveways on private land (including many car parks). In most cases, the law will apply to them and there may be additional rules for particular paths or ways. Some serious driving offences, including drink-driving offences, also apply to all public places, for example public car parks.

Chronically Sick & Disabled Persons Act 1970	CSDPA
Functions of Traffic Wardens Order 1970	FTWO
Greater London (General Powers) Act 1974	GL(GP)A
Highway Act 1835 or 1980 (as indicated)	HA
Horses (Protective Headgear for Young Riders) Act 1990	H(PHYR)A
Horses (Protective Headgear for Young Riders) Regulations 1992	H(PHYR)R
Motor Cycles (Eye Protectors) Regulations 1999	MC(EP)R
Motor Cycles (Protective Helmets) Regulations 1998	MC(PH)R
Motorways Traffic (England & Wales) Regulations 1982	MT(E&W)R
Motorways Traffic (England & Wales) Amended Regulations	MT(E&W)(A)R
Motorways Traffic (Scotland) Regulations 1995	MT(S)R
Motor Vehicles (Driving Licences) Regulations 1999	MV(DL)R
Motor Vehicles (Wearing of Seat Belts) Regulations 1993	MV(WSB)R
Motor Vehicles (Wearing of Seat Belts) (Amendment) Regulations 2006	MV(WSB)(A)R
Motor Vehicles (Wearing of Seat Belts by Children in Front Seats) Regulations 1993	MV(WSBCFS)R
New Roads and Streetworks Act 1991	NRSWA
Pedal Cycles (Construction & Use) Regulations 1983	PCUR
Powers of Criminal Courts (Sentencing) Act 2000	PCC(S)A
Police Reform Act 2002	PRA
Prohibition of Smoking in Certain Premises (Scotland) Regulations 2006 (SI no 90)	PSCP(S)R*
Public Passenger Vehicles Act 1981	PPVA
Road Safety Act 2006	RSA
Road Traffic Act 1984, 1988 or 1991 (as indicated)	RTA
Road Traffic (New Drivers) Act 1995	RT(ND)A
Road Traffic Offenders Act 1988	RTOA
Road Traffic Regulation Act 1984	RTRA
Road Vehicles (Construction & Use) Regulations 1986	CUR
Road Vehicles (Display of Registration Marks) Regulations 2001	RV(DRM)R
Road Vehicles Lighting Regulations 1989	RVLR
Road Vehicles (Registration & Licensing) Regulations 2002	RV(R&L)R
Roads (Scotland) Act 1984	R(S)A
Traffic Management Act 2004	TMA
Traffic Signs Regulations & General Directions 2002	TSRGD
Use of Invalid Carriages on Highways Regulations 1988	UICHR
Vehicle Excise and Registration Act 1994	VERA
Zebra, Pelican and Puffin Pedestrian Crossings Regulations and General Directions 1997	ZPPPCRGD

Acts and regulations from 1988 can be viewed on the Office of Public Sector Information website (www.opsi.gov.uk). Acts and regulations prior to 1988 are only available in their original print format which may be obtained from The Stationery Office as detailed inside the back cover.

* Specific legislation applies to smoking in vehicles which constitute workplaces.

For information visit:

www.smokefreeengland.co.uk

www.clearingtheairscotland.com

www.smokingbanwales.co.uk

5. Penalties

Parliament sets the maximum penalties for road traffic offences. The seriousness of the offence is reflected in the maximum penalty. It is for the courts to decide what sentence to impose according to circumstances.

The penalty table on page 489 indicates some of the main offences, and the associated penalties. There is a wide range of other more specific offences which, for the sake of simplicity, are not shown here. The penalty points and disqualification system is described opposite.

Penalty points and disqualification

The penalty point system is intended to deter drivers and motorcyclists from following unsafe motoring practices. Certain non-motoring offences, e.g. failure to rectify vehicle defects, can also attract penalty points. The court **MUST** order points to be endorsed on the licence according to the fixed number or the range set by Parliament. The accumulation of penalty points acts as a warning to drivers and motorcyclists that they risk disqualification if further offences are committed.

Law RTOA sects 44 & 45

A driver or motorcyclist who accumulates 12 or more penalty points within a three-year period **MUST** be disqualified. This will be for a minimum period of six months, or longer if the driver or motorcyclist has previously been disqualified.

Law RTOA sect 35

For every offence which carries penalty points the court has a discretionary power to order the licence holder to be disqualified. This may be for any period the court thinks fit, but will usually be between a week and a few months.

In the case of serious offences, such as dangerous driving and drink-driving, the court **MUST** order disqualification. The minimum period is 12 months, but for repeat offenders or where the alcohol level is high, it may be longer. For example, a second drink-drive offence in the space of 10 years will result in a minimum of three years' disqualification.

Law RTOA sect 34

Furthermore, in some serious cases, the court **MUST** (in addition to imposing a fixed period of disqualification) order the offender to be disqualified until they pass a driving test. In other cases the court has a discretionary power to order such disqualification. The test may be an ordinary length test or an extended test according to the nature of the offence.

Law RTOA sect 36

New drivers. Special rules as set out below apply for a period of two years from the date of passing their first driving test, to drivers and motorcyclists from

- the UK, EU/EEA, the Isle of Man, the Channel Islands or Gibraltar who passed their first driving test in any of those countries;

- other foreign countries who have to pass a UK driving test to gain a UK licence, in which case the UK driving test is treated as their first driving test; and

- other foreign countries who (without needing a test) exchanged their licence for a UK licence and subsequently passed a

Penalty Table

Offence	Maximum Penalties		Disqualification	Penalty Points
	Imprisonment	**Fine**		
*Causing death by dangerous driving	14 years	Unlimited	Obligatory - 2 years minimum	3-11 (if exceptionally not disqualified)
*Dangerous driving	2 years	Unlimited	Obligatory	3-11 (if exceptionally not disqualified)
*Causing death by careless driving under the influence of drink or drugs	14 years	Unlimited	Obligatory - 2 years minimum	3-11 (if exceptionally not disqualified)
Careless and inconsiderate driving	-	£5,000	Discretionary	3-9
Driving while unfit through drink or drugs or with excess alcohol; or failing to provide a specimen for analysis	6 months	£5,000	Obligatory	3-11 (if exceptionally not disqualified)
Failing to stop after an accident or failing to report an accident	6 months	£5,000	Discretionary	5-10
Driving when disqualified	6 months (12 months in Scotland)	£5,000	Discretionary	6
Driving after refusal or revocation of licence on medical grounds	6 months	£5,000	Discretionary	3-6
Driving without insurance	-	£5,000	Discretionary	6-8
Using a vehicle in a dangerous condition	-	LGV £5,000 PCV £5,000 other £2,500	Obligatory if offence committed within 3 years of a previous conviction for the same offence - 6 months min otherwise discretionary	3 in each case
Failure to have proper control of vehicle or full view of the road and traffic ahead, or using a hand-held mobile phone while driving	-	£1,000 (£2,500 for PCV or goods vehicle)	Discretionary	3
Driving otherwise than in accordance with a licence	-	£1,000	Discretionary	3-6
Speeding	-	£1,000 (£2,500 for motorway offences)	Discretionary	3-6 or 3 (fixed penalty)
Traffic light offences	-	£1,000	Discretionary	3
No MOT certificate	-	£1,000	-	-
Seat belt offences	-	£500	-	-
Dangerous cycling	-	£2,500	-	-
Careless cycling	-	£1,000	-	-
Cycling on pavement	-	£500	-	-
Failing to identify driver of a vehicle	-	£1,000	Discretionary	6

* Where a court disqualifies a person on conviction for one of these offences, it must order an extended retest. The courts also have discretion to order a retest for any other offence which carries penalty points, an extended retest where disqualification is obligatory, and an ordinary test where disqualification is not obligatory.

UK driving test to drive another type of vehicle, in which case the UK driving test is treated as their first driving test. For example a driver who exchanges a foreign licence (car) for a UK licence (car) and who later passes a test to drive another type of vehicle (eg an HGV) will be subject to the special rules.

Where a person subject to the special rules accumulates six or more penalty points before the end of the two year period (including any points acquired before passing the test), their licence will be revoked automatically. To regain the licence they must reapply for a provisional licence and may drive only as a learner until they pass a further driving test (Also see Annex 8 - Safety code for new drivers.)

Law RT(ND)A

Note. This applies even if they pay for offences by fixed penalty. Drivers in the first group (UK, EU/EEA, etc.) who already have a full licence for one type of vehicle are not affected by the special rules if they later pass a test to drive another type of vehicle.

Other consequences of offending

Where an offence is punishable by imprisonment then the vehicle used to commit the offence may be confiscated.

Law PCC(S)A, sect 143

In addition to the penalties a court may decide to impose, the cost of insurance is likely to rise considerably following conviction for a serious driving offence. This is because insurance companies consider such drivers are more likely to be involved in a collision.

Drivers disqualified for drinking and driving twice within 10 years, or once if they are over two and a half times the legal limit, or

those who refused to give a specimen, also have to satisfy the Driver and Vehicle Licensing Agency's Medical Branch that they do not have an alcohol problem and are otherwise fit to drive before their licence is returned at the end of their period of disqualification. Persistent misuse of drugs or alcohol may lead to the withdrawal of a driving licence.

6. Vehicle maintenance, safety and security

Vehicle maintenance

Take special care that lights, brakes, steering, exhaust system, seat belts, demisters, wipers and washers are all working. Also

- lights, indicators, reflectors, and number plates **MUST** be kept clean and clear

- windscreens and windows **MUST** be kept clean and free from obstructions to vision

- lights **MUST** be properly adjusted to prevent dazzling other road users. Extra attention needs to be paid to this if the vehicle is heavily loaded

- exhaust emissions **MUST NOT** exceed prescribed levels

- ensure your seat, seat belt, head restraint and mirrors are adjusted correctly before you drive

- ensure that items of luggage are securely stowed.

Laws RVLR 1989 regs 23 & 27 & CUR 1986, regs 30 & 61

Warning displays. Make sure that you understand the meaning of all warning displays on the vehicle instrument panel. Do not ignore warning signs, they could indicate a dangerous fault developing.

- When you turn the ignition key, warning lights will be illuminated but will go out when the engine starts (except the handbrake warning light). If they do not, or if they come on while you are driving, stop and investigate the problem, as you could have a serious fault.
- If the charge warning light comes on while you are driving, it may mean that the battery isn't charging. This should also be checked as soon as possible to avoid loss of power to lights and other electrical systems.

Window tints. You **MUST NOT** use a vehicle with excessively dark tinting applied to the windscreen, or to the glass in any front window to either side of the driver. Window tinting applied during manufacture complies with the Visual Light Transmittance (VLT) standards. There are no VLT limits for rear windscreens or rear passenger windows.

Laws RTA 1988 sect 42 & CUR reg 32

Tyres. Tyres **MUST** be correctly inflated to the vehicle manufacturer's specification for the load being carried. Always refer to the vehicle's handbook or data. Tyres should also be free from certain cuts and other defects.

Cars, light vans and light trailers **MUST** have a tread depth of at least 1.6 mm across the central three-quarters of the breadth of the tread and around the entire circumference.

Motorcycles, large vehicles and passenger-carrying vehicles **MUST** have a tread depth of at least 1 mm across three-quarters of the breadth of the tread and in a continuous band around the entire circumference.

Mopeds should have visible tread.

Be aware that some vehicle defects can attract penalty points.

Law CUR reg 27

If a tyre bursts while you are driving, try to keep control of your vehicle. Grip the steering wheel firmly and allow the vehicle to roll to a stop at the side of the road.

If you have a flat tyre, stop as soon as it is safe to do so. Only change the tyre if you can do so without putting yourself or others at risk - otherwise call a breakdown service.

Tyre pressures. Check weekly. Do this before your journey, when tyres are cold. Warm or hot tyres may give a misleading reading.

Your brakes and steering will be adversely affected by under-inflated or over-inflated tyres. Excessive or uneven tyre wear may be caused by faults in the braking or suspension systems, or wheels which are out of alignment. Have these faults corrected as soon as possible.

Fluid levels. Check the fluid levels in your vehicle at least weekly. Low brake fluid may result in brake failure and a crash. Make sure you recognise the low fluid warning lights if your vehicle has them fitted.

Before winter. Ensure that the battery is well maintained and that there are appropriate anti-freeze agents in your radiator and windscreen bottle.

Other problems. If your vehicle

- pulls to one side when braking, it is most likely to be a brake fault or incorrectly inflated tyres. Consult a garage or mechanic immediately

- continues to bounce after pushing down on the front or rear, its shock absorbers are worn. Worn shock absorbers can seriously affect the operation of a vehicle and should be replaced

- smells of anything unusual such as burning rubber, petrol or an electrical fault; investigate immediately. Do not risk a fire.

Overheated engines or fire. Most engines are water-cooled. If your engine overheats you should wait until it has cooled naturally. Only then remove the coolant filler cap and add water or other coolant.

If your vehicle catches fire, get the occupants out of the vehicle quickly and to a safe place. Do not attempt to extinguish a fire in the engine compartment, as opening the bonnet will make the fire flare. Call the fire brigade.

Petrol stations/fuel tank/fuel leaks. Ensure that, when filling up your vehicle's tank or any fuel cans you are carrying, you do not spill fuel on the forecourt. Any spilled fuel should be immediately reported to the petrol station attendant. Diesel spillage is dangerous to other road users, particularly motorcyclists, as it will significantly reduce the level of grip between the tyres and road surface.

Double-check for fuel leaks and make sure that

- you do not overfill your fuel tank

- the fuel cap is fastened securely

- the seal in the cap is not torn, perished or missing

- there is no visual damage to the cap or the fuel tank

Emergency fuel caps, if fitted, should form a good seal.

Never smoke, or use a mobile phone, on the forecourt of petrol stations as these are major fire risks and could cause an explosion.

Vehicle security
When you leave your vehicle you should

- remove the ignition key and engage the steering lock

- lock the car, even if you only leave it for a few minutes

- close the windows completely

- never leave children or pets in an unventilated car

- take all contents with you, or lock them in the boot. Remember, for all a thief knows a carrier bag may contain valuables

- never leave vehicle documents in the car.

For extra security fit an anti-theft device such as an alarm or immobiliser. If you are buying a new car it is a good idea to check the level of built-in security features. Consider having your registration number etched on all your car windows. This is a cheap and effective deterrent to professional thieves.

7. First Aid on the road

In the event of an incident, you can do a number of things to help, even if you have had no training.

1. Deal with danger

Further collisions and fire are the main dangers following a crash. Approach any vehicle involved with care. Switch off all engines and, if possible, warn other traffic. Stop anyone from smoking.

2. Get help

Try to get the assistance of bystanders. Get someone to call the appropriate emergency services as soon as possible. They will need to know the exact location of the incident and the number of vehicles involved.

3. Help those involved

DO NOT move casualties still in vehicles unless further danger is threatened. **DO NOT** remove a motorcyclist's helmet unless it is essential. Remember the casualty may be suffering from shock. **DO NOT** give them anything to eat or drink. **DO** try to make them warm and as comfortable as you can, but avoid unnecessary movement. **DO** give reassurance confidently and try not to leave them alone or let them wander into the path of other traffic.

4. Provide emergency care

Remember the letters **DR A B C:**

D - Danger - check that you are not in danger.

R - Response - try to get a response by asking questions and gently shaking their shoulders.

A - Airway - the airway should be clear and kept open. Place one hand on the forehead, two fingers under the chin and gently tilt the head back.

B - Breathing - normal breathing should be established. Once the airway is open check breathing for up to 10 seconds.

C - Compressions - if they are not breathing normally compressions should be administered to maintain circulation; place two hands in the centre of the chest and press down 4-5 cms at a rate of 100/minute. You may only need one hand for a child. Give 30 chest compressions. Then tilt the head back gently, pinch the casualty's nostrils together and place your mouth over theirs. Give two breaths, each lasting one second (use gentle breaths for a small child).

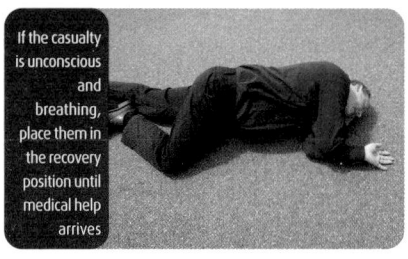

If the casualty is unconscious and breathing, place them in the recovery position until medical help arrives

Bleeding. First check for anything that may be in the wound, such as glass. If there is nothing embedded apply firm pressure over the wound. Take care not to press on the object - build up padding on either side of it. Fasten a pad to the wound with a bandage or length of cloth. Use the cleanest material available. If a limb is bleeding, but not broken, raise it above the level of the heart to reduce the flow of blood. Any restriction of blood circulation for more than a short time could cause long-term injuries.

Burns. Try to cool the burn by dousing it with clean, cold water or similar non-toxic liquid for at least 10 minutes. Do not try to remove anything sticking to the burn.

5. Be prepared

Always carry a first aid kit. You could save a life by learning emergency aid and first aid from a qualified organisation, such as the local ambulance services, the St John Ambulance Association and Brigade, St Andrew's Ambulance Association, the British Red Cross or any suitable qualified body (see page 495 for contact details).

8. Safety code for new drivers

Once you have passed the driving test you will be able to drive on your own. This will provide you with lots of opportunities but you need to remain safe. Even though you have shown you have the skills you need to drive safely, many newly qualified drivers lack experience. You need to continue to develop your skills, especially anticipating other road users' behaviour to avoid having a collision. As many as one new driver in five has some kind of collision in their first year of driving. This code provides advice to help you get through the first twelve months after passing the driving test, when you are most vulnerable, as safely as possible.

- Many of the worst collisions happen at night. Between midnight and 6 am is a time of high risk for new drivers. Avoid driving then unless it's really necessary.

- If you are driving with passengers, you are responsible for their safety. Don't let them distract you or encourage you to take risks. Tell your passengers that you need to concentrate if you are to get to your destination safely.

- Never show off or try to compete with other drivers, particularly if they are driving badly.

- Don't drive if you have consumed any alcohol or taken drugs. Even over-the-counter medicines can affect your ability to drive safely - read the label to see if they may affect your driving.

- Make sure everyone in the car is wearing a seat belt throughout the journey.

- Keep your speed down - many serious collisions happen because the driver loses control, particularly on bends.

- Most new drivers have no experience of driving high-powered or sporty cars. Unless you have learnt to drive in such a vehicle you need to get plenty of experience driving on your own before driving a more powerful car.

- Driving while uninsured is an offence. See Annex 3 for information on types of insurance cover.

REMEMBER that under the New Drivers Act you will have your licence revoked if you get six penalty points on your licence within two years of passing your first driving test. You will need to pass both the theory and practical tests again to get back your full licence.

You could consider taking further training such as Pass Plus, which could also save you money on your insurance, as well as helping you reduce your risk of being involved in a collision. There are three ways to find out more:

- internet - www.passplus.org.uk
- telephone - DSA head office on 0115 936 6504
- email - passplus@dsa.gsi.gov.uk

Other information

Metric conversions

The conversions given throughout *The Highway Code* are rounded but a detailed conversion chart is shown below.

Miles	Kilometres	Miles	Kilometres
1.00	1.61	40.00	64.37
5.00	8.05	45.00	72.42
10.00	16.09	50.00	80.47
15.00	24.14	55.00	88.51
20.00	32.19	60.00	96.56
25.00	40.23	65.00	104.60
30.00	48.28	70.00	112.65
35.00	56.33		

Useful websites

www.sja.org.uk (St John Ambulance Association and Brigade)
www.firstaid.org.uk
(St Andrew's Ambulance Association)
www.redcross.org.uk
(The British Red Cross)
www.dft.gov.uk
www.direct.gov.uk
www.transportoffice.gov.uk
www.highways.gov.uk/traffic info
www.direct.gov.uk/highwaycode
www.larsoa.org.uk
www.collisionreporting.gov.uk
www.askthe.police.uk
www.secureyourmotor.gov.uk
www.parking-appeals.gov.uk
(outside London)
www.parkingandtrafficappeals.gov.uk
(inside London)

Further reading

Best practice
Further information about good driving and riding practice can be found in the Driving Standards Agency books *The Official DSA Guide to Driving - the essential skills* and *The Official DSA Guide to Riding - the essential skills*. Information specifically for drivers of large vehicles can be found in *The Official DSA Guide to Driving Goods Vehicles* and *The Official DSA Guide to Driving Buses and Coaches*.

The Blue Badge Scheme

Information on this scheme can be found on the Department for Transport Website - www.dft.gov.uk

Code of Practice for Horse-Drawn Vehicles

The Code of Practice is available from the Department for Transport, Transport Technology and Standards Division 6, 2nd Floor, Great Minster House, 76 Marsham Street, London SW1P 4DR. Tel 0207 944 2078.

Road Works

A leaflet giving further information on driving through road works can be obtained from Highways Agency Publications, tel 0870 1226 236, quoting reference number HA113/04. For general Highways Agency information, tel 08457 504030 or email ha_info@highways.gsi.gov.uk

Index

S

Answers to Case Study questions on pages 400 - 402

Question1	Look over your shoulder for a final check
Question 2	Slow down Consider using the horn Beware of pedestrians
Question 3	Find a suitable place to stop
Question 4	Go past slowly Give plenty of room
Question 5	There may be another vehicle coming

Other Official DSA Publications

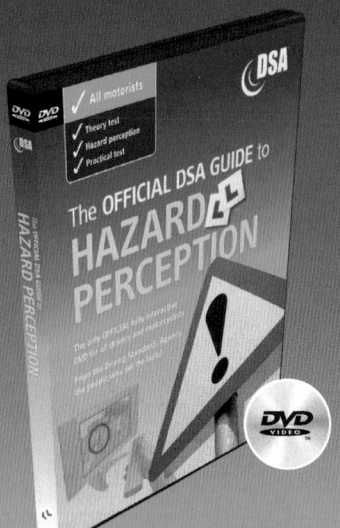

The Official DSA Guide to Hazard Perception DVD

Hazard perception is a vital skill and a key part of today's driving tests. This interactive DVD from the Driving Standards Agency will help you stay safe on the roads.

Includes official DSA video clips and tests your responses to hazards.

ISBN 9780115528651 £15.65

Prepare for your Practical Driving Test – the official DSA guide DVD

Taking away the mystery of what actually happens during your practical driving test, this is the only official interactive DVD which clearly shows you how to reach Level 5 – the practical test pass standard – for each of the 24 key driving skills examined in the test.

The perfect companion to your lessons, from the Driving Standards Agency.

ISBN 9780115528590 £15.65

The **OFFICIAL DSA**
THEORY TEST
for Car Drivers
and The Official Highway Code

2010 WIN A CAR COMPETITION*

TSO, DSA's official publishing partner, is offering you the chance to win a new car.

To enter, simply answer the questions and tell us in 25 words or less how learning to drive will make a difference to your life. The winner will be the entrant who answers the first 3 questions correctly and writes the most apt and original 25 word essay, as decided by the judges.

Please send the entry form to: Win a Car Competition 2010, TSO, Freepost, ANG 4748, Norwich, NR3 1YX (No stamp required).

1. You may only use front fog lights when visibility is reduced to less than what distance?

....

2. What is the legal minimum insurance cover you must have to drive on public roads?

....

3. When may you drive over a footpath?

....

Tie Breaker: Learning to drive will change my life.... (complete in 25 words or less)

....

....

....

....

When are you planning/ hoping to take your theory test?

Within a fortnight ☐ Within a month ☐ In 1-3 months ☐ In 3-6 months ☐
In 6-12 months ☐ In 12+ months ☐

When are you planning/ hoping to take your practical test?

Within a fortnight ☐ Within a month ☐ In 1-3 months ☐ In 3-6 months ☐
In 6-12 months ☐ 12+ months ☐

Do you already own a car?

Yes ☐ No ☐

If Yes, is the car...

New ☐ Second-hand ☐

Do you plan to buy a car when you pass?

Yes ☐ No ☐

If Yes, will the car be...

New ☐ Second-hand ☐

Name of shop or website that you bought this product from?

....

How would you improve this, or any other DSA product?

....

....

Name ....

Address ....

.... Date of birth ....

Daytime tel. .... Email ....

Mobile tel. ....

TSO (The Stationery Office) Ltd is proud to be DSA's official publishing partner

Prices, images and publication dates are correct at time of going to press but may be subject to change without notice.

Account holders should note that all credit card transactions will not be shown on their statements. The personal information provided here will only be used to process your order and keep you informed of related products or services. We will not pass your data on to any third parties.

TSO would like to continue to keep you informed of products and services that may be of interest to you. If you do not wish to receive these updates in future please let us know.

I do not want to receive these updates from TSO in future ☐

I have read, accept and agree to be bound by the Competition Rules

Signature .... Date ....

If you would like us to send you email updates on your specific area(s) of interest register at www.tsoshop.co.uk/signup.

* Terms and conditions apply

Competition Rules

The following rules apply to this competition. By entering this competition, entrants will be deemed to have accepted these rules and to agree to be bound by them.

1. Only one entry will be accepted per purchase of The Official DSA Theory Test book for Car Drivers (and The Official Highway Code).

2. All entries must be on original official entry forms. No photocopies will be accepted.

3. Entries must be received by the Promoter by no later than 5.00pm on Monday, 6 September 2010 (**Closing Date**). Entries must be submitted by ordinary post to the Promoter's free mailing address at: TSO, Freepost, ANG 4748, Norwich, NR3 1YX.

4. The competition will run from 29 June 2009 to 6 September 2010 and one prize shall be awarded to a winner chosen from valid entries received by the Promoter by the Closing Date. No responsibility can be taken by the Promoter for lost, late, misdirected or stolen entries.

5. The prize awarded to the winner will be one car (not necessarily the car pictured), being either a Peugeot 206 1.4 3 door Petrol model or another make and model of approximate equivalent value (£8995 at the time of these rules going to press) to be selected by the Promoter in its absolute discretion. Colour is subject to availability. Insurance and all on the road charges are not included and will be the winner's responsibility. There will be one prize only and accordingly only one winner. The prize cannot be transferred or exchanged and there is no cash alternative.

6. Only entrants over the age of 17 and resident in the United Kingdom are eligible to enter the competition. The Promoter reserves the right to request evidence of proof of age and residence from the winner before any prize will be awarded.

7. The winning entry will be decided by the judges in their absolute discretion from correct entries submitted by eligible entrants received by the Closing Date. A "correct" entry means a fully completed entry, with the first three questions answered correctly, the most apt and original essay and otherwise in compliance with these rules.

8. The winner will be notified by 24 September 2010. Only the winner will be contacted personally via the email address or telephone number they provide.

9. If the winner cannot be contacted by the means provided, the Promoter reserves the right to have the judges decide on an alternative winner from other correct entries received by the Closing Date, using the same criteria as for the original "winner" and subject to these rules.

10. The winner's name will be published on the Promoter's website at www.tso.co.uk on or about 24 September 2010 for a period of approximately 60 days.

11. The prize will be made available within six weeks of the Closing Date by arrangement between the Promoter and the winner, provided that the Promoter shall not be responsible for any delivery costs.

12. By entering this competition, an entrant agrees that if they accept any Prize, they will be deemed to consent to:

    (a) the use for promotional and other purposes (without further payment and except as prohibited by law) of their name, city/town/county of residence, likeness and Prize information; and

    (b) participate in the Promoter's reasonable marketing and promotional activities.

    The entrant agrees that all rights including copyright in all works created by the entrant as part of the competition entry shall be owned by the Promoter absolutely without the need for any payment to the entrant. They further agree to waive unconditionally and irrevocably all moral rights pursuant to the Copyright, Designs and Patents Act of 1988 and under any similar law in force from time to time anywhere in the world in respect of all such works.

13. No entries will be returned to entrants by the Promoter. Therefore, entrants may wish to retain a copy.

14. The Promoter reserves the right to cancel this competition or amend these rules at any stage without prior notice, if deemed necessary in its opinion, especially if circumstances arise outside of its control. Any such cancellation or changes to the rules will be notified on the Promoter's website.

15. This competition is not open to employees or contractors of the Promoter or the Driving Standards Agency or any person directly involved in the organisation or running of the competition, or their direct family members. Any such entries will be invalid.

16. By entering this competition, entrants warrant that all information submitted by them is true and correct and that they are eligible and have legal capacity to enter this competition. The Promoter reserves the right to disqualify any entrant if it has reasonable grounds to believe that the entrant has breached these rules.

17. Any personal data provided in any entry will be dealt with by the Promoter in accordance with the requirements of the Data Protection Act 1998, provided that the winner expressly consents to the information set out in rule 12(a) being used in the manner specified therein.

18. The judges' and the Promoter's decisions in relation to any aspect of this competition are final and no correspondence will be entered into. Neither the judges nor the Promoter will have any liability to any person in relation to their decisions or any damage, loss, injury or disappointment suffered arising from the competition (except to the extent that such liability cannot be limited or excluded by law).

19. The competition and these rules shall be governed by English law.

20. The "Promoter" means The Stationery Office Limited, St Crispins, Duke Street, Norwich, NR3 1PD (the publishers of The Official DSA Learner Range). The judges will be employees of the Promoter.

Other Official DSA Publications available to order

The Official DSA Guide to Driving – the essential skills
Book   ISBN 9780115528170   £12.99
Downloadable PDF*   ISBN 9780115530609   £12.99

The industry standard driving manual packed with advice for learners, experienced motorists and instructors. Includes guidance on essential driving techniques, manoeuvring and defensive driving.

The Official DSA Theory Test for Car Drivers and The Official Highway Code CD-ROM
ISBN 9780115530685   £12.99

Includes all the questions in the theory test question bank you could be asked until summer 2010. Contains information about the new case-study style questions to be introduced from 28 September 2009. The closest experience to the multiple choice part of the theory test.

The Official DSA Complete Theory Test Kit - CD-ROM and DVD
ISBN 9780115530715   £19.99

Prepare for both parts of the theory test. Includes Theory Test for Car Drivers CD-ROM and Hazard Perception DVD. Valid for tests taken until summer 2010. Save over £8.00 on individual prices.

The Official DSA Complete Learner Driver Pack - electronic version
ISBN 9780115530708   £29.99

Provides complete preparation for your theory and practical tests, valid until summer 2010. Includes Theory Test for Car Drivers CD-ROM, Hazard Perception DVD and Prepare for your Practical Driving Test DVD. Save over £14.00 on individual prices.

TSO (The Stationery Office) is proud to be DSA's official publishing partner.

6 Easy Ways To Order:

- Online: Visit www.tsoshop.co.uk/dsa
- Email: Email your order to customer.services@tso.co.uk
- Telephone: Please call 0870 243 0123. Please quote reference CQD when ordering
- Fax: Fax your order to 0870 243 0129
- Post: Marketing, TSO, Freepost, ANG 4748, Norwich NR3 1YX (No stamp required)
- Shops: Available from all good High Street book stores (including TSO shops) or online bookstores. For interactive products please also visit selected computer software retailers.

Prices, covers and publication dates are correct at time of going to press but may be subject to change without notice.

*Available as a downloadable PDF, direct from TSO.
Please visit **www.tsoshop.co.uk/pdf** for more information.
This new electronic format provides immediate access at the press of a button.

information & publishing solutions